Wandering Ghost

The Odyssey of

Lafcadio Hearn

Wandering Ghost

Jonathan Cott

Alfred A. Knopf   New York   1991

THIS IS A BORZOI BOOK PUBLISHED BY ALFRED A. KNOPF, INC.

Grateful acknowledgment is made to the following for permission to reprint previously published material:

New Directions Publishing Corporation: Excerpt from poem by Lady Murasaki Shikibu and excerpt from poem by Ono No Komachi, from One Hundred Poems from the Japanese, translated by Kenneth Rexroth. All rights reserved. Reprinted by permission of New Directions Publishing Corporation.

Princeton University Press: "Ithaka," from C. P. Cavafy: Collected Poems, edited by George Savidis and translated by E. Keeley and P. Sherrard. Copyright © 1975 by E. Keeley and P. Sherrard. Reprinted by permission of Princeton University Press.

Ross-Erikson: Excerpts from the Introduction by Kenneth Rexroth from The Buddhist Writings of Lafcadio Hearn. Introduction copyright © 1977 by Kenneth Rexroth. Reprinted by permission of Ross-Erikson, 223 Via Sevilla, Santa Barbara, CA 93109.

The University of Michigan Press: Poem by Sappho from Poems from the Greek Anthology, translated by Kenneth Rexroth. Published by the University of Michigan Press in 1962. Reprinted by permission of The University of Michigan Press.

Library of Congress Cataloging-in-Publication Data
Cott, Jonathan.
Wandering ghost: the odyssey of Lafcadio Hearn / by Jonathan Cott.—1st ed.
    p. cm.
Includes bibliographical references.
ISBN 0-394-57152-5
1. Hearn, Lafcadio, 1850–1904—Biography.
2. Authors, American—19th century—Biography.
I. Hearn, Lafcadio, 1850–1904. II. Title.
PS1918.C6 1991
813'.4—dc20 90-4412 CIP
[B]

FIRST EDITION

As certain as color
Passes from the petal,
Irrevocable as flesh,
The gazing eye falls through the world.

ONO NO KOMACHI

Contents

Acknowledgments

I AM greatly indebted to Sonny Mehta for publishing my book; to my agent, Michael Carlisle, for having helped get it published; to my editor, Bobbie Bristol, for providing the book with whatever coherence and structure it may have; and to Richard Gere for having invited me in 1987 to spend some time in the region of Japan that Lafcadio Hearn referred to as the "Land of the Gods." Here, in Shimane Prefecture in southwest Honshu, I visited the city of Matsue (450 miles southwest of Tokyo) where Hearn's well-preserved domicile of 1891 (an ancient samurai *yashiki*) and the adjoining Lafcadio Hearn Memorial Museum are both located, and then drove twenty miles west of Matsue to see the Izumo-Taisha Shrine—the oldest and second-holiest site in Japan and a place often visited by Hearn (as well as by thousands of pilgrims every New Year's Day). I owe thanks to Richard not only for allowing me to make my own pilgrimage but also for his constant interest in and encouragement of my work on Koizumi Yakumo (as Hearn is known throughout Japan).

I would also like to thank the following persons who, in various ways, contributed to the writing of my book: Veronica Bay, Elizabeth Bertran, Anna Muñoz Brandon, Tina Chow, Cynthia Crawford, Castle W. Freeman, Jr., Olivier Gérard, Peter M. Grilli, Ann and Lee Katzenbach, Joan Keener, Mrs. Mona Lutz, Melvin Rosenthal, Alexandra Stewart, Natsuko Toda, Iris Weinstein, Hannah Wolsky.

For their assistance with my research, I am grateful to Reiko Sassa, Director of Language Education and the Library at the Japan Society, New York City; to Ms. Sharon Defibough and Robert A. Hull of the Lafcadio Hearn Collection, Alderman Library, the University of Virginia; to Sylvia Metzinger of the Howard-Tilton Memorial Library, Tulane University; to Amy Vladeck Heinrich, Head of Reference and Resource Services at the C. V. Starr East Asian Library, Columbia University; and to the librarians of the Cincinnati Historical Society.

I wish to state that none of the persons mentioned above is responsible in any way for my presentation and views of the life and writings of Lafcadio Hearn as expressed in this book—though I thank them all for making it possible for me to complete *Wandering Ghost: The Odyssey of Lafcadio Hearn.*

A NOTE ABOUT THE ILLUSTRATIONS

The author wishes to thank the University of Virginia Library (Lafcadio Hearn Collection, Clifton Waller Barrett Library, Manuscripts Division) for the following illustrations:

Page xii, drawing of Hearn by C. D. Weldon from E. L. Tinker's *Lafcadio Hearn's American Days;* Page 7, Lafcadio and his aunt, Mrs. Brenane, from G. M. Gould's *Concerning Lafcadio Hearn;* Page 115, photograph of Hearn in New Orleans, 1887.

The sketches by Hearn on pages 36, 37, 113, 120, 127 are from *Letters from the Raven: Being the Correspondence of Lafcadio Hearn with Henry Watkin.*

The drawings by Hearn on pages 130, 131, 150 are from the New Orleans *Item.*

The drawings on pages 168, 174 are by E. L. Tinker from his book *Ladcadio Hearn's American Days.* The sketches by Hearn on pages 190, 191 are from Elizabeth Bisland's *Life and Letters of Lafcadio Hearn.*

The photographs on pages 203 and 205 are from Hearn's *Two Years in the French West Indies.*

The photograph of Hearn with his wife and son on page 239 is from *The Writings of Lafcadio Hearn.*

The sketch by Hearn on page 334 is from his *Japanese Letters.*

The ghost drawing by Hearn on page 355 is from Hearn's notebooks. The letter written by Hearn to his wife on page 390 is from *Life and Letters.*

The sketch by Hearn of the "weeping Jizo" on page 393 is from Kazuo Koizumi's *Father and I: Memories of Lafcadio Hearn.*

Introduction

Real travelers are those who go for the sake of going
And travel light, like balloons.   BAUDELAIRE

For me, it began with a sketch of a small man—seen from the back—wearing a rumpled linen suit and a fedora-type hat, and carrying a small, worn-looking trunk in his left hand and a travel-weary suitcase in his right—the visible side panel of the former embossed with the initials *L.H.*: "Sketch by C. D. Weldon from memory," the caption read, "of how Hearn looked as he was leaving New York for Japan."

It wasn't much of an illustration, hastily drawn in pen-and-ink to accompany the writer Lafcadio Hearn's article "A Winter's Journey to Japan" for the November 1890 issue of *Harper's Magazine*. But its Chaplinesque pathos seemed to express some kind of quiet resignation and sadness, and led me to pin the sketch up on my wall—reminding me that Hearn had been on the road since he was nineteen years old, when he left London for Cincinnati, Ohio (later moving on to New Orleans and Martinique), owning only what he could carry and carrying everything that he owned, like a nomad. Looking at the man with the two pieces of luggage, I felt empathy for this exile and wanderer. Then one day I began to imagine that Lafcadio Hearn was smiling under that fedora, free from possessions and tourist schedules, as he gladly set off on a one-month journey by train and steamer to an unknown world he had long dreamt of—heading west to the East—perhaps for a few weeks, perhaps forever.

In the 1870s Lafcadio Hearn (1850–1904) was Cincinnati's most famous and controversial newspaper reporter. In the 1880s his journalistic depic-

tions of white and black Creole life in New Orleans—along with his cul-
tural criticism, translations of French authors such as Théophile Gautier
and Pierre Loti, and learned feuilletons—were praised by writers as popular in their time as George Washington Cable (well known for his depictions of Creole life in New Orleans), Joel Chandler Harris (author of
the *Uncle Remus* tales), Charles Dudley Warner (coauthor, with Mark
Twain, of *The Gilded Age*), and Joaquin Miller (the poet of *Kit Carson's
Ride*). In New York City, his novels *(Chita* and *Youma)* and his writings
about Martinique were glowingly reviewed by William Dean Howells.
And Hearn contributed regularly to the most distinguished periodicals of
the day: *Harper's Magazine, Century Magazine, Lippincott's Magazine,* and
Atlantic Monthly.

"At the turn of the century," the poet and critic Kenneth Rexroth stated,
"Hearn was considered one of the finest, if not the finest, of American
prose stylists. He was certainly one of the masters of the Stevensonian
style. . . . [His] Japanese writings demonstrate economy, concentration,
and great control of language, with little stylistic exhibitionism. Their attitude of uncritical appreciation for the exotic and the mysterious is as
unmistakably nineteenth century as the fine prose idiom with which it is
consistent." In Germany, literary masters such as Hugo von Hofmannsthal
and Stefan Zweig were enraptured by Hearn's books on Japan, the latter
calling them "something totally unique in the world of art, a miracle of
transplantation, of artificial grafting: the works of an Occidental, yet written by an Oriental."

Yet although Hearn today has a small, devoted following in the United
States and Europe, he is truly a household name only in Japan where, as
Koizumi Yakumo—the name Hearn chose when he became a Japanese
citizen in 1896—he is known to all segments of Japanese society, and is
honored as an adopted son. The Yakumo Society, consisting of about 150
Japanese members nationwide, meets monthly in Matsue and publishes
a journal called *Hearn.* Lafcadio's ghost tales are commonly used by Japanese children in their English-language classes. Japanese television recently presented a series of five hour-long docudramas (starring George
Chakiris as Lafcadio), portraying his life from his days in New Orleans
to his final years in Tokyo. And in 1963, the renowned director Masaki
Kobayashi used three of Hearn's stories (including "The Story of Mimi-
nashi-Hōïchi") as the basis for his film *Kwaidan.*

In the city of Matsue (southwest of Tokyo on the Sea of Japan), Lafcadio Hearn's beloved home—an ex-samurai *yashiki* with three gardens

surrounding the house where Hearn and his wife, Setsu, lived for only about six months in 1891—has been preserved much as the writer described it in his essay "In a Japanese Garden." (The house is owned by the grandson of the man who originally rented it to Hearn when he taught English in the city's middle and normal schools between 1890 and 1891.)

Adjoining this residence, with its "all-reposing peace of nature and the dreams of the sixteenth century"—as Lafcadio put it—is the Lafcadio Hearn Memorial Museum. Originally built in 1933 with financial support from a number of Hearn's appreciative former students and literary admirers, this small museum displays the two pieces of luggage with which the writer arrived in Yokohama, examples of Hearn's extensive long-stemmed pipe collection, the desk and chair from his study in Tokyo, items of clothing worn by Lafcadio and by Setsu, scores of his manuscripts and personal letters, the finest compilation extant of photographs from all periods of his life, and an extensive library of books by and about the author.

The museum also supplies a map of the places and sites often visited by Hearn—many of which, in spite of recently constructed hotels, bowling alleys, and cinemas, still remain as Lafcadio wrote about them: innumerable temples, shrines, and cemeteries; the seventeenth-century Matsue Castle on the summit of its citadel hill; the small *soba-ya* (noodle shop) where he loved to watch the sunset. And one can also catch a glimpse of the people he loved to observe: workers stopping to clap their hands at dawn in front of small Shintō shrines; peddlers of noodles and hot sweet potatoes making their afternoon rounds; fishermen with straw baskets and bamboo poles in their narrow boats on the Ohashi River; peasants with their hoes wading through rice paddies; and mourners climbing up to mountainside cemeteries with offerings of flowers, food, and water for their ancestors.

Although the rock singer Michael Jackson and Beethoven's *Ninth Symphony* are more popular in Japan today than *shakuhachi* (bamboo flute) masters and Nō dramas, it is also true that each spring, workers, businessmen, and governmental ministers rearrange even the busiest schedules in order to sit under cherry trees in nearby city parks for the annual *hanami* ritual (cherry-blossom viewing), drinking saké and singing songs with friends and colleagues about the evanescence of life. And although the late Emperor Hirohito—considered a descendant of Amaterasu Omikami (the Shintō Sun Goddess)—was reported to have worn a treasured Mickey Mouse watch (obtained during a 1970 visit to Disneyland) on all but state occasions, the 124th Emperor of Japan was buried with full Shintō rites. True, the woodcutters of the mountainside village of Yase, who had served for 650 years as the Imperial pallbearers, were for the first time not invited to perform their traditional function; the Emperor's corpse traveled mostly by car, and the villagers had to watch the event on television instead. Yet Japanese sociologists have noted that Shintōism and, along with it, the "imperial cult" are regaining their importance as traditional buttresses of a group-oriented society that is experiencing the deracinating strains on family and clan imposed by the country's global preeminence.

In the years just before and after World War II, many young Japanese found little to admire in what they considered Lafcadio Hearn's "reactionary," recalcitrant notions concerning the "horrors" of the New Japan and its desire to industrialize and modernize as rapidly as possible. These people had forgotten, or not known, that Koizumi Yakumo was a Japanese patriot. As early as the 1890s he talked of a "persecuted" nation "forced . . . to become strong," and expressed his hope of seeing "a United Orient yet bound into one strong alliance against our cruel Western civilization," adding: "If I have been able to do nothing else in my life, I have been able at least to help a little—as a teacher and as a writer, and as an editor—in opposing the growth of what is called society and what is called civilization. It is very little, of course—but the gods ought to love me for it." The gods may have loved Lafcadio Hearn, but the Japanese ruling class was more interested in transforming a tattered postwar nation—condescendingly known for its cheap toys, rubber sandals, and *ramen* noodles—into a colossal producer of semiconductors, fiber-optic cables, computers, cars, and robots, its yen stronger than the dollar, and the Greater East Asia Co-Prosperity Sphere more powerful in peacetime than its original industrial and military formulators would have ever imagined it could be.

Today, nevertheless, one can imagine Lafcadio Hearn finding some truth in the assertion by Japan's leading social critic Shuichi Kato that "A world view which centers on the group and does not include transcendental values implies that accepting the new does not require discarding the old. The confrontation between past and future involves changing an abstract conception of reality and ethical codes to conform with the new realities of the concrete situation. . . . This practical flexibility has been the secret of Japan's ability to modernize without a crisis of cultural integrity. Today, we produce high-tech products and still have an emperor."

As Kenneth Rexroth, moreover, has commented in *The Buddhist Writings of Lafcadio Hearn:*

> In spite of the incredible changes that have taken place in Japan since Hearn's death in 1904, as an informant on Japanese life, literature, and religion he is still amazingly reliable, because beneath the effects of industrialization, war, population explosion, and prosperity much of Japanese life remains unchanged. . . . Two world wars and Japan's astonishing emergence as a modern nation temporarily extinguished the credibility of Hearn's vision of traditional Japanese culture. But both in the West and in Japan interest in the old forms of Japanese culture is increasing. . . . Pet crickets, for example, still command high prices, and more people apply their new prosperity to learning tea ceremony, calligraphy, flower arrangement, and *sumi-e* painting than ever before.

"We Japanese," the twentieth-century poet Yone Noguchi once said, "have been regenerated by [Hearn's] sudden magic and baptized afresh under his transcendental rapture . . . and the ancient beauty which we buried under the dust rose again with a strange yet new splendor." And Professor Inazo Nitobe, author of *Bushido—The Soul of Japan,* asserted that Lafcadio Hearn was "the most eloquent and truthful interpreter of the Japanese mind. . . ."

In 1987 I visited the Lafcadio Hearn Memorial Museum in Matsue and was told that the museum had in its collection more than six hundred volumes by or about the author. Having long admired Hearn's writings on Japan, I realized I knew little about his work or his life before he arrived in Yokohama.

Since almost all of Hearn's books written before 1890 were, and still are, out of print—or difficult to obtain—I made a trip to the Library of Congress, which has about three hundred volumes in its Hearn collection (in addition to much original Hearn material), and spent several days reading his marvelous *Two Years in the French West Indies,* as well as a number of compilations of his numerous journalistic pieces. In one of these collections, *Occidental Gleanings,* I came across the following remark by its editor, Albert Mordell: "Japan gave [Hearn] nothing. . . . He himself, not Japan, is the interesting subject in his writings on Japan. He was so great an observer and had so powerful an imagination and such command of language and so individual a mental outlook, that we may say he only found in Japan the pretexts for exercising his gifts."

Preposterous as this notion was, I soon discovered that far from being merely a writer of precious, overwrought prose sketches *(Fantastics and Other Fancies)* who realized his brilliance and eminence as an essayist *only* in Japan (a commonplace of Hearnian criticism), Lafcadio Hearn had an extraordinary career not only as a journalist but as a novelist, critic, translator, folklorist, professor of English literature, and explicator of Japanese Buddhism. He was also one of the outstanding letter writers of his time.

Considering the full range of Hearn's mostly forgotten body of work, I decided to compile an anthology of complete texts (or lengthy excerpts from) Hearn's articles, essays, letters, and stories, with introductory notes meant to place these writings in the context of Hearn's career, intellectual concerns, and interests. I soon realized, however, that the context of the work was indissolubly linked to Hearn's literary and personal life—one of the most remarkable and fascinating lives of any writer of the late nineteenth century. My anthology therefore began to turn into an informal biographical reader that attempted to present Lafcadio's *voice* from the days he emerged, seemingly out of nowhere, as a newspaper reporter in Cincinnati in 1871 until his death in Japan in 1904—a voice whose strength, volatility, frankness, passion, and subversiveness remained surprisingly consistent in spite of his manic-depressive moods and the protean nature of his identities as Patrick Hearn, Lafcadio Hearn, Koizumi Yakumo.

In allowing this voice to manifest itself, I hoped to present the story of a Greek–Anglo-Irish child abandoned by his parents when he was five years old; who was partly blinded when he was sixteen during a school-boys' game; who felt for most of his life like a social misfit; who, as an adolescent, dared to reject completely his Catholic upbringing because of his ardent belief in the ancient Greek gods; who, at various times of his life, found himself destitute, homeless, and sleeping on the streets and alleyways of London, Cincinnati, and New Orleans; who broke social taboos and antimiscegenation laws with his sexual predilection for mulatto and black women; and who gradually developed into a remarkable, disciplined, mostly self-taught bohemian man of letters—a model for more recent bohemian writers such as Jaime de Angulo, Gary Snyder, and Henry Miller, the last declaring: "My passion for Japan began with Lafcadio Hearn."

In dealing with such a life, about which most casual readers of Hearn knew little or nothing, I also hoped to avoid the often racist, prudish, and provincial comments—as well as the all-embracing reductionist psychologizing (Oedipus complex, inferiority complex, *puer* complex) or etiological theorizing (Hearn's genius/weakness as a function of his myopia)—that pervade many of the previous biographies about a writer whom many critics, at one time or another, have spoken of as "a sensual Romantic," "a decadent aesthete," "a morbid genius," "a rootless cosmopolite," "a bohemian misfit," "a frightened escapist," "a wandering dreamer."

To be a wanderer, the novelist Marguerite Yourcenar once remarked, "requires an ability to take pleasure in the outer spectacle of things combined with a definite willingness to go beyond that spectacle in order to discover the often hidden realities underneath. Every traveler is Ulysses and ought to be Proteus as well."

Lafcadio Hearn was such a wanderer. From his childhood island home of Leucadia (present-day Levkas), it was possible, on a clear day, to catch a glimpse of the island of Ithaca—the legendary birthplace of perhaps the most courageous, inventive, and indomitable wanderer-adventurer of the ancient world—Odysseus, who plied the waters of a Mediterranean encircled (in the sixth-century-B.C. map of the natural philosopher Anaximander) by the ouroboros-shaped River Ocean. Twelve hundred years later, however, Dante described a Ulysses fiercely determined "to explore a greater world, and search the ways of life,/Man's evil and his virtue." He and his sailing companions headed west through the Strait of Gibraltar, the boundary beyond which, so Hercules had ordained, man was not permitted to pass. Ulysses and his crew died at sea in a divinely engendered whirlwind, and Dante placed the striving hero in his *Inferno* for having committed the sin of *curiositas*. Tennyson's Ulysses, on the other hand (one of Lafcadio Hearn's most admired literary heroes), exclaimed, "I cannot rest from travel: I will drink/Life to the lees . . ." and expressed his desire "To follow knowledge like a sinking star,/Beyond the utmost bound of human thought."

Columbus sailed west to find the East. Lafcadio, too, journeyed across the Atlantic to make his fortune, and wound up a vagabond in Cincinnati, as he discovered an America in the period of Primitive Accumulation, when presidents chewed tobacco, politicians were purchased by billionaires who didn't know how to spell, workers were grist for the mills and sacrificial victims for the mines, and most professional writers found their talents undervalued and generally ill-nourished. As Hearn complained: "We little, petty outsiders—gnats hovering about life! . . . There isn't any

more room for us! The world is become methodical as an abacus. . . .
One thing is sure: in another generation there can be no living by dreaming of art."

Finally, with what he called his "Cyclopian eye," Hearn completed his
Ulyssean journey—traveling farther west in order to leave the West behind by crossing the "mysterious, divine Pacific," as Herman Melville
called it, "the tide-beating heart of earth." Lafcadio passed through the
line of his horizon in order to experience—as Dante's Ulysses hoped to
do—"the unpeopled world behind the sun." And there he came upon
and found a home among people whose Emperor was worshipped as a
descendant of the Goddess of the Sun.

With the poet Charles Olson we might well say that "Homer's world
was locked tight in River Ocean which circled it. . . . But in the *Odyssey*
Ulysses is already pushing against the limits, seeking a way out. . . . Homer
was an end of the myth world from which the Mediterranean began. But
in Ulysses he projected the archetype of the West to follow. It was the
creative act of anticipation." So, too, was Lafcadio Hearn's life journey;
for from Greece to Japan, it mirrored the 2,500-year course of Western
civilization. Japan was truly Hearn's Ithaca, in the sense that the modern
Greek poet C. P. Cavafy wrote about it:

>*When you set out for Ithaka*
>*pray that your road's a long one,*
>*full of adventure, full of discovery. . . .*
>
>*Keep Ithaka always in mind.*
>*Arriving there is what you're destined for.*
>*But don't hurry the journey at all.*
>*Better if it goes on for years,*
>*so you're old by the time you reach the island,*
>*wealthy with all you've gained on the way,*
>*not expecting Ithaka to make you rich. . . .*
>
>*And if you find her poor, Ithaka won't have fooled you.*
>*Wise as you'll have become, and so experienced,*
>*You'll have understood by then what an Ithaka means.*

At the end, having been blinded like Polyphemus, tempted by Sirens and
Lotus-Eaters, seduced by dark Nausicaas, and confronted by many external and a few self-created Laestrygonians, Lafcadio Hearn/Koizumi Ya-

kumo understood what his journey meant. His courageous voyage was not an escape but rather a pilgrimage to his origins. For in "his" Japan he found "his" Greece, where he sensed the ancient gods waiting to greet him at the end of his lifetime journey, when he arrived with his two pieces of luggage, on the other side of the world.

Wandering Ghost

The Dream of
A Summer Day

I T   W A S   a sweltering summer day in July 1893—the twenty-sixth year
of Meiji. Pulled in his open *kuruma* (a rickshaw-type passenger vehicle)
by a straw-sandaled runner along the curving and rolling Japanese shoreline from the town of Misumi to the southern city of Kumamoto, the
forty-three-year-old Lafcadio Hearn stared, as if in a trance, at the infinite
blazing blue light of sea, cliffs, and sky, broken only by a few radiant and
motionless white clouds.

Only two days previously, he had escaped the confines of a recently
built, fashionable European hotel in the Open Port city of Nagasaki, which
flaunted an impressive array of rocking chairs, ranks of flower pots filled
with ornamental plants, stylish lamps, and, as he would later write to a
friend, "the seven deadly Sins for waiters."

Having made his exodus by boat, he found respite the next night in a
real Japanese inn—the House of Urashima—where he immediately removed his white duck-cloth suit and army boots, and took his ease in
the manner to which, for a number of years now, he had become accustomed: seated upon cool *tatami* matting, dressed in a *yukata* (a cotton
summer kimono), and waited upon by sweet-voiced chambermaids who,
at that moment, seemed to him like veritable butterfly- or moth-maiden
spirits, "a redemption," he would declare, "from all the sorrows of the
nineteenth century."

Back in his hired *kuruma*, Lafcadio Hearn, his once-black hair and
mustache now turned completely gray, glanced down drowsily at his
hands, in which he held a paper fan, given to him that morning at break-

3

fast as a keepsake by his beautiful innkeeper, a woman as graceful, he recalled, as a dragonfly and with a voice like the tinkling of a crystal wind bell. It was a fan that simply depicted the white rush of an enormous breaking wave on a beach, with seabirds flying exaltedly through the blue skies overhead.

"Now we will go to my father's palace, the Dragon Palace, under the waves of the South."

"No, I must go home to Kumamoto!"

Lafcadio, who had been blinded in his left eye as a child, suddenly opened his dreaming right eye. The day had become oppressively humid, the sea peculiarly silent, the air bathed in iridescent mother-of-pearl light.

As the *kuruma* now traveled—or seemingly floated—through the heat of the day, Lafcadio Hearn thought of the name of the inn where he had spent the previous night, and was reminded of "The Story of Urashima," perhaps the most famous of all Japanese fairy tales. And as he noticed one or two white clouds floating close above in the hazy sky, he imagined them as revenant ghosts of clouds that might have passed that way fourteen hundred summers before when the tale of Urashima had first been written.

Drifting into blue light, and hovering over the summer sea, Lafcadio fell into a trancelike sleep and dreamt he saw a boy on *another* drowsy summer day, letting his rudderless boat float adrift while he stared out at the infinite blue light of sea, cliffs, and sky. In spite of his indolence, the fisher-boy somehow managed to catch a giant tortoise, which he immediately, with a prayer, threw right back into the water, knowing that the creature was sacred to the Dragon God of the Sea. But nothing else came his way. The day got warmer, the sea peculiarly silent; and the fisher-boy Urashima soon felt his eyes closing, his boat drifting on forever.

Then out of the dreaming of the sea rose up a beautiful girl, robed in crimson and blue, with long black hair flowing down her back to her feet. Gliding over the waters she came, and she stood above the sleeping boy in the boat, woke him with a light touch, and said, "Do not be surprised. My father, the Dragon King of the Sea, sent me to you because of your kind heart. For today you set free a tortoise. And now we will go to my father's palace on the island where summer never dies, and I will be your flower-wife if you wish, and we shall live there happily forever."

Then Urashima took one oar and she the other, and they rowed away together south until they arrived at the Palace of the Dragon King of the Sea, an enchanted abode where summer never dies. Here they were married and lived blissfully for three years, until one day Urashima felt an inexplicable and profound desire to visit—just briefly—his aging father and mother.

At this request the Sea God's daughter began to weep, and said to him: "Since you wish to go, of course you must go, even though I fear we shall never see each other again. But I will give you a little box to take with you. It will help you to come back to me if you do what I tell you. Do not open it, no matter what may happen! Because if you open it, you will never be able to come back, and you will never see me again." And she gave him a little lacquered box tied about with a silken cord. Urashima comforted his bride and promised never to open the box—not even to loosen the silken string. Then he passed away through the summer light over the forever-sleeping sea, and the shape of the island where summer never dies faded behind him like a dream. Until before him stood the blue mountains of Japan.

On arriving home, the boy felt something amiss. His father's cottage had disappeared. The trees were strange, the fields were strange, the people's faces were strange. Urashima went to the village graveyard, and there he found his own tombstone and the tombstones of his father and his mother and of many others he had known. He felt himself the victim of some strange illusion, and he walked confusedly back to the beach, carrying in his hand the gift of the Sea God's daughter. Recklessly he broke the promise made to his beloved; he loosened the silken cord and opened the box.

Instantly, without sound, there burst from it a white, cold, spectral vapor that rose in the air like a summer cloud and began to drift away swiftly toward the south, over the silent sea. There was nothing else in the box. And Urashima then knew that he could never again return to his island of summer, and he wept and cried out in despair.

Suddenly he himself began to change. An icy chill shot through his blood, his teeth fell out, his face shriveled, his hair turned white as snow, his limbs withered, his strength ebbed, and he sank down lifeless on the sand.

The *kuruma* was moving quickly along the shore as Lafcadio Hearn rubbed his eyes and dazedly looked up to see numerous white clouds—summer mist that he was certain had escaped from Urashima's box. Slowly he began to return to where he was. On the other side of the road, he noticed recently installed telegraph lines that seemed to be following the *kuruma* at every turn, with thousands of chattering and twittering white-breasted birds perched contentedly on mile after mile of wire. And in the distance he heard the sound of drums being beaten by peasants in every passing, drought-stricken hamlet, hoping to invoke the rain—a sound, echoing back and forth along the shore, that had woken Lafcadio Hearn from his dream of a summer day.

And as he approached his Japanese home, Lafcadio remembered another summer day, long ago and far away:

I have memory of a place and a magical time in which the Sun and the Moon were larger and brighter than now. Whether it was of this life or of some life before I cannot tell. But I know the sky was very much more blue, and nearer to the world,—almost as it seems to become above the masts of a steamer steaming into equatorial summer. The sea was alive, and used to talk,—and the Wind made me cry out for joy when it touched me. Once or twice during other years, in divine days lived among the peaks, I have dreamed just for a moment that the same wind was blowing,—but it was only a remembrance.

Also in that place the clouds were wonderful, and of colors for which there are no names at all,—colors that used to make me hungry and thirsty. I remember, too, that the days were ever so much longer than these days,—and that every day there were new wonders and new pleasures for me. And all that country and time were softly ruled by One who thought only of ways to make me happy. Sometimes I would refuse to be made happy, and that always caused her pain, although she was divine;—and I remember that I tried very hard to be sorry. When day was done, and there fell the great hush of the light before moonrise, she would tell me stories that made me tingle from head to foot with pleasure. I have never heard any other stories half so beautiful. And when the pleasure became too great, she would sing a weird little song which always brought sleep. At last there came a parting day; and she wept, and told me of a charm she had given that I must never, never lose, because it would keep me young, and give me power to return. But I never returned. And the years went; and one day I knew that I had lost the charm, and had become ridiculously old.

Part
One

CHAPTER *1*

*B*lue
*G*host

O N T H E summer morning of June 27, 1850, Patrick Lafcadio Hearn
was born on the Ionian island of Leucadia (then called Santa Maura by
the colonizing British, now called Leucas, Levkas, or Lefkas), about twenty-
five miles due north of the island of Ithaca. On July 8, the infant Lafcadio
was baptized at the Greek Orthodox Church of Santa Paraskevi, with its
simple, windowless, earthen-covered exterior and its tenebrous, incense-
wafting, golden-walled interior embellished with gilded icons of Santa
Barbara, the Virgin, and Jesus Christ—their golden halos and dazzling red
and purple colors illuminated by candlelight.

As his mother held the child in her arms, his limbs were anointed and
his body immersed three times with his face turned toward the East. And,
as the priest intoned: "The servant of God, Patrick Lafcadio Hearn, is
baptized in the name of the Father, Amen, and of the Son, Amen, and of
the Holy Ghost, Amen," the mother made three tiny cuts, each representing one of the powers of the Trinity, in the calf of each of her infant's
legs.

"Do you remember," Lafcadio—forty years later—would write to his
long-lost younger brother, "that dark and beautiful face,—with large, brown
eyes like a wild deer's—that used to bend above your cradle? You do not
remember the voice which told you each night to cross your fingers after
the old Greek Orthodox fashion, and utter the words—'Εν το ονομα του
Πατρος και του Γιου και του 'Αγιου Πνευματος—In the name of the Father, and of the Son, and of the Holy Ghost'? She made, or had made,
three little wounds upon you when a baby,—to place you, according to

her childish faith, under the protection of those three powers, but especially that of Him for whom alone the Nineteenth Century still feels some reverence—*the Lord and Giver of Life*. And you know nothing about her? It is very strange. Perhaps there is much I do not know."

Rosa Antonia Cassimati, born in 1823 on the southernmost Ionian island of Cerigo (known to the Greeks as Cythera), was of noble Cerigote lineage through her father, Anthony Cassimati. Brought up speaking Romaic and Italian, she had no formal education and was illiterate, as were almost all of the countrywomen of her time. It was an era when fathers were not seen walking on the streets of their villages with their own daughters, or husbands with their wives, and when women were kept inside the house as much as possible.

Rosa Cassimati had a childlike, almost theopathic devotion to the mysteries of the Greek Church, and would spend hours looking at icons lit by lone candles in the smoky, perfumed darkness of an empty church. She was also, however, a passionate and romantic girl who, after all, came from Cythera, where Paris and Helen of Troy, fleeing from Menelaus, were said to have found a refuge; the island, according to the poet Hesiod, where "Golden" Aphrodite herself first arose out of the foam of the sea— the most beautiful of the deities, in whose magical embroidered girdle were contained "love, yearning, fond discourse, and beguilement."

Charles Bush Hearn, a surgeon and officer with the British Army Medical Staff, was attached to various regiments on several Ionian islands between 1846 and 1850. (In spite of sporadic popular insurrections, the British did not completely relinquish control of these islands until 1864.) After serving on Zante, Ithaca, and Corfu, Charles Hearn was transferred in April 1848 to an old Venetian castle on Cerigo, overlooking the port of Kapsali and just a short distance from the town of Cerigo itself.

Hearn felt bored and isolated on the island; the local people disliked the British and, though Hearn knew a bit of Greek, avoided social contact with him. He spent much of his spare time alone, walking aimlessly through the streets of Cerigo. One day he caught a glimpse of a beautiful dark-eyed young Greek woman hurrying through a village passageway and, without hesitation, he followed her and introduced himself. To his shock, she looked up and introduced herself to *him*.

Good-looking, well-built, with dark curly hair, heavy eyebrows over slightly protuberant eyes, Charles Hearn was a gregarious, intelligent,

CHARLES HEARN

thirty-year-old surgeon, known to be a capable swordsman and known also for accompanying his lilting tenor versions of Irish and Italian love songs on the guitar. Rosa Cassimati, hardly the ideal Greek daughter, was an impetuous and sometimes unstable twenty-five-year-old woman. Apparently without misgivings, she cast aside the social, moral, and religious strictures of her upbringing and, urgently entreated by the smitten and equally impetuous British army officer, engaged with him in the "works of Aphrodite."

It was not long before Anthony Cassimati discovered that his daughter was pregnant. To avenge the family's honor, Rosa's hotheaded brother, Demetrius, tracked Charles Hearn down and (so Lafcadio would later recount the apocryphal-sounding story) surprised the British surgeon on his medical rounds in the village, stabbing him repeatedly and leaving him for dead. Hearing of Demetrius's deed, Rosa ran distraught and screaming from her home, found Charles lying barely alive in an alleyway, and half-carried, half-dragged him—till she was as bloodied as he—to a cave in the hills, where she nursed her lover back to health.

In June 1849, Charles Hearn was ordered to report to Fort Santa Maura, a military post on the malaria-ridden island of Leucadia, where Rosa Cassimati accompanied him and a month later (July 24, 1849) gave birth out of wedlock to a boy, George Robert Hearn.

Charles Hearn had decided to marry his Cerigote sweetheart, and their subdued nuptials took place on November 25, 1849, before a black-robed Greek Orthodox priest, two witnesses, and several newly made friends from Leucadia. The bride and groom wore crowns of green myrtle on their heads. No parents or relatives of the couple—all of whom disapproved of the liaison—were in attendance.

After only three months of marriage, Charles, who had suddenly been promoted to Staff Surgeon Second Class, was reassigned to Dominica and Grenada in the British West Indies, and thus forced to leave his six-month-old son and once-again-pregnant wife on Leucadia. For two years he avoided informing the British War Office of his marriage, fearing that the scandal of this irregular union might prejudice his career, which he valued more than his paternal responsibilities. He was, moreover, in no hurry to relocate Rosa and his children to Dublin, having learned that his still-unwelcoming mother, Elizabeth Holmes Hearn, was less than eager to assign part of the family estate, the Barony Moycashel, to Charles and the undesirable woman who had ensnared her son.

So Rosa waited. A month before her little boy George Robert's first birthday, the infant became critically ill. And in spite of her appeals for the intercession of Santa Paraskevi—Rosa had rushed the baby to church to kiss the saint's icon—he died on August 17, 1850. Devastated, the mother clung to her faith and sanity by doting on her new child, born just two months before, a dark, strange-looking little boy whose ears were pierced with gold earrings. She called him Patricio or Lafcadio, talked to him in Italian and Romaic, and thought of ways to make him happy.

She took him to explore the island after which he was named. From the white, hot, dusty streets and the bazaar of the main island town of Santa Maura, she would walk with the child in her arms or ride on donkeys past endless fields of olive trees, vineyards, and corn growing on hillside terraces. As he got a bit older, she would take him up to the cliff of the Temple of Apollo, on the southernmost cape of Leucadia. There, amid groves of ilex and cypress, she would stand on the un-wrought altar stones where ceremonies and animal sacrifices to the God of Light had once taken place. We can imagine Rosa raising the child in her arms high above her head, showing him a glimpse of the island of Ithaca not far away—home of the great wanderer of many devices, Odysseus, and of his loyal wife, Penelope, who weaved and unraveled and weaved once again, hoping to put off her suitors until the day her adventurer husband came home to her. And in the air above her, raising his little arms to the sun, Rosa's child—in that supernal Apollonian realm of iridescent light of sea, cliffs, and sky—must have experienced what, when he grew up, he would call "the great Blue Soul of the Unknown . . . that infinite Blue Ghost . . . something into which you would wish to melt utterly away forever."

Years later, on another island, on the other side of the world—looking at the sky, cliffs, and sea—this once-blessed child of heaven would melt into a dream of another summer day . . . and then wake up and have a memory "of a place and a magical time in which the Sun and the Moon were larger and brighter than now. Whether it was of this life or of some life before I cannot tell. But I know the sky was very much more blue, and nearer to the world. . . . And all that country and time were softly ruled by One who thought only of ways to make me happy."

CHAPTER 2

Paradise

Lost

IN JULY 1852, with Charles Hearn still on extended call in the West Indies, his wife and two-year-old child were finally summoned to Dublin to stay on Lower Gardiner Street with part of the Hearn clan, which included Charles's mother, one of her daughters and the latter's husband, and one of her spinster sisters-in-law.

From the island of unending summer, Rosa and Lafcadio now found themselves on an island of short, sunless days, filled with ceaseless drizzle, rain, and fog. The Hearns cast one glance at their new Greek/Romaic–speaking relatives and were duly horrified. That olive-complexioned little boy with gold earrings was more "gypsy" and "Oriental" than English or Irish. And Rosa's arrival was greeted rather as though Anna Magnani had appeared at a very proper English tea party.

The family was astonished to discover that Charles's wife could neither read nor write in *any* language and was perplexed that Rosa communicated so poorly with the interpreter they provided, who couldn't quite make out Rosa's Ionian Greek dialect. The Hearns assumed that Rosa's habitual siestas—a necessity in the blazing, enervating afternoon hours of Cerigo and Leucadia—must surely be a sign of torpor and sloth. Most of all, this virulently anti-Catholic, Anglo-Irish Protestant family was appalled by the Greek woman's passionate belief in saints, her habit of crossing herself in public, and her zealous regard for priests.

It didn't take Rosa Cassimati long to catch the drift of the Hearns' attitude toward her and her son, whom they insisted on calling Patrick, his "Christian" name. No one seemed surprised when she began spending most of her time at the home of the sixty-year-old Mrs. Sarah Holmes Brenane. Mrs. Brenane, the younger, renegade sister of Elizabeth Hearn, had converted to the Roman Catholic Church of her deceased husband. Fastidious, eccentric, childless, peremptory in manner, and fanatically devout, she was the archetype of Victorian widowhood. She sympathized with Rosa's plight as a misunderstood and lonely outsider, and she doted on "Patrick" Hearn. Soon, mother and son were part of the wealthy Brenane household in the Dublin suburb of Rathmines. Rosa accompanied Mrs. Brenane in her large barouche when—clad always in black—she took her daily "airing" to the city to shop or to attend Mass.

In spite of Mrs. Brenane's sometimes peculiar but well-meaning attempts to make Rosa feel at home, the Greek woman suffered from homesickness, grieved for her first child, and missed her husband, who had by then been absent for three years. She was a foreigner in a strange and cold country, and her child was unwelcome in his own father's family. Rosa also began to manifest signs of mental imbalance. She stopped looking after herself, was often disheveled, and suffered increasingly from feelings of depression. She physically abused her son and once tried to kill herself by jumping from an upper story of the Brenane house.

In September of 1853, Charles Hearn, who had been stricken with yellow fever in Grenada, was sent home on extended sick leave. But the ocean voyage invigorated him and improved his health, and when he was finally reunited with his family, everything on the surface at first seemed harmonious. Charles, Rosa, and Lafcadio moved into a house near the Portobello barracks where Charles was stationed. Soon, however, he was spending little time with his wife and son, and Rosa realized that her husband had lost interest in her. Charles could not endure her frequent tantrums and manic episodes, and they argued constantly. So it was with relief that he took up a new military assignment, not knowing what was awaiting him in the trenches of Crimea and at the siege of Sebastopol, where he would witness some of the most horrendous suffering of nineteenth-century warfare.

When he returned, half-alive, to Dublin in 1856, Rosa was gone. Homesick and distraught, she had gone in 1854 to visit relatives in Cerigo. She left four-year-old Lafcadio in the care of his great-aunt, who had personally paid the passage to Greece for both Rosa and a midwife/wet nurse; unbeknownst to Charles Hearn, Rosa had become pregnant with his child shortly before his departure. During the voyage to Greece—probably in the port of Cephalonia—she gave birth to her third son, Daniel James (who would thereafter be known as James).

Two years later, still in Cerigo with her child, Rosa Hearn received word that Charles Hearn had secured an annulment of their marriage on his return from the Crimea. She had not been a signatory to the marriage contract (since, of course, she couldn't write), and because of this technicality the English court ruled that the marriage, though legal abroad, in the Orient, was not valid according to English law.

Outraged, crushed, loath to return to Ireland under any circumstances, Rosa almost immediately decided to marry a Greek of Italian descent named Giovanni Cavallini (who later served as governor under the British on the small island of Cerigotto). There was, however, one cruel, inexorable condition to the engagement: the groom had demanded that Rosa give up custody of and any claim to her two sons by Hearn. James was sent back to Ireland with the wet nurse to be looked after by his father. Lafcadio was to be raised by Mrs. Brenane, who, disgusted by Hearn's annulment of his marriage, had disinherited her nephew and promised Rosa to make the boy one of her heirs.

"I only once remember seeing my brother as a child," Lafcadio wrote later in his life to his half-sister Mrs. Atkinson. "Father had brought me some tin soldiers, and cannon to fire peas. While I was arranging them in order for battle, and preparing to crush them with artillery, a little boy with big eyes was introduced to me as my brother. Concerning the fact of brotherhood, I was totally indifferent—especially for the reason that he seized some of my soldiers, and ran away with them immediately. I followed him; I wrenched the soldiers away from him; I beat him and threw him downstairs; it was quite easy, because he was four years my junior. What afterwards happened I do not know. I have a confused idea that I was scolded and punished. But I never saw my brother again."

Lafcadio never saw his mother again, either. Rosa Cavallini once returned secretly to Ireland to try to see Lafcadio and James, but the Hearn family refused to reveal the children's whereabouts to her. Heartbroken, she returned to the Ionian islands, where she had four other children—two more boys and two girls—by her second husband. Yet, in spite of brief periods of happiness, Rosa's mental state grew increasingly erratic. After one prolonged bout of religious mania, her husband was forced to commit her to the National Mental Asylum at Corfu, where she remained for ten years until her death on December 12, 1882, at the age of fifty-nine.

"With regard to . . . mother's treatment of us," Lafcadio wrote in 1890 to his brother James, "—I must tell you that, even as a child, I used to

wonder at it. But my old grandaunt and others, the family servants especially, would say to me: 'Don't believe anything unkind about your
mother; she loved you all as much as any mother could do; she could
not help herself.' "

Lafcadio once recalled a strange memory of his mother: "One day [my
mother's face] bent over me caressingly. . . . A childish impulse came to
me to slap it. I slapped it—simply to see the result, perhaps. The result
was immediate and severe castigation, and I remember both crying and
feeling I deserved what I got. I felt no resentment, although the aggressor
in such cases is usually the most indignant at consequences."

This confession of childish perversity may have been in part a dis-
placed memory of the behavior of a frequently irrational and physically
abusive mother, herself unloved, dispirited, rejected, on the edge of emotional despair. However, Rosa Cassimati Hearn's dark eyes and dark hair
would come to haunt every aspect of Lafcadio's life. To him she was, and
would always remain, "divine," a volatile Mother goddess. She loved him
in the only way she could—from the depths of her own elemental nature
and spirit; and she was the only person throughout his often mistrusting
life whom he never stopped remembering with love.

"Whatever there is good in me," he told his brother, "came from that
dark race-soul of which we know so little. My love of right, my hate of
wrong;—my admiration for what is beautiful or true;—my capacity for
faith in man or woman;—my sensitiveness to artistic things which give
me whatever little *success I have*;—even that language power whose physical sign is in the large eyes of both of us,—came from Her.

"What if there is 'a skeleton in our closet'? Did not he make it? I think
only of her . . . rarely of him. It is the mother who makes us,—makes at
least all that makes the nobler man: not his strength or powers of calculation, but his heart and power to love. And I would rather have her
portrait *than a fortune*."

Lafcadio had asked his brother to send him a photographic portrait of
their father, saying that he had lost his copy (perhaps intentionally) many
years before. Then, having received it, he wrote back: "When I look on
the portrait . . . with that rigid grim face and steel-steady eyes, I can not
feel much in my life common with his. I suspect I do not love him."

Lafcadio consciously remembered seeing his father no more than five
times when he was a child, and Charles Hearn, uncomfortable around
his son, apparently never showed him any affection. One of their encounters, though, turned out to be quite significant:

One day, my father came to my aunt's house to take me out for a walk. He took me into some quiet street, where the houses were very high— with long flights of steps going up to the front door. Then a lady came down to meet us, all white-robed, with very bright hair—quite slender. I thought her beautiful as an angel, perhaps partly because she kissed me and petted me, and gave me a beautiful book and a toy gun. But my aunt found it out, and took away the book and the gun, and said that was a very wicked woman and my father a very wicked man. She was the woman who afterward became my father's second wife. . . .

Alicia Goslin had been Charles Hearn's sweetheart before he ever went to Greece. They had talked of marrying, but Alicia's parents had persuaded her to marry a wealthier man, a judge named George John Crawford, who then emigrated with his bride to Australia. On his way back to Dublin from the West Indies in 1853, Charles Hearn learned that Alicia's husband had died, and that she and her two children were living in Ireland. While still married to Rosa, Charles renewed his friendship with Alicia, and after his return from the Crimea, the two took up where they had left off fifteen years before. They were married in Dublin in July of 1857, less than a year after Hearn's annulment. That August, Hearn and his new wife left with the First Infantry Regiment for Secunderabad, India, where they lived together until Alicia's death from fever in 1861. Charles occasionally wrote to Lafcadio about serpents and tigers and elephants, but the boy never responded, and he never saw his father again, even though the latter returned to Dublin for a short sick leave in 1862. (Hearn, who had three daughters with Alicia, died of malaria in the Gulf of Suez on November 21, 1866.)

For most of his life, Lafcadio blamed his father and stepmother for betraying and abandoning his mother. "I could not love his . . . children by that woman with bright hair who kissed me as a boy," he would write later to his brother James. "The soul in me is not of him." Lafcadio always insisted on his Greek ancestry as determinative of his character, talent, and soul. He refused to acknowledge an emotional tie between himself and a person who, he felt, had never recognized any ties with *him*, and whose behavior toward his adored mother seemed unforgivable.

Strangely, though, in parts of West Somersetshire and Northumberland, where his father's family had its roots, the name "Hearn" was thought to be of gypsy origin, despite the family's many respectable ecclesiastical and military forebears. Even within the family, a story was told about one of Lafcadio's aunts who came unexpectedly upon a band of gypsies in the Irish countryside. She asked a gypsy to tell her fortune, and the gypsy, after examining her hand carefully, raised the aunt's palm and said, "You're one of us, the proof is *here.*" Moreover, the three daughters of Charles and Alicia Hearn all had Lafcadio's distinctive physiognomy—dark complexion, black hair, aquiline profiles, deeply set eyes—hardly common English features. Lafcadio himself, much later in life, commented on this physical affinity of his half-sisters' and his own children. He was also known to display with pride the mark on his thumb that was supposed to be the infallible sign of Romany descent. That Charles and Lafcadio Hearn were both perpetual wanderers is perhaps more than a coincidence. It is intriguing that the various modifications of the name *Hearn*—Erne, Horne, Hern, Herne, Hearon, Hirn—derive from the Teutonic *irren:* to wander, to stray, to err, to become outlaw; and the Indo-Germanic word *Hirn*—related to the word *errant* (as in *knight errant*)—is said to mean "the brain or organ of the wandering spirit or ghost," a particularly Lafcadian image.

Lafcadio (still known, as long as he lived in the British Isles, as Patrick) was five years old when his father entrusted him to Sarah Brenane as his official guardian. She was then sixty-four years old and knew nothing about children. To her, this little orphan, with his shoulder-length black hair, the faraway look in his increasingly myopic eyes, and the stuffed animal that he clung to, was intended to be the proper *Catholic* Brenane heir that she and her deceased husband had always hoped for.

"At that time," Lafcadio once said, "I was scarcely ever mentioned by name, but only referred to as 'the Child.' " The Child lived in a grand, dark, three-story house with soft carpets on the stairway, four-poster beds, a library, a parlormaid, a footman, and occasional visitors, including priests and stray Catholic converts befriended by Mrs. Brenane. It was also a house filled with shadows.

The Child was inordinately terrified of goblins and ghosts and saw them everywhere, especially in the dark. Mrs. Brenane thought that the best way to have the Child overcome these silly fears was to shut him in his room by himself at night, turn out the lights, and lock the door. Alone in the blackness, the Child would scream when he felt ghosts pulling at the bedclothes. Whenever he cried out, he would be whipped. "But the fear of ghosts," he said later, "was greater than the fear of whippings—*because I could see the ghosts.* The old lady did not believe me; but the servants did, and used to come and comfort me by stealth."

Even when Aunt Sarah took the Child to church, the eerie shapes would present themselves. According to Lafcadio, "The wizened and pointed shapes of the windows immediately terrified me. In their outline I found the form of apparitions that tormented me in sleep;—and at once I began to imagine some dreadful affinity between goblins and Gothic churches." In an attempt to allay his fears, Mrs. Brenane taught the Child some prayers, which he would dutifully parrot back, and gave him small French religious prints edged with lace.

In the Child's bedroom, on the other hand, was something that had belonged to his mother, which so fascinated Lafcadio that he would re- member it all his life:

To the wall of the room in which I slept there was suspended a Greek icon—a miniature painting in oil of the Virgin and Child, warmly colored, and protected by a casing of fine metal that left exposed only the olive- brown faces and hands and feet of the figures. But I fancied that the brown Virgin represented my mother—whom I had almost completely forgotten—and the large-eyed Child, myself. I had been taught to pro- nounce the invocation, *In the name of the Father, and of the Son, and of the Holy Ghost;*—but I did not know what the words signified. One of the appellations, however, seriously interested me: and the first religious question that I remember asking was a question about the *Holy Ghost*. It was the word "Ghost," of course, that had excited my curiosity; and I put the question with fear and trembling because it appeared to relate to a forbidden subject. The answer I cannot clearly recollect;—but it gave me an idea that the Holy Ghost was a *white* ghost, and not in the habit of making faces at small people after dusk. Nevertheless the name filled me with vague suspicion, especially after I had learned to spell it correctly, in a prayer-book; and I discovered a mystery and an awfulness unspeak- able in the capital G. Even now the aspect of that formidable letter will sometimes revive those dim and fearsome imaginings of childhood.

CHAPTER *3*

Renaissance

WITH THE PASSING of dreary winter and the rainy months of spring, Lafcadio would look forward to the bright and happy reality of summer, when the ghosts of Dublin went into hiding. Now seven years old, he began to spend long, contented, mostly sunny months, under the strict but not oppressive supervision of Aunt Sarah, at Tramore on the southern Irish coast; and at Bangor, North Wales. Occasionally he visited his cousins in Cong, County Mayo, where he searched for fairy rings with his favorite cousin, Robert Elwood, who was a year older than himself. There one day they came across a strange, unkempt-looking vagabond harper who began singing a lilting Irish song with a kind of rough tenderness that both frightened and attracted the two boys, and that unexpectedly made Lafcadio cry, suggesting to him for the first time the ambiguous nature of beauty.

At Tramore he listened to the pounding of the sea, which may have reminded him of far-off places and times. He also learned about fishing and boating from an old Wexford fisherman who would regale the boy with sea yarns. And when alone with his nanny—and out of earshot of his aunt—he would listen, entranced, to her melodious Irish brogue as she told stories, legends, and superstitions about banshees, leprechauns, merrows, and changelings.

In Wales, near Bangor, Lafcadio played on wide, sandy beaches and learned to swim. He rode donkey-phaetons, observed Welsh farmers wearing traditional witch hats, and made many visits to a private museum in Bangor, where were displayed South Pacific and Chinese curiosities: a

Fijian spear barbed with shark's teeth, paddles from the Sandwich Islands, and an enormous moon-yellow Chinese metal gong that the owner of the museum would strike, at Lafcadio's request, with a padded drumstick. "And it commenced to sob, like waves upon a low beach. [The man] tapped it again, and it moaned like the wind in a mighty forest of pines. Again, and it commenced to roar, and with each tap the roar grew deeper and deeper, till it seemed like thunder rolling over an abyss in the Cordilleras, or the crashing of Thor's chariot wheels." He also lived with his nanny for a season in the rented cottage of a Carnarvon sea-captain who had been on the China run and had collected an enthralling assortment of statues of oriental gods, porcelain animals, and Eastern grotesqueries, which so fascinated Lafcadio that he would dream of them at night.

At the end of bright summers like these, the shadows of the gloomy Brenane house always loomed large. But Lafcadio had less time now for goblins and ghosts. For Aunt Sarah had installed a live-in tutor to impart to her heir-to-be the dogmas of the Catholic Church, and to teach him the rudiments of reading, writing, and arithmetic. (He had by this time forgotten Italian and Romaic, and now spoke a charming Irish-tinged English.) Lafcadio quickly discovered that he was bored by arithmetic, despised creeds and dogmas, and loved reading and writing.

As he got older, he began to frequent the Brenane library, a room almost no one else ever entered. For hours he would hide away in this musty, quiet, mysterious room, lock the door, and pick out books at random, like an adventurer searching for hidden treasure.

And then it happened:

[At last one day I discovered, in one unexplored corner of our library, several beautiful books about art—great folio books containing figures of gods and of demigods, athletes and heroes, nymphs and fauns and nereids, and all the charming monsters—half-man, half-animal—of Greek mythology.

How my heart leaped and fluttered on that happy day! Breathless I gazed; and the longer that I gazed the more unspeakably lovely those faces and forms appeared. Figure after figure dazzled, astounded, bewitched me. And this new delight was in itself a wonder—also a fear. Something seemed to be thrilling out of those pictured pages—something invisible that made me afraid. I remembered stories of the infernal magic that informed the work of the pagan statuaries. But this superstitious fear

presently yielded to a conviction, or rather intuition—which I could not
possibly have explained—that the gods had been belied *because* they were
beautiful. . . .

And these had been called devils! I adored them!—I loved them!—I
promised to detest forever all who refused them reverence! . . . Oh! The
contrast between that immortal loveliness and the squalor of the saints
and the patriarchs and the prophets of my religious pictures!—a contrast
indeed as of heaven and hell. . . . In that hour the medieval creed seemed
to me the very religion of ugliness and of hate. And as it had been taught
to me, in the weakness of my sickly childhood, it certainly was. . . .

But this new-found delight soon became for me the source of new
sorrows. . . . One day the beautiful books disappeared; and I was afraid
to ask what had become of them. After many weeks they were returned
to their former place; and my joy at seeing them again was of brief duration. All of them had been unmercifully revised. My censors had been
offended by the nakedness of the gods, and had undertaken to correct
that impropriety. Parts of many figures, dryads, naiads, graces, muses had
been . . . erased with a penknife;—I can still recall one beautiful seated
figure, whose breasts had been excised. Evidently "the breasts of the
nymphs in the brake" had been found too charming: dryads, naiads,
graces and muses—all had been rendered breastless. And, in most cases,
drawers had been put on the gods—even upon the tiny Loves—large baggy
bathing-drawers, woven with cross-strokes of a quill-pen, so designed as
to conceal all curves of beauty—especially the long fine thighs. . . . However, in my case, this barbarism proved of some educational value. It
furnished me with many problems of restoration; and I often tried very
hard to reproduce in pencil-drawing the obliterated or the hidden line.
In this I was not successful; but, in spite of the amazing thoroughness
with which every mutilation or effacement had been accomplished, my
patient study of the methods of attack enabled me . . . to understand how
Greek artists had idealized the human figure. . . .

Now after I had learned to know and love the elder gods, the world
again began to glow about me. Glooms that had brooded over it slowly
thinned away. The terror was not yet gone; but I now wanted only reasons to disbelieve all that I feared and hated. In the sunshine, in the green
of the fields, in the blue of the sky, I found a gladness before unknown.
Within myself new thoughts, new imaginings, dim longings for I knew
not what were quickening and thrilling. I looked for beauty, and everywhere found it: in passing faces—in attitudes and motions—in the poise

of plants and trees—in long white clouds—in faint-blue lines of far-off
hills. At moments the simple pleasure of life would quicken to a joy so
large, so deep, that it frightened me. But at other times there would come
to me a new and strange sadness—a shadowy and inexplicable pain.

I had entered into my Renaissance.   ("IDOLATRY")]

Cynics might say that Lafcadio had simply entered early adolescence
(he was only nine or ten years old when his epiphany in the Brenane
library occurred). In any case, it led to a personal rebirth for this with-
drawn, alienated boy, giving him a sense of who he really was and who,
he felt certain, he had somehow always been.

One of the meanings of the Greek word for "truth" (a-letheia) is "no-
forgetting"; and looking back to this moment in his childhood, Lafcadio
embraced this notion of truth with his entire being. "He who receives in
one sudden vision the revelation of the antique beauty," he would declare, "—the unutterable mingling of delight and sadness—he remembers!"
It was a remembering, moreover, that went back further than his Ionian
childhood, a kind of race memory. "Three thousand—four thousand years
ago: it matters not," he stated; "what thrills him now is the shadowing
of what has been, the phantom of rapture forgotten. Without inherited
sense of the meaning of beauty as power, of the worth of it to life and
love, never could the ghost in him perceive, however dimly, the presence
of the gods." The divine humanity and beauty of the ancient Greek spirit—
and not the cold, and sterile piety of Gothic Christianity—would from
now on be his true guiding light—a new paganism.

As time went by, Aunt Sarah, now approaching seventy, began to
realize that her grandnephew was never going to be the kind of good
Roman Catholic she had hoped he would be. Slowly, then surely, both
her emotional and her pecuniary allegiance shifted from Lafcadio to a
young man named Henry Hearn Molyneux, a distant relation of her deceased husband and an even more distant kin of the Hearns. Thirteen
years older than her troubling grandnephew, Henry had already attended
a Catholic commercial college, spoke several foreign languages, was con-
spicuously and almost exaggeratedly devout, and clearly ambitious. Mrs.
Brenane found him inordinately charming, and before long he had become her personal financial adviser—as well as principal beneficiary of
her own investments—as he pursued his own business of importing goods
from the East.

In due time, Sarah Brenane sold her Dublin home, having been persuaded by Henry to spend her last years with him and his wife, Agnes, in Surrey. Soon Henry had also persuaded Mrs. Brenane to assign to one of his wife's relatives the whole of her County Wexford estate—several thousand acres in the baronies of Bantry, Scarawalsh, and Ballaghkeen—which had previously been intended for her grandnephew.

Concerning young Patrick Hearn, Mrs. Brenane convinced herself that she had never really promised that the boy was to be her *sole* heir; she now simply planned to leave him an annuity. And while the delicate estate-transfer negotiations were taking place, Henry Molyneux sought to convince Mrs. Brenane that it would be in Patrick's best interest if he were sent as soon as possible out of the country to study in a school in France. The aunt, feeling some remorse, said that the boy was only twelve years old and had no parents and no family except for her. But knowledge of a foreign language would certainly stand Patrick in good stead, Henry reassured her. Besides, he added, he had already looked into the matter, and the school that Patrick would attend, everyone agreed, was a fine, decent, and upstanding *Catholic* school.

Sarah Brenane could not refuse such a suggestion.

CHAPTER 4

Shades of the Prison-House

T H E Institution Ecclésiastique at Yvetot near Rouen was a well-known and highly regarded church school among many British Catholic parents. To some of its students, however, the Petit Séminaire, as it was generally known, was three-quarters monastery, one-quarter military barracks, administered, as Lafcadio recalled, by "a hateful, venomous-hearted old maid." In later years Lafcadio would compare the school's headmistress to the figure of Madame Beck in Charlotte Brontë's remarkable novel *Villette* ("To attempt to touch her heart was the surest way to rouse her antipathy," Brontë had written, "and to make of her a secret foe. It proved to her that she had no heart to be touched: it reminded her where she was impotent and dead").

The school day began promptly at 5:00 A.M. with mass in chapel and ended with vespers at 9:00 P.M.; meals were eaten in silence and accompanied with readings from the gospels, the lives of the saints, and Daniel's *History of England.* Classes held under the supervision of humorless *curés* in spartan rooms of bare boards and black benches further contributed to Lafcadio's lifelong conviction that Christian education consisted of "conventional dreariness and ugliness and dirty austerities and long faces and Jesuitry and infamous distortion of children's brains."

He was not alone in his acrimonious view. Another witness to the rigidity and baleful atmosphere of the Petit Séminaire was the young Guy de Maupassant, who entered the school just several months after Lafcadio left (the French writer was there as a young boy in 1863–64, and again in 1866–67), and who described the institution in a story called "Une Surprise":

I can never think of the place even now without a shudder. It smelled
of prayers the way a fish-market smells of fish. Oh! That dreary school,
with its eternal religious ceremonies, its freezing Mass every morning, its
periods of meditation, its gospel-recitations, and the reading from pious
books during meals! Oh! Those dreary days passed within those cloister-
ing walls, where nothing was spoken of but God. . . . We lived there in
a narrow, contemplative, unnatural piety—and also in a truly meritorious
state of filth, for I well remember that the boys were made to wash their
feet but three times a year, the night before each vacation. As for baths,
they were as unknown as the name of Victor Hugo. Our masters apparently held them in the greatest contempt.

Lafcadio elatedly said *adieu* to the Petit Séminaire after one year. He
had detested it, but he *had* learned French—well enough so that in later
times he would himself translate works by de Maupassant and others into
English.

In September 1863—again at the recommendation of Henry Molyneux—the thirteen-year-old matriculated at St. Cuthbert's College, Ushaw,
County Durham. A strict Catholic school of three hundred boys which
trained its students both for the priesthood and for university, the institution prided itself on its unhesitating meting out of "stripes innumerable"
for bad conduct, insubordination, and the persistent questioning of received Catholic dogma and ethics. Lafcadio was in for some brutal times.

Regarded as "slightly off his mental balance" (as one of his classmates
put it) by some of the students, Lafcadio found it easier at school to use
the diminutive of his Christian name in order to avoid being teased for a
strange Greek one—in addition to being teased, as he often was, for his
small stature and poor eyesight. More high-spirited than he had ever been
in Ireland or France, the teenage "Paddy" Hearn often provoked whippings by instigating various adolescent escapades, raggings, and pranks—
then laughed off the punishment. His teachers considered him eccentric;
one of them, a future bishop, recalled that Paddy Hearn had let the nail
of the index finger of his right hand grow to great length, then cut it into
the shape of a quill pen and tried to write with it.

Lafcadio was, however, the head of his classes in English composition
for three consecutive years. In the insufferable religion classes, on the
other hand, he continually disturbed the instructor-priests by questioning
the truth of Divine Writ, as well as many accepted teachings, and he
particularly shocked his personal confessor by his admission that he had
often had a fantasy of the devil in the form of a beautiful woman and

that he had gladly yielded himself to her temptations. At which point the priest rose and shouted at the boy, saying: "Let me warn you! Of all things never wish that! You might be more sorry for it than you can possibly believe!"

"Now when he thus spoke," Lafcadio remarked, "his earnestness filled me with a fearful joy;—for I thought all that I wished for might be realized—so serious he looked. And, after that, oh! how I prayed for some pretty gracious devil to come to me, and take my soul in exchange for—! But the merciless succubi all continued to remain in hell!"

Reserving to himself his most basic and deeply felt pagan and Hellenistic ideas, Lafcadio did experience one epiphanic moment at college that may have reawakened in him his ecstatic childhood memories under Leucadian skies (as well as his sense of pagan beauty in Mrs. Brenane's library):

⟦ I remember . . . lying on my back in the grass, gazing into the summer blue above me, and wishing I could melt into it, become a part of it. For these fancies I believe that a religious tutor was innocently responsible; he had tried to explain to me, because of certain dreamy questions, what he termed "the folly and the wickedness of Pantheism," with the result that I immediately became a Pantheist, at the tender age of fifteen. And my imaginings presently led me not only to want the sky for a playground, but also to become the sky! ⟧

With his best friend at St. Cuthbert's, an Irish boy with, strangely enough, the equally tauntable Greek name of Achilles Daunt, Lafcadio would take leisurely walks through the spacious college grounds: "two lads,—absolutely innocent of everything wrong in the world or in life,—living in ideals of duty and dreams of future miracles, and telling each other all their troubles, and bracing each other up."

Achilles Daunt would later reminisce about his old schoolmate:

Knightly feats of arms, combats with gigantic foes in deep forests, low red moons throwing their dim light across desolate spaces, and glinting on the armor of great champions, storms howling over wastes and ghosts shrieking in the gale—these were favorite topics of conversation, and in describing these fancies his language was unusually rich. . . .

A note was handed to me one evening from him as I sat reading in [the] library, inviting me to take a stroll. The style of this epistle was eminently characteristic of his tastes and style:

> Meet me at twelve at the Gothic door,
> Massive and quaint, of the days of yore;
> When the spectral forms of the mighty dead
> Glide by in the moonlight with silent tread;
> When the owl from the branch of the blasted oak
>   Shrieks forth his note so wild,
> And the toad from the marsh echoes with croak
>   In the moonlight soft and mild.
> When the dead in the lonely vaults below
>   Rise up in grim array
> And glide past with footsteps hushed and slow,
>   Weird forms, unknown in day;
> When the dismal death-bells clang so near,
>   Sounding o'er wold and lea,
> And the wail of the spirits strikes the ear
>   Like the moan of the sobbing sea.

In response to a schoolmate's boast about the length of his home address, Lafcadio declared his own to be much longer: "P. L. Hearn, Esq., Ushaw College, near Durham, England, Europe, Eastern Hemisphere, The Earth, Universe, Space, God." For all his far-flung unbounded view of the world (and beyond), however, Lafcadio was an exceedingly myopic teenager. His poor eyesight limited his involvement in any sports activity except for swimming, and made it necessary for him to read with his eyes not more than two or three inches from the printed page.

Then, when he was sixteen, an accident occurred that would change his life forever. It is difficult to know exactly *what* happened, since several stories exist. It may have been that while Lafcadio was playing a rope game called Giant's Stride, the knotted end of the rope was accidentally or intentionally flung at him; or else, as Lafcadio himself stated, he may have been punched by one of his classmates ("They are gentle in English Schools, particularly in Jesuitical schools!"). In either case, his damaged left eye became infected and required an operation in Dublin and consultations with several London optometrists, all to no avail. The eye was now blind, with part of the retina destroyed and the surface of the eye whitened by scar tissue. This colorless, bulbous eye, along with his congenitally protuberant right eye, was a disfigurement that destroyed his already fragile sense of self-confidence and trust in other persons; it also exacerbated his existing obsessions with "the Odd, the Queer, the Strange, the Exotic, the Monstrous"; and forced him to wear glasses (something he had always disliked doing) or use a magnifying glass and small folding telescope in order to see things clearly close up and far away. From then on, Lafcadio would instinctively cover his left eye with his left hand when conversing with someone, and look down or to the left when being photographed.

It took Lafcadio a year to recuperate from his injury and operation. Then in October 1867 he received more bad news. The financially clever Henry Molyneux, who had previously mortgaged Sarah Brenane's County Wexford property for £7,000, had gone bankrupt—Mrs. Brenane along with him—and she now found herself unable to pay Lafcadio's college fees. No other member of the Hearn family had offered to help him complete his schooling. So in 1868, Lafcadio found himself, without money or a job, lodging, at Henry Molyneux's suggestion, in London's East End with a former parlormaid of Aunt Sarah's named Catherine Delaney and her dock-worker husband.

Far from the wooded hills of North Wales, from the meadows, flow-ered lanes, and beaches of Tramore Bay, and from the expansive lawns of St. Cuthbert's, Lafcadio now wandered the dark, gloomy streets of London—and like William Blake before him, saw in every face he met, "marks of weakness, marks of woe." The previously sheltered eighteen-year-old was overwhelmed by the slum-dwellers he encountered (ped-dlers, vagabonds, costermongers, pickpockets, prostitutes), thirty to forty of whom would often be living in a single house. He would later melo-dramatically recall "windows thrown violently open, or shattered to pieces, shrieks of agony, or cries of murder, followed by a heavy plunge in the river." Mrs. Brenane sent the Delaneys a pittance from time to time for Lafcadio's care, but that family had its own cares and paid no attention to where Lafcadio went or what he did. Feeling unwanted, unneeded, unwelcome, and alone, the boarder would take refuge for short periods in workhouses, and for the first time he faced "the wolf's side of life, the ravening side, the apish side; the ugly facets of the monkey puzzle."

There were only a few things that gave Lafcadio comfort during this rootless time: the poetry of Swinburne, which he discovered in a book-store and used to recite aloud to himself on his aimless walks ("Thou hast conquered, O pale Galilean; the world has grown gray from thy breath;/We have drunken of things Lethean, and fed on the fullness of death./Laurel is green for a season, and love is sweet for a day;/But love grows bitter with treason, and laurel outlives not May"); mornings spent sitting on the London docks, gazing for hours at the tall ships ("swift Hermae of traffic—ghosts of the infinite ocean"); and occasional afternoons in the British Museum, where he was drawn to a room of Japanese Buddhas "chambered with forgotten divinities of Egypt or Babylon under the gloom of a pea soup fog."

Henry Molyneux, after much prodding of the Delaneys, received a report from them about the Hearn boy's aimless existence, and, now back once more on his financial feet, decided to do something about Patrick Hearn once and for all. This time there was no need for him to persuade Sarah Brenane; she was now seventy-five years old, and physically and mentally infirm. In the spring of 1869, then, Molyneux's sister, Frances Anne, was living in Cincinnati, Ohio, with her husband, Thomas Cullinan. Without consulting the Hearn boy, Molyneux bought a one-way boat ticket to New York City, called the unmanageable nineteen-year-old to his office, presented him with the ticket and a small amount of money, and instructed him to find his way to Cincinnati. There he promised that the Cullinans would offer Lafcadio all the hospitality, help, and familial advice he would need to start an auspicious and productive new life in the Land of Opportunity.

Lafcadio looked at the ticket, put it in his pocket, and went off to America.

CHAPTER 5

In the Land
of Opportunity

M ARK TWAIN is reported to have said, "When the end of the world comes, I want to be in Cincinnati—it is always ten years behind the times."

The city began in 1788 as a somnolent Ohio River trading post called Losantiville or, alternatively and more colorfully, City Across the Mouth of the Licking River. Preferring to remain a steamboat marketing center rather than becoming a massive railroad hub like the growing metropolis of Chicago, Cincinnati, with its quarter of a million people, was still, in 1869, America's largest inland city.

One fifth of the residents were of German descent and lived "Over-the-Rhine"—north and east of the old Miami Canal—and worked at pork-packing, tanning, soap-manufacturing, and beer-brewing. Scores of breweries were scattered throughout the Cincinnati hills. (Today, only the Hudepohl-Schoenling Brewing Company remains.) There was a large English and Irish contingent, a smaller French and even smaller Jewish one. And there were thousands of impoverished, uprooted blacks—almost all ex-slaves from Kentucky, many of whose pre–Civil War flights to freedom across the Ohio into Cincinnati had been dramatized in Harriet Beecher Stowe's *Uncle Tom's Cabin.*

Most of the black population lived in the overcrowded shanties, hovels, and dens of the mud-inundated and crime-beset neighborhood known as Bucktown (in the vicinity of Sixth and Seventh streets east of Broadway) that overflowed into the open countryside to the east. The rest of the city's blacks—mainly transient stevedores, porters, and deckhands—

found temporary refuge from the river in the warehouse cellars and in-salubrious boarding rooms of the often-flooded, wide-open waterfront district called the Levee.

The more prosperous denizens of Cincinnati—the city of the Long-worths, the Tafts, and the Thompsons—were then in the process of spon-soring the construction of broad avenues, civic-minded monuments, imposing public buildings, expansive and affluent suburbs. Cincinnati took pride in itself as a Midwestern cultural oasis with its thriving news-paper, magazine, and book-publishing companies, its two large theaters and two opera houses, with productions of *opéra comique,* plays by local dramatists, and recitals by renowned European artists. If important cul-tural events took place in the city one or two—or even *ten*—years later than they did in Boston or New York, so be it. No one wished to give up the Southern amenities and gracious pace of Cincinnati life. A city with pride.

When Lafcadio descended from his coach at the Cincinnati train station after his long journey from New York City, an observer might have no-ticed a thin and tired young man, five feet three inches tall, with olive complexion, one enlarged dark-brown eye—the other whitish and blind—wearing thick-lensed glasses, a small mustache resting above a thin mouth, a long aquiline nose, abundant black hair falling in a shock over a square forehead, broad and strong shoulders, delicate hands, and graceful, almost feline, movements. His manner betrayed a shy, hypersensitive, suspicious, and often sullen nature. When he spoke, however, he had an entrancing melodic lilt to his voice. Obviously a person of little means, he wore black clothes that were frayed and badly patched. He had no trade, no profession, no friends. Only the name and address of one Thomas Cul-linan, who turned out to be a cold, inhospitable person with a large family to support and no time or inclination to help a tatterdemalion from the old country. Cullinan invited Lafcadio into his apartment, took a couple of close looks at this short, strange-looking boy, gave him five dollars—courtesy of Sarah Brenane—gruffly wished him good luck, and shoved him out the door.

Alone in an unknown city in the middle of an unknown country, Lafcadio quickly spent his money on smoking tobacco and some second-hand clothes. He also, in a questionable part of town, obtained a small amount of opium to dull the pangs of hunger. Unable to afford even a cheap rooming house, he was forced to sleep on the streets; and when the police rousted him, he made do with grocers' sheds, a boiler, and even dry-goods boxes.

One day, walking aimlessly into a mews, he met some English coachmen who, learning of the boy's situation, allowed him to sleep surreptitiously for a few weeks in a hayloft—even stealing scraps of food for him from their master's house:

I take off my clothes—few and thin—and roll them up into a bundle, to serve me for a pillow: then I creep naked into the hay. . . . Oh, the delight of my hay-bed—the first bed of any sort for many a long night!— oh, the pleasure of the sense of rest! The sweet scent of the hay! . . . Overhead, through a skylight, I see stars—sharply shining: there is frost in the air.

The horses, below, stir heavily at moments, and paw. I hear them breathe; and their breath comes up to me in steam. The warmth of their great bodies fills the building, penetrates the hay, quickens my blood; —their life is my fire.

So contentedly they breathe! . . . They must be aware that I am here— nestling in their hay. But they do not mind;—and for that I am grateful. Grateful, too, for the warmth of their breath, the warmth of their pure bodies, the warmth of their good hay—grateful even for those stirrings which they make in their rest, filling the dark with assurance of large dumb tolerant companionship. . . . I wish I could tell them how thankful I am—how much I like them—what pleasure I feel in the power that proceeds from them, in the sense of force and life that they spread through the silence, like a large warm Soul. . . .

It is better that they cannot understand. For they earn their good food and lodging;—they earn the care that keeps them glossy and beautiful; —they are of use in the world. And of what use in the world am I? . . .

Those sharply shining stars are suns—enormous suns. They must be giving light to multitudes unthinkable of other worlds. . . . In some of those other worlds there must be cities, and creatures resembling horses, and stables for them, and hay, and small things—somewhat like rats or mice—hiding in the hay. . . . I know that there are a hundred millions of suns. The horses do not know. But, nevertheless, they are worth, I have been told, fifteen hundred dollars each: they are superior beings! How much am I worth? . . .

Tomorrow, after they have been fed, I also shall be fed—by kindly stealth;—and I shall not have earned the feeding, in spite of the fact that I know there are hundreds of millions of suns!   ]

Despite this seemingly futile existence, Lafcadio had a sense that there was something greater than himself, his loneliness, his problems; there were hundreds of millions of stars, and somehow he was part of it all. On a more mundane level, moreover, the frontiers of America were expanding; the transcontinental railroad, for instance, had just been completed. So he decided to look for work somewhere . . . or anywhere, becoming, for short periods, a messenger boy, a waiter, a canvasser, and then a boardinghouse servant, lighting fires and shoveling coals in exchange for meals and the privilege of sleeping on the smoking-room floor.

One day, Lafcadio was introduced to an English printer named Henry Watkin—a largely self-taught, freethinking radical who was especially interested in utopian communalism. The slow-speaking forty-five-year-old man took a bemused look at the nineteen-year-old waif and, upon learning that Lafcadio knew no trade, asked:

"Well, my young man, how do you expect to earn a living?" "I don't know." "And what ambition do you nourish?" "To write, sir." "Mercy on us! Better learn something that will put bread in your mouth first; try your hand at writing later on," Watkin advised.

Something about this curious-looking fellow intrigued Watkin. He offered Lafcadio the job of errand boy–janitor in his back-street printmaking shop, instructed him in typesetting, and made a bed of paper shavings in one of the back rooms for him.

For about two months the two comrades worked and lived together (since there was no bedroom in the shop, Mrs. Watkin and her daughter were residing temporarily outside the city), spending hours after dinner talking about books, politics, and religion in Watkin's quiet office—amidst his library of "infidel" books (Tom Paine, Voltaire, Saint-Simon) and pamphlets about deism and atheism. To the stately ticking of a grandfather clock, Lafcadio would hold copies of the *Atlantic Monthly* up close to his face and read aloud to the printer articles by Emerson, Oliver Wendell Holmes, and James Russell Lowell; and after Watkin retired for the night, Lafcadio would stay up reading on his own.

"The old man was something of a Fourierist," Lafcadio said years later about his first friend in Cincinnati, who "preceded [me] into exile by nearly forty years," and through whom "I made acquaintance first with hosts of fantastic heterodoxies. Of Fourier himself, Hepworth Dixon ('Spiritual Wives'), the Spiritualists . . . and the Mormons,—the founders of phalansteries and the founders of free love societies."

The American founding fathers might have been influenced by deist, rationalist, and Masonic ideas, but most Americans after the French Revolution were devout and evangelical Christians. Henry Watkin, however, had a quasi-scientific, agnostic, and

HENRY WATKIN

utopian turn of mind, and he would spend hours telling Lafcadio about the complicated but extraordinary conception of "phalansteries" imagined by the French utopian thinker Charles Fourier (1772–1837). Each phalanstery was to have a common building housing about two thousand individuals on three square miles of land divided into fields, orchards, and gardens. Its residents would be divided into groups of seven persons who performed the tasks of farmers, mechanics, scientists, or artists (the cleaning of privies was left to junior battalions of children)—each person free to move between one group or occupation and another. A believer in the fulfillment of sensual pleasure, Fourier proposed a Chancellery of the Court of Love, Corporations of Love, and a system of organized polygamy. He further posited a cosmology in which the Earth—upon the future attainment of its Great Harmony—would witness corpses transformed into interstellar perfume, the sea into a kind of *citron pressé,* and a "gentler" world of anti-lions, anti-rats, anti-bugs.

Some of Fourier's ideas *were* a bit moonstruck and balmy, Watkin conceded; but newspaper editors like Horace Greeley and Charles A. Dana, writers like Margaret Fuller, James Russell Lowell, John Greenleaf Whittier, and, of course, the residents of Brook Farm, had been won over by at least some of the eccentric French philosopher's more practical suggestions for sexual, economic, and social harmony.

Lafcadio, however, found himself more fascinated by John Humphrey Noyes, founder of the Oneida Community in the late 1840s. At once devout, radical, and learned, Noyes was a rationalist believer who had studied theology at Yale and who espoused a form of apostolic Christianity that embraced the subversive notions of a divinized male-female conception of the Godhead, the equality of men and women, and communal living and communal ownership of property. The Perfectionists, as the Noyes sect called itself, lived and worked together in what became a profitable agricultural and manufacturing settlement in northern New York. They practiced a form of group (or "complex") marriage, a kind of elementary erotic yoga involving orgasm without ejaculation, communal childrearing, vegetarianism, faith healing, controlled eugenic breeding (known as "stripiculture"), group criticism, and community consensus. Like the Quakers, they trusted in the possibility of human goodness.

Lafcadio had certainly never come across ideas like these at the Petit Séminaire or St. Cuthbert's, and was profoundly grateful to Henry Watkin for the "unlearning," as Lafcadio put it, the older man was providing him. Sometimes after work, printer and apprentice took long, leisurely walks across the Ohio River into Kentucky to attend revivalist meetings or lectures on spiritualism frequently held there. Watkin had a tolerant, unprejudiced mind, but he lamented intelligent people who gave themselves over to obvious shams or frauds. The once ghost-obsessed Lafcadio listened with respect to the printer, and soon was observing with amused skepticism the well-contrived shows of the charlatans and mountebanks.

Gone to get my sable plumage plucked

Gradually, the young man took the older man into his confidence and fervently spoke to him about his strange, disordered life; about his passion for the Greek gods; about his sense of religion as epidemic insanity and of Christianity as antagonistic to nature, passion, and justice; and about his antagonism toward (as he put it) "hypocrite" priests, "goblin nuns in black robes," and "civilized" folk who considered themselves so superior to the powerless, the "uncouth," and the "savage" types of the world. Soon Lafcadio was familiarly addressing the sympathetic Watkin as "Old Man" or "Dad," and the printer in his turn would call his pale, dark-haired, moody young apprentice "The Raven," a name inspired by Lafcadio's admiration for Edgar Allan Poe as well as by the evident affinities between that misunderstood author's life and Lafcadio's. For Poe had been orphaned at the age of two, Lafcadio abandoned by his parents at the age of five. Both men had been raised by adults who never understood, accepted, or officially adopted them; both suffered from extreme poverty and rejection and lived as misfits and strangers in society.

Lafcadio, however, now had a friend, an acknowledging, generous "father," whom he would trust and keep for the rest of his life. If the Old Man was not in his printing shop when The Raven showed up in the evening, Lafcadio would leave a little note: "I came to see you—to thank you—to remonstrate with you—to demonstrate matters syllogistically and phlebotomically. GONE!!! Then I departed, wandering among the tombs of Memory, where the Ghouls of the present gnaw the black bones of the Past. Then I returned and crept to the door and listened to see if I could hear the beating of your hideous heart." And at the end of each note Lafcadio would append a penciled or pen-and-ink sketch of a raven.

Lafcadio's eyesight wasn't strong enough to permit him to concentrate for long stretches on typesetting, so Henry Watkin began to help him look for other part-time work. For a while he was hired as a milling clerk in a printing office, as a proofreader for a trade journal, and as a hack author for a weekly family paper in which he brought out anonymously his first published writings, which included serial stories about an indestructible man engendered by chemistry who feeds only on dust and steel filings. He later became the private secretary to Thomas Vickers, a bold, liberal pastor of the Cincinnati Unitarian Church, whom Lafcadio admired greatly, calling him a "hierophantic sage," and for whom he did some clerical and translating work.

He was also spending much of his spare time in the Cincinnati Public Library, which then held about fifty thousand volumes. Here he discovered first editions of those who would become his favorite French writers—Gautier, Baudelaire, Pierre Loti, Gérard de Nerval, and Flaubert—whom he loved for their sensuality, their unconventional ways of perceiving the world, and their ability to extract beauty and tenderness from the iniquitous and repugnant.

In the spring of 1871, Lafcadio received a smug and unfeeling letter from Henry Molyneux, coolly informing him that Mrs. Sarah Brenane had died on January 13. Molyneux had been named sole executor of her estate. There was no mention of a will or of the annuity that Lafcadio had once been promised. Molyneux never wrote to him again.

"Everybody who does me a wrong indirectly does me a right," Lafcadio would later assert. "It strikes me as being possibly a peculiar morbid condition. If it is, I trust that some day the power will come to do something really extraordinary. . . . What is the good of having a morbid sensitive spot if it cannot be utilized to some purpose worth achieving?" And with the severing of the last tie to his family, Lafcadio decided to devote all his energy to the realization of such a purpose.

CHAPTER **6**

A Sensational Reporter

In THE BEGINNING of 1872, Lafcadio was residing in a series of shabby boardinghouses, visiting Watkin almost every evening, and working as a compositor and proofreader for Robert Clarke and Company, a publisher specializing in Americana. He was still employed at this job in October 1872 when, one morning, he mustered up his courage and took a review he had written of Tennyson's *Idylls of the King* to the office of the managing editor of the Cincinnati *Enquirer*, one of the city's two major newspapers. His visit was unannounced.

Twenty years later, that editor, John Cockerill, distinctly recalled his first encounter with Lafcadio: "One day there came to the office a quaint, dark-skinned little fellow, strangely diffident, wearing glasses of great magnifying power and bearing with him evidence that Fortune and he were scarce on nodding terms.

"When admitted, in a soft, shrinking voice he asked if I ever paid for outside contributions. I informed him that I was somewhat restricted in the matter of expenditure, but that I would give consideration to what he had to offer. He drew from under his coat a manuscript, and tremblingly laid it upon my table. Then he stole away like a distorted brownie, leaving behind him an impression that was uncanny and indescribable. . . . Later in the day I looked over the contribution which he had left. I was astonished to find it charmingly written."

Cockerill ran the lengthy review—a paraphrase, discussion, and mostly critical assessment of what Lafcadio considered one of the weaker sections of Tennyson's poem—in three issues of the *Enquirer*. It was Lafcadio's first signed published writing, and he was overjoyed. At twenty-two, he had discovered his vocation, and while still working for Robert Clarke and Company, he enthusiastically set about, in his spare time, covering a wide range of subjects for the newspaper, some suggested by Cockerill, some by the fledgling journalist himself. There were book reviews of works by Thomas Bailey Aldrich (*Marjorie Daw and Other People*) and an especially laudatory notice of Henry James's story "The Last of the Valerii"; interviews with local artists and with a gravedigger named Baldwin; a description of the city's pawnshops and an examination of "The Hebrews of Cincinnati"; and several feature articles that, already at the outset of Lafcadio's career, revealed his fascination with the macabre and the morbid. Characteristic of his work was a half-ironical, half-spellbound account ("Wonders of Assassinations") of a one-legged German man who, after reading Malthus, decided to reduce the overpopulation of the human race by converting his wooden leg into a firearm—fastening to a concealed trigger a string that he controlled from inside his pocket, and in this manner killing several persons before being caught and accidentally blowing himself up.

Lafcadio's first newspaper writings greatly impressed Cockerill with their intelligent, provocative, unconventional approach to their subjects, so that in the early months of 1874 Lafcadio was asked to join the *Enquirer*'s city staff. His salary began at ten dollars a week, and he worked fourteen to sixteen hours a day—from one in the afternoon well until dawn—seven days a week. "Cockerill," Lafcadio recalled, "was a hard master, a tremendous worker, and a born journalist. I think none of us liked him, but we all admired his ability to run things. He used to swear at us, work us half to death (never sparing himself), and he had a rough skill in sarcasm that we were all afraid of. He was fresh from the army, and full of army talk. In a few years he had forced up the circulation of the paper to a very large figure."

Lafcadio himself, known as "Hearn" to his colleagues, who often found him distant, hypersensitive, and unsociable, and as "Paddy" or "O'Hearn" to the police, whose beat he soon began to cover and who occasionally joked with him in Gaelic, threw himself into his work with remarkable energy and motivation. "Hour after hour he would sit at his table," John Cockerill remembered, "his prominent eyes resting as close to the paper as his nose would permit, scratching away with beaver-like diligence and giving me no more annoyance than a bronze ornament. . . . He was poetic, and his whole nature seemed attuned to the beautiful, and he wrote beautifully of things which were neither wholesome nor inspiring."

Edgar Allan Poe once stated that the ascendency of the "sensational" penny papers in the early 1830s had an influence on America "probably beyond all calculation." Poe's own tales of the bizarre and the grotesque were, in part, influenced by the penny papers, though his idiosyncratic, arabesque style transformed this material. Lafcadio, too, could write articles that had the narrative structure of horror tales or ghost stories; and as a fledgling newspaperman he quickly developed a dramatic and bold manner of describing shocking and lurid events for journalistic effect.

For a series of articles that equaled in their creepiness some of Poe's narratives, Lafcadio spent six days and nights in Cincinnati's Tallow District (a noisome, brutal area of hog-pens, slaughterhouses, and charnel houses)—interviewing hundreds of persons in the street, spending hours at court and coroner's hearings, as well as at jail—in order to depict and re-create the brutal Tanyard Murder.

Lafcadio was, first of all, astonished by the "hideous" milieu of the Tallow District itself, but because of space limitations in the *Enquirer*, it was not until a follow-up story a few days later that he was able to give an adequate description of the area in which the crime took place:

[The quarter] is wholly deserted, darksome, desolate; and the stench which pervades its narrow streets suggests only the decay of death. You may walk upon the broken and filthy pavements for squares and squares without seeing any light but that of the street-lamps that gleam like yellow goblin eyes, or hearing the footstep of a human being. The ghoulish grunting of hogs awaiting slaughter, the deep barking of ferocious tannery dogs, the snakish hissing of steam in rendering establishments, and the gurgling, like a continuous death-rattle, of the black and poisonously-foul gutter streams alone break the deathly silence. To right and left nought is visible but tall broad fences or long frame buildings, ghastly in the gleam of whitewash or gloomily black with the grime of a smoky and greasy atmosphere. You can not cross the road without befouling your shoe-leather frightfully. Your own footsteps sound unpleasantly loud, and awake grim, hollow echoes in all directions. The narrow streets and alleys are unevenly checkered by weirdly grotesque shadows, and intersected by shadowy by-ways and deep doorways where murderers might well hide. The deep howling of the dogs in the tannery near by now excites frightful fancies.

The great brutes are alone in the dark yard where the blood-pools have scarcely dried up! Perhaps they miss him [the Tanyard Murder victim,

Herman Schilling]. Perhaps they see in the darkness what no human eye
can see. . . .   ]

Even without this Dickensian mood-setting introduction, the November 9, 1874, front page of the *Enquirer* startled its morning readers by
dispensing with its usual political dispatches and want ads, and presenting instead five unexpected, eye-catching illustrations and nine blazoning
headlines:

VIOLENT CREMATION
SATURDAY NIGHT'S HORRIBLE CRIME
A MAN MURDERED AND BURNED IN A FURNACE
THE TERRIBLE VENGEANCE OF A FATHER
ARREST OF THE SUPPOSED MURDERERS
LINKS OF CIRCUMSTANTIAL EVIDENCE
THE PITIFUL TESTIMONY OF A TREMBLING HORSE
SHOCKING DETAILS OF THE DIABOLISM
STATEMENTS AND CARTE DE VISITE OF THE ACCUSED

Milk curdled and eggs and porridge went cold in thousands of Cincinnati kitchens and dining rooms that morning, as *Enquirer* subscribers put
off eating breakfast in order to read reporter Lafcadio Hearn's horrifying,
feverishly written account of their city's crime of the century. His astonishing, unmediated presentation forced people to *feel* the last stupefying,
agonized moments of the murdered man's existence, and allowed them
to imagine what it would be like to *touch* the half-boiled consistency of
the victim's brains:

["One woe doth tread upon another's heel," so fast they follow. Scarcely
have we done recording the particulars of one of the greatest conflagrations that has occurred in our city for years than we are called upon to
describe the foulest murder that has ever darkened the escutcheon of our
State. A murder so atrocious and so horrible that the soul sickens at its
revolting details—a murder that was probably hastened by the fire; for,
though vengeance could be the only prompter of two of the accused
murderers,

FEAR OF A DREADFUL SECRET

Coming to light may have been partly the impelling motive that urged on the third to the bloody deed, as will be found further along in our story. The scene of the awful deed was H. Freiberg's tannery on Livingston street and Gamble alley, just west of Central avenue, and immediately opposite the ruins of M. Werk & Co.'s candle factory.

Herman Schilling, the murdered man, and Andreas Egner, George Rufer and Frederick Egner, his suspected murderers.

The story as near as we can obtain it, and divested of unnecessary verbiage, is as follows: Herman Schilling, the deceased, has been employed by Mr. Freiberg for some time, and formerly boarded with the elder Egner, who keeps a saloon and boarding-house at No. 153 Findlay street, on the lot immediately west of the tannery, and connected with it by means of a gate. Egner possessed a daughter Julia, about fifteen years of age, whose morals, from common report, were none of the best, and she and the deceased became very intimate. In fact, so intimate did they become that Schilling was found by the father, late one night,

IN HER BEDROOM,

Under circumstances that proved that they were criminally so, and Schilling only escaped the father's vengeance at the time by jumping through the window to the ground and temporary safety. Egner claimed that Schilling had seduced his daughter, which charge was denied by the accused, who, while admitting his criminal connection with the girl, alleged that he was not the first or only one so favored. At all events, the girl became pregnant and died at the Hospital on the 6th of August last from cancer of the vulva, being seven months advanced in pregnancy at the time. The same day Egner and his son Frederick attacked Schilling in the tanyard with oak barrel staves, and in all probability would have killed him then and there but for the interposition of bystanders. Schilling had the Egners arrested for this assault and battery and they were tried and convicted before Squire True, each being fined $50 and costs for the offense, and being held in $200 bonds to keep the peace toward him for one year. After the trial

THE ELDER EGNER SWORE,

In his own bar-room, that he would have Schilling's life for the wrong he had done him, and he has repeated these threats on several occasions since. After the discovery of his criminal intimacy with the girl, Schilling left Egner's house and took his meals thereafter at the house of C. Westenbrock, 126 Findlay street, and sleeping in a room in a shed of the tannery. Last Saturday night Schilling left Westenbrock's house about 10 o'clock for his sleeping apartment, and as far as is now known this was the

LAST TIME HE WAS SEEN ALIVE

By any one who knew him except his murderers. About half past ten o'clock a stout youth of 16, named John Hollerbach, residing on Central avenue, just above Livingston street, came home and entered his residence by the rear of its yard, opening on Gamble alley. He proceeded to his room in the back of the second floor of the dwelling, and disrobed for bed. He had scarcely done so when he heard the noise of a violent scuffle, apparently proceeding from the alley back of his house, and hastily donning his garments again he dashed down stairs, to find that the noise came from the stable of the tannery, and knowing Schilling well he called to him in German: "Herman, is that you?" The reply came, "Yes, John. John, John, come and help me, some one is killing me," uttered as if the speaker was being choked or stifled. "Who is it," was the next query. The answer was so indistinct that nothing could be made of it and Hollerbach shouted "Murder, murder, let that man alone or I will come in and shoot you." No response was made to this threat save the

GURGLING NOISE OF THE STRANGLING MAN,

And Hollerbach frightened almost to death, started out the alley and down Livingston street in quest of a policeman. He saw the light of the lantern of the private watchman of Werk's place, but not knowing that he had the power of arrest, so runs the boy's strange story, he did not call his attention to the matter, and after vainly seeking for a policeman on several streets without calling or making any outcry for them, he returned to his room, passing by the stable where the foul deed had been committed, hearing, he thought, a dragging noise as he went by. Upon regaining his room he was afraid to go to sleep, and sat up all night in fear and trembling.

ABOUT SEVEN O'CLOCK YESTERDAY MORNING,

Schilling's boarding boss, Westenbrock, who is also an employee of Mr. Freiberg, came to the grated Gamble alley gateway of the tannery to groom the horse in the stable. He found the gate locked, and called for Schilling. Of course he received no response, until his repeated calls attracted the attention of Hollerbach, who looked out of his window and said, "I shouldn't wonder if Herman was killed last night." "Come here and climb the gate," said Westenbrock. Hollerbach did as desired, and opening the gate admitted his partner. The pair at once found that a dreadful deed of blood had been committed. The stable showed signs of a desperate conflict, being splashed with gore, while a

SIX-PRONGED PITCHFORK

Standing against its side was smeared with blood and hair, as was a broom and a large stick near by. Traces of blood were found leading from the stable to the door of the boiler-room, a distance of over one hundred feet, and upon examination these traces were found to lead directly to the door of the gas chamber of the furnace. The horror-struck men stood appalled for a moment as the realization of their worst fears burst upon them, and then spread the news with all the speed possible. Messengers were dispatched to the Oliver street Station-house, and Lieutenant Bierbaum arrived on the scene about half-past eight o'clock, accompanied by Officer Knoeppe. It did not take them long to determine that the body of the murdered man had been thrown into the furnace, and, aided by the spectators who had gathered to the scene by hundreds, they dampened the fire with water and then fished for the remains. These were found to consist of the head and a portion of the trunk and intestines, burned to a crisp and beyond recognition. Suspicion at once fell upon the Egners, from the fact that the gate in the fence between the tannery and their yard *was wide open* when Westenbrock and Hollerbach entered the premises.

THEY WERE AT ONCE ARRESTED

And taken to the Oliver street Station-house, where a charge of suspicion of murder was placed against their names. Coroner Maley was notified and responded promptly to the call. No Constable being on the ground, he appointed Samuel Bloom special, and impaneled the following jury: John Cutter, Henry Britt, George Gould, Dennis O'Keefe, John Wessel and B. F. Schott. They adjourned until this morning at nine o'clock, the remains meanwhile being transferred to Habig's undertaking establishment, on West Sixth street. An *Enquirer* reporter visited the establishment some hours later, accompanied by Dr. Maley, and examined all so far discovered of Herman Schilling's charred corpse.

THE HIDEOUS MASS OF REEKING CINDERS,

Despite all the efforts of the brutal murderers to hide their ghastly crime, remain sufficiently intact to bear frightful witness against them.

On lifting the coffin-lid a powerful and penetrating odor, strongly resembling the smell of burnt beef, yet heavier and fouler, filled the room and almost sickened the spectators. But the sight of the black remains was far more sickening. Laid upon the clean white lining of the coffin they rather resembled great shapeless lumps of half-burnt bituminous coal than aught else at the first hurried glance; and only a closer investigation could enable a strong-stomached observer to detect their ghastly character—masses of crumbling human bones, strung together by half-burnt sinews, or glued one upon another by a hideous adhesion of half-molten flesh, boiled brains and jellied blood mingled with coal. The

SKULL HAD BURST LIKE A SHELL

In the fierce furnace-heat; and the whole upper portion seemed as though it had been *blown out* by the steam from the boiling and bubbling brains. Only the posterior portion of the occipital and parietal bones, the inferior and superior maxillary, and some of the face-bones remained—the upper portions of the skull bones being jagged, burnt brown in some spots, and in others charred to black ashes. The brain had all boiled away, save a small wasted lump at the base of the skull about the size of a lemon. It was crisped and still warm to the touch. On pushing the finger through the crisp, the interior felt about the consistency of banana fruit, and the yellow fibers seemed to writhe like worms in the Coroner's hands. The eyes were cooked to bubbled crisps in the blackened sockets, and the bones of the nose were gone, leaving a hideous hole.

So covered were the jaws and lower facial bones with coal, crusted blood and gummy flesh, that the Coroner at first supposed the lower maxillary to have been burned away. On tearing away the frightful skull-mask of mingled flesh and coal and charred gristle, however,

THE GRINNING TEETH SHONE GHASTLY WHITE,

And both jaws were found intact. They were set together so firmly that it was found impossible to separate them, without reducing the whole mass to ashes. For so great had been the heat, that the Coroner was able to crumble one of the upper teeth in his fingers.

Besides the fragments of the skull have been found six ribs of the right side and four of the left; the middle portion of the spinal column; the liver, spleen and kidneys; the pelvic bones; the right and left humerus; the femoral bones, and the tibia and fibula of both legs. The body had burst open at the chest, and the heart and lungs had been entirely consumed. The liver was simply roasted and the kidneys fairly fried. There is a horrible probability that the wretched victim was

FORCED INTO THE FURNACE ALIVE,

And suffered all the agonies of the bitterest death which man can die, while wedged in the flaming flue. His teeth were so terribly clenched that more than one spectator of the hideous skull declared that only the most frightful agony could have set those jaws together. Perhaps, stunned and disabled by the murderous blows of his assailants, the unconscious body of the poor German was forced into the furnace. Perhaps the thrusts of the assassin's pitchfork, wedging him still further into the fiery hell, or perhaps the first agony of burning when his bloody garments took fire, revived him to meet the death of flame. Fancy the shrieks for mercy, the mad expostulation, the frightful fight for life, the superhuman struggles for existence—a century of agony crowded into a moment— the shrieks growing feebler—the desperate struggles dying into feeble writhings. And through all the grim murderers, demoniacally pitiless, devilishly desperate, gasping with their exertions to destroy a poor human life,

LOOKING ON IN SILENT TRIUMPH!

Peering into the furnace until the skull exploded and the steaming body burst, and the fiery flue hissed like a hundred snakes! It may not be true—we hope for poor humanity's sake it cannot be true; but the frightful secrets of that fearful night are known only to the criminals and their God. They may be brought to acknowledge much; but surely never so much as that we have dared to hint at.

A FRESH TRAIL.

Immediately after the arrest of the Egners the police got news that a man named George Rufer, who had been employed in the tannery, had been discharged Saturday evening, and that he had blamed Schilling for his dismissal. Search was made for him at his residence, No. 90 Logan street, but that he had gone out, and his wife, in response to questions, at first stated that he had not left the house after supper. Afterward she convicted herself, saying that he had gone to Spring street, to a friend's house, in company with her, and that he had retired at 10 o'clock.

The news of the terrible affair spread with great celerity, and though its horrible features seemed too awful for belief, for once a story passed through a dozen lips without gathering anything by the transition,

REALITY FOR ONCE DISTANCING

The most fervid imagination. By noon the streets in the vicinity of the scene were thronged with people who eagerly caught at the slightest word dropped by any one conversant with the story of the murder, and repeated it with bated breath to fresh groups of earnest listeners. The day was fine, and in the afternoon hundreds who visited the locality . . . learned of the still more terrible affair, and aided in swelling the crowd that

SWAYED TO AND FRO

Around the tannery like waves of the sea. About half past four o'clock the rain, which had been threatening for some time, began to descend in a lively manner, and this dispersed the throng, much to the relief of the police on guard around the premises.

About five o'clock Lieutenant Birnbaum started out on a fresh search for Rufer. Before he reached his residence, however, he found him on his way to the Station-house, he having been arrested by officers Paulus and Knoeppe at the corner of Logan and Finlay streets. When taken to the station-house he was confronted by Colonel Kiersted, who ordered him to be stripped and examined. His face was scratched and contused in a terrible manner, and presented every appearance of his having been engaged in

A FEARFUL AND PROLONGED STRUGGLE.

He appeared cool and collected, considering the fearful nature of the suspicion against him. His clothing did not present any traces of blood until he had removed his pantaloons; then the knees of his drawers were found

STIFFENED WITH GORE.

He quickly exclaimed: "That is blood from the hides I handled." A gout of blood was also found on the breast of his undershirt.

HIS STORY

Was told partly in broken English and partly in German, and was substantially as follows: "Last Saturday night Mr. Freiberg told me that work was slack, and that he would have to let me go for a few days. Well, after supper I took my little child and I went down to Mr. Egner's and I had a glass of beer, and then I paid Mr. Egner my beer-bill. After I had had a couple of more beers, about nine o'clock, I took my child and started home. I stopped at a frame grocery at the corner of Logan and Findlay and took a couple of glasses more of beer and one of wine, and then I went to bed. Sunday morning I got up about 7 o'clock and after breakfast I started to walk to Columbia to see the superintendent of a furniture factory there about getting a job of work. I could not find the superintendent, as two men told me he lived over the river. I met no one in Columbia that I knew, and I started to walk home after getting some beer. I got tired, and got into the street cars and rode to the Elm street depot and then started home, when I was arrested. I did not have any trouble with Schilling. I last saw him dressing hides when I left the tannery Saturday evening. He had been in the habit of working at night. I did not know where he slept. I once heard Egner talking about Schilling and his daughter Julia's seduction, and he said that Schilling ought to be

RUN THROUGH WITH A PITCHFORK.

Another time I heard the son Fred talking about the same thing, and he said that Schilling ought to have a rope tied around his neck and be

HELD OVER THE HOT FURNACE.

When asked how he accounted for the scratches on his face, he became contradictory, first saying that he got them by jumping from a shed the night of the fire at Werk's factory, then that he refused to give his wife any money Saturday night, and that she and he had a fight, and that she had torn his face with her nails, and again that he had fallen down on the street. He is a man about five feet seven inches high, with a sinewy and strong frame, and is about thirty seven years old.

The most damning report against him is that the deceased, Herman Schilling, was cognizant of the fact that

RUFER HAD SET FIRE

To M. Werk & Co.'s candle factory Friday night last, and that he intended to apprise the police of his information. How true this report is we cannot now state, but if true it would afford conclusive evidence of the reason that inclined him to share in the deep damnation of the murder.

THE ELDER EGNER

Is a German, about forty-three years old, slight and spare in figure, and with a forbidding but determined look. His son is a beardless boy, without any distinguishing characteristics save a sullen look of stolid indifference to his fate. His tale is that he played "tag," "catcher," etc., up till nine o'clock Saturday night, slept soundly during the night, hearing no noise, and awakening at seven o'clock in the morning, and only hearing of the murder about eight o'clock.

Egner keeps a coffee-house and a cooper-shop, just west of the tannery, his saloon being at No. 153 Findlay street.

THE DECEASED,

Herman Schilling, was a native of Westphalia, twenty-five years old, about five feet eight inches high, finely proportioned, ruddy-faced, with dark mustache and cross-eyes. He was generally spoken of yesterday evening as a very good, companionable kind of a man. He was unmarried, and has no relations that we could learn of in this city.

THE PREMISES

On which the bloody deed was enacted comprise a table, harness, carriage and sleeping-room of the deceased, together with two large tan-bark sheds and a boiler shed, in which is situated the furnace wherein Schilling was cremated. The stable adjoins Gamble alley, and is about eight by ten feet square, with a loft not much higher than a man's head. It is occupied by but one horse, and presents every indication of a terrible and bloody struggle. Adjoining it is a room used for storing harness, and it is probable that in this room the murderers lay in wait for their prey. Next, west, is the carriage room; and, by means of a door in its west partition, access is had to the room used by the deceased as his sleeping apartment. These rooms form an offset to the tan-bark sheds, and west of these is the boiler, furnace and engine rooms. Between these buildings and the others of the tannery is a large yard running east and west. To guard the premises are three immense and savage mastiffs.

THE MANNER OF THE MURDER.

Judging by all the evidence the murderers were familiar with the premises and its canine guardians; for, were they not, they could not have gained access to them without encountering the dogs, and being probably torn into fragments by them. They in all probability entered through the gate leading from Egner's to the tanyard, and ensconced themselves in the harness-room, which they knew their victim must pass on his way to his lodging. When he entered, as was his wont, by the small gate opening on Gamble alley, they were peering through the open door of the harness-room awaiting their opportunity. A few more steps in the darkness and silence, and the watchman's throat is suddenly seized with a grasp of iron. Then commences

THE TERRIBLE STRUGGLE FOR LIFE.

The night is pitch dark, fit gloom for the dark deed it veils. The victim is a young and powerful man, muscled like Hercules; but he has been wholly taken by surprise, he is unarmed, and he finds by the strength of the grasp on his throat that his antagonist is more than a match for him in mere brute force. A stunning blow from behind suddenly shows him that he has two enemies to deal with; and then for the first time, perhaps, the terrible knowledge of the fact that his life is sought, first dawns upon him. Then indeed it became a fierce fight for dear life. The stable shows that the victim, despairing of his ability to cope with his savage assailants, sought refuge behind the horse's hoofs: hoping at least to thus gain a moment's time to shriek for help. But here the indications are that the contest was hottest. The side of the stable is in places deeply indented by the prongs of the pitchfork—indented by such thrusts as only immense force could give—thrusts which were designed to let out the life of the victim. It was the noise of this struggle that attracted the attention of young Hollerbach, and—who knows?—but that his version of what he saw and heard of it has yet to be told in full. Certainly it seems singular that he should behave himself in the remarkable manner he states. At the hour he names as the time of the murder a dozen saloons in the immediate vicinity were in full blast and filled with patrons. Aye, even the house in which he slept—no, did not sleep, but watched—has a bar-room in it, which kept open until after midnight, and volunteers to rescue the victim could have been obtained by scores. Mr. John Hollerbach evidently knows much more than he has told of this fearful crime. It is preposterous to think that any man in his sane mind would act as he says he did. When the life of the dying man had so far ebbed that he could no longer resist his fate his murderers thought of the best place to dispose of the body,

THE FURNACE.

Within a hundred feet of the stable is the boiler-room, and this boiler is heated by a furnace of peculiar construction, being built on the principle of an air furnace for melting iron. Its fuel is tanbark, emptied in a grate through two circular openings in its top, and provided with a brick flue through which its gases pass into a chamber underneath the boiler where they are ignited. Into this chamber is a square damper opening of about twelve inches across, and to this narrow door the victim was carried by his slayers. The fire in the furnace had been dampened down, but the villains know well its mechanism, and, forcing the body through the narrow door, they endeavor to push it through into the flue. In this, however, they were balked by its size, and their next work was to arrange the furnace so that its fire would burn the remains to ashes. How well they succeeded our story has told.

THE CIRCUMSTANTIAL EVIDENCE

Is all as yet there is to found a suspicion on, but we must say that it appears to be of the most conclusive kind. Especially is this fact in the case of Andreas Egner.

The grimy boards forming the floor of the loft of the stable are covered with festoons of heavy cobwebs; and through the chinks hay-seed has been constantly drifting down and lodging in the glutinous film spun by the gray spiders below. Moreover, the floor of the stable is thickly covered with poplar shavings. Suspicion being once fastened upon Andreas Egner, search was made in his house for articles of clothing or other things which might serve as a clue for tracing up the crime. A bundle of clothes was one of the first things pounced upon, including an old hat, a pair of low shoes, and a well-worn pair of coarse cassimere pants. The pants bore great stains of candle-grease, but there were no stains of blood, although some strange dark spots warranted a keen investigation. Yet the other garments afforded terrible witness against him. His hat was found to be covered with just such cobwebs and hay-seed as hung from the roof of the stable; and his shoes were found full of the very poplar shavings which covered the stable-floor.

Rufer's clothes, which are also in the hands of the police, afford only

THE EVIDENCE OF BLOOD,

But there is plenty of it. It has stained the bosom of his coarse checked shirt a muddy red. It has trickled in thick streams upon the legs of his jeans, and stained them dark below the knees. He accounts for the blood on his shirt by the fact that it has been a part of his duties in the tannery to handle fresh hides. The gore on his pants he declares to have come from the veins of a chicken which he had killed the night before. There does not seem to be anything more than a general suspicion against the boy Fred Egner.

THE SHUDDERING HORSE.

There are several instances connected with the scene of the horrible tragedy which must come under the head of circumstantial evidence. We have already referred to the great size and ferocity of the dogs guarding the premises, and their peculiar quietness during the performance of the hideous crime as conclusive proof that the murderers must have both been very familiar with the premises and the mastiffs. When we visited the tannery late last evening in company with Messrs. Farny and Duveneck to take sketches of the buildings, we found it impossible to gain entrance by reason of the dogs' ferocity. Another curious fact is the condition in which the horse, the dumb witness of that frightful crime, was found this morning—shuddering and trembling from head to hoofs, his eyes wild with terror. Petting and caressing availed nothing; and the whole forenoon the animal was in a perfect tremor of fear.

THE FIVE-PRONGED FORK,

Used by the murderers either to kill their victim, or to stuff his body into the furnace, was found in the stable, with blood and hair still adhering to it, and a suspender-buckle on the fourth prong. It is curious that a similar suspender-buckle was found among the ashes of the furnace.

Besides the fork, a long stake, sharpened to a spear-like point and dyed at the smaller end with blood, appears to have served in the deed of murder. A small broom had evidently been used to brush up the blood, as it was completely coated with thickly crusted gore. How it happened that the murderers could have been careless enough to leave such damning evidence against them, we can scarcely imagine.

THE LATEST.

John Hollerbach, by order of Chief Kiersted was arrested in his bed at two o'clock this morning by Lieutenant Benninger, and locked up in the Oliver street Station-house as a witness. He stuck to his apocryphal story. In conversation with a reporter this morning Rufer said if he had killed Schilling, he would have put him in a better place—a tank of salt-water under the tannery, where he never would have smelt. Would that tank not be a good place to drag for bloody clothes?

The following witnesses will be examined at the Coroner's inquest this morning: Wm. Hollerbach, Jr., C. Westenbrock, N. Westenbrock, Ban Fruink, Jos. Schlingrop, R. Mellenbrook, Henry Korte, E. Kerr, Wm. Osterhage, Henry Kote, Jr., Isadore Freiberg, Henry Freiberg.

George Rufer stated that his wife was at the house of her sister, Mrs. Peter Eckert, the officers who were sent in search of her having failed to find her at her home on Dunlap street.

Rufer couldn't tell where Mrs. Eckert lived. Lieutenant Wersel, without any guide except that the husband of Mrs. Eckert was a potter, set out in search of her, and after a tramp of three or four miles, calling at a dozen houses, found her on Western Avenue.

She stated that Mrs. Rufer was not with her, had not been with her, that they were not on good terms, and did not visit each other. This leaves the whereabouts of Mrs. Rufer still a mystery.

A little after midnight an officer of the Oliver street Station came running into the station-house with a statement that rumors were afloat that a band had organized to take the prisoners out of their cells and lynch them. A good reserve of police was afterward kept at the station.

Lafcadio's first article on the Tanyard Murder ended at this point, but the story continued for several months. At the trial, Andreas Egner's son turned state's evidence, and the elder Egner and George Rufer received life sentences—though Egner was afterwards pardoned by the state governor on account of his contracting tuberculosis. (He later went insane and died in 1889.)

With its unprecedentedly extensive coverage of the murder and its startling dramatic presentation—more intense and literary than the typical penny paper "shocker"—the *Enquirer* scored a notable journalistic coup; all editions of the November 9 issue quickly sold out. Because of the success of his hastily written article (and several follow-up stories), Lafcadio was immediately given a raise in salary to twenty-five dollars a week. Almost overnight he became known as Cincinnati's most audacious and famous journalist.

During the following years as a newspaper reporter, Lafcadio found that his new status frequently gave him the opportunity to choose many of the subjects he wished to write about, from the grotesque to the genial to the horrifying to the humorous (or a mixture therof). He was furthermore given unusual latitude to experiment with a variety of styles, genres, and approaches: the exposé, the ghost story, the interview, the first-person narrative, the critical review, the prose-poem, and the feuilleton (a melding of personal essay, vignette, and reportage). Often he combined two or more of these forms, and, just as often, he illuminated his articles with a surprising and anomalous scholarly aura that veiled a subversive content.

A police officer's arrest of a streetwalker, and his platitudinous remarks about her seizure ("determination to mitigate the social evil"), finds Lafcadio—on the police beat that particular evening—writing in his notebook: "Arrest of notorious Cyprian." This leads him into an eloquent disquisition ("The Demi-Monde of the Antique World") on the ancient temple courtesans of Aphrodite: on their literary, dance, and musical skills, educational attainments, and physical beauty; and on the worship of the goddess more generally—a worship Lafcadio himself surreptitiously inclined toward. (As he would later exclaim to Watkin: "Let me be the last of the idol worshipers, O Golden Venus, and sacrifice to thee the twin doves thou lovest,—the birds of Paphos and the Cytheridae.") "Certainly the cities of Cyprus," he remarks in his article, "were sinful cities, according to our modern code of ethics; but their sins were splendid sins, sweetened, as Swinburne would say, with the fumes of sacrificial incense—glorified by hierophantic rites, within temples of snowy stone. . . ." Then, thinking of the persecuted, curly-haired Cincinnati streetwalker who has just unsuccessfully tried to commit suicide in her jail cell, Lafcadio concludes: "Poor Cyprian; two thousand years ago you might have been famous—today a triple curse, not of Cyprus, but of society, religion, and nature."

Lafcadio had a penchant for probing areas of perverse interest that were usually unspoken of, or at least unacknowledged, by his readers. He dropped in on a leather warehouse on Main Street to talk with an English tanner about the time in London when he had "the delicate job" of "dressing" a human skin. "They brought us the hide of some murderer . . . and it made a beautiful, soft leather, of a pale color; and I believe that a portion of it was afterward used to bind books with." This "little incident" conjured up in Lafcadio's mind "a train of historical reminiscences" ("Notes on the Utilization of Human Remains") about candles made from human fat, drinking vessels from skulls, utensils from human bones, furniture from skeletons, and weapons from petrified brains. Lafcadio also reminded his readers in a sly aside of the "ludicrous will of a patriotic New Englander . . . wherein may be found a provision to the effect that the corpse of the deceased be flayed and the skin made into a drumhead, and that 'Yankee Doodle' be played thereon every Fourth of July, at sunrise, in the shadow of Bunker Hill Monument. Whether the extraordinary provisions of this will have yet been in any part fulfilled we have not been able to learn."

Perhaps Lafcadio's most charmingly macabre story ("Skulls and Skeletons") from this period concerns an encounter he had with an "articulator of skeletons," whom the reporter designates as Dr. B., and his enthusiastic assistants in the trade—the doctor's ten-year-old son and eight-year-old daughter:

[. . . "I'm always glad to see a reporter about here," said the Doctor [the "articulator of skeletons"], politely ushering the visitor into a small, whitewashed room, neatly furnished but carpetless, and looking out upon a narrow alley running between huge, murky factories. This was the articulator's private work-shop. A huge pine table stood in the center of the apartment, covered with fragments of skeletons in various stages of development; a handsome cabinet-library was placed against the south wall, and a couple of huge tubs, carefully covered, were arranged at the opposite end of the room. What most startled the reporter, however, was the spectacle of two rosy-cheeked, yellow-haired children, evidently sister and brother, and not more than nine and twelve years of age respectively, busily engaged in sorting out a great pile of bleached human bones, tibia, femurs, vertebrae, etc., lying on a bare floor in a corner.

"You see my children help me in my work, sir," said the articulator with a smile of paternal pride. "As fast as I can get the bones bleached they sort them out in little heaps, so that I know just where to put my hand on anything I want. I've taught them the names of the bones, and their position, and all that."

"But you do not mean to say," asked the astounded reporter, "that these children know the names of all those bones!"

"Well, I'll wager you can't puzzle George. Katie's not quite so far advanced; but she can tell you the names of all the larger pieces of the skeleton. I never took much pains to teach Katie, though there's not much use teaching a girl such things, you know; but George has determined to teach all he knows, and he's a pretty good tutor, I can tell you. I'll show you"—he added, picking up a thigh bone. "Come, Katie dear, tell the gentleman what this is."

The child rose, looked at the piece carefully, and answered with a pretty little smile.

"Left femur, pa."

"Correct, and this," holding up another fragment.

"That's right—no a left ilium, pa."

"And this?"

"Tibia"

"Which tibia, darling?"

"I think it's a right one, pa."

"And this?"

"Patella"

"Right or left?"

Here the little creature seemed puzzled. Her brother looked up and whispered:

"Right."

"You see, sir," remarked the father with a smile, "Katie's picked up a great deal about these things for a child of her age. But, Lord! George can take disarticulated vertebrae and number them for you, and he knows the position of all the smaller hand and foot bones. He's helped me out sometimes when I've been puzzled myself."

"How old is he?"

"He'll be eleven in November—nearly two years older than Katie. But this kind of thing seems to come natural to my children. Why, Katie was

rattling skulls about the floor when she was only two or three years old;
and I guess the first toys George ever had were a couple of thigh bones.
Run away into the next room, darlings, till I talk with the gentleman.
"Here," continued the articulator, opening a cabinet and taking out a
finely polished skull in three pieces, "this used to be one of Katie's toys."

It was a small, finely-formed skull, with a peculiarly delicate formation
of the facial bones, and remarkably small and regular teeth, white and
pearly. Some had dropped out here and there.

"Is that a woman's skull," asked the reporter, looking into the eye
sockets.

"Yes, and the skull too, of a very pretty, but very naughty girl—Mattie—
who used to live on Sixth Street." The reporter remembered her well—a
slender, handsome brunette, notable character in Cincinnati fast-life, some
six or seven years before. A wonderful girl she was for balls and buggy
rides, a great dancer and a great singer.

"Died in the Hospital," continued B.—"She was a splendidly-limbed
woman, and I tried to save the body, but didn't succeed very well."

The jaw-bone slipped from the reporter's hand, and fell to the floor
with a crash.

"There they go—two more teeth out!" cried the articulator. "Oh! You
needn't mind; it makes no difference. I can do them in again easily enough.
Pretty little teeth, aren't they?"

"They are indeed. I'd like to know the history of that skull, Doctor."

"Well, I used to be connected with B—— Medical College some years
ago, and when Mattie's body came there I saw at once it would be an
unusually fine subject. So I managed to get it all for myself, and succeeded; my intention being to make a dried specimen of it. I brought the
body up here from the college in two parts and got to work to see if I
could petrify them."

"But wasn't it very unpleasant to have such a hideous thing occupying
this room?"

"Not particularly. It did smell a little, but that didn't much matter, as
I used always to keep the room shut up. Well, I soon found I could only
save the right arm. I had hopes for the left leg, which I kept hanging up
here by the window for nearly a month. But the worms at last got into it
and I had to let it go."

"What did you do with the remains then?"

"Cut all the flesh, tendons, etc., away, and then boiled the bones in
the usual manner to get all the grease out of them! We generally boil them

about twenty-four hours or more, skimming off the grease as it rises. Young persons' bones are never very greasy, and are easily cleaned, but the bones of old people are always greasy, and the older the greasier. High living makes bones awfully greasy."

"And when the bones are well boiled are they ready for articulation?"

"Oh no! They must macerate for six months or a year after."

"Well, how is that done?"

"Why, by leaving them to soak in a covered vessel full of water. The water gradually draws all the grease out through the pores of the bones. We generally bore a hole in the end of the larger bones to let the marrow out, but it is not very easy to do that with the little bones. You see, the boiling does not begin to clean the bones, in fact they will macerate quite as thoroughly although a little slower, without it."

"Why is it necessary to get them so clean?"

"Because they won't bleach if any oily or greasy matter remains to them. Now, I prepared Canby's skeleton for the museum, you may have seen it there, and I had to keep the old man in soak for more than a year. He was a terribly greasy old fellow."

"Well, don't you have to keep changing the water constantly in which the bones are steeping?"

"Goodness, no! Why that would destroy the whole operation."

"Then the water must become abominably foul."

"Frightfully. But then the more putrid it becomes the better it is for maceration. You ought to see some of that water under a microscope— such hideous life, swarming, squirming, wriggling over one another, monstrous and horrible, beyond anything you ever dreamed of. I've got some bones now soaking in those vats there, but I don't like to take covers off and stink the room."

"So you always leave bones macerating for six months?"

"Yes, never less than that. Then I take them out and scrub them with a brush."

"What do they look like when you take them out?"

"Black as a coal. That comes off with scrubbing, however and then I lay them to bleach in the sun. Then a young person's bones will become white as milk; and an old person's yellow-white, or blotched, owing to grease which can not be got rid of. Now that girl's bones came out white as snow; you see she was only twenty-three years old. See how smooth and white and clean that skull is."

"And what do you do with the bones after they are bleached?"

"Sort them, and articulate them with brass wires making hinges at the principal joints. The best specimens of artificial articulation are those in which every joint is flexible as in life. It takes much trouble and time, of course. I built up Canby right in that corner, there, and my children used to help me."

"Are you not afraid of catching some horrid complaint from handling all these nasty bones and things?"

"Not at all. There is not much danger in handling a dead body after decomposition has fairly set in. I have dissected the bodies and macerated the bones of men and women that died of the most horrible diseases, but I never got any harm by it.

"I remember too, having had a funny adventure up here years ago while preparing a body for drying. It was about midnight, and I was working away by the light of a couple of candles at a table covered with bones and skulls and such things just as you see now. I had Mattie L's body up here on the table, or at least the upper half of it—the lower half was hanging up in the window—and I was trying to kill the infernal little white worms with corrosive sublimate. It wasn't much use though, they came swarming out by hundreds, and crawled over my hands and bare arms until I felt ready to vomit and give the job up."

"Now at that time there used to be a morning paper office on the next floor, and that funny old Dutchman who sells sandwiches and sausages to newspaper printers came up with his little tin cans. It seems he had a glass of beer too much in him that evening, and so missed the way and came into my room, the door of which shuts with a spring.

"Well, he came in and the door closed behind him with a bang. He came right up to the table, however, before he noticed anything, and I stood and watched him without moving a muscle. When the actual nature of his position dawned on him, you never saw a man turn so pale. Before him was a table with the rotting upper half of a dead woman's body on it; piles of skulls and bones all around him, and dried human legs and arms and feet dangling from the ceiling, while the whole room smelt like a newly opened grave from the mass of festering flesh on the table. He was too frightened for the moment to do anything but stare at me until I thought his eyes would start from their sockets. My silence, I believe, frightened him terribly. At last I pointed to his sausages with one hand, and then pointed solemnly to a dead woman's thigh with the other. That settled him. He just gave one yell, and went down stairs three steps at a time crying 'Murder.' "

"Papa, dinner is ready," cried Katie, showing her rosy face at the door.

"Coming, darling. Well, you'll excuse me, sir, for the present; but drop up once in a while, and I'll be glad to see you."

Lafcadio's subjects would not always prove to be so ghoulishly cooperative or beguiling. When a group of homeless ragpickers refused to speak with him, he simply described, in the manner of Victor Hugo, the Cincinnati city dump in which they wallowed for food and anything they could use:

A wilderness of filthy desolation walled in by dismal factories; a Golgotha of foul bones and refuse; a great grave-yard for worn-out pots and kettles and smashed glasses, and rotten vegetables and animal filth, and shattered house-hold utensils and abominations unutterable. . . . Here and there evil-featured women, children and hideous old men may be seen toiling and burrowing amid the noisome piles of rottenness—beings frightful as gnomes. . . . Clad in rags fouler than those they unearthed from the decaying filth beneath them, the dump-pickers worked silently side by side, with a noiseless swiftness that seemed goblin-like to one coming upon such a scene for the first time. At a greater distance these miserable creatures, crawling over the dumps on all-fours, looked in their ash-colored garments, like those insects born of decay, which take the hue of the material they feed upon.   ("LES CHIFFONIERS")

In one of his most startling and, to some, least bearable articles ("Balm of Gilead"), he depicted with Zola-esque detail the skinning and boiling of animal carcasses and carrion (dead horses, cattle, sheep, hogs, goats, and dogs) for tallow, grease, lard, and soap at the "Stink Factory" on the outskirts of Cincinnati, whose "compound stench" ("to which at least twenty different forms of animal putrefaction contribute") Lafcadio's hypersensitive olfactory system generously and informatively analyzed as he approached the premises: "The various smells of which it is made up differ greatly in elasticity, in power of penetration and extension; so that while journeying on foot toward the factory . . . the nose is continually assailed by new varieties of stench. First a faint odor, like that of very ancient shoe leather, then a smell as of decaying cats, mingling with the first smell; then a smell resembling that of rotten hides mingling with the two previous smells; and so on as you near the great focus of simon-pure stench itself, by which time the odors have become so multitudinous, so overpowering and so mingled together that the nostrils are numbed beyond the power of further analysis."

Lafcadio's most tough-minded and compelling article in the domain of what he called (and spelled) the "grewsome" unflinchingly observes and contrasts a Gentile and a Jewish slaughterhouse in the Tallow District (the scene of the Tanyard Murder case). In this astonishing report ("Haceldama"—from the New Testament word meaning "field of blood"), Lafcadio describes drinking a proffered glass of animal blood (as consumptives were sometimes recommended to do) in order to convey a sense of the texture and taste of this unusual potation to his readers:

[. . . On a boiling summer day it is not, indeed, a pleasant neighborhood to visit; its very gutters seem foul with the fetor of slaughter, and its atmosphere heavy with the odors of death,—impregnated with globules of blood. Its unpleasantness has rendered it an unfamiliar neighborhood to a large portion of the community, who have no interests in those businesses for which it is famous, and who have no desire to linger longer amid its stenches than they can possibly help. There is very little attention given by a carnivorous community—our Hebrew brethren excepted—as to how the beeves and fatlings which furnish flesh meat for general consumption come by their death, but many a beef-eater would feel more concern regarding his daily diet did he but witness the death agonies of the last bullock slaughtered by his favorite butcher. The flavor, delicacy, and nutritive properties of mutton and beef depend more upon the method of slaughter than is generally supposed, and of this fact a few visits to the Quarter of Shambles would suffice to convince any intelligent observer.

To describe one Gentile slaughter-house is to describe the majority of those in the district—huge frames mostly, often painted black or red (appropriate hues of death), oftener whitewashed, with long, low pens in the rear, offal-gutters traversing the main floor from wall to wall, and great doorways yawning upon the streets in front, and exhaling heavy and deathly aromas. The impression left by a visit to the first is confirmed rather than varied by visits to half a dozen more—an impression of gloom and bad smells; daylight peering through loose planking; the head of a frightened bullock peering over the pen door; blood, thick and black, clotting on the floor, or oozing from the nostrils and throats of dying cattle; entrails, bluey-white and pale yellow; fresh quarters and sides hanging up; butchers, bare-legged and bare-armed, paddling about in the blood; naked feet encrusted with gore, and ill-shaped toes dyed crimson with the red fluid oozing up and clotting between them. Children stare in half terror, half curiosity through the open doorways, and greedy hogs are fattening on the blood and entrails which pass down to them through the offal gutter. Half the slaughter-houses keep hogs for scavengers, and it is to be observed that such hogs are seldom heard to squeal—they only grunt out their deep satisfaction, their sense of repletion and their regret that their cavernous bellies are not larger. The dull thud of the slaughter-er's axe, the bellowing and stamping of terrified cattle, the splash of en-trails flung into the gutter, the click-clack of steel, sharpened upon steel, an occasional curse flung at an unruly cow, and the grunting of the hogs aforesaid are the pleasant sounds which accompany the vision.

All this, however, is the brighter side of the picture—the mere back-ground to darker and fouler things—the general impression unrelieved from its vagueness by certain sharply defined features of horror which linger in the memory of the observer long after their attendant circum-stances have faded out. The inexperience of the half-grown boys, too, often employed as butchers, the torture of maddened steers, the agony of a bullock under a rain of ill-placed blows, are much more unpleasant matters than entrails and odors. It is well, perhaps, that the poor brutes are not gifted with facial expression, and that one of slaughter's greatest horrors is not thus visible in the slaughter-house. But it is certain that they are often aware of the fate in store for them, especially when per-mitted to peer through the pen-door into the slaughter-house, and see what is going on there. We noticed in one instance a strong proof of this fact. There were two cows in a pen; and there was a large square opening in the partition between the pen and the slaughter-house. It was the first slaughter of the day when one of the animals was dragged into the sham-bles and dispatched in a very bungling manner. The remaining cow watched the proceedings as though fascinated with terror—she saw her companion stricken down with the axe, saw the knife enter the throat, saw the blood pouring out, saw the butcher treading on the carcass, and the red fluid gushing out in spurts from the wound with each tramp of the men's naked feet. This part of the tragedy the poor vaccine mind was perhaps unable to fully comprehend, as she had probably never seen blood before, and could not exactly understand what was being done to her sister. Neither is it likely that she understood what those great masses of red and yellow hanging from the ceiling were; for there was no semblance to the living cow in them. But when she beheld the flaying, and the decapitation, and the ghastly, headless trunk, with severed windpipe protruding, and the entrails rolling out of the carcass, and the carcass itself divided and converted into great white and yellow masses of flesh and fat like those others hanging up further away,—then the poor cow must have had a dim understanding of what had happened to her companion, for she bellowed, and kicked, and turned her eyes away from the sickening sight, and perchance puzzled her poor brains in attempts to devise means of escape. Then at last came her turn; and the butchers approached with the fatal noose. But, while the cow had sense enough to be fully aware of the design of the men who approached her, with blood-encrusted arms and crimson feet, she had not sense enough to know that resistance was worse than useless. She was conscious only of danger,—danger of having her head cut off and her inside torn out, and of being turned into great masses of yellow fat and red meat;—and so she made violent demonstrations of brave despair. Wheedling and coaxing were in vain; and the butchers loudly cursed the poor cow. But at last the noose was flung about her neck, and they laid on the rope while she braced herself to resist. Then a great, yellow-haired brute of a man, with very large calves and very ugly feet, seized a pritch, and put out the poor cow's left eye. Still she would not enter the shambles; and the cruel ruffian thrust the iron spike into the other eye, and worked the point about in the socket. Frantic with agony, and trembling in every limb, the blinded and helpless animal leaped forward and butted the door in her pain. It was no trouble now to drag her into the place of slaughter, shivering with torture, and streams of mingled blood and tears rolling down from either eye.

"Got yer eyes sore, didn't ye?—ye d——d infernal beast. Thought I'd bring ye to."

And the brawny butcher brought down the axe, not on the right spot, but on the bleeding eye; and the wretched cow, who had never before, perhaps, known rougher hands than those of the milkmaid, gave such a hideous cry! It was not bellowing or lowing, but a cry between a shriek and a moan,—a cry half human, as of one in the agony of a nightmare, —a cry of prolonged and exquisite torture. The human heart would have heaved in horror at a cry of such anguish—anguish aggravated by the terror of helpless blindness. But the butcher only laughed, and swung the axe again and again in the most unscientific, bungling and brutal way. It took nine heavy blows to fell the miserable cow, all because the butcher knew nothing about his business. At last the poor carcass rolled over, and the knife opened a passage for the blood, and the butchers danced right joyously upon the belly of the cow. With every jump the blood-stream leaped, too, but the blood looked inky, as though turned black with agony, and thus reproaching the black cruelty of the slaughterers. So we found it elsewhere. In half a dozen slaughter-houses we did not find a single butcher who seemed to know his business, or who could fell a bullock with one well directed blow between the eyes. It may have been that we had an unfortunate knack of visiting a slaughter-house at an unpropitious time, but it would rather seem that too little attention is paid to the demands of humanity by employing inhuman and inexperienced men to kill. Such cruelty as we witnessed in the instance of the poor cow which uttered so unnatural a cry, is, we were subsequently informed, not uncommon. In the killing of sheep, too, we have seen men cruel through pure laziness—slowly plunging the knife into the poor creature's throat, and carelessly working it backward and forward, and making three or four efforts to break the vertebrae apart when one energetic effort would have sufficed. If the mutton-eaters and beef-eaters, contemplating their savory steaks and chops, could but know how the animals died that furnished the food—could but guess how every fiber of the tender meat vibrated in exquisite torture but a few hours before, it is doubtful whether they would have had much stomach left for breakfast. Many a cruel butcher is earning good wages for bungling work, who would be more fitly employed in those horrible cannibal markets spoken of by recent African travelers, where human flesh is sold by weight, and human legs and arms dangle in the booths. The fiend who can laugh at the tortures of a blind cow, would certainly find rare amusement in severing a human throat, in watching human eyes roll in blood, and in listening to moans of human pain. And how amusing it would be to pry out a human eye with a pritchet.

Leaving such scenes as these for the interior of a Jewish slaughter-house is actually a pleasant relief. The one we visited was a neat and roomy edifice of brick, airy, well lighted, well ventilated, purified by running water, and it seemed to us less haunted by unsavory odors. The cattle saw nothing of the place of death until brought there for slaughter. Probably the neat and cleanly appearance of the place was partly due to its construction; but one almost felt on entering that the precepts of humanity were obeyed there. Near the office door sat a dark, swarthy man, with curly black beard, handsome aquiline features, and eyes shadowed by peculiarly long lashes—a face peculiarly Hebrew, grave almost to severity, and sternly calm. This was the Shochet, the Jewish butcher.

To be a Shochet a man must be thoroughly versed in the Hebrew doctrine, must be a member of a Hebrew congregation, must be humane, and must be extremely dexterous in the use of the instruments of slaughter. Consequently the Hebrew butchers are without exception an educated and respectable class of people; and, as their profession calls for a dexterity and knowledge not commonly possessed, it is a very profitable profession. Some slaughterers can make two hundred dollars a month. The Shochet above referred to kills (or "cuts," as they generally term it) for nine different establishments, the Jewish houses paying him a regular monthly salary, and the Gentile houses so much a head for every animal slaughtered. The Shochet can command good prices, and is more or less an autocrat in his profession; for, being a scrupulous and religious man, he will permit no interference in his duties. Many of the Gentile houses employ him for the sake of Hebrew custom; but the meat stamped with his mystical seal will find ready purchasers not only among the followers of either faith, but among all who seek for the best with views hygienic or epicurean. Some of our leading hotels will purchase no other beef but that bearing the Shochet's mark.

He is allowed to use but one weapon—the knife; and to kill in but one manner—by severing the throat with one rapid, dexterous stroke. The knives shown to us were peculiar in shape and temper. That for slaughtering bullocks and calves had a blade over two feet in length, of a uniform breadth and thickness throughout, pointless and square at the end; it was a thin blade, thin as that of a small table-knife at the middle part, or a piece of printers' brass rule; it was about three inches in breadth, bright as silver, keen as a razor and tempered so that it would ring like a bell if tapped with the finger-nail. The edge was a peculiar one—not a sloping edge like that of a razor, although quite as keen, but an edge that seemed to roll in from the blade, smooth as French note paper and that one might pass the tip of the finger over gently without being cut. To sharpen such a knife is not an easy matter and requires a peculiar skill. The knife for slaughtering sheep is not larger than a small table-knife; but is shaped, tempered, and edged precisely like the other.

Now, every Shochet must have a certificate from his rabbi before he may practice his calling; and in order to obtain such a certificate he must pass such an examination as will convince his examiner of his fitness and dexterity. He must even sharpen his knife in the rabbi's presence, so as to leave no perceptible roughness on its edge. Pass your finger over the blade of a new pen-knife sharpened in the ordinary manner, and you will receive a painful cut. But the Shochet's blade is even keener, although it will not cut you by a gentle touch; and a wound inflicted by it on a healthy person will heal up without even the ordinary soreness consequent upon other cuts. When the Shochet has answered all questions satisfactorily and demonstrated his fitness for the office, he receives his certificate, and may obtain employment wherever he can.

Before killing an animal he must pass his thumbnail over the edge of the knife, and thus assure himself that the edge is both smooth and sharp, without the least flaw or roughness that might cause unnecessary pain.

He must take heed to inflict the least possible amount of suffering.

He must examine the edge of his knife after killing each animal, and if the edge is not perfectly true, he must either resharpen the knife or use another.

He must never inflict more than one cut, if possible.

He must examine the lungs of beeves and sheep killed by him, and under no condition is he allowed to place his mark upon the meat of an animal not found perfectly healthy in these organs.

And having discharged this duty conscientiously and found the animal healthy, the Shochet stamps the meat with the mystic characters כשר, or in English letters "kosher," signifying sound; adding also, in Hebrew characters, the day and date of slaughter. Cruelty is never practiced in Hebrew slaughter-houses; at least never in the presence of the Shochet. His religion, his humanity, and the hygiene of his profession alike prohibit any unnecessary violence to the poor dumb brutes, and his keen eyes are always watchful.

Fifteen sheep are placed in a row, with their heads on the edge of the offal gutter, the fore legs and one hind leg of each sheep being tied together. The Shochet approaches with his knife between his teeth. With one hand he lifts the head of the first sheep, and with the other gently parts the wool on the throat; then for an instant he presses the head well back with the left hand, and with the right touches the throat with the knife. The sheep jerks its head away with a hissing inhalation, much like the sound involuntarily uttered by a human on the receipt of a slight burn. There was no apparent effort in that slight, rapid movement of the knife, but the blood pours from a clean wound that has severed the neck half-way through. The animal has suffered no more actual pain than that inflicted by a slight burn on the skin. It kicks a little on finding its breath coming so short, snorts a little, and passes quietly away, while the Shochet feels the edge of his blade and seizes another victim. In no instance did we observe more than one rapid cut inflicted, and none of the victims exhibited signs of much pain.

But in the slaughter of bullocks the skill of the Shochet showed best to advantage. Most of the animals were in remarkably good condition, and very tractable; for they had been well used. An attendant entered the pen and slipped a noose about one of the animal's hind legs, while another within pulled at the hoisting apparatus. Resistance to the mechanical power thus employed was soon felt by the animal to be useless, and it found itself in the slaughter-house in an astonished condition. A few more pulls at the rope, and the animal was hoisted up by the leg until it was lying on its back, very much bewildered, but not in the least hurt. Then, while the head was held back by an attendant, the Shochet advanced, and the great, bright knife passed once across the vast neck like a gleam of lightning, while the blood leaped high into the air from a yawning cut six inches deep. It was a bright crimson, a healthy red; and leaped in jets from the neck at each beat of the dying heart, finally growing thicker, and slower, until its ripple on the floor ceased and it coagulated in bright red patches, in color and form miniatures of fleecy clouds reddened by a rosy sunset. The bullock kicked feebly a few times, and died as easily as the sheep had died. To do such execution at one stroke of that light, long, thin blade requires no little art. The Shochet never makes an apparent effort, never changes a muscle of his grave face, never misses the mark. And kosher meat is the tenderest, freshest, healthiest of all. Calves are killed in the same manner, except that they are hoisted up by both hind legs, and allowed to bleed more thoroughly. Even chickens are slain by the Shochet with a knife, and according to laws observed even in that remote antiquity when the smoke of sacrifice ascended in the wilderness, "and the Lord smelled a sweet savor."

It may not be generally known that, like New York, Cincinnati has its blood-drinkers—consumptives and others who daily visit the slaughter-houses to obtain the invigorating draught of ruddy life-elixir, fresh from the veins of beeves. Lawrence's slaughter-house, opposite the Oliver Street Police Station, has its daily visitants who drink blood; and the slaughter-houses of the Loewensteins, on John street, a few squares away, has perhaps half a dozen visitants of the same class. The latter places, indeed, have the principal custom of this kind (if custom it can be termed where the recipient is charged nothing); for the reason that all beeves are slaughtered there by a Shochet. Many who can drink the blood of animals slaughtered according to the Hebrew fashion, can not stomach that of bullocks felled with the axe. The blood of the latter is black and thick and lifeless; that of the former brightly ruddy and clear as new wine.

"We have two ladies and one young man coming here every day to drink blood," observed a slaughter-house proprietor yesterday. "We used to have a great many more, but they got well and strong and stopped coming. One woman came here for a year, and got wonderfully healthy and fat; she used to be a skeleton, a consumptive skeleton. We always slaughter in the Hebrew way; and the blood of cattle so killed is more healthy. It tastes like new milk from the cow."

"Why, did you ever drink it?"

"No, no!—what should I drink it for? I am too fat as it is. And you know"—with a pleasant laugh—"Moses forbid the Hebrews to use blood for a diet."

The Shochet passes by with his long knife. "I am going to cut a bullock now," he observed, "if you want a glass of blood."

It at once occurred to the writer to try the experiment for curiosity's sake, and give the public the benefit of his experience. A large tumbler was rinsed and brought forward, the throat of the bullock severed, and the glass held to the severed veins. It was filled in an instant and handed to us, brimming over with the clear, ruddy life stream which warmed the vessel through and through. There was no odor, no thickening, no consequent feeling of nausea; and the first mouthful swallowed, the glass was easily drained.

And how did it taste? Fancy the richest cream, warm, with a tart sweetness, and the healthy strength of the pure wine "that gladdeneth the heart of man!" It was a draught simply delicious, sweeter than any concoction of the chemist, the confectioner, the winemaker—it was the very elixir of life itself. The popular idea that blood is difficult to drink is an utter fallacy; and the most timid with the warm glass in his hand must be reassured by one glance at its clear contents. He will forget all the familiar feelings of sickness conjured up by that terrible word "blood"; it is not "blood" any longer in his eyes, but rosy life, warm and palpitating with the impulse of the warm heart's last palpitation; it is ruddy, vigorous, healthful life—not the essence, but the protoplasmic fluid itself—turned in an instant from its natural channel. No other earthly draught can rival such crimson cream, and its strength spreads through the veins with the very rapidity of wine. Perhaps the knowledge of its invigorating properties originated that terrible expression, "drunk with blood." That the first draught will create a desire for a second; that a second may create an actual blood-thirstiness in the literal sense of the word; that such a thirst might lead to the worst consequence in a coarse and brutal nature, we are rather inclined to believe is not only possible, but probable. The healthy and vigorous should respect the law of Moses in this regard. Perhaps it was through occasional indulgence in a draught of human blood (before men's veins were poisoned with tobacco and bad liquor), that provoked the monstrous cruelties of certain Augustine Emperors. Perhaps it was such a passion that, as De Quincey has it, left Caligula, while toying with the polished throat of his wife, Caesonia, half distracted between the pleasure of caressing it, which he might do frequently, and of cutting it, which could be enjoyed but once.

What most of Cincinnati's newspaper readers really thought of Lafcadio's unsettling reportage is difficult to determine. The circulation of the *Enquirer* continued to rise during Lafcadio's tenure there, for people have always had an uneasy fascination with the violent and bizarre—though with a story like "Haceldama," subscribers may well have put aside not only their breakfasts but their lunches and dinners as well!

Under the guise of "sensationalism," however, Lafcadio was doing something more. His curiosity and candor were at the heart of almost all of his best articles, much as they are in the shocking and unsentimentalized photographs of accident and murder victims taken by the mid-twentieth-century photojournalist Weegee. But by reporting on and portraying what society took to be unmentionable and unthinkable subjects, Lafcadio (like Weegee) was in fact revealing the unstable nature of the boundary that most of his readers would have sworn existed, incontrovertibly, between "savagery" and "civilization." As Herman Melville's Ishmael would say in *Moby-Dick*—with a true Lafcadian perspective: "Go to the meat-market of a Saturday night and see the crowds of live bipeds staring up at the long rows of dead quadrupeds. Does not that sight take a tooth out of the cannibal's jaw? Cannibals? who is not a cannibal? I tell you it will be more tolerable for the Fejee that salted down a lean missionary in his cellar against a coming famine . . . in the day of judgment, than for thee, civilized and enlightened gourmand, who nailest geese to the ground and feastest on their bloated livers in thy paté-de-foie-gras." And what might at first seem to be Lafcadio's disengaged, dispassionate approach to some of his subjects is often only a function of his unadmonishing, dark-humored, but undeniable outrage and compassion.

When a nineteen-year-old convicted criminal named James Murphy, for example, was about to be hanged in a long-awaited public execution, Lafcadio reported in one of his most trenchant stories ("Gibbeted") how the killing was botched when the rope broke around the boy's neck, under his black hood. As the half-injured prisoner, obviously in shock, opened his eyes inside his darkness, he whispered, "Why, I ain't dead— I ain't dead."

"Are you hurt, my child?" the attending—and now embarrassed—priest asked solicitously.

"No, Father, I'm not dead. . . . What are they going to do with me?"

Lafcadio, who had managed to enter the physician's area to the rear of the scaffold and whose hand was on the boy's wrist, felt his pulse quicken horribly as another rope was prepared.

"Die like a man," the priest whispered to the terrified nineteen-year-old who was now desperately holding on to a crucifix and, screaming, had to be restrained.

On the second time around, after the body fell with a jerk through the trap and the noose tightened, the priest sprinkled holy water on the swinging figure, and Lafcadio again felt the boy's wrist—still hot and moist—as the pulse only gradually grew fainter, and the skin colder.

It had taken seventeen minutes for the prisoner to die, and Lafcadio commented to his readers, "But the facts in the case, as they appeared to the writer, were simply that a poor, ignorant passionate boy, with a fair, coarse face, had in the heat of drunken anger taken away the life of a fellow-being, and paid the penalty of his brief crime, by a hundred days of mental torture, and a hideous death."

In a country of Robber Barons and promises of gold in the pavements and pie in the sky, Lafcadio wrote about ragpickers, impoverished seamstresses, abused children, and terrified inmates in a lunatic asylum. Soon, too, he would be spending much of his time in the black neighborhoods of Bucktown and the Levee.

On his night shifts, he often met up with Henry Watkin, who accompanied Lafcadio on his nocturnal rounds of interviewing saloonkeepers, coroners, mission derelicts, policemen, pickpockets, leech-doctors, and stevedores. And they would wander the city and argue about various subjects, disagreeing, for instance, about polygamy (Lafcadio was against it, Watkin accepted it) but agreeing about their distaste for self-serving religious do-gooders of any creed and for bilkers of the poor and gullible in any guise.

In his quest for truth, Lafcadio once even resorted to a schoolboy's prank by dressing himself up as a woman in order to file one of his least impressive, but still uproariously catty (if misogynistic), reports on a matinée talk—billed as a "lecture for ladies only"—by Edith O'Gorman, the self-styled "Escaped Nun" from a New Jersey convent. Her purpose in her national lecture tour was to titillate the ladies of America with innuendoes and tales of monastic sexual dalliance:

To further the cause of science and to complete the truth of history by a judicious use of "Sweet Sixteen," blonde wigs, trails, veils and brass, your smooth-faced reporter did it. After arraying himself in these strange garments, looking dubiously on No. 8 gloves and No. 9 buttoned boots, he was forcibly impressed with the danger he was to encounter. Remembering, too, the depth of the mud, he went in a carriage, for discretion is the better part, and he was afraid of the sharp eyes of our street Arabs. . . . He lumbered out . . . stepped on his dress. He looked askance at the ticket seller as he tripped up the stairs, and the rude glance of that functionary brought the hot blood to his cheeks. By the time he was inside the portals sacred to "lovely woman" for "this time only," he really began to feel like one—[as] he imagined one [might] feel.

The prurient females began coming in, in squads of five and six, and popping up out of one seat into another because they were right next to some women they didn't like. But, taking it altogether, there was a good deal of hobnobbing—being met together for a common purpose—and a virtuous-looking female on our right kept nudging us in a sisterly kind of way till we were ashamed. By the time the flush brought to our cheeks by the rude man below had subsided, it was blanched by a new and more terrible episode—"There's a man!"

Your reporter knew that it was [he]. These accursed No. 8's had betrayed him. His limbs trembled, his teeth chattered, and he thought he said damn. The female to his right thought he said shame. He waited to be sacrificed on the altar of outraged virtue, but seeing the indignant eyes looking in another direction . . . he knew he was safe.

The hall filled up. The Nun trotted out. The little buzz subsided. Each little angel twisted herself into a comfortable shape—one school girl near us sat on her foot—and each beaming eye was turned to see the Escaped—each ear intent on hearing the "lecture for ladies only." Just then a baby cooed, and after silencing it at nature's font, the mother looked happy, and Edith began. She told of how good she was, how all the naughty, naughty things other little girls knew she never dreamed of, and then—oh, she made your reporter blush and wish that he had stayed away. The ladies all tittered. Then she got moral and prosy, and one or two virtuous middle-aged ladies left the hall. (It is not known whether they got their money back, but it is safe to say that they applied for it.) Everybody began to look bored and disappointed. Sly Edith—cunning little creature—saw this, and then she looked around furtively, slipped to all the doors, and as she came back with her finger on her lips, the eyes, mouth and ears of each divinity stood open and Edith began: "I'll tell you about Sister"—[she gave her name, we refrain]. . . . Then she told about this sister, but your representative was blushing so that he hasn't got over it yet. . . .

A trusting public expects information, but modesty forbids. The women enjoyed it and seemed in a degree happy—the dear things—and they cried and made [a] cunning little sound with their ruby lips that means sympathy and horror combined; and Edith floated off the stage in a blaze of glory, as it were. There were some very pretty attempts at applause, and, considering the little practice they have, the darling little feet stamped bravely. Altogether it was a most enjoyable afternoon, and we have no doubt the half dozen little four-year-olds profited by it. . . .

("FEMININE CURIOSITY")]

Less like a prankster and more like a serious investigative journalist, Lafcadio began writing a series of crusading articles exposing: a "baby farm" in which a doctor, paid to care for illegitimate infants, allowed them to die instead; a "medical institute" that awarded diplomas to students after a twenty-four-hour course; the swindling activities of Miss Tennessee Claflin's cultlike "little freaks of free love" and her quack dispensary; various groups of temperance advocates; self-aggrandizing Christian evangelists and missionaries (the latter would become one of Lafcadio's lifelong *bêtes noires);* and numerous fraudulent mediums, spirit photographers, and spiritualists. Notable among these last was a certain Madame

Raphael, "a very fat dwarf, about four feet three inches high; with an immensely high forehead, small cunning eyes without eyebrows; a non-descript nose, and a mouth that strongly resembles an equatorial line drawn across a greasy hemisphere."

It was easy for Lafcadio to expose fake clairvoyants like Madame Raphael. But he met his match in a session—fake or real, he never managed to figure out—with a trumpet medium named Mrs. Smith. On this occasion he found himself speaking with the spirit of his dead father, to whom, for the first and last time in his life, Lafcadio granted forgive-ness—at least for the benefit of his engrossed readers ("Among the Spirits"):

〖

> "Be thou a spirit of health, or goblin damn'd,
> Bring with thee airs from Heaven or blasts from Hell,
> Be thy intents wicked or charitable,
> Thou com'st in such questionable shape
> That I will speak to thee."
>
> "I am thy father's spirit,
> Doom'd for a certain term to walk the night."
>   —HAMLET, ACT I, SCENE III.

After his last visit to No. 16 Barr street, the reporter resolved to go through a course of purification before again presuming to enter that ghostly tem-ple; for his spiritualistic friend had maliciously suggested that the spirits objected to him as being physically and psychically filthy. He began by taking a bath, and washed himself seven times in a mystic manner. More-over, he promised to abstain from tobacco, to live on mush and milk, to wear a clean shirt, to black his boots every morning, and to forswear swearing. Alas for the fragility of such promises, so aptly compared to pie-crusts! He longed after the flesh-pots of Egypt, and devoured beefsteak rare the very next morning; he neglected his linen; and he found it hard to confine himself to five cigars a day. However, he actually succeeded in sticking to his last resolution for six long and weary days; but happening to look at the office clock last Friday afternoon, and finding himself twenty minutes behind time for the seance, he unfortunately said something at the very last moment that the recording angel must have put down in black and white. It was therefore with horrible qualms of conscience that he entered Mrs. Smith's parlor.

The reporter was kindly received by the medium, who looked younger and prettier than ever. "Your last report was a very fair one," she said, smiling; "but you made some dreadful mistakes in describing that room upstairs. The windows are *not* at the north side, and the closet is *not* in the west wall, and there *is* a carpet upon the floor."

The reporter apologized for the inaccuracy, and promised to correct it, excusing himself at the same time for his unpunctuality.

"My husband has not yet come home from the gallery," said the medium [Mr. Smith is a photographer]; but this lady, Mrs.——, will take his place in the circle.

The lady to whom the reporter was now introduced looks much more like a medium than Mrs. Smith. She is not tall, but of a [robust] physique . . . with dark hair and steady, piercing black eyes, a rather high forehead, and lips indicative of great power of will. She is evidently a person of much force of character, yet withal of a frank and kindly manner. The reporter regrets being unable to give her name—especially as her husband happens to be a prominent citizen of Cincinnati. After some brief conversation the three proceeded upstairs and commenced preparations for the seance.

"You don't like to tie Mrs. Smith yourself, I believe?" said the black-eyed lady, with a peculiar smile.

"Indeed I had rather not," pleaded the reporter; "I don't know how."

"Well, you must at least fasten the robe behind the chair; and you must examine the room. You can tack down her dress to the floor if you like, and tie her feet to the chair."

The reporter declined to act upon the last two somewhat malicious suggestions; but he examined the room, and tied the rope as desired. The preparations made were similar to those described in his last report; the medium's dress being nailed to the floor; the doors locked and fastened with pen-knives, etc. Then the tin trumpet was placed in the middle of the floor, but out of the reach of any one in the circle; the gas was put out, and the sitting commenced. It may be as well to mention here that the reporter took good care to satisfy himself that the medium was securely fastened, at the same time remarking, that so far as he was personally concerned his possible convictions would not be weakened or strengthened by the fact of Mrs. Smith being fettered or unfettered; but that having to lay a statement before the public it were just as well that the usual course was adopted. Mrs.—— observed that the spirits preferred that the medium should be tied.

For nearly an hour the circle waited for news from the Spirit-world, at first beguiling the time with conversation, and a little singing in which all joined. The musical hymn with the well-known refrain—

> On the other side of Jordan,
> In the green fields of Eden,
> There is rest for the weary,
> There is rest for you—

was sung several times, and also several other pieces; but the spirits appeared to be unwilling. The conversation gradually slackened, until the circle sat in a dreary silence, interrupted only by the occasional cries of children in the street at play, or the rumble of a passing vehicle.

"I really hope we are not going to be disappointed this time," said the medium, finally breaking the silence. "It would be too bad."

"I wish Mr. Mitchel would come and speak to the gentleman," said Mrs.——.

"Who is Mr. Mitchel?" asked the reporter.

"Why," answered the medium, "a spirit, of course."

"Yes; but I meant to ask what he was before he became a spirit."

"Well, he says he is the brother of Professor Mitchel—the astronomer, that used to live here, you know. He first began to communicate with us nearly six years ago, when he told us some very strange things about a little private affair of our own—things we didn't know anything about beforehand—and he also told us the name of a man who he said could give us further information. Father was a strict church-member at that time, and did not, of course, believe in Spiritualism; but he went after this man just for curiosity, and found him at last after a good deal of trouble. The man was a kind of artist—used to touch up pictures. He told my father everything that the spirit had referred to. Mitchel nearly always attends our sittings now; and sometimes you would be surprised at the manifestations he gives. He will talk in a loud, deep voice—just like a person in the flesh, and sing, and stamp on the floor."

"I think," said Mrs.——, "that we are talking too much. When you talk, Mary, it makes you too positive. We had better sing something. Don't you know some song?"—to the reporter.

The reporter sang some songs in a very dismal voice, until the bells announced that it was six o'clock. An hour and a quarter had passed away.

"The spirits are going to do something, I know," suddenly exclaimed Mrs.——, in tones of quiet satisfaction. "I feel an unusually strong influence. They will certainly lift that trumpet. Do you feel the influence strongly, Mary?"

"Not as strong as I generally do," answered the medium.

"Do you feel the influence?"—to the reporter.

"I have no idea what the 'influence' is like—except from reading Bulwer Lytton's fantastic tales. He speaks of such an influence in one of his horrid stories as a 'ghastly exhalation' rising through the floor—a vague, but awful description, isn't it? How does the influence affect you?"

"Why, a strange kind of numbness creeps all over me, as if my whole body was 'going to sleep' in the sense that one's foot is said to go to sleep. This feeling is accompanied by a curious sense of *expansion*, as it were: my hands, for instance, seem to increase in size. But I can not describe the feeling properly. Ah! I felt a hand laid on my arm this moment. We had better continue singing; the spirits like it."

Suddenly the reporter distinctly felt the fingers of a hand touching, first the lower part of his right thigh, and then his knee in a rapid succession of taps. The taps seemed to be given by the first finger and thumb of a right hand—a heavy, strong hand—which closed as they touched the reporter's thigh, as though in the attempt to pinch slightly without hurting. The sensation, at the same time, was extremely peculiar, each tap being followed by a very faint shock as of electricity. The reporter naturally started.

"Did you touch me, Mrs. ——?"

"No, sir. You had better take hold of my hands."

The reporter did so, but the ghostly touches were continued, and the strange shocks accompanying them became stronger. Mrs. Smith still sat at the opposite side of the room, occasionally talking while the spectral hands were tapping the reporter's knee. He endeavored to catch hold of them, holding both of Mrs.——'s hands with his right, and seeking the ghostly hands with his left. But he could not touch them. Then another hand, a very small one, was laid upon the upper part of his right arm, and closed its fingers upon the limb for an instant, sending a peculiar, but not disagreeable, thrill through the reporter's frame.

The trumpet then began to move along the floor, making a strange tinkling sound as it passed over the carpet. Then came a succession of faint taps, which sounded as though made by the index-finger of a hand.

"The spirit wants to say something, evidently," said Mrs.——. "Do you want anything?"—to the spirit.

"Yes."—[three taps.]

"What is it?"

[No answer.]

"Are we sitting right?"

"No!"—[a single emphatic tap.]

"What is the matter?"

[No answer.]

At that moment the trumpet was raised from the floor, and struck the reporter heavily on the right thigh three times. Then it repeated the operation on his knee.

"Perhaps somebody has their legs crossed," said Mrs.——. "Have you, sir?"

"Yes." The reporter had had his right leg crossed over his left for some time. He uncrossed them at once.

"You must not sit that way according to the rules of the seance. The spirits don't like it. Is it all right now?"—to the spirit.

Three emphatic taps; and three blows with the trumpet on both of the reporter's knees. The touch of the trumpet did not produce the peculiar shock caused by the touch of the fingers. A moment after, the spirit laid the trumpet down in its first position and departed.

"I wonder if that could have been Mitchel?" said Mrs.——.

The state of affairs had now become really interesting. After a minute or two the trumpet was moved again, but this time with apparent difficulty, as though the ghostly fingers were too unsubstantial for the task.

"I guess that's Maudie," said the medium.

"No; I should rather think it is one of this gentleman's relatives—the spirit is so weak. It is always weak the first time it tries to speak."

The tinkling noise seemed to move in the direction of the medium. Then there came a distinct sound of *kisses*—kisses in quick succession, as though coming from the small, chubby lips of a child; and the word "Mamma" was repeated in a distinct, soft whisper.

"Ah! That's Maudie," said the medium. "What is it, darling?"

"Why isn't papa here?"

"If we knew you wished to speak to him, darling, we would not have formed the circle without him."

"Won't you bring some flowers next time?"

"Yes, dear."

The spirit then seemed to go to Mrs.——, and kissed her. The child-voice asked once more for flowers; and the trumpet was returned to its place.

Again the reporter felt a hand laid upon his knee—a strong, heavy hand, like the hand of a man, and the touch was accompanied by the same strange electric thrill as before. The trumpet was again raised. It was first laid on the visitor's knees, and then brought over to where the medium was sitting. A voice spoke through it in a deep, hoarse whisper.

"Some spirit wishes to speak with the gentleman," said the medium.

The trumpet then appeared to be brought to within about four inches of the reporter's face, and the voice addressed him by a name by which he is unknown to his friends in this country, but which he at once recognized. The reporter did not mention this fact to the medium for private reasons; and no one but himself caught the name. The greater part of the sentence following was indistinguishable; but the word "father" was distinctly uttered.

"Do I understand you to say that you are my father?"

"Yes"—[feebly].

"Please give your name."

[Two indistinguishable whispers.]

"Your full name, please."

Three indistinct whispers. The whispers sounded much like the full name, but the reporter wished to hear it distinctly given. The middle name is a curious one, and the reporter's father never was in America, or known to any person in this country, so far as can be ascertained.

"Please try again?"

"Charles"—the rest indistinguishable.

Several more unsuccessful efforts were made. Then a whisper came— "I shall try to grow stronger," and the trumpet was laid down.

In about a minute it came again, and the voice clearly and distinctly uttered the full name:

"Charles Bush H——."

"That is the name."

"I am your father, P——."

"Have you any word for me?"

"Yes."

"What is it?"

"Forgive me"—in a long whisper.

"I have nothing to forgive."

"You have, indeed"—very faintly.

"What is it?"

"You know well"—distinctly.

"Will you write it?"

"I don't know how."

"There is a pencil and paper upon the table."

"I will try. I will try to grow stronger."

The trumpet was replaced for several minutes, after which the spirit returned.

"I wronged you: forgive me"—a loud, distinct whisper.

"I do not consider that you have."

"It would be better not to contradict the spirit," interrupted the medium, "until it has explained matters."

"I do not wish to contradict the spirit in the sense you imply," answered the reporter. *"I thoroughly understand the circumstance alluded to; but I wish to explain that I have long ceased to consider it as a wrong done to me."* To the spirit—"Please state explicitly the circumstance you refer to.

"Am I to understand that you prefer not to speak of it in the circle?"

"Yes."

"Will you write it?"

"I will try."

The trumpet was once more replaced. After waiting a few minutes the reporter, inadvertently, and, he believes, noiselessly *crossed his feet in the dark;* and to his surprise immediately received a heavy blow from the trumpet on the *left* foot, which happened to be the uppermost. The trumpet rang again with the stroke, and was violently tapped, as with strong fingers. It is needless to say that the reporter uncrossed his feet without delay.

"That must be Mr. Mitchel," said Mrs.——.

"Is that you, Mitchel?" inquired the medium.

"Yes; the father wishes to speak with his son. He would write to him, but he has not yet learned the law by which that can be done." This was spoken in the loud, deep, clear voice of a vigorous man.

"Will he be able to write?"

"Not yet. But it *can* be done"—with a remarkably strong emphasis upon the word in italics. The voice seemed to come from the floor, immediately at the reporter's feet.

In a short time the former voice again spoke; but only to testify pleasure "at meeting my son," and promising to endeavor to gain strength for a more satisfactory communication. Then followed a sound as of footsteps, moving around the reporter's chair, and seeming to die away in the direction of the wall—heavy footfalls, as of a man; yet the slight floor did not respond to the heavy tread by the faintest vibration.

"You had better ask Mr. Mitchel to assist your father," said Mrs.——. "He will answer any questions you may wish to put."

"You are better acquainted with Mr. Mitchel than I am," answered the reporter. "Be kind enough to ask him for me."

"Mr. Mitchel," said the lady, "will you please let this gentleman know what his father wishes to say?"

No answer.

"This is a reporter, Mr. Mitchel. He intends to publish his experience at this seance."

"Humph!" said the spirit, in a slightly sarcastic manner.

"Don't you think it would help our cause, Mr. Mitchel?"

A long, weary sigh, and a succession of taps upon the trumpet.

Just at that moment a loud knock sounded upon the door; the trumpet fell upon the carpet with a loud crash, as if dropped from the ceiling. The spell was broken.

"Ah! that spoils our sitting for the remainder of the evening," said Mrs.——, turning up the gas, and opening the door to admit Mr. Smith.

"Why, it is after seven o'clock," said that gentleman. "I am sorry to have broken up the sitting, but I did not suppose you were having any manifestations."

The seance had lasted more than two hours.

Mrs. Smith was still sitting, exactly as she had been tied previous to the performance; her dress strongly nailed down to the floor; and the ropes fastened exactly as they had been before the *seance commenced*. The reporter examined the knots he had made, and found them intact.

In conclusion the author of this statement wishes to inform the readers that he has endeavored to lay before them a plain, unvarnished report of facts. He can offer no explanation of them, but leaves the reader to his own conclusions. It may be well to mention, however, that the words uttered by the Voice regarding something it refused to explain more fully appeared to allude to a rather curious bit of private family history. The reporter can not conceive of any possible means by which the secret of the name given by the Voice could have come to the knowledge of either of the lady mediums present—especially as even the steps necessary to produce mesmeric clairvoyance had not been taken. The person supposed to speak to the visitor had spent the greater part of his life in Hindostan, and had been buried at sea in the Mediterranean in 1866. Neither of the parties concerned have, or ever did have, any relatives or connections, however distant, in the United States.

CHAPTER 7

*B*lack
and *W*hite

E ARLY IN his journalistic career, Lafcadio realized that while it was acceptable to write about drinking the blood of an animal for an article on slaughterhouses, it was not advisable to admit to having tried opium, even when one was describing small opium dens in the city and concluding that opium addiction was a "disease." (In fact, Lafcadio, like many of the French writers he admired, would later, surreptitiously, experiment with opium and hashish, though he never became addicted to either.) He also understood that when he wrote an article enumerating the charms of a naked artist's model in a painter's studio, he had to represent her as having *limbs* instead of legs, a *bosom* instead of breasts, and as being *unclad* instead of nude. In any case, of course, he would be—and indeed was—accused of lewdness simply because his subject was "inappropriate."

For in spite of the openness of the American press, the period was still the Victorian era—a time of euphemisms, concealment, prudishness, and sanctimoniousness, when it was acceptable for a newspaper to convey the precise details of an unusually brutal and grotesque murder but not appropriate for a magazine in San Francisco, for example, to serialize Bret Harte's story "The Luck of Roaring Camp" because the character of the mother in the book—a mining-camp prostitute—might shock the "sentiments" of the journal's subscribers.

For all its renown as the city that gave safe haven to runaway slaves before and during the Civil War, postwar Cincinnati was strictly segregated. Blacks avoided Fourth Street, the suburbs, and the German enclaves Over-the-Rhine. In turn, whites practiced an early form of "benign neglect" with regard to their "colored" citizens. Chary policemen, who patrolled in pairs, and intrepid single white men, who entered the Levee to frequent its ladies of the night, made up the ghetto's few encounters with members of the city's establishment. Sex (and sometimes drugs), as usual, was what broke the ice separating white from black, black from white.

The hypocrisy with regard to the facts of sex and race in nineteenth-century America hardly bears recapitulation. The United States was the only country in the New World that carried its laws against miscegenation (so common on slave plantations) from its colonial period into its national era, and these antimiscegenation laws were declared unconstitutional by the Supreme Court only in 1967. Before then, more than half the states of the union for varying lengths of time distinguished themselves (along with South Africa, Australia, and Nazi Germany) by trying legally to keep the doctrine of racial purity alive. Depending on whether a person was one-fourth, one-eighth, or one-sixteenth black, he or she might be white in one state but black in another. In 1938 a Louisiana court annulled the marriage of a white man to a woman whose great-great-grandmother was black. In Oregon, at one time, a person with less than a fourth of a black strain in a direct white line was considered white and could marry a white person, but could not marry a mulatto or a quadroon. In Colorado's past, mixed marriages were once legal in the southern part of the state but punishable by two years' imprisonment in the northern part. In Ohio, mixed marriages were prohibited between the years 1861 and 1877. In Virginia, where the white proportion of a person's racial strain required for him to qualify as white was legally increased three times beginning in 1866, one might have been *unimpeachably* white in 1866 (assuming one were less than one-fourth black), but *unquestionably* black in 1932 if one— or perhaps one's mean-spirited neighbor—could dig back and find a black relative in one's past even a thousand years before! One might simply wish to dismiss such laws as atavistic race madness, if it were not that millions of people's lives were, and still are, destroyed by them and the attitude behind them.

Certainly Lafcadio, who was himself a hybrid genetically, can hardly have taken seriously the laws regarding relations between the races in the state of Ohio. And, indeed, it is plain that he had failed to heed them, because one summer afternoon in August 1875, he reported for work at the *Enquirer* as usual, only to find himself summarily fired. The reason given: the reporter's "deplorable moral habits."

Lafcadio knew that a few of his colleagues on the paper were jealous of his success and had never understood his aloofness; they, certainly, would not have been unhappy to see him leave. Neither, of course, would the ever-growing number of religious pretenders and out-of-work spirit mediums the journalist had exposed, some of whom had friends in influential places. But it was ultimately a deputation of pothouse city politicians who were Lafcadio's undoing. Increasingly aggravated by many of his embarrassing reports on barely disguised "nameless crimes," they put pressure on the publisher of the *Enquirer* to get rid of Hearn. The means by which they accomplished their mission so successfully was their discovery that the star reporter had not only been cohabiting with a "woman of color" for four years, but had actually married her.

Sometime between meeting Henry Watkin and being hired by the *Enquirer,* Lafcadio had taken lodgings in a cheap boardinghouse at the northeast corner of McFarland and Plum streets. Working in the kitchen as a cook was a beautiful half-black girl named Alethea Foley. Lafcadio avoided the endless, wearying living-room palaver of the other boarders, and instead always managed to find a way into the kitchen, or onto the kitchen stairway, to converse with Alethea about her life. While she cooked on her breaks, she told him that her father had been an Irish slaveholder whose plantation was near Maysville, Kentucky. Her mother had been a slave. When her father's white daughter had married, Alethea had been given to her as a wedding present. After the Civil War she worked for several families in and around Maysville, had an illegitimate child by a Scotsman named Anderson, and then, impoverished, moved to Cincinnati with her son, William, who was now four years old.

Lafcadio told Alethea that he, too, had had an Irish father who had sired him and then abandoned him and his Greek mother, who in her turn had left him to be brought up by a religiously fanatical great-aunt. Lafcadio was now twenty-two years old, Alethea eighteen. Both of them, Lafcadio pointed out, were alone in the world; both had suffered and been mistreated and abused. They had, Lafcadio was certain, a kind of bond with each other. And, starved for affection, Lafcadio asked Alethea to be his lover. Eventually, she agreed. He called her "Mattie" as a nickname.

Only Henry Watkin and a couple of other of Lafcadio's trusted newspaper colleagues knew about the liaison. For almost four years he and Mattie were together during the few hours each morning or night when Lafcadio had finished work. Without ever naming her or suggesting his relationship to her, he even managed to describe and give a portrait of

Alethea and her powers of "ghost-seeing" (somewhat similar to Lafcadio's own when he was a child) in one of his *Enquirer* articles ("Some Strange Experience"):

["They do say the dead never come back again," she observed half dreamingly; "but then I have seen such queer things!"

She was a healthy, well built country girl, whom the most critical must have called good looking, robust and ruddy, despite the toil of life in a boarding-house kitchen, but with a strangely thoughtful expression in her large dark eyes, as though she were ever watching the motions of Somebody who cast no shadow, and was invisible to all others. Spiritualists were wont to regard her as a strong "medium," although she had a peculiar dislike of being so regarded. She had never learned to read or write, but possessed naturally a wonderful wealth of verbal description, a more than ordinarily vivid memory, and a gift of conversation which would have charmed an Italian *improvisatore*. These things we learned during an idle half hour passed one summer's evening in her company on the kitchen stairs; while the boarders lounged on the porch in the moonlight, and the hall lamp created flickering shadows along the varnished corridors, and the hungry rats held squeaking carnival in the dark dining-room. To the weird earnestness of the story-teller, the melody of her low, soft voice, and the enthralling charm of her conversation, we cannot attempt to do justice; nor shall we even undertake to report her own mysterious narrative word for word, but only to convey to the reader those impressions of it which linger in the writer's memory.

"The first thing I can remember about ghost-people," she said, "happened to me when I was quite a little child. It was in Bracken County, Kentucky, on a farm, between Dover and Augusta—about half way between the towns—for I remember a great big stone that was set up on the road just above the farm, which they called the 'Half-way Stone,' and it had a big letter H cut on it. The farm-house was away back from the river, in a lonely place, among woods of beech and sugar-trees; and was one of the weirdest old buildings you ever saw. It was built before there were any nails used out West; so you can imagine how old it was; and I heard that the family who first built it had many a terrible fight with the Indians. Before the house ran a rocky lane full of gutters and mud holes; and behind it was a great apple orchard, where very few apples grew, because no one took care of the trees. Great slimy, creeping plants had grown up about them, and strangled them; and the pathways were almost grown over with high weeds, and strong rank grass; and owls lived in some of the trees, but the family seemed to be afraid to shoot them. At the end of the orchard yawned a great, deep well, unused for many years; cats and dogs and rabbits had found graves in the fetid black water; the stones were green with moss and slime; the bucket was covered with moss; and great black snakes which lived in holes in the sides of the well used to wriggle out on sunny days and blink their wicked, slimy eyes at the house. This well was at the mouth of a deep hollow, choked up with elder-brush and those creeping plants that can never be killed, and there were black-snakes, garter-snakes and dry-land moccasins living there. Near the hollow on the other side flowed a clear "branch" of water, over a bed of soft blue clay, which we used to roll into "slate pencils" and make mud pies of. One time we wanted to make a little mill-dam there, to drown some geese in, and while digging into the blue clay with a grubbing-hoe we found four great big Mexican dollars buried there. We did not know what they were then, and we brought them to the farmhouse, where they took them from us. Some time afterwards two men came and bought the piece of ground where we had found the money, and they set to digging; but nothing more was ever found there.

"The farmhouse looked as if it had been built a hundred years ago, but those who built it built well and strong, for it was sound from roof to foundation. Many of the big trees in the orchard, planted by them, had rotted and died, and the bark was peeling off over nests of the gray wood-lice that burrowed under it; but the old house was still strong. It was a very queer, antiquated structure, with ghostly looking gables, and great limestone chimneys towered up at each end of it. There were four big rooms, two up stairs and two down stairs, and a little kitchen built against the house, making a fifth room; there were five old-fashioned doors of heavy planking, and there were eight or ten narrow windows, with ever so many tiny panes of glass in them. The house was built of heavy sarsaparilla logs, with floors of black walnut, and walls ceiled with blue ash; and there were no shelves, but only recesses in the walls—small, square recesses, where books and little things were kept. The clapboards were fastened down on the roof with wooden pegs, and the flooring was pegged down to the sleepers. Between the planking and the logs of the south room on the first floor there was an old Revolutionary musket built into the wall. The north room, next to this, was never occupied.

"I remember that room well; for the door was often open, although no one of the family ever entered it since an old lady named Frankie Boyd had died there, years before, of consumption. She had lingered a long time, and coughed a great deal, and used to spit on the wall beside the bed. The bed was an old-time piece of furniture, with posters; and all the furniture was old-fashioned. There was an old-fashioned clothes-chest with legs; an old-fashioned rocking-chair, with great heavy rockers; and an old-fashioned spinning-wheel. One of the old lady's dresses, a black dress, still hung on the wall where she had placed it the last time she had taken it off; but it had become so old and moth-eaten that a touch would have crumbled it like so much burnt paper. The dust was thick on the floor, so thick that the foot would leave an impression in it; and the windows were yellow like parchment for want of cleaning.

"They said that the old lady used to walk about that room, and that no one could sleep there. Doors used to open and shut without the touch of human hands; and all night long the sound of that rocking-chair rocking, and of the spinning-wheel humming, could be heard through the house. That was why nobody ever went into that room. But the ghost of Frankie Boyd was not the only ghost there. The house had once been owned by the Paddy family, and Lee Paddy, the "old man," and all his children, had died in the room used when I was there for a kitchen, and had been buried in the family graveyard, on the north side of the house, under the shadow of a great locust tree. After Frankie Boyd died the house fell into the hands of her nephew, a man named Bean, who had a rich father, a scientific old gentleman, in Lewis County. Both father and son were queer people, and the old man's eccentricity at one time nearly lost him his life. Some one killed an immense blacksnake on his farm, and the scientific Mr. Bean had it cooked for dinner after the manner of cooking salmon. Then he invited a friendly neighbor to dine with him. They say that the neighbor was delighted with the repast, and declared that he had never eaten finer salmon. But when old Bean told him that he had eaten a blacksnake which John killed yesterday morning, the shock nearly killed him, and he staggered home to get his shot-gun. Bean did not dare to leave his home for weeks afterwards.

"After the death of Frankie Boyd, the old farmhouse in Bracken County of course became a weirder and ghostlier place than ever—a scary place, as the slaves around there used to call it. It was a dreadfully creaky place, and no one could pass out or down the old staircase without making a prodigious creaking and crackling. Now at all hours of the day or night those stairs creaked and creaked, and doors opened and banged, and steps echoed overhead in the room upstairs. I was a very little girl then and had a little boy-playmate, who used to run about with me all over the farm, digging in the blue clay, running after the fowls, watching the great snakes that glided about the noisome well, climbing the strangled apple trees in search of withered and shrunken apples, and throwing pebbles at the great, ugly horned owls that used to sit there among the creepers, blinking with their great yellow eyes. We did not know why the house was haunted by such odd noises; and the old Negro servants were strictly forbidden to tell us anything about the queer things that walked about there. But, nevertheless, we had a perfect horror of the house; we dreaded to be left in it alone; we never entered it on sunny days, except at meal time, and when foul weather forced us to stay in-doors the folks often found us sitting down and crying in a corner. We could not at first tell why we cried, further than that we were afraid of something undefinable—a vague fear always weighed upon us like a night-mare. They told us to go upstairs, one evening after dark, and we had to go without a light. Something came after us, and stepped up the stairs behind us, and touched our heads, and followed us into the room, and seemed to sob and moan. We screamed with fear, and the folks ran up with a lantern and took us down stairs again. Some one used also to play with the rusty old musket that had been built into the wall, and would get under the black walnut floor, knocking loudly and long; and all the time the rocking-chair creaked and thumped in the north room. Bean had got used to it all; but he seldom went up stairs, and the books in the old recesses became black with layers of clammy dust, and the spiders spun thick, glutinous webs across the windows.

"It came to pass about six months after the dead had followed us into the dark room upstairs, that a great storm came down through the woods, wrestling with the ancient trees, tearing away the serpent-creepers in the garden, swelling the springs to torrents, and the old farmhouse rattled through all its dry bones. The great limestone chimneys and the main building stood the test bravely; but the little kitchen building where all the Paddy family had died, was shattered from clapboards to doorstep. It had been built in a very curious fashion, a fashion passed away and forgotten; and the cunning of modern house builders could not rebuild it. So they pulled it down, log by log, and brought destruction upon many spider colonies, and mice nests, and serpent holes; building a new pine-wood structure in its place, with modern doors and windows. And from that time the strange noises ceased and the dead seemed to rest, except in the room where the yellow spittle had dried upon the walls and the old-fashioned furniture had become hoary with years of dust. The steps on the staircase died away forever, and the knocking beneath the floor ceased.

"But I must not forget to tell you one more curious thing about the place. There was a hen-house near the grave of the Paddy family; and the hens were great in multitude, and laid eggs by hundreds. Somehow or other we could scarcely ever get any eggs for all that. The hens were thin, spectral birds, which looked as if they had been worn out by anxiety and disappointment. Something or other used to steal their eggs the moment they were laid; and what it was no one ever pretended to know. The old Negro cook hinted that the ghosts of the Paddy family sucked the eggs; but as we could never find even an egg-shell, this supposition did not hold good. Traps were laid for pole-cats, weasels, coons, and every variety of wild egg-thieves; but none were ever seen there or caught; and the poultry ceased to propagate their species, so that fresh relays of poultry had to be purchased ever and anon. I don't know whether the old farm-house still stands, or whether Bachelor Bean has been gathered to his fathers, for it is many years since I left there to live with friends at Dover. . . ."

In some ways—probably on account of his family history—Lafcadio's ideas concerning love relationships were quite Victorian: if you had a long-term involvement with a woman, you should marry her. So, early in 1874, he proposed to Mattie. She understood, however, that Lafcadio was prompted more by a sense of duty than by desire, and she furthermore warned him that he would be socially and professionally ostracized if the marriage was ever publicly revealed. Lafcadio was undeterred: he was used to feeling repudiated and excluded, and what did his private life have to do with his professional competence? But he *was* astounded when he could find no one to accompany him to the marriage bureau in order to obtain a marriage license (for which, he was to discover, he had to swear that Alethea was white), and equally distressed when at least one minister refused to perform the ceremony. How could a wedding ceremony be illegal in a democracy?

Eventually, a courageous black Episcopalian minister agreed to officiate, and the nuptials took place at the home of one of Mattie's black friends on June 14, 1874. The bride could not help sensing the groom's deter-

mined attitude of obligation and duty, and the ceremony was consequently a less than joyful occasion. When Mattie, her son, William, and
Lafcadio now began to live together in their own apartment for the first
time, the result was a disaster. She complained about her husband's long
working hours and his "morose and silent disposition." He reproached
her for never ironing his clothes properly and also criticized her cooking—
though he had never minded it at the boardinghouse where they had first
met.

Several months after the wedding, the couple decided to separate. (Their
union, in the eyes of the state, had been legally null and void from the
beginning.) Mattie soon began to quarrel with her friends, she negligently
lost most of her belongings, she spent money recklessly, and she began
to engage in violent arguments, threatening one woman with a razor.
Lafcadio was giving Mattie a five-dollar weekly allowance and thought he
had convinced her to live with her son in the country—only to find out
that she had soon returned to Cincinnati in order to frequent some of the
toughest streets in Bucktown. Like Lafcadio's own mother, Mattie would
lead a life increasingly chaotic and painful until, in 1880, she married a
black man named John Kleintank—though she was to separate from him,
too.

One might decide to see the relationship between Lafcadio and Mattie
as a recapitulation of Charles Hearn's relationship with Rosa Cassimati
(as the Bible declares, "The fathers have eaten sour grapes and the children's teeth are set on edge"). Like Rosa, Mattie was a volatile, culturally
deracinated, often disturbed woman. But Lafcadio did not abandon his
wife for another woman, and he stayed with Mattie for three years—longer
than this homeless writer, with his obviously wounded sense of reci-
procity, would stay with anyone for another two decades. He was moved
by her childlike vulnerability and racial victimization. As he wrote to
Watkin about the time of his separation:

I have been much more troubled about Mattie than you have any idea
of; and the prospect of leaving her to ruin herself is something I can
scarcely bear. Whatever I may have said or done, I love her,—more I
fancy than I will ever love any woman; and somehow the lower she falls,
the fonder I feel of her. I think I have been unjust to her—unjust in
marrying her at all—lifting her up only to let her fall lower than ever. Had
I never taken her, she would suffer far less in going to the devil. . . .

She is so utterly helpless, and yet so proud and wilful, that I don't know what to do, except to cry about her. I was very foolish to have done anything for her when she refused to stay in the country. I ought to have made her go back there by leaving her without resources. I fear she has been lying to me in order to hide other things she has done. . . .

There is so much innocent childish goodness in her after all. . . .

Lafcadio's first response to the shock of learning that he had been fired by the *Enquirer* (almost a year after his breakup with Mattie) was to rush impetuously out of the office—followed by a sympathetic colleague—and head toward the Miami Canal at the Vine Street Bridge, where he had to be forcibly held back from jumping—a suicide attempt that would un- doubtedly have failed in any event because of the shallowness of the water and Lafcadio's adeptness as a swimmer.

He wandered the streets for days, having no idea of what to do next. Within a month, however, the *Commercial,* the daily rival of the *Enquirer,* disregarded gossip and local prejudice and offered Lafcadio a job. (The *Enquirer,* too, soon offered to rehire him, but Lafcadio wouldn't hear of it.) He produced for the *Commercial* some of his best "sensational" stories ("Haceldama" and "Gibbeted," for example). But one afternoon during a bitter cold spell, Lafcadio decided simply to write a short meditation on the varied crystallized shapes and patterns that he found himself staring at on the windows of the city ("Frost Fancies"):

During the intense cold of the past forty-eight hours, the great panes of large plate-glass windows throughout the city presented scenes of such beauty as the artistic Spirit of the Frost seldom favors us with. The crys- tallizations were frequently on a gigantic scale—in likeness of such ara- besque vegetation, although colorless, as somehow awakened fancies of strange fretwork about the moresque arches of the crystal palaces de- scribed in the *Arabian Nights.* Sometimes they presented such a combi- nation of variedly intricate patterns, as to suggest a possible source for the fantastic scroll-work designs employed by the monkish masters of medieval illumination in the decoration of their famous missals and manuscripts. There were double volutes of sharp-edged leaf design, such as occasionally formed a design for elegant vase handles with the antique proficients in the ceramic art; damascene patterns, broken by irregular

markings like Cufic characters on a scimitar-blade; feathery interweavings
of inimitable delicacy, such as might form elfin plumage for the wings of
a frost-spirit; spectral mosses, surpassing in their ephemeral beauty the
most velvety growths of our vegetable world; ghost ferns, whose loveliness attracts the eye, but fades into airy nothingness under the breath of
the admirer; evanescent shrubs of some fairy species, undreamt of in our
botanical science; and snowy plumes, fit to grace the helmet of a phantom-
knight, shaming the richest art of devisers in rare heraldic emblems. At
moments the December sun intensified the brilliancy of these corusca-
tions of frost-fire: lance-rays of solar flame, shivered into myriad sparkles
against the flittering mail of interwoven crystals, tinged all the scintillating
work with a fairy-faint reflection of such iridescence as flames upon a
humming bird's bosom. The splendor of the frost-work was yesterday
everywhere a matter of curious comment, and such a variety of pattern—
often of a peculiarly "large-leaved" design—has not been seen for years
in the city. On [one] street, was a very beautiful and peculiar specimen
of crystallization in a shop window. It presented the aspect of narrow-
bladed wild grasses, thickly growing, and luxuriant; stems shot up bare
to a certain height, when leaves sprouted from them on either side, bending suddenly downward at a sharp angle shortly after leaving the stem,
in exquisite rivalry of nature. But at a certain height the pattern lost distinctness, and blended into a sharply bristling wilderness of grass-blades,
so that the general effect, like that of a rough etching, was best observable
at a short distance. The unearthly artist who created the scene, however,
was not content with rivaling nature, for his wild grasses terminated beautifully but weirdly in a wild fantasy of leaf scrolls, which resembled nothing in the world of green things growing.   ]

For another article, Lafcadio recklessly volunteered to accompany a
famous steeplejack named Joseph Roderiguez Weston, who made an appearance at the *Commercial* offices and announced his intention to climb
to the summit of the spire of the Cathedral of St.-Peter-in-Chains, the
highest structure in Cincinnati, and ingenuously asked if any reporter
wanted to join him.

Lafcadio's description of being hauled on Weston's back to the top of
the cathedral, and of perching, terrified, on the arm of the cross as if he
were sitting on top of the world, takes on a wonderful comic quality
when the reader remembers that the hair-raising adventure is happening

to a one-eyed, myopic, five-foot-three-inch reporter. Lafcadio later confided to a friend that he omitted mentioning in the article ("Steeple Climbers") the "Mephistophelian delight" he felt when, from his cathedral aerie, he "piddled on the universe."

¶ Joseph Roderiguez Weston, the daring steeple climber, who recently affixed the green wreaths and tri-colored banner to the cross of the Cathedral spire, called at the *Commercial* office a few days ago and expressed the desire that a reporter should accompany him on his next trip to the giddy summit, when he should remove the temporary decorations there placed in honor of the Archbishop's Golden Jubilee. Such a proposition could not well be accepted without considerable hesitancy—a hesitancy partly consequent upon the consciousness of personal risk, and partly owing to the probable nature of the public verdict upon such undertakings. The novel and rare experiences of such a trip, coupled with the knowledge that a correct description of them could not fail to elicit some public interest, and that the hardy enterprise of the professional climbers themselves could only be done justice to by temporarily sharing their dangers, ultimately proved sufficient inducements to a *Commercial* reporter to attempt the experiment. The ascent was fixed for 4 o'clock yesterday afternoon, at which time Mr. Weston, accompanied by John Klein, of the Globe Slating Company, who is no less daring a climber than his experienced comrade, called at the office with a buggy for a representative of the *Commercial.* Each of the party had previously prepared for the event by changing his ordinary dress for a worn-out suit. Mr. Peter Depretz, also of the firm of John Klein & Co., awaited us at the Cathedral with all the necessary climbing apparatus,—ropes, grappling-ladders, block and tackle, etc.

It is scarcely necessary to observe that the writer, wholly inexperienced in the art of hazardous climbing, did not start out upon such an undertaking without considerable trepidation, notwithstanding the reiterated assurances of his guide that nothing was to be feared in view of the secure arrangements and first-class apparatus; and when we drove under the Cathedral spire itself, towering symmetrically against the clear blue, pillar piled on pillar, and cornice succeeding cornice, up to the last long, bare peak of white stone, it was impossible to quell a little fluttering of the heart. The lightning-rod appeared like a tiny black line, slender as a spider's thread; the lofty flag, floating in the afternoon breeze, seemed from below no larger than a kerchief of colored silk; and the great stone cross

itself, wreathed with evergreens, looked far too small to afford foothold
on its summit for any human being. The fantastic and shadowy interior
of the spire itself was calculated to increase rather than to lighten the
novice's weight of anxiety. With the doors of the Cathedral closed, we
groped our way up the winding stairs of stone in ebon darkness, passing
above the choir, through an iron door, which slides portcullis fashion,
and whereof the purpose is to cut off connection between the spire and
the main building in case of a conflagration. Here the spiral stairway of
stone ceased, and a gas jet being lighted, revealed a seemingly interminable series of octagonal stone chambers above, rising above one another
in lessening perspective, separated only by floors of open beam or plank
work, and lighted, far up, by a dim gray light struggling through louver
windows. The cold, bare walls of rough stone seemed to sweat a chilly
sweat under the gas-light, which revealed clinging to them growths of
those tiny fungi which thrive even in darkness. The walls at this point
are eight feet in thickness, massive as those of a feudal donjon-keep; and
flights of grimy wooden stairs, narrow and often unsteady, creep in a
long-drawn-out spiral around the interior. Looking down from the bal-
ustrade an abyss of gloom alone is visible; the beams of the stair-structure
are thickened on their upper surface with inches of colorless dust; the
panels of the iron door are edged on the lower groove with a deep layer
of detached rust; the wooden steps creak and shriek as the foot falls on
them; and far up above, in the deep darkness, the solemn pulsations of
the great clock's iron heart are weirdly audible, monotonously awful,
as the footfall of Something coming up the stairs of a haunted house. "I
have heard the beating of that clock," said the steeple-climber, "on wild,
wintry nights, when I had to go aloft to fix something and the goblin
sound almost frightened me. It sounds gruesome in the dark."

Again and again gas jets were lighted and stairs climbed, until the light
of day struggled faintly in upon us, the beating of the clock grew louder,
and the great weights became visible, floating and swaying above. The
tower now narrowed, and we crawled rather than climbed among beams,
through holes, and into the heart of the clock itself, like animalculæ creeping amid the machinery of an old-fashioned chronometer, until we stood
among the bells. Thence we watched in the gray dimness the life-springs
of the huge time-keeper working and shuddering. The bells were rusty;
their tongues were rough with red decay. Suddenly the chimes boomed
out around us; an iron arm arose in the gloom and smote the great bell
twice; it was half-past 4 o'clock.

We crawled up between the lips of the bells to another and again another wooden stair and stood one hundred and fifty feet above the pavement, in an octagonal chamber, lighted by eight louver windows. From one of these, on the eastern side, had been removed the huge wooden lattice which at once serves to keep out foul weather, and to throw down the sound of church bells into the bosom of the city. And from below struggled faintly to our ears the distant din of traffic, the rumble of wagons, the hoof-beats of horses and the buzz of the City Buildings. Spires and cornices seemed to rise almost under our feet; the river's silver flickered from the south, and the yellow canal crawled beneath its bridges away to the rolling purple of the hills in the north.

"Must we climb out through this window?" was our first nervous interrogation.

"Oh, yes," replied Weston. "It can't be done any other way."

Above projected a huge cornice, below was nothing but a sheer precipice of smooth stone. The writer saw and trembled, and inwardly wished himself at home; and when Peter Depretz got out of the window to execute a dance on the narrow cornice underneath for the purpose of inspiring us with courage, the fear only increased. Then a young man clambered up to a loophole within, Klein fastened the steel hooks of a grappling ladder to the cornice, which projected twenty-five feet above us, and the top rung of the vibrating stairway was made fast to a rope, which the young assistant tied firmly about a beam within. But the ladder swung backward and forward over the precipice, until we began to experience the familiar feeling of nightmare.

After having read that hideous but most artistically Gothic romance by Victor Hugo, *The Dwarf of Notre Dame,* one is apt to have a frightful nightmare about steeple-climbing, and we remember such unpleasant experience. The dreamer finds himself, perhaps, straddling a stone dragon at a vast altitude from the gabled city below; the clouds float far beneath him; the ravens shriek in his ears; above him springs into the very vault of heaven a vast peak of carven stone—a precipice roughened only with gargoyles, griffins, hippogriffs, dragons—all the hideous imaginations of the medieval sculptors. He flees from a pursuing monster below, and climbs the dizzy eminence above with frantic despair. The diabolic pursuer pauses, to grin with satiated rage at his victim's agony of fear. Suddenly the gargoyles grin; the stony monsters open their giant mouths; the vast steeple trembles with awful animation; the gargoyle seizes the fugitive's heel with his teeth. The victim shrieks and falls into the abyss of peaked roof below, bounding from carven projections, wheeling, turning,

circling, ricochetting in the ghastly fall. There is no more intense fear than
this fear of falling in nightmare, and the spectacle of the swaying ladder
without the Cathedral steeple yesterday produced a wide-awake realization of that horrible fancy.

"Take a good drink of whisky," observed Weston, proffering a well
filled flask; "it will give you nerve without producing giddiness, since you
seem frightened."

Then Weston produced a thick leathern strap, and buckled it tightly
about the reporter's waist, also fastening a strong harness strap under and
over his right thigh. To these straps the end of a new rope was made fast,
and one other end passed up the ladder to the loophole window, twenty-
five feet above, where it was taken in and tied to a beam. Klein then ran
up the ladder, which shuddered under him as though trying to shake
him off and down on the stone steps of the facade below, and Weston
endeavored to induce the reporter to follow. The latter was by that time
in a shivering fit and on the point of backing down, when Depretz seized
him by the thigh and pulled him outward, with a gruff "Confound you,
come out or I'll pull you out!" Then he came out and went up the quivering ladder, feeling all the while as though the steeple were reeling.

On arriving at the cornice above, a strong rope stretched through the
loophole window afforded an excellent hand-rail; then the ladder was
pulled up, made fast to another cornice above, and the climbing operation
repeated for another twenty-five feet. We then found ourselves perched
on the narrow cornice at the base of the tall, bare peak, whence the flag
was flying fifty feet further up. It may be worth while to mention here
that all the party had encased their feet in India-rubber, which clings well
to roughened stone, and facilitates the work of climbing. The ladder was
left hanging to the cornice by its iron teeth for the descent.

Weston then clambered up the slope of the spire with the agility of a
monkey, planting his feet against the stone and ascending the lightning-
rod hand over hand. Arrived at the summit, he bestrode the cross, low-
ered a third rope, with which he hauled up a block-and-tackle and a
larger rope, and made preparations for our ascent. The block-and-tackle
was firmly bound over the arms of the cross, the large rope riven through
it and fastened below around the reporter's chest, while the lighter rope
was tied to the leathern belt about his loins, to serve as a stay-rope in
case of accident. Then seizing the lightning-rod the work of ascent was
rendered comparatively easy. Just below the cross there is a little cornice
which affords a temporary foothold, and thence it was not difficult, with

the aid of the lightning-rod, to climb into the arms of the cross, when the
novice was tied to the lightning-rod itself. The northern arm of the cross
served admirably for a footstool and the summit for a seat. It is cut
octagonally, with facets upon the summit, converging cut-diamond style
to a little point. The summit of the cross has a surface equivalent to about
two feet square.

Fear gradually passed off while thus seated, and it was possible to turn
and look in any direction over the city. From the great height, two hundred and twenty-five feet, every portion of the city encircled by the hills
was distinctly visible. The City Buildings and the surrounding edifices
seemed dwarfed to toy-houses; the circular fountain-basin of the City
Park seemed like a ring of muddy water at the foot of the Cathedral; the
summits of the Synagogue's minarets were visible below; in every direction the city lay out in regular squares like an elaborate map. For three
or four blocks, north, south, east and west, the centers of thoroughfares
were distinctly visible, with wagon-teams, buggies and carriages straggling
along, apparently no larger than flies. The crowds below, with faces up-
turned to the cross, were lilliputians; even with a small opera glass it was
difficult to distinguish faces. All the Plum street canal bridges from the
elbow eastward, were plainly visible; Mill Creek shimmered with a golden
gleam in the west, and the Ohio curved in blue serpentine in the south.
We seemed to stand above the city smoke and the evening mists; sounds
from below came faintly to the ear, like echoes of another world; the tone
of the giant clock below striking the chimes and the hour of five, were
weird and thin; the least whisper was audible; the sky seemed nearer,
and the ripple of fleecy clouds, coming up from the west, in white breaker
lines against the sea of azure, seemed purer and clearer than ordinary.
From our eminence it was impossible to obtain, by looking down, any
accurate idea of the prodigious height—the foreshortening of the spire, to
the last cornice we had left, gave it the appearance of being but ten or
twelve feet high.

"Suppose," we horrifically observed, "that the cross should give way,
and fall down!"

"See!" replied Weston, giving the summit a violent shake with both
hands—"she rocks!"

It was true; the cross trembled and shuddered an instant, and then
gave four distinct rocks—earthquake tremblings they seemed to us. Another shake caused it to rock still more violently, and shook us in our
seats.

"For God's sake," we frantically yelled, "stop!"

"It's perfectly safe," observed Weston, apologetically. "I rocked it just to show you that it was safe. If it didn't rock it would be out of plumb. All properly built stone spires rock, and wooden spires rock horribly."

"Suppose," we again suggested, "that the steeple should take fire below us!"

"Then I should run down the lightning rod and carry you on my back."

"Besides," observed Klein, "the steeple is as solid as the everlasting hills. The fire might burn out the wooden shell within, but the heat would escape through the windows, and we could get to the windward side of the cross, you know."

The flags and wreaths were carefully detached, and the copper-barbed top of the lightning rod, which had been removed for the decorations, was replaced in its socket. Then Weston took a small flag and threw it down. It was awful to watch its descent. It flew and flew in circles, described somersaults, trembled, collapsed, extended, and finally, after many seconds, flattened out on the roof.

"I want you to stand up on the top of the cross, right on the top," exclaimed Weston, commencing to detach the cords which held the reporter to the lightning-rod. His indifference to danger inspired the visitor with sufficient confidence to perform the feat, and extend his arms for an instant 225 feet above *terra firma*. Suddenly the reporter caught sight of something that caused him to clutch the lightning-rod convulsively and sit down. Weston's braces were adorned with great brazen buckles, which bore in ghastly bas-relief the outlines of a skull and crossbones.

"What on earth do you wear such ill-omened things for?" we asked.

"Oh," replied he, laughing and dancing on the northern arm of the cross, "I thought I'd get smashed up some day, and took a fancy to these suspenders, as they serve to remind me of my probable fate. You seem to believe in omens. Well, I tell you I never like to do climbing on Friday, although I know it's all foolishness."

After inspecting the initials of the climbers cut into the summit of the cross, we performed a descent which seemed far easier than the ascent. As we re-entered the belfry the clock boomed out six times, and the "Angelus" chimed in measured strokes of deeply vibrating music from the big bell. The mists climbed higher as the sun commenced to sink in a glory of mingled gold and purple, and a long streamer of ruby light flamed over the western hills. "That is a lovely view," exclaimed Weston, "but I think it is not so fine as the bird's eye view of the city by night,

sparkling with ten thousand lights. You must come up on the cross some
fine night with me."

The reporter shivered and departed.   ]

Lafcadio's most important journalistic pieces during this period were
twelve sketches and articles in which he explored and described the
world (invisible to white Cincinnatians) of Bucktown and the Levee—one
of the few depictions we have of black life in a border city during the
post–Civil War period. Here, as in those other fringe areas he was so
drawn to, Lafcadio found the violent, the perverse, the impoverished, the
rejected. But here, too, he experienced a perilous, vital world of comings
and goings, piety and lawlessness, gaiety and misery—a world that somehow derived strength from its afflictions.

Instinctively, Lafcadio covered the waterfront and Bucktown with a
kind of inchoate, improvised folkloristic perspective. In spite of his only
partially successful attempts to replicate black street and waterfront speech
and his occasional descent into racial stereotype, his rapidly written articles present mostly clear-sighted views by a sympathetic and fascinated
outsider of an African-American culture and its rich tradition of songs,
dances, stories, poetry, charms, superstitions, proverbs, customs. Lafcadio
was not tempted to glorify the appalling living conditions, poverty, violence, and degradation he observed in Bucktown, a stamping ground of
pimps, prostitutes, thieves, and morphine addicts which was sinking
gradually under its own weight into the mud of the Ohio. But at night,
the writer could perceive the eerie, haunting allurement of the ghetto,
with its shadow-figures flitting in and out of its rows and alleys:

[Bucktown is nothing if not seen by gaslight. Then it presents a most
striking effect of fantastic *chiar'oscuro;* its frames seem to own dorésque
façades—a mass of many-angled shadows in the background, relieved in
front by long gleams of light on some obtruding post or porch or wooden
stairway; its doorways yawn in blackness, like entrances to some interminable labyrinth; the jagged outline of its dwellings against the sky seems
the part of some mighty wreck; its tortuous ways are filled with long
shadows of the weirdest goblin form. The houses with lighted windows
appear to possess an animate individuality, a character, a sentient consciousness, a face; and to stare with pale-yellow eyes and hungry door-

mouth all agape at the lonely passer-by, as though desiring to devour
him.   ("PARIAH PEOPLE") ∄

It was, nevertheless, in the ballrooms and dives of Bucktown and the
roustabout bars on the Levee where Lafcadio understood that a valid
urban culture—what "civilized" nineteenth-century social scientists, unlike Lafcadio, denigrated as "primitive" and "savage"—could not be restricted to the parlor and the concert hall but might also be looked for
and found in juke joints and in riverfront saloons ("Levee Life"):

∄ Along the river-banks on either side of the levee slope, where the brown
water year after year climbs up to the ruined sidewalks, and pours into
the warehouse cellars, and paints their grimy walls with streaks of water-
weed green, may be studied a most curious and interesting phase of life—
the life of a community within a community,—a society of wanderers
who have haunts but not homes, and who are only connected with the
static society surrounding them by the common bond of State and municipal law. . . . [On] a cool spring evening, when the levee is bathed in
moonlight, and the torch-basket lights dance redly upon the water, and
the clear air vibrates to the sonorous music of the deep-toned steam-
whistle, and the sound of wild banjo-thrumming floats out through the
open doors of the levee dance-houses, then it is perhaps that one can
best observe the peculiarities of this grotesquely-picturesque roustabout
life.

Probably less than one-third of the stevedores and 'longshoremen employed in our river traffic are white; but the calling now really belongs
by right to the Negroes, who are by far the best roustabouts and are
unrivaled as firemen. The white stevedores are generally tramps, willing
to work only through fear of the Work-house; or, sometimes laborers
unable to obtain other employment, and glad to earn money for the time
being at any employment. On board the boats, the whites and blacks
mess separately and work under different mates, there being on an average about twenty-five roustabouts to every boat which unloads at the
Cincinnati levee. Cotton boats running on the Lower Mississippi will
often carry sixty or seventy deck hands, who can some seasons earn from
forty-five dollars to sixty dollars per month. On the Ohio boats the average wages paid to roustabouts will not exceed $30 per month. 'Long-

shoremen earn fifteen and twenty cents per hour, according to the season. These are frequently hired by Irish contractors, who undertake to unload a boat at so much per package; but the first-class boats generally contract with the 'longshoremen directly through the mate, and sometimes pay twenty-five cents per hour for such labor. "Before Freedom," as the colored folks say, white laborers performed most of the roustabout labor on the steamboats; the Negroes are now gradually monopolizing the calling, chiefly by reason of their peculiar fitness for it. Generally speaking, they are the best porters in the world; and in the cotton States, it is not uncommon, we are told, to see Negro levee hands, for a wager, carry five-hundred-pound cotton-bales on their backs to the wharfboat. River men, today, are recognizing the superior value of Negro labor in steamboat traffic, and the colored roustabouts are now better treated, probably, than they have been since the war. Under the present laws, too, they are better protected. It used at one time to be a common thing for some ruffianly mate to ship sixty or seventy stevedores, and, after the boat had taken in all her freight, to hand the poor fellows their money and land them at some small town, or even in the woods, hundreds of miles from their home. This can be done no longer with legal impunity.

Roustabout life in the truest sense is, then, the life of the colored population of the Rows, and, partly, of Bucktown—blacks and mulattoes from all parts of the States, but chiefly from Kentucky and Eastern Virginia, where most of them appear to have toiled on the plantations before Freedom; and echoes of the old plantation life still live in their songs and their pastimes. You may hear old Kentucky slave songs chanted nightly on the steamboats, in that wild, half-melancholy key peculiar to the natural music of the African race; and you may see the old slave dances nightly performed to the air of some ancient Virginia-reel in the dance-houses of Sausage Row, or the "ball-rooms" of Bucktown. There is an intense uniqueness about all this pariah existence; its boundaries are most definitely fixed; its enjoyments are wholly sensual, and many of them are marked by peculiarities of a strictly local character. Many of their songs, which have never appeared in print, treat of levee life in Cincinnati, of all the popular steamboats running on the "Muddy Water," and of the favorite roustabout haunts on the river bank and in Bucktown. To collect these curious songs, or even all the most popular of them, would be a labor of months, and even then a difficult one, for the colored roustabouts are in the highest degree suspicious of a man who approaches them with a note-book and pencil. Occasionally, however, one can induce an intel-

ligent steamboatman to sing a few river songs by an innocent bribe in
the shape of a cigar or a drink, and this we attempted to do with considerable success during a few spare evenings last week, first, in a popular
roustabout haunt on Broadway, near Sixth, and afterward in a dingy frame
cottage near the corner of Sixth and Culvert streets. Unfortunately some
of the most curious of these songs are not of a character to admit of
publication in the columns of a daily newspaper; but others which we
can present to our readers may prove interesting. Of these the following
song, "Number Ninety-Nine," was at one time immensely popular with
the steamboatmen. The original resort referred to was situated on Sixth
and Culvert street, where Kirk's building now stands. We present the
song with some necessary emendations:

> *"You may talk about yer railroads,*
> *Yer steamboats and can-el*
> *If 't hadn't been for Liza Jane*
> *There wouldn't a bin no hell.*
> *Chorus—Oh, ain't I gone, gone, gone,*
> *Oh, ain't I gone, gone, gone,*
> *Oh, ain't I gone, gone, gone,*
> *Way down de ribber road.*

> *"Whar do you get yer whisky?*
> *Whar do you get yer rum?*
> *I got it down in Bucktown,*
> *At Number Ninety-nine.*
> *Chorus—Oh, ain't I gone, gone, gone, &c.*

> *"I went down to Bucktown,*
> *Nebber was dar before,*
> *Great big niggah knocked me down,*
> *But Katy barred the door.*
> *Chorus—Oh, ain't I gone, gone, gone, &c.*

> *"She hugged me, she kissed me,*
> *She tole me not to cry;*
> *She said I was de sweetest thing*
> *Dat ebber libbed or died.*
> *Chorus—Oh, ain't I gone, gone, gone, &c. . . . ."*

The most melancholy of all these plaintive airs is that to which the
song "Let her go by" is commonly sung. It is generally sung on leaving

port, and sometimes with an affecting pathos inspired of the hour, while
the sweet-hearts of the singers watch the vessel gliding down stream.

> *I'm going away to New Orleans!*
>   *Good-bye, my lover, good-bye!*
> *I'm going away to New Orleans!*
>   *Good-bye, my lover, good-bye!*
>   *Oh, let her go by!*
>
> *She's on her way to New Orleans!*
>   *Good-bye, my lover, good-bye!*
> *She bound to pass the Robert E. Lee,*
>   *Good-bye, my lover, good-bye!*
>   *Oh, let her go by!*
>
> *I'll make dis trip and I'll make no more!*
>   *Good-bye, my lover, good-bye!*
> *I'll roll dese barrels, I'll roll no more!*
>   *Good-bye, my lover, good-bye!*
>   *Oh, let her go by!*
>
> *An' if you are not true to me,*
>   *Farewell, my lover, farewell!*
> *An' if you are not true to me,*
>   *Farewell, my lover, farewell!*
>   *Oh, let her go by!*

But the most famous songs in vogue among the roustabouts is "Limber
Jim," or "Shiloh." Very few know it all by heart, which is not wonderful
when we consider that it requires something like twenty minutes to sing
"Limber Jim" from beginning to end, and that the whole song, if printed
in full, would fill two columns of the *Commercial*. The only person in the
city who can sing the song through, we believe, is a colored laborer living
near Sixth and Culvert streets, who "run on the river" for years, and
acquired so much of a reputation by singing "Limber Jim," that he has
been nicknamed after the mythical individual aforesaid, and is now known
by no other name. He keeps a little resort in Bucktown, which is known
as "Limber Jim's," and has a fair reputation for one dwelling in that
locality. Jim very good-naturedly sang the song for us a few nights ago,
and we took down some of the most striking verses for the benefit of our
readers. The air is wonderfully quick and lively, and the chorus is quite
exciting. The leading singer sings the whole song, excepting the chorus,

"Shiloh," which dissyllable is generally chanted by twenty or thirty voices of abysmal depth at the same time with a sound like the roar of twenty Chinese gongs struck with tremendous force and precision. A great part of "Limber Jim" is very profane, and some of it not quite fit to print. We can give only about one-tenth part of it. The chorus is frequently accompanied with that wonderfully rapid slapping of thighs and hips known as "patting Juba."

> Nigger an' a white man playing seven-up,
> White man played an ace; an' Nigger feared to take it up,
> White man played ace an' Nigger played a nine,
> White man died, an' Nigger went blind.
>
> Limber Jim,
>   [All.] Shiloh!
> Talk it agin,
>   [All.] Shiloh!
> Walk back in love,
>   [All.] Shiloh!
> You turtle-dove,
>   [All.] Shiloh!
>
> Went down the ribber, couldn't get across;
> Hopped on a rebel louse; thought 'twas a hoss,
> Oh lor', gals, 't ain't no lie,
> Lice in Camp Chase big enough to cry,—
>   Limber Jim, &c.
>
> Bridle up a rat, sir; saddle up a cat,
> Please han' me down my Leghorn hat,
> Went to see widow; widow warn't home;
> Saw to her daughter,—she gave me honeycomb.
>   Limber Jim, &c.
>
> Jay-bird sittin' on a swinging limb,
> Winked at me an' I winked at him,
> Up with a rock an' struck him on the shin,
> G—d d—n yer soul, don't wink agin.
>   Limber Jim, &c.
>
> Some folks says that a rebel can't steal,
> I found twenty in my corn-fiel',
> Sich pullin' of shucks an' tearin' of corn!—

Nebber saw the like since I was born.
  Limber Jim, &c.

John Morgan come to Danville and cut a mighty dash,
Las' time I saw him, he was under whip an' lash;
'Long come a rebel at a sweepin' pace,
Whar 're ye goin', Mr. Rebel? "I'm goin' to Camp Chase."
  Limber Jim, &c.

Way beyond de sun and de moon,
White gal tole me I were too soon,
White gal tole me I come too soon,
An' Nigger gal called me an ole d—d fool.
  Limber Jim, &c.

Eighteen pennies hidden in a fence,
Cynthiana gals ain't got no sense;
Every time they go from home
Comb thar heads wid an ole jaw bone.
  Limber Jim, &c.

Had a little wife an' didn' inten' to keep her;
Showed her a flatboat an' sent her down de ribber;
Head like a fodder-shock, mout' like a shovel,
Put yerself wid yaller gal, put yerself in trouble.
  Limber Jim, &c.

I went down to Dinah's house, Dinah was in bed,
Hoisted de window an' poked out her head;
T'rowed, an' I hit in her de eyeball,—bim;
"Walk back, Mr. Nigger; don't do dat agin."
  Limber Jim, &c. . . .

One fact worth mentioning about these Negro singers is, that they can mimic the Irish accent to a degree of perfection which an American, Englishman or German could not hope to acquire. At the request of Patrolman Tighe and his partner, the same evening that we interviewed Limber Jim, a very dark mulatto, named Jim Delaney, sang for us in capital style that famous Irish ditty known as "The hat me fahther wor-re." Yet Jim, notwithstanding his name, has little or no Irish blood in his veins; nor has his companion, Jim Harris, who joined in the rollicking chorus:

  " 'Tis the raylics of ould dacency,
    The hat me fahther wor-r-re."

Jim Delaney would certainly make a reputation for Irish specialties in a minstrel troupe; his mimicry of Irish character is absolutely perfect, and he possesses a voice of great flexibility, depth and volume. He "runs" on the river.

On the southeast corner of Culvert and Sixth streets, opposite to the house in which we were thus entertained by Limber Jim and his friends, stands Kirk's building, now occupied jointly by Kirk and Ryan. Two stories beneath this building is now the most popular dance-house of the colored steamboatmen and their "girls." . . . The amount of patronage it receives depends almost wholly upon the condition of the river traffic; during the greater part of the week the attendance is somewhat slim, but when the New Orleans boats come in the place is crowded to overflowing. Besides the admittance fee of ten cents, an additional dime is charged to all the men for every set danced—the said dime to be expended in "treating partners." When the times are hard and money scarce, the girls often pay the fees for their men in order to make up sets.

With its unplastered and windowless limestone walls; sanded floor; ruined ceiling, half plank, half cracked plaster; a dingy black counter in one corner, and rude benches ranged along the walls, this dancing-room presented rather an outlandish aspect when we visited it. At the corner of the room opposite "the bar," a long bench was placed, with its face to the wall; and upon the back of this bench, with their feet inwardly reclining upon the seat, sat the musicians. A well-dressed, neatly-built mulatto picked the banjo, and a somewhat lighter colored musician led the music with a fiddle, which he played remarkably well and with great spirit. A short, stout Negress, illy dressed, with a rather good-natured face and a bed shawl tied about her head, played the bass viol, and that with no inexperienced hand. This woman is known to the police as Anna Nun.

The dancers were in sooth a motley crew; the neat dresses of the girls strongly contrasting with the rags of the poorer roustabouts, some of whom were clad only in shirt, pants and shocking hats. Several wickedly handsome women were smoking stogies. Bill Williams, a good-natured black giant, who keeps a Bucktown saloon, acted for a while as Master of Ceremonies. George Moore, the colored Democrat who killed, last election day, the leader of a party who attacked his house, figured to advantage in the dance, possessing wonderful activity in spite of his heavy bulk. The best performer on the floor was a stumpy little roustabout named Jem Scott, who is a marvelous jig-dancer, and can waltz with a tumbler full of water on his head without spilling a drop. One-fourth of the women present were white, including two girls only about seventeen years old, but bearing physiognomical evidence of precocious vice. The best-looking girl in the room was a tall, lithe quadroon named Mary Brown, with auburn hair, gray eyes, a very fair skin, and an air of quiet innocence wholly at variance with her reputation. A short, supple mulatto girl, with a blue ribbon in her hair, who attracted considerable admiration, and was famous for dancing "breakdowns," had but recently served a term in the penitentiary for grand larceny. Another woman present, a gigantic Negress, wearing a red plaid shawl, and remarkable for an immense head of frizzly hair, was, we were informed, one of the most adroit thieves known to the police. It was a favorite trick of hers to pick a pocket while dancing, and hide the stolen money in her hair.

"How many of those present do you suppose carry knives?" we asked Patrolman Tighe.

"All of them," was the reply. "All the men, and women, too, carry knives or razors; and many of them pistols as well. But they seldom quarrel, except about a girl. Their great vice is thieving; and the fights down here are generally brought about by white roughs who have no business in this part of town except crime."

The musicians struck up that weird, wild, lively air, known perhaps to many of our readers as the "Devil's Dream," and in which "the musical ghost of a cat chasing the spectral ghost of a rat" is represented by a succession of "miauls" and "squeaks" on the fiddle. The dancers danced a double quadrille, at first, silently and rapidly; but warming with the wild spirit of the music, leaped and shouted, swinging each other off the floor, and keeping time with a precision which shook the building in time to the music. The women, we noticed, almost invariably embraced the men about the neck in swinging, the men clasping them about the waist. Sometimes the men advancing leaped and crossed legs with a double shuffle, and with almost sightless rapidity. Then the music changed to an old Virginia reel, and the dancing, changing likewise, presented the most grotesque spectacle imaginable. The dancing became wild; men patted juba and shouted, the Negro women danced with the most fantastic grace, their bodies describing almost incredible curves forward and backward; limbs intertwined rapidly in a wrestle with each other and with the music; the room presented a tide of swaying bodies and tossing arms, and flying hair. The white female dancers seemed heavy, cumbersome, ungainly by contrast with their dark companions; the spirit of the music was not upon them; they were abnormal to the life about them. Once more the music changed—to some popular Negro air, with the chorus—

"Don't get weary,
I'm goin' home."

The musicians began to sing; the dancers joined in; and the dance terminated with a roar of song, stamping of feet, "patting juba," shouting, laughing, reeling. Even the curious spectators involuntarily kept time with their feet; it was the very drunkenness of music, the intoxication of the dance. Amid such scenes does the roustabout find his heaven; and this heaven is certainly not to be despised. . . .

With the exception of Ryan's dance-house, and one or two Bucktown lodging-houses, the roustabouts generally haunt the Rows, principally Sausage Row, from Broadway to Ludlow street. Rat Row, from Walnut to Main, is more especially the home of the white tramps and roustabouts. Here is situated the celebrated "Blazing Stump," otherwise called St. James Restaurant, which is kept by a Hollander, named Venneman. Venneman accommodates only white men, and endeavors to keep an orderly house; but the "Blazing Stump" must always remain a resort for thieves, burglars, and criminals of every description. The "Stump" is No. 13 Rat Row. No. 16 is a lodging house for colored roustabouts, kept by James Madison. No. 12 is a policy shop [a gambling parlor], although it pretends to be a saloon; and the business is so cunningly conducted that the police can not, without special privilege, succeed in closing up the business. No. 10, which used to be known as Buckner's, is another haunt for colored roust- abouts. They have a pet crow attached to the establishment, which is very plucky, and can whip all the cats and dogs in the neighborhood. It wad- dles about on the sidewalk of sunny days, pecking fiercely at any stranger who meddles with it, but the moment it sees the patrolmen coming along the levee it runs into the house.

No. 7—Goodman's clothing store—is said to be a "fence." At the west end of the row is Captain Dilg's celebrated hostelry, a popular and hos- pitable house, frequented by pilots and the most respectable class of river men. At the eastern terminus of the row is the well known Alhambra saloon, a great resort for colored steamboatmen, where large profits are realized on cigars and whisky of the cheapest kind. The contractors who hire roustabouts frequently have a private understanding with the pro- prietor of some levee coffee-house or saloon, and always go there to pay off their hands. Then the first one treats, then another, and so on until all the money just made by a day's heavy labor is lying in the counter drawer, and the roustabouts are helplessly boozy.

Of the two rows Sausage Row is perhaps the most famous. No. 1 is kept by old Barney Hodke, who has made quite a reputation by keeping a perfectly orderly house in a very disorderly neighborhood. No. 2 is Cottonbrook's clothing store, *alias* the "American Clothing Store," whereof the proprietor is said to have made a fortune by selling cheap clothing to the Negro stevedores. No. 3 is Mrs. Sweeney's saloon and boarding-house, an orderly establishment for the entertainment of river men. No. 4 is an eating- and lodging-house for roustabouts, kept by Frank Fortner, a white man. No. 6 is a barber-shop for colored folks, with a clothing-store next to it. No. 7 is a house of ill-fame, kept by a white woman, Mary Pearl, who boards several unfortunate white girls. This is a great resort for colored men.

No. 8 is Maggie Sperlock's. Maggie has another saloon in Bucktown. She is a very fat and kind-hearted old mulatto woman, who is bringing up half a dozen illegitimate children, abandoned by their parents. One of these, a very pretty boy, is said to be the son of a white lady, who moves in good society, by a colored man.

No. 9 is now Chris. Meyer's; it was known as "Schwabe Kate's" when Meyer's wife lived. This is the great resort for German tramps.

Next in order comes a barber-shop and shooting-gallery—"Long Branch" and "Saratoga." These used to be occupied by Pickett.

A few doors east of this is Chas. Redman's saloon, kept by a crippled soldier. This is another great roustabout haunt, where robberies are occasionally committed. And a little further east is Pickett's new hotel. On these two rows Officers Brazil and Knox have made no less than two hundred and fifty-six arrests during the past two years. The most troublesome element is, of course, among the white tramps. . . .

Generally speaking, the women give very little trouble. Some of the white girls now living in Pickett's barracks or in Bucktown brothels are of respectable parentage. Two of the most notorious are sisters, who have a sad history. They are yet rather handsome. All these women are morphine eaters, and their greatest dread is to be sent to the Work-house, and being thus deprived of this stimulant. Some who were sent to the Work-house, we were told, had died there from want of it. The white girls of the Row soon die, however, under any circumstances; their lives are often fairly burnt out with poisonous whisky and reckless dissipation before they have haunted the levee more than two or three years. After a fashion, the roustabouts treat their women kindly, with a rough good nature that is peculiar to them; many of the women are really married. But faithfulness to a roustabout husband is considered quite an impossible virtue on the levee. The stevedores are mostly too improvident and too lazy to support their "gals." While the men are off on a trip, a girl will always talk about what she will be able to buy "when my man comes back—if he has any money." When the lover does come back, sometimes after a month's absence, he will perhaps present his "gal" with fifty cents, or at most a dollar, and thinks he has done generously by her. We are speaking in general terms, of course, and alluding to the mass of the colored roust-abouts who "run on the river" all their lives, and have no other calling. It is needless to say that there are thrifty and industrious stevedores who support their families well, and will finally leave the river for some more lucrative employment.

Such is a glimpse of roustabout life. They know of no other life; they can understand no other pleasures. Their whole existence is one vision of anticipated animal pleasure or of animal misery; of giant toil under the fervid summer sun; of toil under the icy glare of the winter moon; of fiery drinks and drunken dreams; of the madness of music and the intoxication of fantastic dances; of white and dark mistresses awaiting their coming at the levees, with waving of brightly colored garments; of the deep music of the great steam whistles; of the torch-basket fires redly dancing upon the purple water, the white stars sailing overhead, the passing lights of well known cabins along the dark river banks, and the mighty panting of the iron heart of the great vessel, bearing them day after day and night after night to fresh scenes of human frailty, and nearer to that Dim Levee slope, where weird boats ever discharge ghostly freight, and depart empty. ▌

CHAPTER 8

Swallow
Flying South

W H E N Lafcadio got off the train in Cincinnati in 1869, he had no friends, no lodgings, no trade, and only the dimmest intimations of a vocation. Overcoming his poor eyesight and his debilitating tendency toward shyness and mistrust, he had quickly learned the journalist's craft and become known as the city's most audacious and talented reporter. He had worked about sixteen hours a day, seven days a week, for five years, spending most of his time in smoky, gaslit offices and often not returning home until dawn. He had explored both the surface and the underside of Cincinnati life. By the early fall of 1877, this life had taken its toll. Lafcadio was often ill and exhausted by the relentless pace demanded in his work. Sometimes he would find himself staring at the Ohio River on a cold, gray, gusty afternoon, and would have to bring himself back from daydreaming about the bright-green banks of the Nile or the wine-dark seas of his childhood.

Feeling increasingly disengaged from his journalistic duties, Lafcadio turned to translating some of the short stories of the French romantic writer Théophile Gautier (1811–1872). For a half-hour early in the morning in the *Commercial* offices, he would forget his journalistic assignments, open *Une Nuit de Cléopâtre* or *La Morte Amoureuse,* and enter worlds where stars—in Gautier's words—disclosed "their chalices of gold in the azure of the firmament"; where the waters of the Nile, "rippling under an oblique beam of light, [shone] with the dull gleam of the quicksilvered side of a mirror, or like a damascened blade." Here were realms of ancient gods who, Lafcadio himself stated, "loved life and youth and beauty and pleasure" and of "eidolons of ages vanished and civilizations passed away"—all "painted in words" by an imagination that, Lafcadio felt, never lost sight of "picturesque fact . . . minute details . . . studied accuracy."

Most of all, Gautier revealed to the loveless Lafcadio a world of bewitching and erotic female presences: gorgeous dream-lovers, demon-lovers, and phantom-lovers, whom Gautier himself would amiably describe as the "graceful *succubi* that haunt the happy slumbers of youth." Lafcadio himself was still haunted by Mattie, whom in his mind he now saw as a kind of succuba; for he had in some sense transformed a beautiful ex-slave girl (and his first serious lover) into his own type of *femme fatale* (tempestuous, irresponsible, childlike, demanding). Even separated from her, he discovered that he was unable to break his bond with Mattie, whom he loved but could not live with (nor she with him). Yet her hold on him would continue as long as he stayed in Cincinnati.

Lafcadio was still furious that he had been fired from the *Enquirer* because of his marriage; this city ("beastly Cincinnati," he once called it) was hardly a purveyor of equality, as it claimed to be. He considered himself, as he wrote to a friend, "ostracized, tabooed, outlawed." Furthermore, the Ionian-born reporter hated the freezing Cincinnati winters, which adversely affected his health. He also felt that his writing career could go no further here. As he wrote to Henry Watkin: "It is time for a fellow to get out of Cincinnati when they begin to call it the Paris of America." Lafcadio was burnt out. Like the characters in Gautier's stories, he needed "new pleasures and fresh sensations."

Late one night—2:00 A.M. in the *Commercial* offices—he took a break from his writing to listen to his city editor, Edwin Henderson, quietly reminisce about the magnolia groves, bougainvilleas, oleander trees, magnolia blossoms, and sweet-voiced mockingbirds of the Gulf Coast, the part of America that Henderson loved the most. At that moment, Lafcadio decided to move to New Orleans, with its subtropical climate, Latin and Creole cultures, and gracious and leisurely style and manners . . . the ideal place, he fantasized, to rest, read, study, translate, write for an occasional magazine, and perhaps, one day, work on a book or two. He wanted, and needed, to live under blue skies once again.

One morning in October 1877, Lafcadio—accompanied by Edwin Henderson, *Commercial* publisher Murat Halsted, and his loyal friend Henry Watkin—made his way to a platform of the Cincinnati train station. Henderson, who carried Lafcadio's one suitcase, had provided him with a ticket to Memphis, where he was to board the steamboat *Thompson Dean* to New Orleans. (Lafcadio had agreed to write a series of letters from that city as the *Commercial*'s Southern correspondent, though he had no signed contract with the paper to that effect.)

He would miss his "Old Man," promised to write Watkin from Memphis, and asked that he send news about Mattie to him. He would miss Mattie, too, despite their difficult estrangement. He would miss the camaraderie of three or four journalist friends. In spite of the bittersweet nostalgia he felt upon leaving, however, Lafcadio was certain that going south was the right thing to do.

When his train arrived in Memphis, he learned that his steamboat had not yet left New Orleans for the first half of its round-trip journey to Memphis and back. Without other means to continue the journey, Lafcadio found himself all alone in a strange city—bringing back memories of his first days in London and Cincinnati. "Getting damned poor," he wrote unhappily on a postcard to Watkin: "Board two dollars per day. Trouble and confusion. Flabbergasted. Mixed up. Knocked into a cocked hat."

Dislocated, dissociated, caught between his past and future, Lafcadio started to fall into a deep depression, suffering what he would later call a nervous breakdown, moving from one dreary boarding room to another. He wrote despairingly to Watkin:

My room is carpetless and much larger than your office. Old blocked-up stairways come up here and there through the floor or down through the ceiling, and they suddenly disappear. There is a great red daub on one wall as though made by a bloody hand when somebody was staggering down the stairway. There are only a few panes of glass in the windows. I am the first tenant of the room for fifteen years. Spiders are busy spinning their dusty tapestries in every corner, and between the banisters of the old stairways. The planks of the floor are sprung, and when I walk along the room at night it sounds as though Something or Somebody was following me in the dark. And then being in the third story makes it much more ghostly. . . .

I suppose you will not laugh if I tell you that I have been crying a good deal of nights,—just like I used to do when a college boy returned from vacation. It is a lonely feeling, this, of finding oneself alone in a strange city, where you never meet a face that you know; and when all the faces you did know seem to have been dead faces, disappeared for an indefinite time. I have not travelled enough the last eight years, I suppose: it does not do to become attached insensibly to places and persons. . . .

Being unable to read without pain or indeed to find anything to while the time away, I cannot succeed in keeping away one fancy that is always trying to haunt me. I never dwelt much upon it even to you latterly, but it has become an absolute torture recently. I feel all the time as if I saw Mattie looking at me or following me and the thought comes to me of the little present she made me and a little woolly lock of hair she sent me, and her despairing effort to speak to me once more. . . .

Well, I suppose you are right. I live in and by extremes and am on an extreme now. I write extremely often, because I feel alone and extremely alone. By and by, if I get well, I shall write only by weeks; and with time perhaps only by months; and when at last comes the rush of business and busy newspaper work, only by years,—until the times and places of old friendship are forgotten, and old faces have become dim as dreams, and these little spider-threads of attachments will finally yield to the long strain of a thousand miles.

In the fog, he walked like a ghost along the Mississippi waterfront, "dreaming solemnly of the Memphis of the Nile." Instead, he found empty warehouses with shattered windows, derelict hotels, and dilapidated buildings. In his own distraught state he bought an easily obtainable pistol that he planned to keep with his money under his pillow. Feeling mistrustful of everybody and everything, however, he carried the gun everywhere, particularly on his aimless, lonely walks along the rocky country lanes on the outskirts of Memphis, where on one occasion, he took several wild potshots at a sadistic drunk who was torturing a kitten by the side of the road. (Lafcadio, who could describe a slaughterhouse with sangfroid, could not abide cruelty to cats.)

When the *Thompson Dean* finally arrived in Memphis about two weeks late, Lafcadio shakily got on board—overwrought, anxious, mentally exhausted. "I am slowly, very slowly, getting better," he noted several days downriver on a postcard to Watkin, as he sat on cotton bales on the steamboat's deck and watched the Mississippi widening until it looked to him like the Ganges. He rose at dawn to see a sunrise of pale gold and green glowing over fringes of cottonwood and cypress trees, observed cotton fields with their fluttering white bolls, caught sight of the mouths of bayous and swamps of gray Spanish moss, and gazed at decaying river mansions with their broad, moldering verandas and porches.

Every day the sky became bluer, the clouds whiter, the river browner, the air warmer. Finally the *Thompson Dean* steamed up to the mighty levee of New Orleans—the Gate of the Tropics! Lafcadio, his soul revived, his vision renewed, wrote rhapsodically to Watkin: "The wealth of a world is here,—unworked gold in the ore, one might say; the paradise of the South is here, deserted and half in ruins. I never beheld anything so beautiful and so sad. When I saw it first—sunrise over Louisiana—the tears sprang to my eyes. It was like young death,—a dead bride crowned with orange flowers,—a dead face that asked for a kiss. I cannot say how fair and rich and beautiful this dead South is. It has fascinated me. I have resolved to live in it; I could not leave it for that chill and damp northern life again."

Part

Two

CHAPTER 1

The Bride
Stripped Bare

W H E N Lafcadio arrived in New Orleans on November 12, 1877, he immediately walked northeast, crossing Canal Street into the Vieux Carré, and suddenly experienced a *coup de foudre:* he had come home.

"It is not an easy thing to describe one's first impressions of New Orleans," he wrote in a dispatch to the Cincinnati *Commercial,* "for while it actually resembles no other city upon the face of the earth, yet it recalls vague memories of a hundred cities. It owns suggestions of towns in Italy, and in Spain, of cities in England and in Germany, or seaports in the Mediterranean, and of seaports in the tropics. . . . I fancy that the power of fascination which New Orleans exercises upon foreigners is due no less to this peculiar characteristic than to the tropical beauty of the city itself. Whencesoever the traveler may have come, he may find in the Crescent City some memory of his home—some recollection of his Fatherland—some remembrance of something he loves."

During the next two months, Lafcadio explored this city of verandas, piazzas, and balconies; of sloping tile roofs and windows adorned with battened shutters and wrought-iron arabesque designs; and gardens embowered with palm and fig trees, myrtles and cedars, luxuriant shrubs, and an astonishing variety of fragrant, vibrantly hued flowers. A morning stroll through the French Market overwhelmed him with its displays of pomegranates, red bananas, pale green grapes, fresh dates, delftware, porcelain, silks, muslins, hills of shrimps, and pyramids of oysters. "One may see almost everything, and buy almost anything in the French Market; and he must have a hard heart or an empty pocket who can always withstand the softly syllabled request of some bright-eyed Creole girl to buy something that he does not want."

During the day, Lafcadio no longer had his Cincinnati chills or coughs; at night, however, he became a victim of the insidious, all-pervading dampness of the night dew and fog of this city built on marshes:

It descends from the clouds and arises from the soil simultaneously; it exudes from wood-work; it perspires from stone. It is spectral, mysterious, inexplicable. Strong walls and stout doors can not keep it from entering; windows and doors can not exclude it. You might as well try to lock out a ghost. Bolts of steel and barriers of stone are equally unavailing, and the stone moulders, and the steel is smitten with red leprosy. The chill sweat pouring down from the walls, soaks into plank floors, and the cunning of the paper-hanger is useless here. Carpets become so thoroughly wet with the invisible rain that they utter soughy, marshy sounds under the foot.

In this waterlogged city, Lafcadio observed that even the dead could not be buried underground, only "vaulted up" above ground in enclosed two-foot-square "pigeon tubes," which were then inserted in walls of white stone. And hanging on these walls or suspended from the lids of the catacombs he saw wreaths of faded leaves and garlands of withered flowers "crumbling to colorless dust—offerings lest the ghosts of the dead be totally forgotten."

"I have spoken with enthusiasm of the beauty of New Orleans," Lafcadio informed his Cincinnati *Commercial* readers, and now he added: "I must speak with pain of her decay. The city is fading, moldering, crumbling—slowly but certainly . . . in the midst of the ruined paradise of Louisiana." The New Orleans Walt Whitman had visited as a newspaperman in 1848, with its "strange vivacity and *rattle*," was still known everywhere as "the Queen City of the Mississippi," but Lafcadio now saw it thirty years later as "a dead bride crowned with orange flowers." New Orleans's fall to Admiral David Farragut in 1862, her humiliating occupation by Union troops, the exploitation at the hands of scalawags and carpetbaggers, the recurrent outbreaks of yellow fever, municipal corruption and high taxes, and the disintegration of the slave-based economy had all served to render the city stagnant and bankrupt.

Lafcadio's "dear old French houses" with their verandas, peaked gables, and dormer windows were gradually being torn down to make way
for "hideous modern structures." But the ravished "bride" was, to the
groom, still "fair and rich and beautiful," since Lafcadio preferred "ven-
omous . . . tropical lilies" to "the frail and icy-white lilies of the north."

In a sense, New Orleans was the embodiment of the Romantic notion
Lafcadio had always responded to in the work of Gautier and Baudelaire—
indissolubly linking beauty and sadness, beauty and decay, beauty and
pain, beauty and death. *La Ville Fatale.* But, more significantly, it was "the
divine breath of the ocean" that ineluctably drew the sea-bewitched Lafcadio to this southern port. For here, merchant-adventurers from the
Mediterranean and the Levant—descendants of the great wanderer from
Ithaca—now "anchored their lives," far from "the awakening rumble of
traffic and 'the city sickening of its own thick breath.' "

"It is true," Lafcadio admitted, "that you can not hear the voice of the
hoary breakers in the moonlight,—only the long-panting of the cotton
presses, the shouting of the boats calling upon each other through the
tropical night, and the ceaseless song of night birds and crickets. But the
sea ships, with their white wings folded, are slumbering at the wharves;
the sea-winds are blowing through the moon-lit streets, and from the
South arises that wondrous, pale glow, like the far reflection of the emerald green of the ocean. So that the Greek sailor, awaking from the vision
of winds and waves, may join three fingers of his right hand, after the
manner of the Eastern Church, and cross himself, and sleep again in
peace."

CHAPTER 2

Starting
Over

Raven livelli al~
228 Baronne St~

L AFCADIO arrived in New Orleans with twenty dollars, most of which he gave as a down payment to the landlady of the cheapest furnished room he could find, located at 228 Baronne Street in the American section of town. He expected to be remunerated fairly for the fourteen articles he was writing for the Cincinnati *Commerical*. (He would receive in all only twenty-five dollars for his efforts.) Somehow he managed to live in New Orleans for twenty cents a day, making his rounds of the city, like the grasshopper in Aesop's fable, giving no thought to how he was going to survive the winter. Soon he had to sell his clothes and few possessions, then was forced to give up his lodgings. Eventually he wound up as a drifter living in cheap rooms, often camping out on park benches in the French Market—engaging, out of desperation, in con games, scams, and street hustles just trying to scrape together five or ten cents a day to buy himself some bread and orange tea. ("Have been cheated and swindled considerably; and have cheated and swindled others in retaliation," he confessed to Watkin. "We are about even.")

With the coming of the spring of 1878, New Orleans suffered the last of its decimating yellow fever epidemics. The miasma of contagion hung over the city, its air pervaded with the disinfectant odor of quicklime poured into the streets' gutters and with the haze of smoke from small fires and the booming sounds of cannons, which were thought to decontaminate the disease-laden atmosphere. Entire families and boarding households died within days of being stricken and were quickly buried in common graves—their deaths announced on notices attached to doorposts, telegraph poles, or the pillars of verandas. Almost seven thousand persons succumbed to the disease that spring.

In his transient and weakened state, Lafcadio came down with dengue fever, a less virulent form of yellow jack, and was admitted to a charity hospital, where he recovered in about a week. But a lingering mental depression—a typical aftereffect of dengue—exacerbated his already gloomy state of mind. Increasingly, too, he began to *look* like a battered raven. "You would scarcely know me now," he informed Watkin, "for my face is thinner than a knife and my skin very dark. The Southern sun has turned me into a mulatto. I have ceased to wear spectacles, and my hair is wild and ghastly."

After seven months of trying unsuccessfully to find work, living on and off the street, suffering from dengue and marsh fever plus a mild case of malaria, Lafcadio felt as destitute as he had during his most demoralized days in London and Cincinnati. He thought of blowing his brains out or of throwing himself into the Mississippi. He had fallen from the zenith of manic-love for this "Paradise of the South" to the nadir of loathing for a city of dying dreams ("Damn New Orleans!—wish I'd never seen it. I am thinking of going to Texas . . . to Dallas or Waco.")

Not long before his twenty-eighth birthday, Lafcadio, in a lengthy letter to Watkin, reflected with pitiless and astute self-analysis on his entire life:

[Dear Old Man: . . . Looking back at the file of these twenty-eight years, which grow more shadowy in receding, I can remember and distinguish the features of at least twenty. There is an alarming similarity of misery in all their faces; and however misty the face, the outlines of misery are remarkably perceptible. Each, too, seems to be a record of similar events,— thwarting of will and desire in every natural way, ill success in every aim, denial of almost every special wish, compulsion to act upon the principle that everything agreeable was wrong and everything disagreeable right, unpleasant recognition of self-weakness and inability to win success by individual force,—not to mention enormous addenda in the line of novel and wholly unexpected disappointments. Somehow or other, whenever I succeeded in an undertaking, the fruit acquired seemed tasteless and vapid; but usually, when one step more would have been victory, some extraordinary and unanticipated obstacle rose up in impassability. I must acknowledge, however, that, as a general rule, the unexpected obstacle was usually erected by myself;—some loss of temper, impatience, extra-sensitiveness, betrayed and indulged instead of concealed, might be credited with a large majority of failures.

Without a renovation of individuality, however, I really can see no prospect, beyond the twenty-eighth year, of better years—the years seem to grow worse in regular succession. As to the renovation,—it is hardly possible: don't you think so? Sometimes I think small people without great wills and great energies have no business trying to do much in this wonderful country; the successful men all appear to have gigantic shoulders and preponderant deportments. When I look into the private histories of the young men who achieved success in the special line I have been vainly endeavoring to follow to some termination, I find they generally hanged themselves or starved to death, while their publishers made enormous fortunes and world-wide reputations after their unfortunate and idealistic customers were dead. There were a few exceptions, but these exceptions were cases of extraordinary personal vigor and vital force. So while my whole nature urges me to continue as I have begun, I see nothing in prospect except starvation, sickness, artificial wants, which I shall never be wealthy enough to even partially gratify, and perhaps utter despair at the end. Then again, while I have not yet lost all confidence in myself, I feel strongly doubtful whether I shall ever have means or leisure to develop the latent (possible) ability within me to do something decently meritorious. Perhaps, had I not been constrained to ambition by necessity, I should never have had any such yearnings about the unattainable and iridescent bubbles of literary success. But that has nothing to do with the question. Such is the proposition now: how can I get out of hell when I have got halfway down to the bottom of it? Can I carry on any kind of business? I can fancy that I see you throw back your head and wag your beard with a hearty laugh at the mere idea, the preposterous idea!

Can I keep any single situation for any great length of time? You know I can't,—couldn't stand it; hate the mere idea of it,—something horribly disagreeable would be sure to happen. Then again, I can't even stay in one place for any healthy period of time. I can't stay anywhere without getting in trouble. And my heart always feels like a bird, fluttering impatiently for the migrating season. I think I could be quite happy if I were a swallow and could have a summer nest in the ear of an Egyptian colossus or a broken capital of the Parthenon.

I know just exactly what I should like to do,—to wander forever here and there until I got very old and apish and grey, and died,—just to wander where I pleased and keep myself to myself, and never bother anybody. But that I can't do. Then what in the name of the Nine Incarnations of Vishnu, can I do? Please try to tell me. . . .   ]

"Danger itself fosters the rescuing power," a poet once wrote. Lafcadio put it another way: "Somehow or other, when a man gets right down in the dirt he jumps up again."

In Lafcadio's case, his aphorism was both metaphoric and a statement of fact: Desperate circumstances had driven the once-fastidious journalist to take shelter in grimy rooms or on park benches. His one linen suit was now badly soiled and wearing thin. Living as he did, loitering or wandering aimlessly around the Old Quarter in his ludicrously oversized, wide-brimmed hat (as protection from the sun), and looking to all the world like a comic *clochard,* Lafcadio found himself deeply "down in the dirt."

Then one afternoon, Lafcadio wandered in his usual blur into the path of a newspaper editor whom he had met upon arrival in New Orleans. Sizing up this down-and-out journalist, the editor generously made an appointment for Lafcadio to see Mark Bigney, the one-man editorial staff of a four-page daily paper called the *Item.* Bigney urgently needed editorial assistance to keep the unprofitable paper afloat, lest it be abandoned by its owner, Colonel John Fairfax. The Colonel had heard rumors about Lafcadio's suspect views on the "Negro question," and he insisted on personally interviewing this undoubted "radical Republican" from Cincinnati.

Lafcadio did not make a brilliant first impression. "That odd, rolling eye of his," the Colonel recalled, "was the only thing you could see at first—enormous, protruding. After you got used to that eye, you saw that his other features were good, and his face refined. But, in addition, when he first presented himself here he was miserably dressed, and even his hands were grimy and his nails black." The gem needed a good deal of cleaning and polishing . . . but so did the ailing *Item*—and the Cincinnati journalist's ability was never in doubt. (His reputation as that city's premier reporter had followed him to New Orleans.) On June 15, 1878, Lafcadio was hired as assistant editor at a salary of ten dollars a week. Within a month it was obvious to readers that the *Item* was a transformed newspaper.

Lafcadio's basic work consisted in what Walt Whitman, during his days as a newspaperman for the New Orleans *Crescent*, had referred to as "making up the news"—going through out-of-town newspapers with pen and scissors and reprinting articles of note—which occupied the *Item*'s new editor for several hours a day. But in line with his former journalistic practices and proclivities, Lafcadio also went back to writing about the darker side of the city—body-snatchings, morbid suicides, and, in one report, the phenomenon of people who talked to themselves in the street ("The City of Dreams"):

Latterly it has been said that if New Orleans has any special mania which distinguishes it from other cities, it is the mania of "talking to one's self." It were useless to deny so widely recognized a fact as the propensity of people in New Orleans to perambulate their native streets conversing only with themselves. And strangers visiting us have said: "The people of New Orleans are inclined to madness; they converse continually with themselves, which is a sign of insanity." Is it that the people are being driven mad by stupid legislation and business losses and outrageous taxes? God only knows! But they do talk either to themselves or to viewless beings or to the sleepy shadows that fling jagged bits of darkness across the streets on sunny days.

They are comparatively many, these lovers of solitary musing; and usually seek the quiet of the most deserted streets—those streets to which the Secret Police of the East give the ominous name of *dead streets*. Perhaps one might say as well, *streets of the dead*.

At one time we took a special interest in watching those wandering and murmuring spirits. They are of various ages; but most generally advanced in years. The action of the younger men or women is usually quick and nervous; that of the older, slow and meditative. The former often speak angrily as if brooding over some wrong; the latter, rather in sorrow than in anger. All of which is quite natural and to be expected from those who talk to themselves.

What do they talk about?

That is a matter not always easy to find out. The hard echo of a brisk footstep on the pavement, even the sudden fluttering of a leafy shadow, seems often sufficient to break the reverie; the speaker looks about him like one awakened from a dream, gazes with a half-timid kind of suspicion at those who pass by, as if fearing to have been overheard; and walks off at a quicker gait. To study the character of these people perfectly, one must wear rubber shoes.

It would be cruel to wear india-rubber shoes for such a purpose; it would also be despicable. Therefore we cannot fully answer the question—

What are they talking about?

But occasionally the most innocent passer-by cannot fail to catch a word or two—sometimes strangely full of meaning, sometimes meaning-less. We have heard such words. Occasionally vast sums of money were mentioned—billions, quintillions!—a sure sign that the speaker was finan-cially stripped, and had little hope of favors from the goddess Fortuna. Sometimes we heard odd curses—men cursing themselves, and others, nameless places and nameless people, unknown memories and unknown misfortunes. Sometimes they spoke cheerfully, and laughed to themselves softly;—but this was seldom, very, very seldom.

Before the epidemic we fancied that the majority of these conversations with airy nothings were upon the subject of money. Indeed, most of the fragmentary mutterings which reached us seemed related to dreams of wealth—wild, vague, and fantastic—such dreams as are dreamed by those who have lost all and hope for nothing, but who seek consolation in the splendor of dreams of the Impossible.

Then came the burning summer with its burning scourges of fever;—under the raw, merciless, dizzy sunlight, and the pitilessly clear infinite of warm blue above, the mutterers still wandered the silent streets, seeking out the bits of shadow, as Arabs oases in a world of yellow sand;—and they talked more than ever to themselves and to the shadows, to the vast void above and to the whispering trees that dropped in the mighty heat.

So the months rolled dryly and fiercely by; the sun rose each day with the same glory of angry heat; and the sky glowed each evening with the glare of molten brass. And the talkers became fewer; but they seemed to talk much more than they ever had before done. They talked to the black streamers that fluttered weirdly at the handles of muffled bells, and to ghostly white things hung to cottage doors and to the long processions that rumbled ominously toward the Places of Tombs.

Sometimes it seemed that one heard a sound of sobbing—stifled sob-bing; as if a man were swallowing a bitter grief with bitter determination—but this was perhaps imaginary; for there were so many strange sounds in that strange summer that no one could well trust his ears.

The summer waned; and yet it seemed at last as though the number of those who talked to invisible things became greater. They *did* become greater in number. There was no doubt of it remaining before the first cold wind came from the far North, boisterous and wild as though suddenly freed from some Arctic enchanter. And the numbers of the mysterious ones waxed greater.

Then at intervals their words fell upon our ears; and it seemed that the character of them had undergone a change—no longer expressing ideas of wealth. They had ceased to speak in our hearing of money. They spoke of the dead—and muttered remembered words uttered by other tongues—and asked information from waving shadows and white walls regarding people that God only knows anything about.

Perhaps they remembered that the only witnesses of some last interview were the same white walls and waving shadows. And the shadows lay there at just the same angle—well, perhaps, the angle was a little sharper—and they were waving just as dreamily as then. And perhaps a time might come in which all Shadows that have been must answer all questions put to them.

Seeing and hearing these things, we somehow ceased to marvel that some people dwelling in the city of New Orleans should speak mysteriously and hold audible converse with their own thoughts; forasmuch as we, also, dreaming among the shadows, spoke aloud to our own hearts, until awakened by an echo of unanswered words.   ]

In Lafcadio, the *Item* also found its first book critic—a particularly erudite and controversial one—who habitually lambasted the popular and sentimental "Southern novel" and who eventually announced publicly to all publishers that "The *Item* will not hereafter notice fourth-rate novels, stupid volumes of poetry, and whatever is generally termed 'Trash' in more than one line, if at all." He *did*, however, review and praise fiction by Bret Harte and Emile Zola, and works such as John Addington Symonds's *Greek Poetry, Cantes Flamencos* (a collection of anonymous gypsy ballads), and Sir Edwin Arnold's *The Light of Asia*, a grandiloquent, epic retelling in blank verse of the life of Buddha written, according to Lafcadio, "for the purpose of teaching the Occident to appreciate those marvelous ethical beauties which the religion of Gotama certainly possesses for any unbiased thinker." This "noble" book "perfumed" Lafcadio's mind "as with the incense of a strangely new and beautiful worship."

It was in New Orleans that he first began to read and write about the tenets of the "higher Buddhism" for several newspapers and magazines. To friends and in newspaper editorials he asserted: "What are the heavens of all Christian fancies, after all, but Nirvana,—extinction of individuality in the eternal interblending of man with divinity? . . . And the life and agony and death of universes, are these not pictured forth in the Oriental teachings that all things appear and disappear alternatively with the slumber or the awakening, the night or the day, of the Self-Existent? . . . I have an idea that the Right Man could now revolutionize the whole Occidental religious world by preaching the Oriental faith."

Sentiments like these outraged many New Orleans clergymen and provoked them to preach sermons against Lafcadio and the newspapers he wrote for, claiming that they were "Infidel sheets" for purveying such anti-Christian ideas. The churches also attacked Lafcadio's book reviews on Sanskrit literature, suggesting that it, too, was connected to the Buddhist menace.

Lafcadio's various editors began to find themselves pressured about the pro-Buddhist sentiments expressed in their publications, and tried to convince their writer to modify or even change his views. Lafcadio, however, who felt as if he were back in Ushaw College flying in the face of repressive priests, was not cowed: "Buddhism has been of incalculable service to mankind by creating an ideal of goodness and love and of a beauty so holy that even the skepticism of the nineteenth century bows low in reverence before it."

With his new job at the *Item*, Lafcadio recovered his physical health, regaining the weight and some of the mental stability he had lost during his debilitating homeless existence just a couple of months before. But his harrowing underground experiences had aggravated what he himself admitted was "a badly-balanced nervous make-up." As Julia Wetherall, a poet and the wife of one of Lafcadio's editors who knew him well during his New Orleans days, recalled: "His character presented strange contrasts. He was warm-hearted and affectionate, though at the same time extremely prone to distrustfulness; often suspecting his best friends of a design to slight or injure him. Hearn was not a good judge of character, and would often accuse quite simple and harmless persons of deep, dark subtlety."

Just as Lafcadio was beginning to develop a sense of equilibrium in his life, he was temporarily but painfully unbalanced by ocular troubles. "The Raven has not found letter-writing a pleasant occupation lately," he informed Henry Watkin. "It has had some trouble; It has also been studying very hard; It has had Its literary work doubled, and It has had little leisure time, as Its grotesque and fantastic Eye is not yet in a healthy condition."

Faced with seemingly insuperable problems, Lafcadio often dealt with them—after anger and pity ran their course—by regarding them with an illuminating (and sometimes perverse) sense of humor, or by transforming them into creative occasions. In one of his book review/editorials ("Artistic Value of Myopia"), he tried to come to terms with his baneful nearsightedness by seeing in it the possibilities of an esthetic principle—that of "suggestion" and "depth":

Probably more than one reader, on coming to page 15 of Philip Gilbert Hamerton's delightful book, *Landscape*, was startled by the author's irrefutable statement that "the possession of very good eyesight may be a hindrance to those feelings of sublimity that exalt the poetic imagination." The fact is, that the impressiveness of natural scenery depends a great deal upon the apparent predominance of *mass* over *detail*, to borrow Mr. Hamerton's own words; the more visible the details of a large object—a mountain, a tower, a forest-wall—the less grand and impressive that object. The more apparently uniform the mass, the larger it seems to loom; the vaguer a shadow-space, the deeper it appears. An impression of weirdness—such as that obtainable in a Louisiana or Florida swamp-forest, or, much more, in those primeval and impenetrable forest-deeps described so powerfully by Humboldt—is stronger in proportion to the spectator's indifference to lesser detail. The real effect of the scene must be a *general* one to be understood. In painting, the artist does not attempt microscopic minutiæ in treating forest-forms; he simply attempts to render the effect of the masses, with their characteristic generalities of shadow and color. It is for this reason the photograph can never supplant the painting—not even when the art of photographing natural colors shall have been discovered. Mr. Hamerton cites the example of a mountain, which always seems more imposing when wreathed in mists or half veiled by clouds, than when cutting sharply against the horizon with a strong light upon it. Half the secret of Doré's power as an illustrator was his exaggerated perception of this fact—his comprehension of the artistic witchcraft of *suggestion*. And since the perception of details depends vastly upon the quality of eyesight, a landscape necessarily suggests less to the keen-sighted man than to the myope. The keener the view, the less depth in the impression produced. There is no possibility of mysterious attraction in wooded deeps or mountain recesses for the eye that, like the eye of the hawk, pierces shadows and can note the separate quiver of each leaf. Far-seeing persons can, to a certain degree, comprehend this by recalling the impressions given in twilight by certain unfamiliar, or even by familiar objects—such as furniture and clothing in a half-lighted room. The suggestiveness of the forms vanishes immediately upon the making of a strong light. Again, attractive objects viewed vaguely through a morning or evening haze, or at a great distance, often totally lose artistic character when a telescope is directed upon them.

In the February number of *Harper's Magazine* we find a very clever and amusing poem by the scholarly Andrew Lang upon this very theme. The writer, after describing the christening-gifts of various kindly fairies, tells us that the wicked one said:

> "I shall be avenged on you.
> My child, you shall grow up nearsighted!"
>   With magic juices did she lave
> Mine eyes, and wrought her wicked pleasure.
>   Well, of all the gifts the Fairies gave,
> Hers is the present that I treasure!
>
> The bore, whom others fear and flee,
>   I do not fear, I do not flee him;
> I pass him calm as calm can be;
>   I do not cut—I do not see him!
> And with my feeble eyes and dim,
>   Where you see patchy fields and fences,
> For me the mists of Turner swim—
>   My "azure distance" soon commences!
> Nay, as I blink about the streets
>   Of the befogged and miry city,
> Why, almost every girl one meets
>   Seems preternaturally pretty!
> "Try spectacles," one's friends intone;
>   "You'll see the world correctly through them."
> But I have visions of my own
>   And not for worlds would I undo them!

This is quite witty and quite consoling to myopes, even as a cynical development of Philip Gilbert Hamerton's artistic philosophy. Still, it does not follow that the myope necessarily possesses the poetic faculty or feeling;—neither does it imply that the presbyope necessarily lacks it. If among French writers, for example, Gautier was notably near-sighted, Victor Hugo had an eye keen as a bird's. It is true that a knowledge of the effect of short sightedness on the imagination may be of benefit to a near-sighted man, who, possessing artistic qualities, can learn to take all possible advantage of his myopia—to utilize his physical disability to a good purpose; but the long-sighted artist need not be at a loss to find equally powerful sources of inspiration—he can seek them in morning mists, evening fogs, or those wonderful hazes of summer afternoons, when the land sends up all its vapors to the sun, like a smoke of gold. Baudelaire in his *Curiosités Esthétiques*, made an attempt to prove that the greatest schools of painting were evolved among hazy surroundings—Dutch fogs, Venetian mists, and the vapors of Italian marsh lands.

The evolutionary tendency would indicate for future man a keener vision than he at present possesses; and a finer perception of color—for while there may be certain small emotional advantages connected with myopia, it is a serious hindrance in practical life. What effect keener sight will have on the artistic powers of the future man can only be imagined— but an increasing tendency to realism in art is certainly perceptible; and perhaps an interesting chapter could be written upon the possible results to art of perfected optical instruments. The subject also suggests another idea—that the total inability of a certain class of highly educated persons to feel interest in a certain kind of art-production may be partly accounted for by the possession of such keen visual perception as necessarily suppresses the sensation of breadth of effect, either in landscape or verbal description.

Lafcadio himself had drawn and sketched throughout his life. Although a Daumier or Doré he certainly was not, when the *Item* found itself in a particularly acute financial situation, it was the one-eyed assistant editor who came to the rescue by thinking up the idea of executing nearly two hundred woodcuts—illustrations of New Or-

leans types such as street musicians, costermongers, washerwomen, tramps, sailors, and boys on
velocipedes. The *Item* printed these simple but
striking cartoons—the first to appear in a
Southern newspaper—on its front pages and the
result was an immediate increase in circulation.

THE UNSPEAKABLE VELOCIPEDE

For the sake of his financial portfolio, Lafcadio
should doubtless have continued his career as an
illustrator. Carving woodcuts, however, wearied
his eye, and after six months he called it quits,
preferring to use his spare time translating works by his beloved French
authors—as well as others by recent discoveries (for him) such as Gérard
de Nerval, Anatole France, and the writer who was to become his greatest
literary influence, Pierre Loti, from whose works Lafcadio translated more
than twenty passages for New Orleans newspapers.

Loti was the *nom de plume* of the Breton Louis Marie Julien Viaud
(1850–1923), who traveled the world as a lieutenant in the French navy,
while producing numerous impressionistic novels that Lafcadio felt were
"a series of exotic word paintings unlike anything else ever written."
Lafcadio identified with Loti's rapid "mental and nervous organization,"
finding in him a soul that comprehended nature "like the ancient Finnish
singers [the source for Elias Lönnrot's great Finnish epic the *Kalevala*], or
the pre-Islamic Arabians." He also admired Loti's curiosity about the customs of non-Western societies and his descriptions of his romantic and
erotic liaisons with scores of alluring native girls.

Loti was capable of great moral courage, as shown, for example, by his
bold and outspoken criticism of French military atrocities in Indochina,
which prompted a yearlong suspension from the navy. Many of his novels, on the other hand, today seem blatantly amoral, campy, and
adolescent:

> It was one tropical midday, silent and burning, when I saw my little
> sweetheart Rarahu for the first time in my life. The young Tahitian girls,
> accustomed to bathe in the brook of Fataoua, overcome with heat and
> sleep, were lying upon the grass of its banks, their feet dipping in the
> clear, cool water. The shadow of the thick verdure fell upon us, vertically
> and without motion; great butterflies of velvet black, marked with large
> scabby-colored spots, flew heavily around us or even perched upon us,
> as if their silky wings were too heavy to bear them away; the air was
> filled with enervating and unfamiliar odors; and I gently allowed myself

to sink into this soft, sweet life, to abandon myself to the charms of Oceanica.

In the background of the picture, suddenly the branches of the mimosas and guavas opened, a gentle sound of rustling leaves was heard, and two little girls appeared, examining the situation with the mien of mice coming out of their holes.

They were crowned with garlands of leaves, which protected their pretty heads against the heat of the sun; their loins were tightly girt with *pareos* [brightly colored national dress of Tahiti, often worn from the waist down] with broad yellow stripes on a blue ground; their tawny torsos were slenderly graceful and naked; their hair long, black and loosely flowing. There were no Europeans, no strangers, nothing disquieting in sight. So the two little ones lay down under the cascade, which began to sport noisily around them. The prettiest was Rarahu; the other, Tiahoui, was her friend and confidante.

—"Loti," said Queen Pomare, addressing me a month later, in her deep hoarse voice—

"Loti, why do you not marry little Rarahu of the Apire district?—I assure you it would be the best thing to do, and would give you more friends in the country."

It was under the royal veranda that this question was put to me. I was lying at full length on a mat, holding in my hand five cards my friend Teria had just dealt out to me;—before me lay at full length my fantastic partner the Queen, who was passionately fond of *ecarte:* She was clad in a dressing-gown of yellow with great black flowers on it, and smoked a long cigarette of pandanus, made of a single leaf rolled upon itself. Two attendant girls, wearing wreaths of jasmine flowers in their hair, marked our points, shuffled our cards, and aided us with their advice, while leaning in kindly curiosity over our shoulders. . . .

—"Marry the little Rarahu of the Apire district!" The proposition taking me by surprise, gave me much food for reflection.

I need hardly say that the Queen, who was a very intelligent and sensible person, did not propose to me any such marriage as that which according to European laws fetters for life. She was full of indulgencies for the easy morals of her country, although she often strove to render them more correct and more conformable with Christian principles. It was, therefore, only a Tahitian marriage which was proposed to me. I could not find in my heart any serious objection to this desire of the Queen, and the little Rarahu of the Apire district was such a charming little creature!   (FROM *Le Mariage de Loti,* TRANSLATED BY LAFCADIO HEARN)

Despite their sentimentality, the vistas and experiences Pierre Loti presented in his books coincided with Lafcadio's own reveries; and the colors, sounds, tastes, and scents brought to such sensuous life in Loti's novels suggested to Lafcadio ways of describing unusual landscapes and sensations—all of which he hoped, and was determined, to experience firsthand.

CHAPTER *3*

Creole

Days

I SUPPOSE I have changed a little," Lafcadio wrote to Henry Watkin at the beginning of his fifth year in New Orleans. "Less despondent, but less hopeful; wiser a little and more silent; less nervous, but less merry; more systematic and perhaps a good deal more selfish. Not strictly economical, but coming to it steadily; and in leisure hours studying the theories of the East . . . the teachings of the wise concerning absorption and emanation, the illusions of existence. . . . And still there is in life much sweetness and much pleasure in the accomplishment of a fixed purpose."

At the end of 1881, Lafcadio was offered an editorial job on the New Orleans *Times-Democrat,* the most successful paper in the South. His duties were simply to publish translations of articles, editorials, and reviews from the French and Spanish newspapers and to contribute one or two editorials a week on subjects of his choosing. His salary was to be thirty dollars a week.

This unusually accommodating arrangement was the idea of the paper's owner and editor-in-chief Page Baker, a successful businessman with a deep regard for literature who admired Lafcadio's brilliance and liked him personally. Lafcadio was naturally grateful to his "tall, fine eagle-faced, primitive Aryan-type" boss. Baker directed his pertinacious composing-room editors and printers to disregard *Times-Democrat* style, and let Lafcadio's articles be set exactly as they were written and punctuated—leaving intact, in particular, the journalist's habitual and characteristic use of semicolons or commas followed by a dash. And he allowed

Lafcadio to write about arcane subjects such as Ferdinand Lassalle (the father of German socialism), the Tuareg tribes of the northern Sahara, the elaborate ritual of orthodox Jewish funerals, the beauties of Sanskrit poetry, and the life of the twelfth-century Moslem saint Sidi Abd-El-Kader El Djel-Lani.

Lafcadio's relaxed working schedule gave him time to finish his translations of the stories of Gautier that he had begun in his Cincinnati days. His attempts to find a publisher for a collection of these tales, however, proved futile, and he finally decided to subsidize their publication by saving up $150 and begrudgingly paying this sum to R. Worthington, a New York publisher. In April 1882, Worthington brought out Lafcadio's first book, his translation of Théophile Gautier's *One of Cleopatra's Nights and Other Fantastic Romances*. The few periodicals and newspapers that reviewed it expressed shock at the sensuality of the tales and the sentiments of the translator, whose prefatory note stated: "Naturally, a writer of this kind [Gautier] pays small regard to the demands of prudery. His work being that of the artist, he claims the privilege of the sculptor and the painter in delineations of the beautiful. A perfect human body is to him the most beautiful of objects. He does not seek to veil its loveliness with cumbrous drapery; he delights to behold it and depict it in its 'divine nudity.' "

Lafcadio continued to translate from French newspapers for the *Times-Democrat*. But in order to translate news reports from Spanish and South American papers, he was encouraged by Page Baker to pursue language studies with an eccentric young Mexican scholar named José de Jesus y Preciado ("a Mexican youth with a very curious Indian face . . . We have become *compañeros"*) who, according to Lafcadio, spoke the language "with that long, soft languid South American Creole accent that is so much more pleasant than the harsher accent of Spain," and who was certain he could hold the interest of his brilliant pupil by presenting him with many engaging dialogues to recite and memorize:

¿Tiene V. un leoncito?	Have you a small lion?
No señor, pero tengo un fero perro.	No: but I've an ugly dog.
¿Tiene V. un muchachona?	Have you a big strapping girl?
No: pero tengo un hombrecillo.	No: but I've a miserable little man.

The opportunity to study was to Lafcadio the supreme happiness. To make up for what he regarded as the "deficiencies" of his formal education, he soon began spending most of his salary in amassing a two-thousand-dollar library, purchasing secondhand, rare, and out-of-print titles from New Orleans booksellers, along with special editions from Parisian publishers (like the forty-two-volume *Bibliothèque Orientale El-zévirienne*).

His ever-growing, ecumenical collection, which he moved with him from one lodging to another, contained works on Japanese art, Chinese legends, Arabic folktales, Jewish mysticism, Persian history, French and English literature, Eastern religions, comparative mythology, anthropology, ethnology, geology, and astronomy. ("I never read a book which does not powerfully impress the imagination; but whatever contains novel, curious, potent imagery I always read, no matter what the subject. When the soil of fancy is really well enriched with innumerable fallen leaves, the flowers of language grow spontaneously.") From these volumes Lafcadio extracted and made his own renditions of folktales, legends, and myths from Egyptian, Talmudic, Arabic, Polynesian, and Finnish traditions, collecting them in his second published book, *Stray Leaves from Strange Literature* (1884). He then elaborated six Chinese ghost stories into a volume called *Some Chinese Ghosts* (1887), which he later described as the "early work of a man who tried to understand the Far East from books—and couldn't, but then the real purpose of the stories was only artistic."

One of Lafcadio's principal interests in New Orleans was reflected in his large collection of Creole dictionaries, grammars, and books of Creole legends and folklore from both the French West Indies and Louisiana. Not content to depend only on book knowledge, however, he set out to teach himself the local Creole patois, referred to superciliously by "the invading *Amerikain*" (Lafcadio's phrase and spelling) as *Gumbo* or *Gombo*.

In New Orleans, Creole was still being spoken in the *Vié faubon* (as black Creole children called those oldest parts of New Orleans at the farthest remove from the river and the American section of town south of Canal Street). And it was in this area that, for three years, Lafcadio rented rooms in a number of dilapidated Creole houses—with their damp brick walls decorated with cracks and green with age, their large yards filled with plants and cacti, and often shared by cats, rabbits, dogs, geese, and a seraglio of hens.

"Let us suppose you are dwelling in one of the curious and crumbling houses of the old quarter of town," he wrote in a newspaper sketch, "and that some evening while dreaming over a pipe as you rock your chair upon the gallery, the large-eyed children of the habitation gather about you, cooing one unto the other in creole like so many yellow doves. Invariably you will then hear the severe maternal admonition, 'Allons, Marie! Eugène! faut pas parler créole devant monsieur; parlez Français, donc!' Creole must not be spoken in the presence of 'monsieur'; he must be addressed in good French, the colonial French of Louisiana that has been so much softened by tropicalization." But Lafcadio loved the Creole patois, describing it as "the offspring of linguistic miscegenation, an offspring which exhibits but a very faint shade of African color, and nevertheless possesses a strangely supple comeliness by virtue of the very intercrossing which created it, like a beautiful octoroon."

Living in the Old Quarter, Lafcadio could listen to a multitude of linguistic intercrossings just outside his windows. At dawn he woke up to the street cries of fig and cantaloupe peddlers, fan-sellers, clothes pole hawkers, and the Gascon charcoal-drivers in their broken-down wagons:

Black—coalee-coaly!
   Coaly-coaly; coaly-coaly; coal-coal-coal.
   Coaly-coaly!
   Coal-ee! Nice!
   Cha'coal!
   Twenty-five! Whew!
   O charco-oh-oh-oh-oh-oh-lee!
   Oh-lee!
   Oh-lee-e!
   [You get some coal in your mout', young fellow, if you don't keep it shut.]
   Pretty coalee-oh-ee!
   Char-coal
   Cha-ah-ah-ahr-coal!
   Coaly-coaly!
   Charbon! du charbon, Madame! Bon charbon? Point! Ai-ai! Tonnerre
de Dieu!
   Char-r-r-r-r-r-rbon!
   A-a-a-a-a-w! High-ya-a-ah! High-yah!
   Vingt-cinq! Nice coalee! Coalee!
   Coaly-coal-coal!
   Pretty coaly!
   Charbon de Paris!
   De Paris, Madame; de Paris!

Lafcadio became friendly with the bonnes vieilles Negresses of the Quarter, with their white fichus and plaided tignons, who sat in the street,

singing out the names of their proffered sweets: *Bons calas touts chauds
. . . Baton d' amande . . . Blanches tablettes à la fleur d'oranger.* From these
women and from other residents of the Quarter, many of them immi-
grants from the French West Indies, Lafcadio learned many Creole proverbs (later published in his book *Gombo Zhèbes,* published in 1885):

> *"Derrière chien, c'est chien; devant chien, c'est 'Monsieur Chien.' "*
> "Behind dog's back, it is *dog;* but before dog it is 'Mr. Dog.' "

> *"Bef pas jamain ca die savane 'merci.' "*
> "The ox never says, 'thank you,' to the meadow."

> *"Crapaud pas tini chimise, ous v'le li poter caneçon,"*—
> "The frog has no shirt, yet you want him to wear drawers."

And Lafcadio gathered a large assortment of Creole-patois ditties, airs,
songs, and their often playful, bizarre refrains:

"Si to té 'tit zozo	"If thou wert a little bird,
Et moi-même mo té fusil	And I were a little gun,
Mo sré tchoué toi,—Boum!	I would shoot thee—*bang!*
Ah, cher bijou	Ah, dear little
D'acajou,	Mahogany jewel,
Mol 'aimin vous	I love thee as a little pig loves
Comme cochon aimin la boue!"	the mud."

Lafcadio noticed with regret that in New Orleans, the Creole patois
was surviving "like some plant that has almost ceased to flower, though
the green has not yet departed from its leaves." What he gathered in the
Vieux Carré were "scattered petals of folklore, few entire blossoms." But
he was pleased when he came across mothers still teaching their children
"the old songs—heirlooms of melody resonant with fetich words—threads
of tune strung with *grigris* from the Ivory Coast."

Lafcadio had a more difficult time ingratiating himself with the white
Creole community, those native-born descendants of the early Spanish
and French colonial settlers. Lafcadio found this world impenetrably antique, with its insular, proud, formal, ornately courteous manners, its feudal customs, and its slow, languorous existence, lived behind closed
doors—as if the crude bustle of the *Américains,* south of Canal Street, were
far off in another country:

⟦ An atmosphere of tranquillity and quiet happiness seemed to envelop the old house, which had formerly belonged to a rich planter. Like many of the Creole houses, the façade presented a commonplace and unattractive aspect. The great green doors of the arched entrance were closed; and the green shutters of the balconied windows were half shut, like sleepy eyes lazily gazing upon the busy street below or the cottony patches of light clouds which floated slowly, slowly across the deep blue of the sky above. But beyond the gates lay a little Paradise. The great court, deep and broad, was framed in tropical green; vines embraced the white pillars of the piazza, and creeping plants climbed up the tinted walls to peer into the upper windows with their flower-eyes of flaming scarlet. Banana-trees nodded sleepily their plumes of emerald green at the farther end of the garden; vines smothered the windows of the dining-room, and formed a bower of cool green about the hospitable door; an aged fig-tree, whose gnarled arms trembled under the weight of honeyed fruit, shadowed the square of bright lawn which formed a natural carpet in the midst; and at intervals were stationed along the walks in large porcelain vases—like barbaric sentinels in sentry-boxes—gorgeous broad-leaved things, with leaves fantastic and barbed and flowers brilliant as hummingbirds. A fountain murmured faintly near the entrance of the western piazza; and there came from the shadows of the fig-tree the sweet and plaintive cooing of amorous doves. Without, cotton-floats might rumble, and street-cars vulgarly jingle their bells; but these were mere echoes of the harsh outer world which disturbed not the delicious quiet within—where sat, in old-fashioned chairs, good old-fashioned people who spoke the tongue of other times, and observed many quaint and knightly courtesies forgotten in this material era. Without, roared the Iron Age, the angry waves of American traffic; within, one heard only the murmur of the languid fountain, the sound of deeply musical voices conversing in the languages of Paris and Madrid, the playful chatter of dark-haired children lisping in sweet and many-voweled Creole, and through it all, the soft, caressing coo of doves. Without, it was the year 1879; within, it was the epoch of the Spanish Domination. A guitar lay upon the rustic bench near the fountain, where it had evidently been forgotten, and a silk fan beside it; a European periodical, with graceful etchings, hung upon the back of a rocking-chair at the door, through which one caught glimpses of a snowy table bearing bottles of good Bordeaux, and inhaled the odor of rich West India tobacco. And yet some people wonder that some other people never care to cross Canal Street. ("A CREOLE COURTYARD") ⟧

CHAPTER 4

Voodoo
Nights

W H E N Lafcadio went out foraging throughout the Vieux Carré for proverbs and songs, he would occasionally come across a weird, unintelligible scrap of verse like *"Tig, tig, malaboin/La chelema che tango/Redjoum!"* And when he asked what it meant, he would get as an answer a smile, a shrug, and the noncommittal comment, *"Mais c'est Voudoo, ça; je n'en sais rien!"* But for the indefatigably curious journalist and amateur folklorist living in the voodoo capital of the United States, that could never have been the end of the subject.

Years before in Cincinnati, Lafcadio had written about a necromancer and voodoo high priest of the Levee named Jot, who dispensed love spells and talismans; and the journalist had visited this *obi*-man's den, which was filled with huge colonies of spiders and their "forests of webs." Lafcadio had also researched and published an article about voodoo sorcerers and their use of some kind of "potent corrosive poison, secretly administered . . . a secret septic poison . . . that left no trace discoverable by most skilful chemists" (possibly similar to the toxin derived from puffer fish that Haitian sorcerers are known to use to achieve the effect of zombification).

According to Professor Robert Farris Thompson, voodoo (or *vodun*), "which was first elaborated in Haiti . . . is one of the signal achievements of people of African descent in the western hemisphere: a vibrant, sophisticated synthesis of the traditional religions of Dahomey, Yorubaland, and Kongo with an infusion of Roman Catholicism." According to Farris Thompson, the resulting Creole religion had two parts: one called *Rada* ("the 'cool' side of vodun, being associated with the achievement of peace and reconciliation") and *Petro* ("the hot side, being associated with the spiritual fire of charms for healing and for attacking evil forces").

The entire subject fascinated Lafcadio. Now in New Orleans, after much searching, he located a supposed voodoo priestess who agreed, for a fee, to chant a voodoo incantation—"one of the weirdest and strangest performances ever heard by the writer . . . with a wild and melancholy sweetness":

> *Heru mande, heru mande, heru mande,*
>   *Tigi li papa,*
> *Heru mande,*
>   *Tigi li papa,*
> *Heru mande,*
>   *Heru mande, heru mande,*
> *Do se dans godo*
>   *Ah tingonai ye;*
> *Ah tingonai ye, ah tingonai ye,*
>   *Ah ouai ya, ah ouai ya,*
> *Do se dans godo*
>   *Ah tingonai ye*
> *Tigi li papa*

Lafcadio then had the good fortune to make contact with the two most important and fascinating practitioners of voodoo and hoodoo (a system of divination, magic, and herbalism) in the history of New Orleans: Marie Laveau (the Queen of Voodoo) and her sometime rival, Jean Montanet (the King of Hoodoo). The latter, who died in his late nineties in August of 1885, was known variously as Jean La Ficelle, Jean Latanié, Jean Racine, Jean Grisgris, Jean Macaque, Jean Bayou, "Voodoo John," or "Doctor John." Lafcadio called him "The Last of the Voudoos," and upon his death wrote a biographical tribute of him:

It may reasonably be doubted whether any other Negro of African birth who lived in the South had a more extraordinary career than that of Jean Montanet. He was a native of Senegal, and claimed to have been a prince's son, in proof of which he was wont to call attention to a number of parallel scars on his cheek, extending in curves from the edge of either temple to the corner of the lips. This fact seems to me partly confirmatory of his statement, as Berenger-Feraud dwells at some length on the fact that the Bambaras, who are probably the finest Negro race in Senegal, all wear such disfigurations. The scars are made by gashing the cheeks during infancy, and are considered a sign of race. Three parallel scars mark the freemen of the tribe; four distinguish their captives or slaves. Now Jean's face had, I am told, three scars, which would prove him a free-born Bambara, or at least a member of some free tribe allied to the Bambaras, and living upon their territory. At all events, Jean possessed physical characteristics answering to those by which the French ethnologists in Senegal distinguish the Bambaras. He was of middle height, very strongly built, with broad shoulders, well-developed muscles, an inky black skin, retreating forehead, small bright eyes, a very flat nose, and a woolly beard, gray only during the last few years of his long life. He had a resonant voice and a very authoritative manner.

At an early age he was kidnapped by Spanish slavers, who sold him at some Spanish port, whence he was ultimately shipped to Cuba. His West-Indian master taught him to be an excellent cook, ultimately became attached to him, and made him a present of his freedom. Jean soon afterward engaged on some Spanish vessel as ship's cook, and in the exercise of this calling voyaged considerably in both hemispheres. Finally tiring of the sea, he left his ship at New Orleans, and began life on shore as a cotton-roller. His physical strength gave him considerable advantage above his fellow-blacks; and his employers also discovered that he wielded some peculiar occult influence over the Negroes, which made him valuable as an overseer or gang leader. Jean, in short, possessed the mysterious *obi* power, the existence of which has been recognized in most slave-holding communities, and with which many a West-Indian planter has been compelled by force of circumstances to effect a compromise. Accordingly Jean was permitted many liberties which other blacks, although free, would never have presumed to take. Soon it became rumored that he was a seer of no small powers, and that he could tell the future by the marks upon bales of cotton. I have never been able to learn the details of this queer method of telling fortunes; but Jean became so successful in the exercise of it that thousands of colored people flocked to him for predictions and counsel, and even white people, moved by curiosity or by doubt, paid him to prophesy for them. Finally he became wealthy enough to abandon the levee and purchase a large tract of property on the Bayou Road, where he built a house. His land extended from Prieur Street on the Bayou Road as far as Roman, covering the greater portion of an extensive square, now well built up. In those days it was a marshy green plain, with a few scattered habitations.

At his new home Jean continued the practice of fortune-telling, but combined it with the profession of Creole medicine, and of arts still more mysterious. By-and-by his reputation became so great that he was able to demand and obtain immense fees. People of both races and both sexes thronged to see him—many coming even from far-away Creole towns in the parishes, and well-dressed women, closely veiled, often knocked at his door. Parties paid from ten to twenty dollars for advice, for herb medicines, for recipes to make the hair grow, for cataplasms supposed to possess mysterious virtues, but really made with scraps of shoe leather triturated into paste, for advice what ticket to buy in the Havana Lottery, for aid to recover stolen goods, for love powers, for counsel in family troubles, for charms by which to obtain revenge upon an enemy. Once Jean received a fee of fifty dollars for a potion. "It was water," he said to a Creole confidant, "with some common herbs boiled in it. I hurt nobody; but if folks want to give me fifty dollars, I take the fifty dollars every time!" His office furniture consisted of a table, a chair, a picture of the Virgin Mary, an elephant's tusk, some shells which he said were African shells and enabled him to read the future, and a pack of cards in each of which a small hole had been burned. About his person he always carried two small bones wrapped around with a black string, which bones he really appeared to revere as fetiches. Wax candles were burned during his performances; and as he bought a whole box of them every few days during "flush times," one can imagine how large the number of his clients must have been. They poured money into his hands so generously that he became worth at least $50,000!

Then, indeed, did this possible son of a Bambara prince begin to live more grandly than any black potentate of Senegal. He had his carriage and pair, worthy of a planter, and his blooded saddle-horse, which he rode well, attired in a gaudy Spanish costume, and seated upon an elaborately decorated Mexican saddle. At home, where he ate and drank only the best—scorning claret worth less than a dollar the litre—he continued to find his simple furniture good enough for him; but he had at least fifteen wives—a harem worthy of Boubakar-Segou. White folks might have called them by a less honorific name, but Jean declared them his legitimate spouses according to African ritual. One of the curious features in modern slavery was the ownership of blacks by freedmen of their own color, and these Negro slave-holders were usually savage and merciless masters. Jean was not; but it was by right of slave purchase that he obtained most of his wives, who bore him children in great multitude. Finally he managed to woo and win a white woman of the lowest class, who might have been, after a fashion, the Sultana-Validé of this Seraglio. On grand occasions Jean used to distribute largess among the colored population of his neighborhood in the shape of food—bowls of *gombo* or dishes of *jimbalaya*. He did it for popularity's sake in those days, perhaps; but in after-years, during the great epidemics, he did it for charity, even when so much reduced in circumstances that he was himself obliged to cook the food to be given away.

But Jean's greatness did not fail to entail certain cares. He did not know what to do with his money. He had no faith in banks, and had seen too much of the darker side of life to have much faith in human nature. For many years he kept his money under-ground, burying or taking it up at night only, occasionally concealing large sums so well that he could never find them again himself; and now, after many years, people still believe there are treasures entombed somewhere in the neighborhood of Prieur Street and Bayou Road. All business negotiations of a serious character caused him much worry, and as he found many willing to take advantage of his ignorance, he probably felt small remorse for certain questionable actions of his own. He was notoriously bad pay, and part of his property was seized at last to cover a debt. Then, in an evil hour, he asked a man without scruples to teach him how to write, believing that financial misfortunes were mostly due to ignorance of the alphabet. After he had learned to write his name, he was innocent enough one day to place his signature by request at the bottom of a blank sheet of paper, and, lo! his real estate passed from his possession in some horribly mysterious way. Still he had some money left, and made heroic efforts to retrieve his fortunes. He bought other property, and he invested desperately in lottery tickets. The lottery craze finally came upon him, and had far more to do with his ultimate ruin than his losses in the grocery, the shoe-maker's shop, and other establishments into which he had put several thousand dollars as the silent partner of people who cheated him. He might certainly have continued to make a good living, since people still sent for him to cure them with his herbs, or went to see him to have their fortunes told; but all his earnings were wasted in tempting fortune. After a score of seizures and a long succession of evictions, he was at last obliged to seek hospitality from some of his numerous children; and of all he had once owned nothing remained to him but his African shells, his elephant's tusk, and the sewing-machine table that had served him to tell fortunes and to burn wax candles upon. . . .

("THE LAST OF THE VOUDOOS")

Lafcadio also met and interviewed the most legendary figure of that period, Marie Laveau. Born in 1794, the illegitimate daughter of a Creole planter and one of his mulatto slaves, this charismatic and strong-willed quadroon girl started her career as a coiffeuse, with access to the "best" homes in the Vieux Carré. This enabled her to supplement her income by acting as a go-between, carrying *billets doux* and arranging clandestine rendezvous for her well-to-do white clients. She eventually became the proprietress of a famous, lavishly appointed bordello, the Maison Blanche (among others); and through a network of intelligence agents among the black servants to the city's rich, she was able to exploit the secrets of New Orleans society, using blackmail to protect the houses of prostitution she controlled.

Marie's grandmother and mother had both been conjurers—adepts of hoodoo. Marie, however, showed no interest in following their example until one night when, legend has it, a rattlesnake entered her bedroom and "spoke" to her. Whereupon Marie decided to study with a renowned hoodoo doctor named Alexander. Soon she was teaching her teacher.

She then began a flourishing business in the manufacture and sale of a wide range of charms and herbal medicines. Admired and feared for her powers of healing and hexing as well as for her psychic and fortune-telling abilities, Marie became renowned as a kind of combination *mambo-witch-shamaness*, who was consulted by both blacks and whites. One wealthy Creole family bought her a house at 1020 St. Anne Street in gratitude for her magical intervention in the court trial of their son. She also gained a local reputation as a saint for tending to wounded soldiers during the Battle of New Orleans in 1815, for nursing the victims of yellow fever epidemics, and for providing food and amulets to the prisoners on death row in the parish jail.

Marie soon attained prominence far beyond the confines of New Orleans. Queen Victoria apparently sent a request to the Queen of Conjure to help her on a private matter (the nature of which remains a secret to this day), for which the English monarch, upon a satisfactory conclusion to the business, gave Marie a beautiful cashmere scarf and a large fee "for services rendered." (Her supposed visits, however, from Aaron Burr, Louis

Philippe, and Lafayette are simply part of the fantastic folklore that gradually grew up about her.)

Marie lived in St. Anne Street and in a house at Bayou St. John with,
at different times, two husbands and a tribe of fifteen or more of her own
children, as well as a brood of grandchildren. One of her daughters, born
in 1827, was also named Marie (or *Ti Marie*)—creating confusion for
biographers, who, even today, often write about both mother and daughter as if they were one person—and was initiated in a voodoo ceremony
as her mother's successor.

Queen Marie officiated at the yearly public voodoo celebration held on
St. John's Eve (June 23) at the place where Bayou St. John enters Lake
Pontchartrain. Bedecked in a colorful shawl, satin skirts, necklaces of amber, malachite, and turquoise, and with a snake draped around her shoulders, Marie organized a fete, attended by several thousand persons in the
midst of hundreds of blazing pine-knot fires, that featured ecstatic dancing
to the accompaniment of goatskin drums, bone castanets, bamboo flutes,
and two-string fiddles. Elements of Catholic ritual also figured in the fete,
as did drink and food (gumbo and rice) and all kinds of marvels and
magical happenings. To these events Marie invited certain journalists, police officials, and members of the white New Orleans establishment,
thereby safeguarding the privacy and secrecy of her orgiastic ceremonies
in the backyard of her St. Anne Street cottage, as well as of the midnight
rituals of the authentic New Orleans voodoo cult—a worship blending
devotions to West African gods and Catholic saints, and held in the
cypress swamps around a makeshift altar with candlelight.

There, Marie ministered as high priestess to a select group of followers
in ceremonies of wild rum-drinking, impassioned incantations, serpent
worship, frenzied trance-dancing during which the gods would "mount"
(or "possess") the participants, fervent prayers to the Virgin Mary, and
animal sacrifices. Only true initiates—those who had undergone a stren-
uous rite of purification, fasting, days of isolation, and bloodletting—were
allowed to participate in cult meetings. Lafcadio was never a witness to
these rituals. Indeed, only three outside accounts of these events appeared
in print. By the 1880s, moreover, the true New Orleans voodoo ceremo-
nial, along with the religious cult, had died out. Only the magic remained.

Both fascinated and repelled by voodoo magic, Lafcadio was one of
the last writers to have interviewed Queen Marie, who died on June 16,
1881. She had attained a position of wealth and authority rare for any
female in nineteenth-century America and had given a sense of identity

and pride to thousands of her people. She kept alive the customs, beliefs, and spiritual power of the black African heritage as it had been brought to New Orleans by the slaves and free blacks of the French West Indies.

When Lafcadio met the Queen of Voodoo, she was in her late eighties, with wild gray tresses hanging about her yellowish neck, her body bowed and withered as she sat in a rocking chair, surrounded by her children, grandchildren, and great-grandchildren, but with the spark of the Spirit still illuminating her sunken eyes and revealing an inextirpable expression of imperiousness, concentration, and mental power. But it was from her daughter Marie—then in her early fifties—that he learned much of what he knew about voodoo magic in New Orleans:

⟦ . . . The fear of what are styled "Voudoo charms" is much more widely spread in Louisiana than any one who had conversed only with educated residents might suppose; and the most familiar superstition of this class is the belief in what I might call *pillow magic*, which is the supposed art of causing wasting sicknesses or even death by putting certain objects into the pillow of the bed in which the hated person sleeps. Feather pillows are supposed to be particularly well adapted to this kind of witchcraft. It is believed that by secret spells a "Voudoo" can cause some monstrous kind of bird or nondescript animal to shape itself into being out of the pillow feathers—like the *tupilek* of the Esquimau *iliseenek* (witchcraft). It grows very slowly, and by night only; but when completely formed, the person who has been using the pillow dies. Another practice of pillow witchcraft consists in tearing a living bird asunder—usually a cock—and putting portions of the wings into the pillow. A third form of the black-art is confined to putting certain charms or fetiches—consisting of bones, hair, feathers, rags, strings, or some fantastic combination of these and other trifling objects—into any sort of a pillow used by the party whom it is desired to injure. The pure Africanism of this practice needs no comment. Any exact idea concerning the use of each particular kind of charm I have not been able to discover; and I doubt whether those who practise such fetichism know the original African beliefs connected with it. Some say that putting grains of corn into a child's pillow "prevents it from growing any more"; others declare that a bit of cloth in a grown person's pillow will cause wasting sickness; but different parties questioned by me gave each a different signification to the use of similar charms. Putting an open pair of scissors under the pillow before going to bed is supposed to insure a pleasant sleep in spite of fetiches; but the surest way to provide against being "hoodooed," as American residents call it, is to open one's pillow from time to time. If any charms are found, they must be first sprinkled with salt, then burned. A Spanish resident told me that her eldest daughter had been unable to sleep for weeks, owing to a fetich that had been put into her pillow by a spiteful colored domestic. After the object had been duly exorcised and burned, all the young lady's restlessness departed. A friend of mine living in one of the country parishes once found a tow string in his pillow, into the fibers of which a great number of feather stems had either been introduced or had introduced themselves. He wished to retain it as a curiosity, but no sooner did he exhibit it to some acquaintance than it was denounced as a Voudoo "trick," and my friend was actually compelled to burn it in the presence of witnesses. Everybody knows or ought to know that feathers in pillows have a natural tendency to cling and form clots or lumps of more or less curious form, but the discovery of these in some New Orleans households is enough to create a panic. They are viewed as incipient Voudoo *tupileks*. The sign of the cross is made over them by Catholics, and they are promptly committed to the flames.

Pillow magic alone, however, is far from being the only recognized form of maleficent Negro witchcraft. Placing charms before the entrance of a house or room, or throwing them over a wall into a yard, is believed to be a deadly practice. When a charm is laid before a room door or hall door, oil is often poured on the floor or pavement in front of the threshold. It is supposed that whoever *crosses an oil line* falls into the power of the Voudoos. To break the oil charm, sand or salt should be strewn upon it. Only a few days before [I wrote] this article a very intelligent Spaniard told me that shortly after having discharged a dishonest colored servant he found before his bedroom door one evening a pool of oil with a charm lying in the middle of it, and a candle burning near it. The charm contained some bones, feathers, hairs, and rags—all wrapped together with a string—and a dime. No superstitious person would have dared to use that dime; but my friend, not being superstitious, forthwith put it into his pocket.

The presence of that coin I can only attempt to explain by calling attention to another very interesting superstition connected with New Orleans fetichism. The Negroes believe that in order to make an evil charm operate it is necessary *to sacrifice something.* Wine and cake are left occasionally in dark rooms, or candies are scattered over the sidewalk, by those who want to make their fetich hurt somebody. If food or sweet-meats are thus thrown away, they must be abandoned without a parting glance; the witch or wizard must not look back while engaged in the sacrifice.

Scattering dirt before a door, or making certain figures on the wall of a house with chalk, or crumbling dry leaves with the fingers and scattering the fragments before a residence, are also forms of a maleficent conjuring which sometimes cause serious annoyance. Happily the conjurers are almost as afraid of the counter-charms as the most superstitious persons are of the conjuring. An incident which occurred recently in one of the streets of the old quarter known as "Spanish Town" afforded me ocular proof of the fact. Through malice or thoughtlessness, or possibly in obe-dience to secret orders, a young Negro girl had been tearing up some leaves and scattering them on the sidewalk in front of a cottage occupied by a French family. Just as she had dropped the last leaf the irate French woman rushed out with a broom and a handful of salt, and began to sweep away the leaves, after having flung salt both upon them and upon the little Negress. The latter actually screamed with fright, and cried out, *"Oh, pas jeté plis disel après moin, madame! pas bisoin jeté disel après moin; mo pas pé vini icite encore"* (Oh, madam, don't throw any more salt after me; you needn't throw any more salt after me; I won't come here any more). . . .   ("NEW ORLEANS SUPERSTITIONS")]

CHAPTER 5

Some Friends
Along the Way

I HAVE BEEN a demophobe for years," Lafcadio once confessed, "—dread crowds and hate unsympathetic characters most unspeakably. I have only been once to a theatre in New Orleans;—to hear Patti [Adelina Patti, the most popular coloratura soprano of her time] sing, and I got out after she had sung one song. I can't be much of a pleasure to any one. Here I visit a few friends steadily for a couple of months;—then disappear for six. Can't help it;—just a nervous condition that renders effort unpleasant."

When a six-year-old boy who had just attended one of the first New Orleans performances of *H.M.S. Pinafore* was introduced to Lafcadio, he blurted out, "My Lord, Grandma, here comes Dick Dead Eye himself!" Children, however, were always to be forgiven their thoughtlessness; adults, almost never. Lafcadio found very few people who would tolerate his "susceptibilities, weaknesses, sensitivenesses, which renders it impossible to adapt myself to the ordinary *milieu;* I have to make one of my own, wherever I go, and never mingle with that already made."

Page Baker's sister-in-law, Julia Wetherall, once commented about Lafcadio's distrustful nature. "At all events," she stated, "he was not happy, or calculated to make others happy. Charming as he could be at times, one sensed that he was not 'good to tie to.' There was none of that staunchness which is the backbone of friendship." Lafcadio considered Page Baker, his boss at the *Times-Democrat*, a "very noble and lovable friend"; yet less than a year after departing New Orleans, he wrote a letter to another friend in which he compared Baker to a chamber pot. For his part, Baker later remarked that Lafcadio was "a rare genius and, in some respects, a most extraordinary human being, but taken altogether he was quite impossible."

Perceived and misperceived slights, petty and malicious gossip, unexpressed resentment and unrealistic expectations, and the need to break off a relationship before it was broken off *for* him, all contributed to Lafcadio's characterological wariness with regard to making and keeping friends. Yet considering this, it should be noted that it was in New Orleans that he first led the full, variegated social life of a bohemian writer. While Lafcadio was occasionally furtive and secretive, he was also capable of being open and outgoing, and with a number of remarkable persons he became warm companions, some for a brief period, one of them for a lifetime.

The latter of these was a young woman named Elizabeth Bisland—the tall, striking, self-possessed, and ambitious daughter of a Louisiana family whose plantation had become impoverished after the war. Bisland came to New Orleans at the age of seventeen in order to make her fortune as a journalist. She was already aware of Lafcadio's work, having read in the *Item* one of his prose-poetic sketches—to which he gave the name "Fantastics"—and was overwhelmed by the romantic ardor of the writer's style and sensibility. Lafcadio's sketch was entitled "A Dead Love":

He knew no rest; for all his dreams were haunted by her; and when he sought love, she came as the dead come between the living. So that, weary of his life, he passed away at last in the fevered summer of a tropical city; dying with her name upon his lips. And his face was no more seen in the palm-shadowed streets; but the sun rose and sank as before.

And that vague phantom life, which sometimes lives and thinks in the tomb where the body moulders, lingered and thought within the narrow marble bed where they laid him with the pious hope—*que en paz descanse!*

Yet so weary of his life had the wanderer been that he could not even find the repose of the dead. And while the body sank into dust the phantom man found no rest in the darkness, and thought to himself, "I am even too weary to rest!"

There was a fissure in the wall of the tomb. And through it, and through the meshes of the web that a spider had spun across it, the dead looked, and saw the summer sky blazing like amethyst; the palms swaying in the breezes from the sea; the flowers in the shadows of the sepulchres; the opal fires of the horizon; the birds that sang, and the river that rolled its whispering waves between tall palms and vast-leaved plants to the heaving emerald of the Spanish Main. The voices of women and sounds of argentine laughter and of footsteps and of music, and of merriment, also came through the fissure in the wall of the tomb; sometimes also the noise of the swift feet of horses, and afar off the drowsy murmur made by the toiling heart of the city. So that the dead wished to live again; seeing that there was no rest in the tomb. . . .

The stars in their silent courses looked down through the crannies of the tomb and passed on; the birds sang above him and flew to other lands; the lizards ran noiselessly above his bed of stone and as noiselessly departed; the spider at last ceased to renew her web of magical silk; the years came and went as before, but for the dead there was no rest!

And it came to pass that after many tropical moons had waxed and waned, and the summer was come, with a presence sweet as a fair woman's—making the drowsy air odorous about her—that she whose name was uttered by his lips when the Shadow of Death fell upon him, came to that city of palms, and to the ancient place of burial, and even to the tomb that was nameless.

And he knew the whisper of her robes; and from the heart of the dead man a flower sprang and passed through the fissure in the wall of the tomb and blossomed before her and breathed out its soul in passionate sweetness.

But she, knowing it not, passed by; and the sound of her footsteps died away forever!

"A Dead Love" belonged to what Lafcadio would, in later years, refer to as his Period of Gush. It was, nevertheless, this particular Gautier-influenced, Orphic vignette of a love stronger than death that stirred the seventeen-year-old Elizabeth Bisland to arrange a meeting with its author. Her beauty, nervous intelligence, and obviously unfeigned enthusiasm for his work made Lafcadio uncomfortable and distant.

Elizabeth herself submitted some short articles and poems to the *Times-Democrat,* and was soon writing for the paper on a regular basis; nor did it take her long to become a fixture of New Orleans society. At one point, she fell victim to yellow fever, and she was ministered to day and night, in the small, quaint hotel where she resided, by a concerned Lafcadio.

When she recovered, however, he reverted to his habitual polite coolness toward her.

Asked by an acquaintance to give his opinion of her, Lafcadio responded: "Tall, fair-skinned, large black eyes, and dark hair. Some call her beautiful; others, pretty; I don't think her either one or the other; but she is decidedly attractive physically and intellectually. Otherwise she is selfish, unfeeling, hard, cunning, vindictive: a woman that will make inferno in any husband's life, unless he have a character of tremendous force."

In her early twenties, Elizabeth Bisland moved to New York to become assistant editor of *Cosmopolitan Magazine,* and in 1891, she married a successful businessman named Charles W. Wetmore. Lafcadio would remember Elizabeth, for whom he cared more than he could admit, as a voice and a thought, *"une jeune fille un peu farouche . . . who* came into New Orleans from the country . . . and was so kind to a particular variety of savage, that he could not understand—and was afraid." He carried a photograph of her wherever he went: "On the opposite wall is the shadow of a beautiful and wonderful person, whom I knew long ago in the strange city of New Orleans," he wrote to her many years later.

Upon his death, Elizabeth Bisland published the first and still the most reverential biography of Lafcadio Hearn, remembering and describing him with sympathy, devotion, perspicacity, and humor:

About five feet three inches in height, with unusually broad and powerful shoulders for such a stature, there was an almost feminine grace and lightness in his step and movements. His feet were small and well-shaped, but he wore invariably the most clumsy and neglected shoes, and his whole dress was peculiar. His favorite coat, both winter and summer, was a heavy double-breasted "reefer," while the size of his wide-brimmed, soft-crowned hat was a standing joke among his friends. The rest of his garments were apparently purchased for the sake of durability rather than beauty, with the exception of his linen, which, even in days of the direst poverty, was always fresh and good. Indeed a peculiar physical cleanliness was characteristic of him—that cleanliness of uncontaminated savages and wild animals, which has the air of being so essential and innate as to make the best-groomed men and domesticated beasts seem almost frowzy by contrast. His hands were very delicate and supple, with quick timid movements that were yet full of charm, and his voice was musical and very soft. He spoke always in short sentences, and the manner of his speech was very modest and deferential. His head was quite remarkably beautiful; the profile both bold and delicate, with admirable modelling of the nose, lips, and chin. The brow was square, and full above the eyes, and the complexion a clear smooth olive. The enormous work which he demanded of his vision had enlarged beyond its natural size the eye upon which he depended for sight, but originally, before the accident—whose disfiguring effect he magnified and was exaggeratedly sensitive about—his eyes must have been handsome, for they were large, of a dark liquid brown, and heavily lashed. In conversation he frequently, almost instinctively, placed his hand over the injured eye to conceal it from his companion.

Though he was abnormally shy, particularly with strangers and women, this was not obvious in any awkwardness of manner; he was composed and dignified, though extremely silent and reserved until his confidence was obtained. With those whom he loved and trusted, his voice and mental attitude were caressing, affectionate, and confiding, though with even these some chance look or tone or gesture would alarm him into sudden and silent flight, after which he might be invisible for days or weeks, appearing again as silently and suddenly, with no explanation of his having so abruptly taken wing. In spite of his limited sight he appeared to have the power to divine by some extra sense the slightest change of expression in the faces of those with whom he talked, and no object or tint escaped his observation. One of his habits while talking was to walk about, touching softly the furnishings of the room, or the flowers of the garden, picking up small objects for study with his pocket-glass, and meantime pouring out a stream of brilliant talk in a soft, half-apologetic tone, with constant deference to the opinions of his companions. Any idea advanced he received with respect, however much he might differ, and if a phrase or suggestion appealed to him his face lit with a most delightful irradiation of pleasure, and he never forgot it.

A more delightful or—at times—more fantastically witty companion it would be impossible to imagine, but it is equally impossible to attempt to convey his astounding sensitiveness. To remain on good terms with him it was necessary to be as patient and wary as one who stalks the hermit thrush to its nest. Any expression of anger or harshness to any one drove him to flight, any story of moral or physical pain sent him quivering away, and a look of ennui or resentment, even if but a passing emotion, and indulged in while his back was turned, was immediately conveyed to his consciousness in some occult fashion and he was off in an instant. Any attempt to detain or explain only increased the length of his absence. A description of his eccentricities of manner would be misleading if the result were to convey an impression of neurotic debility, for with this extreme sensitiveness was combined vigor of mind and body to an unusual degree—the delicacy was only of the spirit.

While living in Cincinnati, Lafcadio had come across and been deeply moved by a story in *Scribner's Magazine* entitled "Jean-ah Poquelin," which was about an old Creole gentleman unable to adjust to the modern world. Lafcadio was determined to meet the author, George Washington Cable, when he came to live in the South. Six years older than the new arrival from Ohio, Cable, like Lafcadio, was a man of small stature, a mostly self-taught man of letters, a onetime journalist, a novelist, and a critic of Southern race relations.

Born in New Orleans and twice wounded as a Confederate cavalryman during the Civil War, Cable was hardly the "good old boy" his war record might imply. His father's family had granted freedom to its slaves before the war, and his mother was of New England Puritan stock. George supported his writing, as well as his widowed mother, wife, and children, by working as a clerk and accountant at the cotton exchange. He had earlier quit his job on the New Orleans *Picayune,* for which he had written articles about Creole life, rather than "aiding the devil" by having to edit the theatrical column.

In 1884 Mark Twain invited Cable, whom he regarded as "the South's finest literary genius," to join him on a four-month reading tour of the United States. The tall, white-suited Twain led his bearded, diminutive partner onstage by the hand, like a little brother. Twain told a few billiard-room jokes, read his story about the jumping frog Dan'l Webster and selections from his soon-to-be published novel *The Adventures of Huckleberry Finn.* Then Cable sang songs in Creole patois in a high-pitched voice, accompanying himself on guitar, or told stories like "Posson Jane" and "Mademoiselle Delphine." Audiences—especially northern ones—loved Cable's portrayals of "exotic" Creole and Cajun characters and his mimickings of their accents and dialects. Twain did too, but he was exasperated by Cable's religious eccentricities, especially his strict keeping of the Sabbath, which led the agnostic Missourian to complain that Cable had taught him "to abhor and detest the Sabbath-day and hunt up new and troublesome ways to dishonor it." His Southern friend, Twain grumbled, "had his littleness, like Napoleon," but of course he was a "brave soul and a great man."

Similarly, Lafcadio had little patience for Cable's rigid Puritanism; nevertheless he admired his musical, folkloristic, and literary abilities. The two met up two or three nights a week to swap Creole poems and stories, then strolled through the Old Quarter to observe Creole street dancers and stop to listen to many of the black singers, as Cable notated the melodies and Lafcadio wrote down the words.

Cable's respect for Lafcadio was such that he arranged for him to contribute articles to national publications such as the *Century* and *Harper's Weekly.* Lafcadio, for his part, glowingly reviewed each of Cable's books in the *Item* and the *Times-Democrat,* knowing that in doing so he was alienating himself from the French Creole community, which detested Cable and considered him a traitor to his city and his race. They particularly despised the novels *The Grandissimes* (1880) and *Dr. Sevier* (1885) and were outraged by the outlandish dialect attributed to them and their forebears, by Cable's suggestion that French Creole blood had been intermingled with that of blacks, Indians, and harlots, and by what they thought was the glorification of "free men of color" at their expense.

In fact, Cable found inspiration in both black and white Creole culture. Indeed Cable's writings—often in spite of themselves—are most convincing and moving when they simply describe the minute particulars of everyday French Creole life and the sensuous atmosphere of that existence. He disapproved, however, of the arrogant complacency, racism, and sexual hypocrisy of the Catholic Creole aristocrats, many of whose ancestors had once been inmates in French jails and whose fortunes derived from slave labor.

Lafcadio's public defense of Cable and his writings never wavered, but after Cable returned to New Orleans from his successful tour with Mark Twain, Lafcadio felt that his former collaborator had become somewhat distant toward him, while Cable felt Lafcadio was acting rude and hostile toward *him.* Their friendship never recovered from these reciprocal slights. And when Lafcadio heard that his journalist friend H. E. Krehbiel, the music critic for the New York *Herald,* had plans to write a book with Cable on Creole folksong (a collaboration he had originally encouraged), his feelings of sibling jealousy became all too obvious ("Here is the only Creole song I know of with an African refrain *that is still sung,*" he wrote Krehbiel; "—don't show it to C., it is one of *our* treasures") and made any possibility of reconciliation impossible.

Lafcadio would now complain privately about being "used" by "the great churchman" with his "awful faith . . . which to me represents an undeveloped mental structure." Yet he would continue to respect Cable's moral courage and folkloristic knowledge, as well as his early literary and critical works drawing on and bringing to life a culture (languorous, technologically backward, proud) whose values and language were disdained by the fast-moving, financially aggressive *Américains*. Even Cable confessed the regrets he felt on the passing of a truly distinctive world: "There are reasons—who can deny it?—why we should be glad that the schoolmaster is abroad in Louisiana, teaching English. But the danger is, that somewhere in the future lurks a day when the Creole will leave these lovable drolleries behind him, and speak our tongue with the same dull correctness with which it is delivered in the British House of Lords. May . . . that time be very far away!"

Lafcadio's work in the *Times-Democrat* attracted the attention of a missionary Catholic priest, Père Adrien Emmanuel Rouquette. Père Rouquette was born in 1813 to one of New Orleans's oldest Creole families. An adventurous child, Adrien ran away at the age of five to join the Choctaw Indians, but was "rescued" by his father. As a young man, he was sent overseas to study law in France. Returning to New Orleans, he again haunted the Choctaw woods, where, under the influence of Chateaubriand's 1801 novel *Atala,* he fell in love with an Indian girl named Oushola ("the Bird Singer"). Caught between parental disapproval and his own indecisiveness, Adrien delayed—and Oushola died of consumption. Heartbroken, he returned to finish his law studies, dropped out of university, led a life of dissipation, and became a writer. His first of three books of verse, *Les Savannes* (romantic descriptions of the Louisiana swamps), was praised by Sainte-Beuve and Thomas Moore, who called Rouquette "the Lamartine of America." Unable to accept "civilized" nineteenth-century life in Louisiana, Adrien entered the seminary to study for the priesthood, and was ordained in 1845. For fourteen years he officiated at St. Louis Cathedral, preaching eloquent and controversial sermons against slavery. Eventually he returned to live among his beloved Choctaw as a missionary—the last of the Blackrobe Fathers. His hair grew down to his shoulders, he spoke the Choctaw language, and he wore Indian dress except when celebrating the Mass.

By the time Lafcadio had arrived in New Orleans, Père Rouquette had been in the woods for almost twenty years. The priest admired Lafcadio's editorials and articles about Creole folklore and French literature and devised an ingenious way of introducing himself. He published a poem in Creole French in the Catholic paper *Le Propagateur,* certain that Lafcadio, who read all the local French papers, would see it. The verse, a kind of "personals notice," began:

> *To papa, li sorti péi-Anglé*
> *Mé to mama, li sorti ile la Gréce.*
> *Pour to vini oir moin, zami Boklé*
> *Li minnin toi, avek plin politesse.*

("Your papa came from England," writes Père Rouquette, "Your mama came from Greece./If you want to come visit me, my friend Buckley/Will bring you here with courtesy." The good Father then promises to receive "L.H." in his little house and show him what life in the woods is like.)

Lafcadio was astonished when he read the poem, and in spite of his well-known abhorrence of missionaries and the Catholic Church, his prejudice was overcome by his curiosity. He visited the priest, not in the woods, but in his tiny room at the Presbyter in New Orleans, where he spent entire nights smoking his pipe and conversing with the elderly Father about French poetry, Creole songs, and Choctaw music. Seeing the unmistakably heterodox, pantheistic inner lining of this good old soul's priestly garb, Lafcadio wrote an unreservedly enthusiastic review in the *Item* of Père Rouquette's *La Nouvelle Atala* (1879) and of the man himself:

We have before us the advance pages of a romance which we do not hesitate to term the most idyllic work in the literature of La.—a creation inspired by the Spirit of forest solitudes,—a prose poem melodious as an autumn wind chanting a language, mystic and unwritten, through woods of pine. Fresh and pure as that unfettered wind, fragrant as wild flowers, there is a strange charm about this story unlike anything perhaps, except the magic of Chateaubriand. . . .

None but one whose life had been passed in communion with nature and all her moods could have written such a book;—it seems to have the very odor of a pine forest; and on turning its pages a breeze from the prairie seems to aid the fingers of the reader.

Aside from the religious idea which permeates, like a leaven, the whole structure of the volume, *La Nouvelle Atala* offers a curious study from a purely literary point of view. It reflects the spirit of a life,—a most unique and strange life, such as will doubtless never be lived again in this country; the life of a missionary so enamoured with nature and solitude, and of the simple and healthy existence of those who call him Blackrobe Father, that he has become even as one of them, as an Indian appellation teaches us;—a priest whose temple is the forest, with the cloud-frescoed heaven for its roof, and for its aisles, the pillared magnificence of the pines,—whose God is the God of the wilderness, the Great Spirit over-shadowing the desert. . . .

Lafcadio and the Father inevitably had one too many arguments about Rouquette's phonetic system of writing Creole verse ("an abomination," Lafcadio would call it), about religious doctrine and the priest's fanatical arguments in favor of chastity, and about what he felt was Lafcadio's immoral way of life. They also must have had words about Rouquette's pseudonymously printed pamphlet attacking G. W. Cable's novel *The Grandissimes,* and describing its author as "a pert, waggish, flippant, some-what bold upstart, brazen-faced witling" who was "a High-Priest of Negro-Voudouism." The pamphlet uncharitably concluded with an insinuation, in French Creole dialect, that Cable participated in voodoo dances and fathered half-breed children.

From then on, Lafcadio, who was still a good friend of Cable's, never mentioned Père Rouquette's name or writings, either negatively or posi-tively, in any of his journalistic reviews or articles. In spite of the priest's defensive pride in his Creole ancestry, his lifetime commitment and de-votion to the "first" Louisianans made him, in Lafcadio's eyes, one of the most remarkable exemplars of the romantic life he had ever met.

In 1883, William D. O'Connor—ardent abolitionist poet, novelist, critic from New England, and great friend and defender of Walt Whitman—happened to read an anonymous essay credited to the New Orleans *Times-Democrat* about the French painter and illustrator Gustave Doré. He was so impressed by the essay that he dashed off a laudatory letter about it and its author to Page Baker, who passed the note on to the anonymous Lafcadio, who thus acquired a pen pal ("a rare literary friend," he called him). The correspondence between the two, who never met in person, lasted for five years.

Both men exchanged books and ideas, and assessed each other's tem-peraments. "I am quite curious about you," Lafcadio wrote O'Connor. "Seems to me you must be like your handwriting,—firmly knit, large, strong, and keen;—with delicate perceptions, (of course I know *that,* anyhow!) well-developed ideas of order and system, and great continuity of purpose and a disposition as level and even as the hand you write. If my little scraggy hand tells you anything, you ought to recognize in it a very small, erratic, eccentric, irregular, impulsive, variable, nervous disposition,—almost exactly your antitype in everything—except the love of the beautiful."

O'Connor, with his Irish warmth, critical exuberance, radical enthusiasms, and passionate sensibility, encouraged the usually reticent and wary Lafcadio to open himself up. One day in 1883, O'Connor sent Lafcadio a copy of *The Good Gray Poet,* his brilliant and polemical essay on *Leaves of Grass.* Lafcadio had a copy of Whitman's then-scandalous masterpiece in his library and had read the book many times, but always with a certain ambivalence because his Victorian sense of poetic form and *mesure* bristled at Whitman's looseness of line and at the "shagginess" and "Calibanishness" of the poet's expression. Throughout his life, Lafcadio sometimes damned Whitman, sometimes extolled him ("My idea of him is not consciously stable," he admitted), but he always admired "the rude nobility of the man." O'Connor's pamphlet forced Lafcadio to reevaluate Whitman—as if it brought out the expansive, Whitmanian part of himself. He wrote to O'Connor:

Your beautiful little book came like a valued supplement to an edition of *Leaves of Grass* in my library. I have always *secretly* admired Whitman, and would have liked on more than one occasion to express my opinion in public print. But in journalism this is not easy to do. There is no possibility of praising Whitman unreservedly in the ordinary newspaper, whose proprietors always tell you to remember that their paper "goes into respectable families," or accuse you of loving obscene literature if you attempt controversy. Journalism is not really a literary profession. The journalist of to-day is obliged to hold himself ready to serve any cause—like the condottieri of feudal Italy, or the free captains of other countries. If he can enrich himself sufficiently to acquire comparative independence in this really *nefarious* profession, then, indeed, he is able freely to utter his heart's sentiments and indulge his tastes, like that aesthetic and wicked Giovanni Malatesta whose life Yriarte has written.

I do not think that I could ever place so lofty an estimate upon the poet's work, however, as you give—although no doubt rests in my mind as to your critical superiority. I think that Genius must have greater attributes than mere creative power to be called to the front rank—the thing created must be beautiful; it does not satisfy me if the material be rich. I cannot content myself with ores and rough jewels. I want to see the gold purified and wrought into marvellous fantastic shapes; I want to see the jewels cut into roses of facets, or turned as by Greek cunning into faultless witchery of nude loveliness. And Whitman's gold seems to me in the ore: his diamonds and emeralds in the rough. Would Homer be Homer to us but for the billowy roar of his mighty verse—the perfect cadence of his song that has the regularity of ocean-diapason? I think not. And did not all the Titans of antique literature polish their lines, chisel their words, according to severest laws of art? Whitman's is indeed a Titanic voice; but it seems to me the voice of the giant beneath the volcano—half stifled, half uttered—roaring betimes because articulation is impossible.

Beauty there is, but it must be sought for, it does not flash out from hastily turned leaves: it only comes to one after full and thoughtful perusal, like a great mystery whose key-word may only be found after long study. But the reward is worth the pain. That beauty is cosmical—it is world-beauty;—there is something of the antique pantheism in the book, and something larger too, expanding to the stars and beyond. What most charms me, however, is that which is most earthy and of the earth. I was amused at some of the criticisms—especially that in the *Critic*—to the effect that Mr. Whitman might have some taste for natural beauty, etc., *as an animal has!* Ah! that was a fine touch! Now it is just the animalism of the work which constitutes its great force to me—not a brutal animalism, but a *human* animalism, such as the thoughts of antique poets reveal to us: the inexplicable delight of being, the intoxication of perfect health, the unutterable pleasures of breathing mountain-wind; of gazing at a blue sky, of leaping into clear deep water and drifting with a swimmer's dreamy confidence down the current, with strange thoughts that drift faster. Communion with Nature teaches philosophy to those who love that communion; and Nature imposes silence sometimes, that we may be forced to think:—the men of the plains say little. "You don't feel like talking out there," I heard one say: "the silence makes you silent." Such a man could not tell us just what he thought under that vastness, in the heart of that silence: but Whitman tells us for him. And he also tells us what we ought to think, or to remember, about things which are not of the wilderness but of the city. He is an animal, if the *Critic* pleases, but a human animal— not a camel that weeps and sobs at the sight of the city's gates. He is rude, joyous, fearless, artless—a singer who knows nothing of musical law, but whose voice is as the voice of Pan. And in the violent magnetism of the man, the great vital energy of his work, the rugged and ingenuous kindliness of his speech, the vast joy of his song, the discernment by him of the Universal Life—I cannot help imagining that I perceive something of the antique sylvan deity, the faun or the satyr. Not the distorted satyr of modern cheap classics: but the ancient and godly one, "inseparably connected with the worship of Dionysus," and sharing with that divinity the powers of healing, saving, and foretelling, not less than the orgiastic pleasures over which the androgynous god presided.

I see great beauty in Whitman, great force, great cosmical truths sung of in mystical words; but the singer seems to me nevertheless *barbaric*. You have called him a bard. He is! But his bard-songs are like the improvisations of a savage skald, or a forest Druid: immense the thought! mighty the words! but the music is wild, harsh, rude, primæval. I cannot believe it will endure as a great work endures: I cannot think the bard is a creator, but only a precursor—only the voice of one crying in the wilderness—*Make straight the path for the Great Singer who is to come after me!* . . . And therefore even though I may differ from you in the nature of my appreciation of Whitman I love the soul of his work, and I think it a duty to give all possible aid and recognition to his literary priesthood. Whatsoever you do to defend, to elevate, to glorify his work you do for the literature of the future, for the cause of poetical liberty, for the cause of mental freedom. Your book is doubly beautiful to me, therefore: and I believe it will endure to be consulted in future times, when men shall write the "History of the Literary Movement of 1900," as men have already written the *Histoire du Romantisme*.   ]

Dr. Rudolph Matas, a graduate of the College of Physicians and Surgeons at Tulane University, editor of the *New Orleans Medical and Surgical Journal,* and professor of surgery at Tulane Medical Department, sought out Lafcadio in 1882 after admiring for a long time his work on the *Times-Democrat* and inquiring of a journalist friend, "Who writes those wonderful things—translations, weird sketches, and remarkable editorials—in your paper?" The friend replied, "A queer little chap, very shy—but I'll manage for you to meet him."

"He was deeply interested in Arabian studies at that time," Matas commented about his first encounters with Lafcadio, "and I was able to give him some curious facts about the practice of medicine among the Arabs, which happened to be exactly what he was seeking. Not only did he read every book on Arabia which he could find, but he actually practiced the Arabic script, and he used to write me fantastic notes, addressing me as if I had been an Arab chief":

⟦ In the Name of the Most Merciful God!
ALI-BEN—ABU'L-HAZAM—ALKARSHI—BEN—NASIS—AL—MATAS
MOHAMMED—IBN—ACHMED—ALMARAKSHI—IBN AL MATAS.
Abdallah-Ibn—Achmed—Diaeddin (El Beithar ben Matas)
AbdurrahmanoMohammed ibn Ali ibn Achmed Al Hanisi Almatas
    God only Knows the Truth!
    God is the Strongest.

Dear Doctor:—I return, with sincere thanks, these Creole notes so kindly procured for me. They are well worth preserving for more scientific utilization than I am capable of. Verily, they may yet be found useful even as the samples of Ibn El-Beithar, greatest of Hispano-Moresque herbologists—perchance, for all thou knowest, some grave ancestor of thine—discoursing at once of metaphysics and of botanical mysteries,—of Allah and the Prophet's Camel, and of the human stomach,—healing the body with herbs, and the soul with beautiful teachings,—with sweet words odorous as the musk of the Tartar.
[Some Arabic]
May Allah make eternal thy memory, and the traces of thy passage through the desert of this world [Arabic signs].
May he give thee His strong help, and His salvation, perfect, eternal—perfumed with musk and with amber. And the gratitude of the Faithful. ⟧

Rudolpho—as Lafcadio called his multilingual friend—was twenty-two when he met the thirty-three-year-old writer, and "Leocadio"—as the doctor called him—became his patient (Matas treated a severe local inflammation of Lafcadio's good right eye that had caused him to become temporarily blind). Lafcadio called Matas "almost a brother," an "ideal confrère," and he was soon the writer's most trusted confidant in New Orleans. Uncharacteristically, Lafcadio felt able to discuss intimate details of his sexual and personal life during his nightly strolls through the Spanish Quarter with his unjudgmental, dispassionate companion. As Dr. Matas later described Lafcadio:

Both in taste and temperament he was morbid, and in many respects abnormal—in the great development of his genius in certain directions, and also in his limitations and deficiencies in other lines. His nature towered like a cloud-topping mountain on one side, while on others it was not only undeveloped—it was a cavity! I understood this better, perhaps, than others of his friends, knowing as I did the pathology of such natures, and for that reason our intercourse was singularly free and candid, for Hearn revealed himself to me with a frankness and unconventionality which would have startled another. I never judged him by conventional standards. I listened to the brilliant, erratic, intemperate outpourings of his mind, aware of his eccentricities without allowing them to blind me to the beauty and value of his really marvelous nature. For example, he would bitterly denounce his enemies—or fancied enemies—for he had an obsession of persecution—in language that was frightful to listen to—inventing unheard-of tortures for those whom he deemed plotters against him. Yet in reality he was as gentle and as tender-hearted as a woman—and as passionately affectionate. But there was an almost feminine jealousy in his nature, too, and a sensitiveness that was exaggerated to a degree that caused him untold suffering. He was singularly and unaffectedly modest about his work—curiously anxious to know the real opinion of those whose judgment he valued, on any work which he had done, while impatient of flattery or "lionizing." Yet with all his modesty he had, even in those days of his first successes, a high and proud respect for his work.

Matas welcomed Lafcadio into his Spanish Creole household and introduced him to his wife, who provided him with a wealth of information on Creole cooking (Lafcadio included many of her recipes in his book *La Cuisine Créole,* published in 1885) and folklore. She was especially knowledgeable about folk remedies, and passed along various cures for chills and fevers (tea prepared with the leaves of the pepper plant, snakeroot in whiskey, or cayenne peppers placed in one's shoes every day for nine days); for tetanus (a poultice of boiled cockroaches placed over the wound); for heart palpitations (teas made with asparagus, or wild sage, or parsley root); for nausea (the interior of a fowl's gizzard, boiled with tea); and for typhoid fever (cutting open a live pigeon and applying it to the patient's head).

Lafcadio remained close to Matas and his wife for several more years before the inevitable and seemingly gratuitous rupture took place. Until then, Lafcadio found in Rudolph Matas an ideal friend and a man of integrity and pride who, because of his Spanish blood, refused to fight in the Spanish-American War, and to whom Lafcadio once wrote: "I would rather have one line from you than sixty columns of notices."

Most Americans and Creoles had no contact with or interest in each other, and lived in their separate districts as if the others' quarter, in Lafcadio's words, "were a portion of Tibet or Patagonia." Lafcadio spent almost all of his time south of Canal Street in the Creole districts, and he was an unlikely participant in anything as "refined" as a salon. If it had not been for Mrs. A. C. Durno, whose house on Constance Street was a gathering place for the American literati of the city, Lafcadio would certainly have spent little time at her house, making "literary" small talk sitting on the arched veranda or in her parlour. For Lafcadio, *parlour* was one of the most obscene seven-letter words in the English language—as he made clear in an *Item* editorial:

¶ "Please step into the parlour, sir, and take a seat," has always been to us the most horrible condemnation to mental suffering that could be inflicted within a short time. We remember an experience of our own in this city some years ago. There was at that time a gentleman residing here whom we wished to see on a matter very important to our own private interests. We visited the house; and the servants of course said, "Please step into the parlour, etc." We stepped into the parlour. Through the dismal gloaming which filtered in through the shutters left ajar and the dark blinds between curtains as sombre as funeral hangings, we caught a glimpse of a chair, even as a man fallen overboard by night sometimes catches through the gloom the glimpse of a broken spar. After our eyes had become partially accustomed to the light, we beheld what we had beheld in many other dismal parlours, the awfully respectable furniture that is only used on state occasions;—the oil cloth piano cover;—the revolving stool on which the young lady sits to torture the instrument, while miserable young men sit around her torturing their brains what to say when she gets done;—the inevitable spittoon which is never spit into;—the chandelier which has never been lit since it was put up;—the frightful pictures in which we were unhappy enough to recognize attempted copies of something we had seen in the original;—the "oil-paintings" turned out by wholesale to the order of New York speculators;—the villainously featureless clock;—the abominable things in delft and plaster of Paris on the mantel-piece;—the card basket in which no cards are ever placed;—the books on the center table which no human being would care to read. We had no time to wait; we left with an apologetic message. Again we visited that house in a cheerful mood, and departed haunted by seven blue devils. Yea! a third time also we visited that house; and on this last occasion we did not dare to leave an apologetic message—it would have looked too ridiculous. We simply "folded our tents like Arabs and silently stole away"—until we got to the next corner. Then we ran, lest somebody might come after us and call us back into that nightmarish room. We never saw that gentleman. Rather than see him at the cost of remaining in such a parlour, we would prefer to give up the ghost without ever seeing him. We must conclude with the heartiest support of the *Telegraph's* suggestion, "Cut the parlour's throat, and give the hide to the children to romp in."   ("THAT PARLOUR!")]

It was in the Durno parlor, nonetheless, that Lafcadio found himself charmed by his "talented, unassuming, kind-hearted" hostess, and particularly fascinated by her nephew, Lieutenant Oscar Terry Crosby, a West Point graduate who had been detailed to New Orleans. Handsome, worldly, yet intellectual and sensitive, Crosby seemed to Lafcadio to be able to reconcile a life of the mind with a life of deeds in a manner quite inspiring. Only he could convince Lafcadio, cringing in a corner of the room, to enter into the midst of a gathering, where his conversational brilliance would dazzle all the guests. And it was Lieutenant Crosby who changed Lafcadio's life by talking to him enthusiastically one evening about the writings of Herbert Spencer, the English philosopher and social scientist who was attempting to apply the law and principle of evolution to all aspects of human life and to all branches of knowledge, including biology, psychology, and ethics. Crosby pressed upon Lafcadio his copy of Spencer's *First Principles*, about which Lafcadio shortly wrote to his friend William O'Connor: "A very positive change has been effected in my opinions by the study of Herbert Spencer. He has completely converted me away from all 'isms, or sympathies with 'isms: at the same time he has filled me with the vague but omnipotent consolation of the Great Doubt. I can no longer give adhesion to the belief in human automatism,—and that positive skepticism that imposes itself upon an undisciplined mind has been eternally dissipated in my case." To several friends, moreover, Lafcadio spoke of Spencer in ecstatic and apocalyptic terms as "the mind that could expound with equal lucidity, and by the same universal formula, the history of a gnat or the history of a sun" or as "the Writer of the New Bible, the Prophet of the New Religion, the Teacher of the Eternal Truth . . . inspired by the Spirit of the Universe, as in another Pentecost of Fire."

Reading Spencer's dry, colorless prose somehow provided Lafcadio with an ineffable vision of cosmic consciousness—much like his pantheistic epiphany when he was sixteen years old—and a quasi-Buddhistic sense of illumination that he attributed to the study of Spencer's *Synthetic Philosophy:* "A memory of long ago . . . I am walking upon a granite pavement that rings like iron, between buildings of granite bathed in the light of a cloudless noon. . . . Suddenly, an odd feeling comes to me, with a sort of tingling shock,—a feeling, or suspicion, of universal illusion. The pavement, the bulks of hewn stone, the iron rails, and all things visible, are dreams! Light, color, form, weight, solidity—all sensed existences—are but phantoms of being, manifestations only of one infinite ghostliness for which the language of man has not any word. . . ."

It was through Spencer, too, that Lafcadio now perceived the painful events of a deracinated life as part of a universal process leading the human species—if not necessarily the individual ego—toward a distant but beneficent end, and teaching a new reverence for all forms of faith. In Herbert Spencer, Lafcadio found a meaning and an intellectual support for his previous intuitions and feelings. And he would always be grateful to Lieutenant Crosby, the archetypal synthesis of brawn and brains, for provoking this revelation by playing the Angel Gabriel one evening in 1885 in a parlor in New Orleans.

Mrs. Margaret Courtney was the owner of a boardinghouse at 68 Gasquet Street. An Irish-American woman in her sixties, she provided Lafcadio with three meals a day starting in 1881 when he decided to abandon the Vieux Carré. He had lived in that district for four years, moving from one romantic but damp and decaying rooming house to another, falling prey to malarial fevers and other illnesses and eating at unwholesome neighborhood greasy spoons. "I am growing very weary of the Creole quarter," Lafcadio confessed, "and I think I shall pull up stakes and fly to the garden district where orange trees are, but where Latin tongues are not spoken."

In exchange for Creole charm, Lafcadio now found Irish warmth and caring. The nurturing Mrs. Courtney immediately took to this lonesome, eccentric writer with the trace of the brogue in his mellifluous speech. Lafcadio, who boarded a few blocks from the Courtney house, paid a dollar a day for her delicious home cooking, and in addition she sewed his shirts, darned his socks, bathed his often-irritated right eye with egg white, and even set up a little cubbyhole in the annex behind her house so that he could eat quietly and privately. (In order to be able to see and cut his food properly, Lafcadio had to sit with his good eye only a few inches from the plate, which caused him great embarrassment.) Mrs. Courtney also prepared meals for him before his occasional dinner engagements so that he could graciously forgo the main course in restaurants or at dining-room tables, saying that he really wasn't very hungry that evening, that a glass of wine would certainly do.

◄68 GASQUET►

Under Mrs. Courtney's regimen, Lafcadio gained weight and strength and became more resistant to colds and fevers. He had not experienced this kind of solicitous, motherly looking-after since his summertime childhood days with his nanny in Tramore more than twenty years before. So much did he enjoy the old-country atmosphere at Gasquet Street that he moved his few belongings—an old leather bag stuffed with clothes and an enormous wooden trunk containing his ever-growing library—into a rooming house on the corner of Robertson and Gasquet, the closest lodging to Mrs. Courtney's he could find.

Lafcadio lived in two small second-floor corner rooms. The larger one served as his monastic bedroom/study and was simply furnished with a single bed and mosquito netting, two chairs, and a trunk. Having no desk, Lafcadio used to place his suitcase on the edge of his trunk, in such a way that it could be tilted up and down as he wrote—his right eye following, at a distance of an inch or two, the purple calligraphic lines of ink his pen spun onto sheets of yellow paper.

Or if he wanted to read, Lafcadio would place his book, leverlike, on his suitcase, and engage in an early version of speed reading. As Dr. Matas described it: "While others read sentences, he read paragraphs, chapters— in the time it would take an ordinary reader to finish a chapter, he would have read the whole book. And this in spite of his defective vision. With his one great near-sighted eye roving over the page, he seemed to absorb the meaning of the author—to reach his thought and divine his message with incredible rapidity. . . . Swiftly as he read, it would be found on questioning him afterward that nothing worth while had been overlooked, and he could refer back and find any passage unerringly."

Lafcadio worked at the newspaper in the morning, wrote and read in the afternoon, and sometimes went for a swim in Lake Pontchartrain. Back in his rooms, he would put on a linen suit and one of his oversized fedora-type hats—making him look, as someone once said, like a giant mushroom—and stroll to Gasquet Street. The air was filled with the scent of magnolia and jasmine, and Lafcadio passed the cottages of the wanton district, in whose midst he lived, enticed by the sight of the "frails" and *horizontales* behind half-opened doors and shutters, readying themselves for the night ahead or sitting on their doorsteps and murmuring sweet nothings to the passing stranger, who arrived at Mrs. Courtney's in high spirits and with a large appetite.

Mrs. Courtney almost always found time to sit with Lafcadio up in his little annex cubbyhole, serve him his dinner, and cut the beefsteak or leg of mutton for him. When she was too busy to do so, her vivacious twelve-year-old daughter Ella gladly took her place. After the meal, Ella would beg Lafcadio to tell her one of his wonderful stories about goblins or Greek gods or mysterious, exotic places. So Lafcadio would sit on the doorstep of the annex, smoking his pipe, with Ella at his feet, and say: "This, Ella, is the tale Abu Mohammed el Hassan, son of Amr, recounted when he returned from one of his voyages":

[. . . A vessel returning from India, met with an accident on the way; and the captain found himself obliged to make for a certain little island, without any water and without any wood upon it. There the sailors discharged all the cargo, and the vessel remained there until the damages she had received were repaired. Then all the bales of merchandise were taken aboard again, and stored away; and everything was prepared for the voyage. Just about this time came the feast of Neurouz (New Year's); and the passengers determined to celebrate it on shore. For this purpose they brought to the beach all the old rags, palm leaves, and kindling they could find on board the ship; and with these they made a bonfire on the island. Suddenly the island trembled and quaked beneath their feet. Not being far from the water all were able to reach it, jump in and cling to the boats.

At the same moment, the island sank into the waves, producing so mighty an eddy in the ocean, that they narrowly escaped being carried down with it, and were only able to save their lives with the greatest difficulty. . . . Now that island was only a turtle sleeping at the surface of the sea; awakened by the scorching heat of the fire, it had dived down to save itself. . . .

These are very big fibs of course, Ella, but you must remember that old Arab captains had really seen very wonderful things and only exaggerated what they actually saw and heard.　　　　　　　　　　　　　　　]]

Mrs. Courtney sometimes came by and stood unobtrusively on the porch, listening to these Arabian sea-captain tales or to stories of Hindu deities. She would cross herself and exclaim, "Ah! and I pray God every night on my knees to make you a good Catholic, Mr. Hearn; and you an Irishman, too!" And chuckling, Lafcadio never put up an argument, saying, "I'm glad you pray to your God for me, Mrs. Courtney. Don't stop."

Between the main house and the annex was a courtyard much like the one in Edgar Degas' mysterious *Children on a Doorstep,* painted in 1872 when the artist came to New Orleans to visit his mother's family. In this work of browns and ochres, a young girl, like Ella, stares down dreamily from a porch at a cluster of children sitting in front of a courtyard, empty except for one small dog. But Mrs. Courtney's courtyard was inhabited by many creatures, among whom Lafcadio had a number of favored friends: a fearless tiny mouse who joined the writer for dinner and to whom he always provided a modest portion of his meal; an old turtle that he professed to have trained to come when it was called and to depart when it was bid adieu; a gray tabby kitten named Nanny that Lafcadio had saved from drowning. There was also a colony of ants that continually streamed from the house to the annex and back again, which he sometimes spent an hour silently observing, until Mrs. Courtney looked out of the kitchen window and asked, "And sure, is there anythin' botherin' you, Mr. Hearn?" "No, Mrs. Courtney," Lafcadio replied quietly, like a child in a trance; "I'm only watching the ants. They seem so superior to us. They never fight among themselves, or backbite, or loaf. They're always working, working for the common good of their community. At a second's notice they are willing to sacrifice their lives—everything—to the general welfare. People are not like this. The propriety and morality of the ant is far higher than that of the human."

Mrs. Courtney was by now used to the idiosyncrasies of her Irish young man . . . but ants? She had even noticed Lafcadio carefully pulling ants out of the sugar bowl, then releasing them onto the floor! And a few weeks later, she saw that Lafcadio had written a curious article entitled "News of Ants" in the *Times-Democrat:*

⟦ "He who shall eat an ant," says the *Talmud,* "shall be flogged five times with forty stripes save one." This would seem to have been inspired less by respect for the ant, than by the belief in its peculiar legal uncleanliness as a creeping thing, and especially as a scavenger. Still the wisest of Hebrew kings much respected ants, as more than one Oriental tradition tells us, and as His own words (Prov. xxx., 24) would indicate. These words referred especially to one of the most wonderful species of ants, The Harvesters, whom Sir John Lubbock treats of in his recent very curious books. The grain stores collected by this species are indeed so important that the Mishnic sages made Talmudic laws concerning them,—discussing at much length whether such stores belong by right rather to the gleaners or to the owner of the field, but paying little attention to the moral right of the ants. In all ages since men began to write books reference has been made to the wonderful intelligence and ingenuity of ants; but it is really only of late years that we have been able to learn the particulars of their curious life, and the degree of civilization to which they have arrived.

Huber is perhaps the most interesting of established authorities in this branch of entomology, so vast in itself;—it was largely from him that Michelet drew the materials for that strangely fascinating essay upon the Republic of the Ants, in *L'Insecte.* Huber's researches have also been popularized in many other ways since. But the subject is so huge, and so interesting, that every addition to its literature by a real scientist is merely as the addition of one paragraph to the first chapter of a colossal work to be yet written. Sir John Lubbock's new work contains few discoveries, but these are of uncommon importance, and his work has already excited entomologists in France and Germany.

To the public, of course, who have daily opportunities of observing the habits of these ubiquitous creatures, the most interesting portion of Sir John Lubbock's work will be that treating of the intelligence of ants. Whether he simply confirms the observations of others in this direction, or reveals himself as a pioneer, he is equally fascinating. The results of his experiences certainly deserve universal study.

We spoke above of the harvesting ants; but even those are common-place creatures enough compared with the Agricultural Ants of Texas, which the great entomologist tells us about. Michelet, speaking of the termites—erroneously termed White Ants—states that their civilization is superior to that of the aborigines of the countries they inhabit. Certainly as much might be said of the Agricultural Ants; for their civilization will compare very favorably with that of the most respectable Indian races who inhabited Texas. They clear spaces of ground around their little city, and appear to plant these spaces with ant-rice (*Aristida oligaultra*), a plant of which they are exceedingly fond. This they regularly harvest and store up. A very curious fact regarding all sorts of grain stores kept by ants is that the grains never germinate. The ants have discovered some secret method of preventing such germination, and science has not yet been able to wrest the secret from them. But just so soon as the grain is taken away from the ants it will germinate.

The relation between the ants and those helpless little green insects, the aphides, is generally well-known. The aphides are the milch cows of the ants, who keep them in herds. But what is not generally known is that the ants often build little cowsheds over them, and erect little mud walls around their pastures, and nurse their young, just as a cowherd attends to young calves. The ants always keep a supply of aphis-eggs on hand, and if the little republic is threatened with danger, the soldier ants keep the enemy back while the rest try to run away with their young and with their stock of aphis-eggs to a place of safety.

Nor is it generally known that besides the aphides the ants keep many other queer little creatures, some appear to be mere *pets,* the cats and dogs of ant-life. Others are blind beetles, which appear to furnish the ant with some kind of milk. These beetles have learned to beg for food just like pets. They tap the ants with their antennae in a peculiar way when they are hungry, and the ants feed them—putting the food into their mouths as we feed babies or kittens. Then there are also tiny little ants of a peculiar species, which bigger ants keep like little monkeys. These climb upon the shoulders of their masters and ride upon their backs when they go out. Sir John Lubbock has also discovered that ants have regular athletic amusements—Olympian or Pythian games.

Their slave systems are well known. Some species of red ants cannot live without slaves. In return for the services of the blacks they protect the latter against their enemies—make raids for them. Between master and slaves the kindliest relations appear to subsist. Whoever has read anything about ants knows these things. But what is far more novel and extraordinary is the discovery that this social system, this antique slave-republic, is founded upon a moral and civil law probably quite as sharply defined for the ants as the ancient social laws governing an Etruscan or Hellenic city. Mr. Grote has declared that no society can exist without a moral law; morality is a necessity of society. The ants have a very complicated society, and sound ethical principles. Their god, their idol, is of course their queen, upon whom the future of the community depends. As Lubbock's observations upon this matter extend over a period of seven years, they are probably the most perfect of the sort ever made.

Barbaric indeed are Assyrian monarchies of wasps and the Roman empires of bees compared with the Greek republics of the ants. In their communities, populous as the cities of Magna Græcia, the division of labor is perfect, the utmost order prevails, the least quarrel never occurs between brothers—even in a Sybaris or Crotona of 500,000 souls. They have their days of temple worship, too, their hours of merry orgies, their Isthmian or Pythian games. Each helps the other. A sick ant is nursed, a wounded ant is doctored, a drowned ant is pulled out of the water and revived.

But the laws of the community respecting strangers are severe as those of the antique city, according to the archæologist De Coulanges. A stranger is not allowed to enter the city, any more than in early times would a Spartan be permitted to obtain a citizenship in Athens. A friend, returned even from a long captivity, is recognized, honored and welcomed like Ulysses. Communities of the same race may make war, Sybaris may be destroyed by Crotona. There is no doubt that ants have a language. They convey news to each other. Sir John Lubbock tells us of many ways in which they may be made useful to man. He believes they make progress also—intellectual progress. Perhaps when the race of man has perished in some vast cataclysm, such as destroyed the monsters of geologic eras, some ants may found a new and peculiar civilization of their own.   ]

Mrs. Courtney had a nephew, Denny Corcoran, a former neighborhood gang leader who had once run away to the West Indies to escape a gang-related murder charge (of which he was subsequently acquitted). A pistol-toting, knife-wielding, three-hundred-pound street bully who made his living by keeping voters "in line" for the political bosses on election days,

Denny would frequently visit his aunt, who had a modicum of familial affection for her "bad, bad" nephew.

Chatting with Denny about his experiences in the West Indies, Lafcadio took an immediate liking to this rowdy but simple and ingenuous behemoth. ("I'd give all the brains in my head for the size and strength of your body," Lafcadio used to say, enviously, to Denny, like a teenage weakling wishing he were Charles Atlas or The Incredible Hulk.)

Soon Denny would come by his aunt's house once or twice a week after dinner to pick up his new friend for a night out on the town. "Don't let Mr. Hearn get into any trouble, Denny," Mrs. Courtney would say. "And be sure you don't leave him until you get back to his door!" And Denny would reassure her, saying, "Don't worry, Aunt Maggie, they'll do nuthin' to him until they get me!"

It was a dangerous neighborhood that Denny and Lafcadio walked through, with its nightly street murders and robberies; but formidable-

DENNY CORCORAN

looking bodyguard nobly protected vulnerable-looking companion as they made their way through the Wild Side and into the bawdy district, where Denny was remarkably familiar with the best and newest brothels. By law, the Cyprians of New Orleans were compelled to wear, at the minimum, "a shift and a pair of stockings." So in addition to ultradiaphanous shifts, the ladies of the night embellished their prosaic uniforms with multicolored high-heeled shoes and garter belts.

As the morbidly shy Lafcadio stood at a distance, his gregarious friend approached the decorative girls at the open doors of the various premises and chatted them up, then drew his companion inside toward the sound of music and laughter and the ever-present and overwhelming scent of patchouli.

Lafcadio depended upon Denny's sharp-eyed suggestions for his night-time paramour (for Denny knew that Lafcadio had a preference for dark-skinned Mediterranean or African women), then agreed to meet his Virgil of the Underworld at a certain hour in the smoke-filled parlor. Later, the slightly dazed comrades would leave the bawdy district, and, with Lafcadio holding on to Denny's arm, the unlikely twosome would stroll through the bumpy, gaslit streets in the cool early-morning breeze until they found a moonlit park and sat down on a bench under a magnolia tree. One can imagine a relaxed, inspired Lafcadio beginning to expound to the drowsy giant beside him about the relationship between sexuality and history, pointing out that without the influence of the former on the latter there could be no real greatness, since every noble mind is made fruitful by its virility.

"Are you following me, Denny?" Lafcadio asked, nudging the figure with half-closed eyes sitting next to him.

"Shoore, shoore, Mr. Hearn," he replied.

So the energized Lafcadio might have gone on to describe the difference between American and French literature, telling his comrade (who hardly knew how to read) that if he studied any first-rate American novel he would find that it was a mere report of facts and fancies in which love only appears as a drop of flavor sprinkled upon an otherwise vapid dish. But in a fine French romance, my friend, passion is the *motive* and its consequence, the *effect* as well as the cause, the *dish* as well as the flavor . . . and the least drop of that flavor has the intoxicating sweetness of Persian rose-essence!

Denny would nod occasionally, or nod off, especially on the odd night when he had taken a more than half-willing Lafcadio into an illicit opium den whose aftereffects may well have contributed to some of the dreamier, over-wrought descriptive passages that appeared occasionally in Lafcadio's work during this period (". . . Acres upon acres of silvered corpses with eyes plucked out;—overshadowing stratus-cloud of wings and claws and shrieking feathered throats! . . .").

Brothel-wise and down-to-earth, Denny sometimes forgot that his hyperimaginative companion could barely distinguish what "house" he was entering or what "beauty" he was admiring. A Don Quixote in the bawdy district, Lafcadio sometimes mistook a plain dark-eyed "wench" for his version of the Dulcinea del Toboso ("her forehead the Elysian fields, her eyebrows two celestial arches, her cheeks two beds of roses"). An embarrassed Don Lafcadio once confided to a friend:

You know, I'm afraid I made an awful fool of myself. Ten days ago I visited a house of harlotry and there I saw a most beautiful woman. Her face had a look of perfect innocence and her features were faultlessly Greek. She made a tremendous impression on me. I did not believe that a woman could influence me so much. I looked at her with reverence, and I left before I had hardly touched her hand. But when I went home her face dogged me—I could not get her look of perfect innocence out of my mind. I could not sleep. I sat down and wrote a letter. I told her how much I suffered to see her in such surroundings, and I knew it was against her will that she was forced into such a life. I offered her my help, money, everything I had, to assist her to escape and to start afresh in another existence better suited to the woman she really was. I phrased it as delicately and considerately as I knew how. I could not have shown a queen more deference. And now I have just found out—she laughed when she got it and read it to the other girls mid screams of merriment. They took it as a joke and it didn't stop there. My letter has been travelling from hand to hand through the whole district.   ]

But Lafcadio's loyal squire never made fun of his nearsighted and brainy mate: "Mr. Hearn," said Denny, "he loved statues and, beggin' yer pardon, de nooder de better, and he offen sit in de park and tell me about 'em. I didn't know nuthin' he was talkin' about, but I loved him."

CHAPTER 6

In the Shadow
of the Ethiopian

A T T H E E N D of his destitute first year in New Orleans, Lafcadio had assured Henry Watkin that he had been "an awfully good boy . . . and have no news to tell you of amours or curious experiences. . . . No one could lead a more monastic life than I have done here. . . . For a year [the Raven] hath not smoked a cigar; and Its morals are exemplary. . . . It has seen little of wine and women in this city."

Even after he became the assistant editor of the *Item,* he confessed to Watkin:

❲ I never felt so funny in my whole life. I have no ambition, no loves, no anxieties,—sometimes a vague unrest without a motive, sometimes a feeling as if my heart was winged and trying to soar away, sometimes a vague longing for pleasurable wanderings, sometimes a half-crazy passion for a great night with wine and women and music. But these are much like flitting dreams, and amount to little. . . .

Life here is so lazy,—nights are so liquid with tropic moonlight,—days are so splendid with green and gold,—summer is so languid with perfume and warmth,—that I hardly know whether I am dreaming or awake. It is all a dream here, I suppose, and will seem a dream even after the sharp awakening of another voyage, the immortal gods only know where. Ah! Gods! beautiful Gods of antiquity! One can only feel you, and know you, and believe in you, after living in this sweet, golden air. What is the good of dreaming about earthly women, when one is in love with marble, and ivory, and the bronzes of two thousand years ago? Let me be the last of the idol-worshippers, O golden Venus, and sacrifice to thee the twin doves thou lovest,—the birds of Paphos,—the Cytheridae!   ]

Not long afterward, however, Lafcadio's feverish dream became reality, and he was engaging in the "Works of Aphrodite" with the Cyprians of New Orleans—those guest-loving ladies of the night with whom he felt so at ease. Under the heady influence of Aphrodite, Lafcadio's self-admitted "meanness," "suspiciousness," and "melancholy" gave way—at least temporarily—to an often rhapsodic acceptance of sexuality. To W. D. O'Connor he wrote:

[I do not find it possible to persuade myself that the "mad excess of love" should not be indulged in by mankind. It is *immemorial* as you say; —Love was the creator of all the great thoughts and great deeds of men in all ages. I felt somewhat startled when I first read the earliest Aryan literature to find how little the human heart had changed in so many thousand years;—the women of the great Indian epics and lyrics are not less lovable than the ideal beauties of modern romance. All the great poems of the world are but so many necklaces of word-jewelry for the throat of the *Venus Urania;* and all history is illuminated by the *Eternal Feminine,* even as the world's circle in Egyptian mythology is irradiated by Neith, curving her luminous woman's body from horizon to horizon. And has not this "mad excess" sometimes served a good purpose? I like that legend of magnificent prostitution in Perron's *Femmes Arabes,* according to which a battle was won and a vast nomad people saved from extinction by the action of the beauties of the tribe, who showed themselves unclad to the hesitating warriors and promised their embraces to the survivors, —of whom not over-many were left. Neither do I think that passion necessarily tends to enervate a people. There is an intimate relation between Strength, Health, and Beauty; they are ethnologically interlinked in one embrace,—like the *Charities.* I fancy the stout soldiers who followed Xenophon were far better judges of physical beauty than the voluptuaries of Corinth;—the greatest of the exploits of Heracles was surely an amorous one. I don't like Bacon's ideas about love: they should be adopted only by statesmen or others to whom it is a duty to remain passionless, lest some woman entice them to destruction. Has it not sometimes occurred to you that it is only in the senescent epoch of a nation's life that love disappears?—there were no grand loves during the enormous debauch of which Rome died, nor in all that Byzantine orgy interrupted by the lightning of Moslem swords. . . . Again, after all, what else do we live for—ephemeræ that we are? Who was it that called life "a sudden light between two darknesses"? "Ye know not," saith Krishna, in the *Bhagavad-Gita,* "either the moment of life's beginning or the moment of its ending: only the middle may ye perceive." It is even so: we are ephemeræ, seeking only the pleasure of a golden moment before passing out of the glow into the gloom. Would not Love make a very good religion? I doubt if mankind will ever cease to have faith—in the aggregate; but I fancy the era *must* come when the superior intelligences will ask themselves of what avail are the noblest heroisms and self-denials, since even the constellations are surely burning out, and all forms are destined to melt back into that infinite darkness of death and of life which is called by so many different names. Perhaps, too, all those myriads of suns are only golden swarms of ephemeræ of a larger growth and a larger day, whose movements of attraction are due to some "mad excess of love."

And to his strict, Methodist-raised friend Henry Edward Krehbiel —music critic of the Cincinnati *Gazette* and, later, of the New York *Herald*— Lafcadio wrote an astonishingly frank letter:

My dear Krehbiel,—Pray remember that your ancestors were the very Goths and Vandals who destroyed the marvels of Greek art which even Roman ignorance and ferocity had spared; and I perceive by your last letter that you possess still traces of that Gothic spirit which detests all beauty that is not beautiful with the fantastic and unearthly beauty that is Gothic.

You cannot make a Goth out of a Greek, nor can you change the blood in my veins by speaking to me of a something vague and gnostic and mystic which you deem superior to all that any Latin mind could conceive.

I grant the existence and the weird charm of the beauty that Gothic minds conceived; but I do not see less beauty in what was conceived by the passion and poetry of other races of mankind. This is a cosmopolitan art era: and you must not judge everything which claims art-merit by a Gothic standard. . . .

Now I am with the Latin; I live in a Latin city;—I seldom hear the English tongue except when I enter the office for a few brief hours. I eat and drink and sleep with members of the races you detest like the son of Odin that you are. I see beauty here all around me—a strange, tropical, intoxicating beauty. I consider it my artistic duty to let myself be absorbed into this new life, and study its form and color and passion. And my impressions I occasionally put into the form of the little fantastics which disgust you so much, because they are not of the Æsir and Jötunheim. Were I able to live in Norway, I should try also to intoxicate myself with the Spirit of the Land, and I might write of the Saga singers—

> From whose lips in music rolled
> The Hamavel of Odin old,
> With sounds mysterious as the roar
> Of ocean on a storm-beat shore.

The law of true art, even according to the Greek idea, is to seek beauty wherever it is to be found, and separate it from the dross of life as gold from ore. You do not see beauty in animal passion;—yet passion was the inspiring breath of Greek art and the mother of language; and its gratification is the act of a creator, and the divinest rite of Nature's temple. ∄

When Elizabeth Bisland published her *Life and Letters of Lafcadio Hearn* in 1906, she substituted the word "converse" for the word "sleep" in Lafcadio's comment to Krehbiel that "I eat and drink and sleep with members of the races you detest. . . ." A half-century later, even Elizabeth Stevenson's meticulously researched biography of the writer has Lafcadio "conversing" with his tropical sirens—as if his passional life in New Orleans were nothing more than an early version of *Ma Nuit Chez Maude*.

After Lafcadio's death, a sardonic H. E. Krehbiel wrote one of their mutual friends about how he had sent a letter to Elizabeth Bisland Wetmore to illustrate "a Hearn characteristic," and in it recounted to her "the story of how [Lafcadio] and Jerry [Jere Cochran, a reporter on the Cincinnati *Commercial*] had gone to a whorehouse, and agreed to be downstairs at a certain time, but H. not showing up, J. got impatient and went to his room where he found Hearn with his girl, she naked in the middle of the floor, he walking around and around her, his one eye six inches from her, admiring her fine lines. Mrs. W. only laughed and said that was reasonable,—it went to prove that Hearn's interest in Negro women was purely aesthetic. The little beast! (H., not Mrs. W.!)."

In fact, all of Lafcadio's American and English biographers have attempted, in one way or another, to deny, conceal, or repudiate the writer's sexual proclivities—this in spite of the comment by Julia Wetherall, Page Baker's sister-in-law, that Lafcadio "was a man of strongly sensual nature, and made no pretence of leading an ideal life." (As if a sensual nature precluded an ideal life!)

Albert Mordell asserts, for example, that the writer's enormous journalistic output—including his numerous French and Spanish translations—and wide range of intellectual interests "prove he did not have much leisure time for dissipation or low company." And E. L. Tinker describes what he sees as Lafcadio's "queer burst of gaiety" upon being introduced to one of New Orleans's unique social institutions, the quadroon ball.

Before the war, the city's rich young white men flocked to these gala affairs to mingle with the girls whom an English visitor at that period described as "the most beautiful he had ever seen" with their "full, dark, liquid eyes, lips of coral, teeth of pearl, sylph-like features, and such beautifully rounded limbs and exquisite gait and manners that they might furnish models for a Venus or a Hebe."

Making a dutiful appearance at the rival (and staid) fetes for the white belles of New Orleans, which often took place on the same evenings as the quadroon galas, the debonair Lotharios would then rush off to the quadroon festivities, which were attended by elegant courtesans in Parisian headdresses and radiantly colored gowns and by quadroon and octoroon girls, thirteen and fourteen years of age, hoping to be "placed" under the protection of a rich young man—a planter's son, perhaps. And when such a desirable young man singled out his chosen mistress, he would approach the girl's mother (in attendance as a chaperone), and make an arrangement with her to establish a home for her daughter in the Vieux Carré's quadroon quarter (near the Ramparts below Orleans Street), as well as to provide her with an allowance, money for the Parisian education of his male offspring, a legacy in case of his own death, and a cash settlement in the event of his probable legal marriage to a "proper" New Orleans white girl.

With the impoverishment of the postwar New Orleans Creole aristocracy and the racially and sexually more restrictive ways of the Yankee "colonizers," the quadroon ball lost most of its glamour and acceptability. The event Lafcadio attended in an old manor on Bienville Street was one of the last of its kind and was organized by a noted New Orleans procuress named Hermina. (Years before, Marie Laveau had hosted much more lavish balls in her Maison Blanche bordello.) Indifferent to the institution's fall from grace, Lafcadio was swept off his feet by the girls, the music, the atmosphere of the affair.

Writing in 1924, the usually open-minded E. L. Tinker, commenting on Lafcadio's behavior at this ball, asks: "What explanation can there be of this timid, shrinking, sensitive soul suddenly blossoming forth as a forward squire of dames, and dames, at that, whose complexion ran from dull gold to soft cream? Of course the obvious one is that the man's frank sensuousness was strong enough to dominate all his other traits; but a more subtle and more likely explanation lies in certain of his psychological peculiarities. He was mentally incapable of adapting himself to the ordinary conditions of life and coping with them successfully. Psychiatrists would have classed him, today, under the heading of 'Defective Personality.' "

Nina Kennard in her 1912 biography bewails the "depths" to which Lafcadio sank in the "episode" with Mattie Foley, a fall the author attributes to her subject's "unbalanced mental equipment," since his "brain was abnormal by inheritance. . . . The fancy for mulattos, Creoles, and Orientals, which he displayed all his life," Kennard explains, "is most likely to be accounted for as an inheritance from his Arabian and Oriental ancestors on his mother's side. He but took up the dropped threads of his barbaric ancestry." And thus, Kennard states emphatically, "on sifting all available evidence there is no doubt that while doing reporter's work for the *Enquirer* he fell under the 'Shadow of the Ethiopian.' "

Lafcadio's consistently bigoted biographers all agree, in the words of Elizabeth Stevenson, that he "could not be quite normal in his relations with those of the other sex whom he thought his equals and whom he was most desperately anxious to please. He was sure he could not please, so his practice was to back off like an awkward crab or to exaggerate deference to the point of caricature. It was only sometimes with women of an entirely different background that he could forget that he was not acceptable." Or, as some other commentators (Drs. Cohn and Deutsch in their biography of Rudolph Matas) have less reticently postulated, Lafcadio, unable to enter into normal human contacts, sought friendships with "dwellers in dives," since only "in the presence of such social inferiors as the cribhouse prostitutes was the burden eased." He was even said to have had a sexual escapade either with the Queen of Voodoo herself—even though Marie Laveau when Lafcadio met her was in her eighties, withered, frail, and unable to move from her rocking chair—or with her fifty-odd-year-old daughter Marie, a possible but unsubstantiated liaison.

After his eye accident when he was a teenager, Lafcadio certainly felt he was deformed and unattractive. Julia Wetherall reports that "when told that a young woman had said she had expected to find Mr. Hearn a bent and withered scholar and was surprised to find him a fine-looking, vigorous man, he replied bitterly that she was probably ridiculing him." His self-image was as fragile as his sensitivities were pregnable. Yet Elizabeth Bisland found his head "quite remarkably beautiful," and Julia Wetherall thought his profile "handsome."

Years earlier in Cincinnati, Mrs. Ellen Freeman, the forty-one-year-old wife of a prominent physician, had fallen hopelessly in love with the twenty-six-year-old writer. At first, Lafcadio was flattered by her correspondence, to which he responded with his own series of letters, the first evidence of his remarkable epistolary abilities. To the overardent Mrs. Freeman he wrote: "I am not by nature cold,—quite the reverse, indeed, as many a bitter experience taught me; and I beg you to attribute my manner rather to overcaution than to indifference to the feelings of others. Why, do we not all wear masks in this great carnival mummery of life, in which we all dance and smile disguisedly, until the midnight of our allotted pleasure time comes; and the King-Skeleton commands, 'Masks off—show your skulls'?"

Lafcadio was involved with Mattie at the time, yet Mrs. Freeman would not simply accept the platonic relationship that was all Lafcadio offered her. Confiding in Henry Watkin, who told her she was obsessed with a phantom, she made a bizarre request: she begged Watkin to put Lafcadio to sleep with a sedative so that she could come to his bed, look at his face, wrap him in a silk quilt, hold his head in her arms, then leave quietly before he awoke. This was rejected by the appalled printer ("A fine healthy woman, in the prime of life . . . and yet indulging a sickly sentimentality, that could only be looked for in a simple school girl of seventeen"), and Lafcadio himself was finally driven to take harsh measures to reject her.

In response to a photograph of herself that Ellen Freeman sent to him, Lafcadio wrote a final missive to her—a shockingly cruel and misogynistic tirade that reveals an almost violently insensitive aspect of Lafcadio's character:

⟦ I do not like the picture at all,—in fact I cannot find words to express how much I dislike it.

You were never physically attractive to me; you are neither graceful, and you evidently know nothing of the laws or properties of beauty. Otherwise you could not have sent me such a picture, as it could only disgust me.

Whatever liking I have had for you, it has never been of such a picture as that. It is unutterably coarse and gross and beefy. It is simply unendurable.

Not that I object to low dresses—or even to utter absence of dress, when the unveiling reveals attractions which the eye of the artist loves as something shapely and beautiful. I have an instinctive and cultivated knowledge of what physical beauty is, and anything in direct violation of my taste and knowledge—like your picture—simply sickens me. I have studied every limb and line in the bodies of fifty young women, and more; and know what form is and beauty is. You must not think me a fool. You are a fine woman in regard to health and strength; you are not handsome or even a tolerably goodlooking woman physically, and your picture is simply horrible, horrible.

This is plain speaking; but I think it is necessary for you. You cannot make yourself physically attractive to me. I am an artist, a connoisseur, a student of beauty, and it is very hard to please me.

Don't disgust me, please—

Yours truly,

L. Hearn ⟧

Julia Wetherall once commented that Lafcadio "was not fond of conventionality, and shrank with misgiving from ladies who must be addressed in terms of 'polite conversation.' " (His horror of the "parlour.") Lafcadio himself complained that "the churches, the societies, the organizations, the cliques, the humbugs are all working against the man who tries to preserve independence of thought and action. Outside of these one cannot obtain a woman's society, and if obtained one is forever buried in the mediocrity to which she belongs." Presented with a woman of Mrs. Ellen Freeman's class or the proper young Southern women with

their polished *bons mots,* Lafcadio immediately made his excuses and
headed for the bordello, an institution created not just for "defective personalities" like himself (and French writers like Flaubert, Baudelaire,
Sainte-Beuve, *et. al.*) but for a defective social and sexual order that rigidly
defined people's morals for them. (Said William Blake: "Consider this, O
mortal Man, O worm of sixty winters . . . /Consider Sexual Organization
& hide thee in the dust.") The real reason, however, for the biographers'
Sturm und Drang about Lafcadio's morals is not so much that he
frequented the bawdy district but that given the choice between a fair-
skinned woman and a dark-skinned woman, he inevitably and instinctively chose the latter.

Lafcadio may have considered it his "artistic duty," as he told Henry
Krehbiel, "to let myself be absorbed into this new life, and study its form
and color and passion"—just as Walt Whitman had once admitted,
"Doubtless I could not have perceived the universe, or written one of my
poems, if I had not freely given myself to comrades, to love." But Whitman had been dismissed from his job at the Indian Affairs Bureau in
Washington, D.C., on account of his "outrageous and offensive" homo-
erotic verse; and Lafcadio had been fired from the Cincinnati *Enquirer* for
his marriage to his "Ethiopian." Such a life was not without its perils in
the U.S.A.

Visiting America in 1833, the English writer E. S. Abdy stated: "As for
the bugbear of amalgamation about which so much is said as to sicken
every European who visits this country, the only question he will ask
himself when he sees its effect everywhere from Maine to Mexico is, will
it be brought about by marriage or concubinage? Shall the future occu-
pants of the New World owe their existence to virtue or to vice?"

The answer was: to "vice"—and to hypocrisy and bigotry, as antimiscegenation and other laws restricting the rights of blacks and free men
and women of color began to multiply in Louisiana under American rule.
The end of the war would not make much difference in the status quo
for women of mixed blood. As the Englishwoman Fanny Kemble wrote
in 1863, "In New Orleans a class of unhappy females exists whose mingled blood does not prevent their being remarkable for their beauty and
with whom no *gentleman* in that city shrinks from associating." But if
Lafcadio had become seriously involved with one of these women—or if
his nighttime escapades with Denny Corcoran had gained wide cur-
rency—he would have become a social pariah in racially segregated New
Orleans and would have again lost his job, as well as many of his friends.
(As he wrote to Watkin in November 1877: ". . . you cannot imagine how

utterly the news of that thing [his marriage to Mattie] would ruin me here. . . . The prejudice here is unutterably bitter, and bottomlessly deep. . . .")

Walt Whitman was "cautious" and "furtive" in making clear his feelings for his beloved "roughs." Emily Dickinson advised: "Tell all the truth but tell it slant." Which is what Lafcadio did, particularly in the rhetorically subtle and charming editorial he wrote for the *Item* in 1878, a little masterpiece of equivocation in which the "golden" Aphrodite ends up with the dark hazel eyes of the South:

The *Picayune* of Sunday contained a pretty translation (by "Q") of some Spanish fancies in regard to blondes and brunettes—discussing the character of the fair woman as compared with the dark woman, rather than the respective physical charms of the contrasting types. The author, himself a Spaniard, ventures at last to express his preference for the darker style of beauty, and his decision is commendably loyal, and well supported by the opinions of poets and of artists.

Yet how much remains to be said in favor of the fair woman! The Greeks, who were surely master-judges of beauty, made fair the limbs and the locks of their marble divinities; and even in these years women have maddened in the presence of an antique Apollo, because the old gods could not or would not repeat the miracle of Pygmalion and transform polished marble to palpitating flesh. Was not Venus called "the Golden"? The artists of antiquity gilded her hair. The locks of Phœbus were bright and flamboyant, as became the lord of the Sun. Aurora was fair-tressed and pink-fleshed, and twelve of the Horæ were as—

"Daughters of Sunrise, shaped of fire and snow."

Most of the glorious old gods were represented with golden hair; and the dainty flesh tints given to their statues are supposed to have been tints of exceeding fairness. For the fair beauty surely comes nearest to our ideal of divinity—a loveliness typical of light and life and immortality—a comeliness as of golden summer and golden suns. We can imagine a seraph only with tresses of waving light and radiant limbs! and fancy most readily realizes the Angel in the blonde woman. We might picture Lilith as a brunette; but Eve we dare not think of save as the loveliest of blondes—a blonde as "blonde as wheat"—blonde as Rowena or Elfrida.

Semiramis, Cleopatra, Faustina, Zenobia, Esther, Messalina, were brunettes; yet fairness seems to us more queenly than olivaceous darkness. Phryne and Rhodope were fair; but were not Laïs and Thaïs and Archianassa and many others brunettes? Laïs was a model for Apelles; but Phryne alone dared in her own person to personify Venus Anadyomene before all Eleusis.

Perhaps we feel more reverence for blonde beauty not only because it seems a reflection of celestial loveliness, but because it bears with it the suggestion of force and will and strength and royalty. It is the beauty of the Druidess and of the Viking's daughter—the glory of the North, cold, fresh, strong, and immortal. It may be cold as the beauty of an ice crystal; but it has the supernatural radiance of auroral lights.

White beauty inspires awe, like the calm beauty of the gods. Dark beauty—save in the purest Oriental types—inspires only love. Men might pray, like Kingsley's Viking, that a fair-haired beauty would honor them by trampling upon them. But unless the darker beauty own the falcon eyes and delicate aquiline nose of Balkis, Queen of Sheba, "perfect love casteth out fear."

The beauty of the North seldom inspires affection unmixed with awe. It is the charm of the priestess of Freya—the charm of the sorceresses of Scandinavia. When Venus appeared to Anchises as a Greek maiden, he feared not to embrace her; but his knees smote together with fear when the goddess became divinely fair, and her dark curls "kindled into sunny rings." The beauty of the North is a witchery.

When gazing into black eyes, one finds depth and softness and sweetness; but the depth is vague and lost in shadows of mystery. You can penetrate only so far and no further into the soul. But the northern blue or gray eye is more mysterious and unfathomable in the deeps of its transparency. Beyond the cool surface of amethyst or night-blue shines a deep of deeps, illimitable as Space, interminable as Time. The dark eye intoxicates like Cyprian wine; but the gray eye, like hasheesh, makes giddy the soul, as though leaning over the verge of Eternity, beyond the fields of stars and the courses of the comets.

The poets have spoken but timidly of blonde beauty; they have spoken with enthusiasm of that comeliness which blends Moresque grace with Gothic strength, the beauty which is Spanish. They have sung much of the Orient, and the flowers of the seraglio, and the bayadères of Hindoostan. Perhaps they might have sung more of the fair woman, but that they are overawed by her as by the splendor of a Statue of Snow. Had Godiva been a brunette we might have known more about her.

All the most famous canticles of love have been devoted to the darker

types of beauty—the ebon hair and velvet eye and olive tint of the brunette—that tender brown tint which suggests the color-tone of antique
marbles mellowed by time. The greatest of love songs is Solomon's song
of the Sulamitess—or the song of songs; and the Sulamitess was a brunette. "I am black but beautiful, O ye daughters of Jerusalem, as the tents
of Kedar—or as the curtains of Solomon."

It is the beauty of the eyes of the Sulamitess which is praised by
Solomon, above all her other charms—more even than "the stature like
unto a palm-tree"—"the neck like unto a tower of ivory"—or the little
white teeth, "like a flock of sheep which cometh up from the shearing,
whereof every one beareth twins, and none is barren among them." For
the dark eye is the eye of love itself—surely the eyes of Eros were dark.
It is the eye of the gazelle, the fawn, the dove, "Thou art all fair, my
beloved, thou art all fair; thou hast dove's eyes. . . .

"O my dove that art in the clefts of the rock, in the secret hiding-
places of the stairs, let me see thy face, let me hear thy voice, for sweet
is thy voice, and thy countenance is comely! . . .

"Eyes like the eyes of doves by the river's waters, washed with milk."
So sang Solomon, even before any one knew the additional enchantment
of a dark eye shining beneath a mantilla or flashing from behind a fan.

And our Spanish gentleman's gallant preference for the dark eye is half
shared by ourselves. Cold Athena had golden hair and gray eyes; but
Venus may have had eyes of golden hazel under her bright hair—that
liquid, limpid, languishing Southern hazel, which always demands love
and always obtains it.   ("FAIR WOMEN AND DARK WOMEN")]

Ten years later, while living in another country and no longer bound
by the South's legal or social constraints with regard to race, Lafcadio
unequivocally spoke his mind about this subject, making it clear that, in
some sense, his attraction to the "darkness" of women was a function of
his dislike of the "fairness" of Western civilization:

[And now I will presume to express my opinion about another heresy,
—that a white skin is most beautiful. I think it is the *least* beautiful. The
Greeks never made a *white* statue,—they were always painted. . . .

But to appreciate the beauty of colored skins, it is not simply enough
to travel,—one must become familiar with the sight of them through

months and years. (So strong our prejudices are!) And at last when you perceive there are human skins of real gold (living statues of gold, with *blue hair,* like the Carib half-breeds!),—and all fruit tints of skins,—orange, and yellow, and peach-red, and lustrous browns of countless shades;— and all colors of metal, too,—bronzes of every tone,—one begins to doubt whether a white skin is so fine! . . .

Now for jet-black,—the smooth velvety black skin that remains cold as a lizard under the tropical sun.

It seems to me extremely beautiful. If it is beautiful in Art, why should it not be beautiful in Nature? As a matter of fact, it *is,* and has been so acknowledged even by the most prejudiced slave-owning races.

Either Stanley—or Livingstone, perhaps—told the world that after long living in Africa the sight of white faces produced something like fear. (And the Evil Spirits of Africa are white.)—Well, even after a few months alone with black faces, I have felt that feeling of uncomfortableness at the sight of white faces. Something ghostly, terrible seemed to have come into those faces that I never even imagined possible before. I felt for a moment *the black man's terror of the white.* At least I think I partly realized what it was.

You remember the Romans lost their first battles with the North through sheer fear. *Oculi caerulii et truces,—rutilae comae,—magna corpora!*—The fairer,—the weirder,—the more spectral,—the more terrible. Beauty there is in the North, of its kind. But it is surely not comparable with the wonderful beauty of color in other races.

(TO BASIL HALL CHAMBERLAIN, MARCH 6, 1894)]

miss Bisland's
Creole Chaperone

CHAPTER 7

The Man Who
Loved Islands

AS CAPTIVATING and enticing as he often found New Orleans, Lafcadio occasionally longed for the "voices of birds, whisper of leaves, milky quivering of stars, laughing of streams, odors of pine and of savage flowers, shadows of flying clouds, winds triumphantly free."

In 1883 he convinced *Harper's Weekly* to let him explore the southern shore of Lake Borgne—just east of New Orleans, and flowing into Chandeleur Sound—with its "shuddering reeds and banneretted grass," out of which rose, on slender supports, the strange houses of the isolated Tagalog fishermen (who were originally from Luzon in the Philippines). That same year he also traveled for the *Times-Democrat* into the Teche country (the Southern Louisiana bayou that served as the setting for Longfellow's *Evangeline*) to describe its astonishing world of Spanish moss:

It streams from the heads and limbs of the oaks; from the many-elbowed cypress skeletons it hangs like decaying rags of green. It creates suggestions of gibbets and of corpses, of rotten rigging, of the tattered sails of ships "drifting with the dead to shores where all is dumb." Under the sunlight it has also countless pleasant forms—the tresses of slumbering dryads, the draperies flung out upon some vast woodland-holiday by skill of merry elves. Under the moon, losing its green, every form of goblinry, every fancy of ghastliness, every grimness of witchcraft, every horror of death, are mocked by it. . . . It is as though this land were yet weeping for Pan,—as though all the forests and streams had not ceased after more than a thousand years to lament the passing away of the sylvan gods and nymphs of the antique world.   ]

In the summer of 1884 Lafcadio, exhausted from overwork and from mild but recurrent bouts of an enervating malarial fever, took a month's paid vacation—his first as a working journalist—on a little island at the mouth of Caminada Bay in the Gulf of Mexico called Grand Isle. Arriving at a former Creole plantation that was now a hotel (Krantz's Hotel), Lafcadio threw his bag into his whitewashed cabin and then walked quickly to the beach where, like a child of the sea, he gave himself over to the gusting winds, the pounding waves, the sparkling light, the azure-golden air. He had not seen the sea since his arrival in America.

With the "hymns of winds and sea" and the "prayers of birds" in his ears, Lafcadio went swimming three or four times a day, sometimes starting out before dawn to view "the blossoming of the vast and mystical Rose of Sunrise" and letting the "Soul of the Sea" mingle with his own, vivifying, strengthening, and inspiring him.

When he wasn't at the beach, Lafcadio, assiduously avoiding the hotel guests, ingratiated himself with some of the local inhabitants of Grand Isle—a population of several hundred, mostly descendants of the pirates of Barataria Bay who spoke to Lafcadio in a slow, guttural French and occasionally invited him into their weatherbeaten cottages.

His favorite acquaintance was a Basque fisherman who entertained his inquisitive guest in his enormous living room filled with suspended nets and tackles, a marine clock and compass. In this shiplike ambiance, the Basque regaled Lafcadio with stories of Grand Isle, reminiscences of his youth in France and Algeria, and theories about the Cabala, while his beautiful, curly-haired, barefooted daughter served them drinks.

Elizabeth Bisland arrived on Grand Isle during Lafcadio's stay. He was friendly and charming in her company, and did a series of sketches of her on the beach. But he was obsessed by the fisherman's daughter, Marie, in whose presence he felt somehow "face to face with a beauty that existed in the Tertiary epoch,—300,000 years ago,—the beauty of the most ancient branch of humanity,—the oldest of the world's races!"

Carried away by his fantasy and his unrequited feelings for Marie (he would have preferred her name to have been something "more ancient, more pagan—a primitive name whereof the meaning is forgotten, and the etymology undiscernable") he later wrote a short "anthropological, evolutional, osteological love-story after the fashion of Pierre Loti ("Torn Letters"): ". . . The wind lifts her long loose hair across my face,—as inviting me to inhale its perfume. Exquisite and indescribable perfume of youth! what flower-ghost prisoned in crystal owneth so delicate a magic as thou? Unnumbered the songs which celebrate the breath of blossoms, the scent of gardens,—yet what blossom-soul, what flower-witchery might charm the sense like the odor of a woman's hair, the natural perfume of beauty, the fresh and delicious fragrance of youth? . . ."

The perfumed maiden taught Lafcadio how to say *ene maiteya* ("my beloved" in Basque); and for a spell he seriously thought of staying on Grand Isle forever with his would-be child bride, living out Lafcadio's favorite lines from Tennyson: "I will take some savage woman, she shall rear my dusky race. /Iron-jointed, supple-sinewed, they shall dive, and they shall run, /Catch the wild goat by the hair, and hurl their lances in the sun;/Whistle back the parrot's call, and leap the rainbows of the brooks, /Not with blinded eyesight poring over miserable books."

The end of his vacation month approached, however, and Lafcadio knew he would have to leave behind his *maiteya* and depart with only his fantasy. "Soon," he wrote to Page Baker, "all this will be a dream: —the white cottages shadowed with leafy green—the languid rocking-chairs upon the old-fashioned gallery—the cows that look into one's window with the rising sun—the dog and the mule trotting down the flower-edged road . . . the pleasure of sleeping with doors and windows open to the sea and its everlasting song—the exhilaration of rising with the rim of the sun. . . . And then we must return to the dust and the roar of New Orleans, to hear the rumble of wagons instead of the rumble of breakers, and to smell the smell of ancient gutters instead of the sharp sweet scent of pure sea wind. . . . One *lives* here. In New Orleans one only exists."

In the city where he only existed, Lafcadio dreamt constantly of Grand Isle. Page Baker allowed him to take occasional short trips back to the island, where he breathed the pure sea wind, caught fleeting glimpses of his indifferent muse, and sat in his cottage, its door open to the comings and goings of tree frogs, mud daubers, and garter snakes. Here he wrote articles for the *Times-Democrat* and jotted down notes on Grand Isle itself for some as yet unrevealed, undefined literary project he knew would manifest itself. "So I wait for the poet's pentecost," he declared to Rudolph Matas, "—the inspiration of nature, the descent of the Tongues of Fire. And I think they will come, when the wild skies brighten, and the sun of the Mexical Gulf reappears for his worshippers. . . ."

Then in the spring of 1886, back in New Orleans, Lafcadio chanced to recall an evening spent with George Washington Cable three years before when the latter had talked about the famous hurricane of August 10, 1856, during which an enormous tidal wave had destroyed most of Île Dernière, an island located forty miles west of Grand Isle. As the wave smashed onto the coast, the guests of a popular beachfront hotel were obliviously waltzing in the ballroom, and as the wooden structure was swept from its foundations, all of the dancers were washed out to sea. On the beach a fisherman found a little Creole girl lying in her dead mother's arms and brought her into his home where he and his childless wife raised her. Years later a visiting Creole hunter noticed the girl, recognized a familial trinket she was wearing, and took her back to New Orleans. But the girl's real family and her strange new world felt so alien to her that she escaped at the first opportunity, returned to Île Dernière, married a native fisherman, and raised a family.

Suddenly, the *matter* of a story took shape in Lafcadio's mind—a tale of a little Creole girl named Chita, her foster-parents Feliu and Carmen, and her real father Julien, who rediscovers and loses his daughter at the moment of his death in a hurricane on Last Island. "Well, you remember my ancient dream of a poetical prose," he wrote excitedly to H. E. Krehbiel, "—compositions to satisfy an old Greek ear,—like chants wrought in a huge measure, wider than the widest line of a Sanskrit composition, and just a little irregular, like Ocean rhythm. I really think I will be able to realize it at last."

A sixty-page, three-part novella, *Chita* (subtitled *A Memory of Last Island*) was Lafcadio's hyperlyrical, rhapsodic homage to water, wind, sky, and the beauty of islands. It was immediately accepted by *Harper's Weekly* and published as a book by Harper and Brothers in 1889. Extremely popular in the late nineteenth century, forgotten in the twentieth, *Chita* has recently been called—by the critic Guy Davenport—"a lost classic" of

American literature, fusing "French narrative as perfected by Prosper Mérimée, Pierre Loti, and Guy de Maupassant with Winslow Homer."

Despite his tendency to lapse into sentimentality and bathos in his
depiction of character, Lafcadio in *Chita* achieves a poetical prose which
imitates the mesmerizing movement of tides and waves to suggest an
impressionistic sense of the mystery of the primordial sea. Here Chita
explores her island world:

⟦ . . . she began to learn the life of the coast.

With her acquisition of another tongue, there came to her also the
understanding of many things relating to the world of the sea. She mem-
orized with novel delight much that was told her day by day concerning
the nature surrounding her—many secrets of the air, many of those signs
of heaven which the dwellers in cities cannot comprehend because the
atmosphere is thickened and made stagnant above them—cannot even
watch because the horizon is hidden from their eyes by walls, and by
weary avenues of trees with whitewashed trunks. She learned by listening,
by asking, by observing also, how to know the signs that foretell wild
weather:—tremendous sunsets, scuddings and bridgings of cloud—
sharpening and darkening of the sea-line—and the shriek of gulls flashing
to land in level flight, out of a still transparent sky—and halos about the
moon.

She learned where the sea-birds, with white bosoms and brown wings,
made their hidden nests of sand—and where the cranes waded for their
prey—and where the beautiful wild-ducks, plumaged in satiny lilac and
silken green, found their food—and where the best reeds grew to furnish
stems for Feliu's red-clay pipe—and where the ruddy sea-beams were
most often tossed upon the shore—and how the gray pelicans fished all
together, like men—moving in far-extending semi-circles, beating the flood
with their wings to drive the fish before them.

And from Carmen she learned the fables and the sayings of the sea—
the proverbs about its deafness, its avarice, its treachery, its terrific power—
especially one that haunted her for all time thereafter: *Si quieres aprender
á orar, entra en el mar* (If thou wouldst learn to pray, go to the sea). She
learned why the sea is salt—how "the tears of women made the waves
of the sea"—and how the sea has "no friends"—and how the cat's eyes
change with the tides. . . .

• • •

She saw the quivering pinkness of waters curled by the breath of the morning—under the deepening of the dawn—like a far fluttering and scattering of rose-leaves of fire;—

Saw the shoreless, cloudless, marvelous double-circling azure of perfect summer days—twin glories of infinite deeps interreflected, while the Soul of the World lay still, suffused with a jewel-light, as of vaporized sapphire;—

Saw the Sea shift color—"change sheets"—when the viewless Wizard of the Wind breathed upon its face, and made it green;—

Saw the immeasurable panics—noiseless, scintillant—which silver, summer after summer, curved leagues of beach with bodies of little fish— the yearly massacre of migrating populations, nations of sea-trout, driven from their element by terror;—and the winnowing of shark-fins—and the rushing of porpoises—and the rising of the *grande-écaille,* like a pillar of flame—and the diving and pitching and fighting of the frigates and the gulls—and the armored hordes of crabs swarming out to clear the slope after the carnage and the gorging had been done;—

Saw the Dreams of the Sky—scudding mockeries of ridged foam—and shadowy stratification of capes and coasts and promontories long-drawn-out—and imageries, multicolored, of mountain frondage, and sierras whitening above sierras—and phantom islands ringed around with lagoons of glory;—

Saw the toppling and smouldering of cloud-worlds after the enormous conflagration of sunsets—incandescence ruining into darkness; and after it a moving and climbing of stars among the blacknesses—like searching lamps;—

Saw the deep kindle countless ghostly candles as for mysterious night-festival—and a luminous billowing under a black sky, and effervescences of fire, and the twirling and crawling of phosphoric foam;—

Saw the mesmerism of the Moon;—saw the enchanted tides self-heaped in muttering obeisance before her.

Often she heard the Music of the Marsh through the night: an infinity of flutings and tinklings made by tiny amphibia—like the low blowing of numberless little tin horns, the clanking of billions of little bells;—and, at intervals, profound tones, vibrant and heavy, as of a bass-viol—the orchestra of the great frogs! And interweaving with it all, one continuous shrilling—keen as the steel speech of a saw—the stridulous telegraphy of crickets.

But always—always, dreaming or awake, she heard the huge blind Sea chanting that mystic and eternal hymn, which none may hear without awe, which no musician can learn;—. . . .

And the tumultuous ocean terrified her more and more: it filled her sleep with enormous nightmare;—it came upon her in dreams, mountain-shadowing—holding her with its spell, smothering her power of outcry, heaping itself to the stars.

Carmen became alarmed;—she feared that the nervous and delicate child might die in one of those moaning dreams out of which she had to arouse her, night after night. But Feliu, answering her anxiety with one of his favorite proverbs, suggested a heroic remedy:

"The world is like the sea: those who do not know how to swim in it are drowned;—and the sea is like the world," he added. . . . "Chita must learn to swim!"

And he found the time to teach her. Each morning, at sunrise, he took her into the water. She was less terrified the first time than Carmen thought she would be;—she seemed to feel confidence in Feliu; although she screamed piteously before her first ducking at his hands. His teaching was not gentle. He would carry her out, perched upon his shoulder, until the water rose to his own neck; and there he would throw her from him, and let her struggle to reach him again as best she could. The first few mornings she had to be pulled out almost at once; but after that Feliu showed her less mercy, and helped her only when he saw she was really in danger. He attempted no other instruction until she had learned that in order to save herself from being half choked by the salt water, she must not scream; and by the time she became habituated to these austere experiences, she had already learned by instinct alone how to keep herself afloat for a while, how to paddle a little with her hands. Then he commenced to train her to use them—to lift them well out and throw them forward as if reaching, to dip them as the blade of an oar is dipped at an angle, without loud splashing;—and he showed her also how to use her feet. She learned rapidly and astonishingly well. In less than two months Feliu felt really proud at the progress made by his tiny pupil: it was a delight to watch her lifting her slender arms above the water in swift, easy curves, with the same fine grace that marked all her other natural motions. Later on he taught her not to fear the sea even when it growled a little—how to ride a swell, how to face a breaker, how to dive. She only needed practice thereafter; and Carmen, who could also swim, finding the child's health improving marvelously under this new discipline, took good care that Chita should practice whenever the mornings were not too cold, or the water too rough.

With the first thrill of delight at finding herself able to glide over the water unassisted, the child's superstitious terror of the sea passed away. Even for the adult there are few physical joys keener than the exultation of the swimmer;—how much greater the same glee as newly felt by an imaginative child—a child, whose vivid fancy can lend unutterable value to the most insignificant trifles, can transform a weed-patch to an Eden! . . . Of her own accord she would ask for her morning bath, as soon as she opened her eyes;—it even required some severity to prevent her from remaining in the water too long. The sea appeared to her as something that had become tame for her sake, something that loved her in a huge rough way; a tremendous playmate, whom she no longer feared to see come bounding and barking to lick her feet. And, little by little, she also learned the wonderful healing and caressing power of the monster, whose cool embrace at once dispelled all drowsiness, feverishness, weariness—even after the sultriest nights when the air had seemed to burn, and the mosquitoes had filled the chamber with a sound as of water boiling in many kettles. And on mornings when the sea was in too wicked a humor to be played with, how she felt the loss of her loved sport, and prayed for calm! Her delicate constitution changed;—the soft, pale flesh became firm and brown, the meagre limbs rounded into robust symmetry, the thin cheeks grew peachy with richer life; for the strength of the sea had entered into her; the sharp breath of the sea had renewed and brightened her young blood. . . .

. . . Thou primordial Sea, the awfulness of whose antiquity hath stricken all mythology dumb;—thou most wrinkled living Sea, the millions of whose years outnumber even the multitude of thy hoary motions;—thou omniform and most mysterious Sea, mother of the monsters and the gods—whence thine eternal youth? Still do thy waters hold the infinite thrill of that Spirit which brooded above their face in the Beginning!—still is thy quickening breath an elixir unto them that flee to thee for life—like the breath of young girls, like the breath of children, prescribed for the senescent by magicians of old—prescribed unto weazened elders in the books of the Wizards.

CHAPTER 8

*R*estless *F*arewell

Having spent ten years in New Orleans, a restless Lafcadio considered that it was time to move on. Even two years after arriving, he had complained in a letter to Henry Krehbiel:

I am very weary of New Orleans. The first delightful impression it produced has vanished. The city of my dreams, bathed in the gold of eternal summer, and perfumed with the amorous odors of orange flowers, has vanished like one of those phantom cities of Spanish America, swallowed up centuries ago by earthquakes, but reappearing at long intervals to deluded travellers. What remains is something horrible like the tombs here—material and moral rottenness which no pen can do justice to. You must have read some of those medieval legends in which an amorous youth finds the beautiful witch he has embraced all through the night crumble into a mass of calcined bones and ashes in the morning. Well, I feel like such a one, and almost regret that, unlike the victims of these diabolical illusions, I do not find my hair whitened and my limbs withered by sudden age; for I enjoy exuberant vitality and still seem to myself like one buried alive or left alone in some city cursed with desolation like that described by Sinbad the Sailor. No literary circle here; no jovial coterie of journalists; no associates save those vampire ones of which the less said the better. And the thought—Where must all this end?—may be laughed off in the daytime, but always returns to haunt me like a ghost in the night.

This mood disappeared with new work, new interests, new accomplishments, new friends. Then another depressive spell would bring with it more distrust, a deeper sense of betrayal. "There is such a delightful pleasantness about the *first* relations with people in strange places," Lafcadio would say, "—before you have made any rival, excited any ill will, incurred anybody's displeasure. Stay long enough in any one place and the illusion is over: you have to sift this society through the meshes of your nerves, and find perhaps one good friendship too large to pass through." In a sense, then, friendship and any ties that bind were unwanted barriers to his wanderlust. As he had once admitted to Watkin: "I have not travelled enough the last eight years, I suppose; it does not do to become attached insensibly to places and persons."

As his life progressed, Lafcadio understood that he would always be a stranger in the world: "I ought never to have been born in this century, I think sometimes, because I live forever in dreams of other centuries and other faiths and other ethics,—dreams rudely broken by the sound of cursing in the street below." Yet his estrangement from the conventional life strengthened his intense, childlike curiosity and fueled his desire to travel: "Once in a while I feel the spirit of restlessness upon me, when the Spanish ships come in from Costa Rica and the islands of the West Indies. I fancy that some day, I shall wander down to the levee, and creep on board, and sail away to God knows where. I am so hungry to see those quaint cities of the Conquistadores and to hear the sandalled sentinels crying through the night—*Sereño alerto!—sereño alerto!*—just as they did two hundred years ago."

One day Mexico was his El Dorado ("where no one ever lights a fire, and where one has only to go into the sun when he is too cold, into the shade when he is too warm"); another day Havana was the perfect place to establish a *meson de los estrangeros.* "I would give anything to be a literary Columbus," Lafcadio declared, "—to discover a Romantic America in some West Indian or North African or Oriental region,—to describe the life that is only fully treated of in universal geographies or ethnological researches. . . . If I could only become a Consul at Bagdad, Algiers, Ispahan, Benares, Samarkand, Nippo, Bangkok, Ninh-Binh,—or any part of the world where ordinary Christians do not like to go! . . . O, that I were a travelling shoemaker, or a player upon the sambuke!"

Lafcadio's fantasies inevitably urged him to move away from a hypocritical and materialistic civilization he was growing to detest. "This is not a country to dream in," his friend Krehbiel once said to him, "but to get rich or go to the poorhouse." Mark Twain called the era "The Gilded Age," and mocked its worship of "Gold and Greenbacks and Stock—father, son, and the ghost of same." Speculators and confidence men, the Ku Klux Klan, the Tweed Ring—it seemed a world for characters like Herman Melville's Paul Jones: "Intrepid, unprincipled, reckless, predatory, with boundless ambition, civilized in externals but a savage at heart. . . ." Even Walt Whitman, who drew inspiration from the American city's hustle, energy, and the effect of world-transforming inventions like the steam engine, the telegraph, and the Atlantic cable, talked bitterly of the "rabid, feverish itching for change" and of "that father of restlessness, the Devil."

"Little phantoms of men," Lafcadio asserted, "are blown about like down in the storms of the human struggle: they have not enough weight to keep them in place." As a self-described "word-artist in embryo," he knew that in spite of Page Baker's indulgent treatment of him, he was still a "gilded slave of newspaper work," a word-fly entrapped in the web of the cash nexus. (The cracks in his friendship with Baker were beginning to show, and he resented Baker's continuing attempts to tone down his editorial meditations on Buddhism.) "In sooth," he wrote to Henry Watkin, "a man on a daily newspaper is as a grain of mustard seed." To William O'Connor he complained, "Journalism dwarfs, stifles, emasculates thought and style," and to Henry Krehbiel he asserted, "When you voluntarily convert yourself into a part of the machinery of a great daily newspaper, you must revolve and keep revolving with the wheels; you play the man in the treadmill. The more you involve yourself the more difficult it will be for you to escape."

Refusing to compromise in the face of this loss of self-esteem, Lafcadio spoke of the necessity for a personal commitment to the *true* bohemian ideal of the holy fire of art and the creative act:

Under all the levity of Henri Murger's picturesque Bohemianism [Murger's *Scènes de la Vie de Bohème* was the basis for Puccini's *La Bohème*], there is a serious philosophy apparent which elevates the characters of his romance to heroism. They follow one principle faithfully,—so faithfully that only the strong survived the ordeal,—never to abandon the pursuit of an artistic vocation for any other occupation however lucrative,—not even when she [Art] remained apparently deaf and blind to her worshippers. . . . So long as one can live and pursue his natural vocation in art, it is a duty with him never to abandon it if he believes that he has within him the elements of final success. Every time he labors at aught that is not of art, he robs the divinity of what belongs to her.   ]

On a springlike day in January 1887, Lafcadio was rummaging through the shelves of Fournier's secondhand bookshop on Royal Street when a pretty young Creole woman with black hair and brown eyes approached him, introduced herself as Leona Queyrouze, and said breathlessly, "I know you are Mr. Hearn, I saw a picture of you in the *Times-Democrat,* I've wanted so much to meet you, I admire your work greatly, could I impose on you perhaps to look at some verse I've been writing?"

Lafcadio was about to extricate himself as politely as possible, but the intensity of her passion and the sweetness of her importunate tone charmed him. "So you are one of the bees," he replied to her instead, "that come to the garden for flowers with the golden dust to make the divine honey and the tiny goblets of amber colored wax that hold it?"

"I am afraid," she responded, "there shall be little left for me. But the garden is large and the flowers are plentiful."

As Lafcadio accompanied her home, Leona noticed that the condition of his eyes gave them the "fixity of glance and introspective stare of statues . . . and cast a sphinx-like expression over his features." She prevailed upon Lafcadio to take several pages of her writing and to call on her again. It was to be the last friendship he made in New Orleans. On his next visit he told her, frankly but gently, that her quasi–blank verse was "so much prose measured off—*not* poetry." Leona took the criticism well, for she respected his opinions and perceptions. When she invited him to visit her again, he sensed that matters might get out of hand. Fascinated but detached, Lafcadio told her, "I would like to look upon you as a younger brother. Would you mind?" To this strange request she replied that she would not mind, even though she did.

Leona Queyrouze was hardly the typical overprotected Catholic Creole girl. A constant companion of her broad-minded father, she was the only female member of the *Athénée Louisianais,* a society that studied and promoted French language and literature, and to which she had contributed a scholarly paper on Racine. In addition to writing poetry, Leona played the piano, sang old Creole songs, and fenced.

Lafcadio was intrigued by this remarkable, independent-minded young woman with whom he could converse about literary matters, dazzling her with his eloquent commentaries, and who tutored him, in turn, on the correct pronunciation of black Creole proverbs. As Lafcadio later described her, Leona was "all fire and nerves and scintillation; a tropical being in mind and physique, and I could never be to her what I should like to be." He was attracted to her, but he was impatient to travel and had definitely made up his mind to leave "this quaint and ruinous city . . . this land of perfume and dreams. . . . I came here to enjoy romance, and I have had my fill." He urgently craved new horizons for his work, and now dreamed of going to live in a place like the French West Indies where he hoped to be able to develop his writing full-time.

In May 1887, Lafcadio resigned amicably from the *Times-Democrat*. He stored his books with Rudolph Matas and said good-bye to former neighbors and current friends: Denny Corcoran, Page Baker, Julia Wetherall, Mrs. Courtney, Mrs. Durno, Lieutenant Crosby, and, finally, to a tearful Leona Queyrouze. Leona claimed to possess second sight, but she had not foreseen the possibility of Lafcadio's departure, and upon first learning of it she had let him know that she was hurt and angry. Lafcadio responded in a note: "Medea, the beautiful witch-maiden, heard of a certain shepherd who kept bees which manufactured a particular sort of honey. She sent for him to come and tell her about the bees. He went for that purpose; but Medea sang him songs, and looked at him; and entangled all the web of his thought, and made his head feel as if many hives of bees were in it—so that he was never able to tell her anything about the honey. It was all her own fault that she never became a bee-keeper."

On his farewell visit to Leona, Lafcadio spoke strangely, she thought, for a man on his way to seek new peoples and new worlds. He said: "Do not seek inspiration merely around you in the exterior world and its powerful vibrations which fill our senses with the ecstasy of beauty. It is in the psychical depths of our own Self that we must look to find treasures which Aladdin's lamp never could have revealed."

Then he kissed her good-bye and set out with his one dilapidated leather suitcase.

Part

Three

CHAPTER 1

Paradise Regained

Lafcadio left New Orleans by train in early June 1887. Stopping off in Cincinnati, he appeared unannounced at Henry Watkin's print shop late one morning. On beholding The Raven at his front door, the now white-haired Old Man wept as he embraced Lafcadio; and the two of them spent the afternoon catching up on each other after their ten-year separation. (Unbeknownst to him, Mattie had remarried in 1880, but there is no record of whether he or Watkin spoke of her that day.) Lafcadio chose to see no one else in Cincinnati and caught the early-evening train to New York City, where he stayed for several weeks with Henry Krehbiel and his wife in their apartment on West Fifty-seventh Street. From there he wrote Watkin a deeply felt letter reflecting on their reunion:

Dear Old Man:

A delightful trip brought me safe and sound to New York, where my dear friend Krehbiel was waiting to take me to his cosy home. I cannot tell you how much our little meeting delighted me, or how much I regretted to depart so soon, or how differently I regarded our old friendship from my old way of looking at it. I was too young, too foolish, and too selfish to know you as you are, when we used to be together. Ten years made little exterior change in me, but a great deal of heart-change; and I saw you as you are,—noble and true and frank and generous, and felt I loved you more than I ever did before; felt also how much I owed you, and will always owe you,—and understood how much allowance you had made for all my horrid, foolish ways when I used to be with you. Well, I am sure to see you again. I am having one of the most delightful holidays here I ever had in my life; and I expect to stay a few weeks. If it were not for the terrible winters, I should like to live in New York. Some day I suppose I shall have to spend a good deal of my time here. The houses eleven stories high, that seem trying to climb into the moon,—the tremendous streets and roads,—the cascading thunder of the awful torrent of life,—the sense of wealth-force and mind-power that oppresses the stranger here,—all these form so colossal a contrast with the inert and warmly colored Southern life that I know not how to express my impression. I can only think that I have found superb material for a future story, in which the influence of New York on a Southern mind may be described. Well, new as these things may seem to me, they are, no doubt, old and uninteresting to you,—so that I shall not bore you with my impressions. I will look forward to our next meeting, when during a longer stay in Cin. I can tell you such little experiences of my trip as may please you. I want to get into that dear little shop of yours again. I dreamed of it the other night, and heard the ticking of the old clock like a man's feet treading on pavement far away; and I saw the Sphinx, with the mother and child in her arms, move her monstrous head, and observe: "The sky in New York is grey!"

When I woke up it *was* grey, and it remained grey until to-day. Even now it is not like our summer blue. It looks higher and paler and colder. We are nearer to God in the South, just as we are nearer to Death in that terrible and splendid heat of the Gulf Coast. When I write God, of course I mean only the World-Soul, the mighty and sweetest life of Nature, the great Blue Ghost, the Holy Ghost which fills planets and hearts with beauty.

Believe me, Dear Old Dad,
Affectionately, your son,

                                                        Lafcadio Hearn

These were the kindest words Lafcadio ever wrote about Manhattan—the only island he ever grew to detest. (Lafcadio was never able to embrace Walt Whitman's enthusiastic notion of the "great democratic island city . . . glistening in sunshine, with such New World atmosphere, vista and action!") Even in his first flush of amazement at the city's "wealth-force and mind-power"—a momentary seduction after years of the "inertness" of the South—his pervasive sense of the "greyness" of the North (common as well to Dublin, London, and Cincinnati) prompted him to make a hasty exit.

In July, Lafcadio boarded the S.S. *Barracouta*—a "long, narrow, graceful steel steamer, with two masts, and yellow chimney"—on a cruise with ports of call at St. Croix, St. Kitts, Montserrat, Dominica, Martinique, Barbados, Trinidad, Tobago, St. Lucia, and British Guiana. Each day they sailed farther south, the sea became bluer, the air warmer. After a week, Lafcadio, an anomaly amidst the planters and gold prospectors, was the only person who observed the "first tropical visitor" boarding the ship: "A wonderful fly, shining black; his wings seem ribbed and jointed with silver, his head is jewel-green, with exquisitely cut emeralds for eyes."

By the time the boat reached the Windward Islands, Lafcadio's eyes and mind were hopelessly intoxicated by the "delirium of color,—abysses of light, and delightful displays of nakedness." To Dr. Matas who had constantly and adamantly warned his impetuous patient/friend about the dangers of syphilis, Lafcadio admitted that his "great and good resolves" came to a "furious termination" at St. Pierre, Martinique (where, coincidentally, Paul Gauguin was at that time painting the "Apples of Paradise" of that sensuous port town). As Lafcadio put it to his *"querido amigo"* in New Orleans:

The air had been one warm caress for a week,—loaded with strange perfumes, from the blue volcanic lands. The sea was tepid; the trail of the boat at night was a torrent of fire.

And everybody got lazy and drowsy and full of dreams;—when the men talked, it was of women; when they slept, air-shapes came to whisper things which were not holy. And all the way, the memories of the North became colder and whiter and less interesting; and the terror of those various *cocci* concerning which you warned me became less.

As, under a perpendicular sun, I wandered down the narrow, curious, yellow painted streets of Martinique, I looked about me; and lo! the fear of the g—coccus wholly passed away. . . . In a little while I ceased to be in the street; under the guidance of a half-naked mulatto I had found my way into the upper chamber of a queer building, overlooking a court full of cabbage-palms and breadfruit trees;—there was a girl there,—the tallest and most generally appetizing possible to conceive,—a Martinique octoroon. I thought once or twice of salutary advice; but only in such a dreamy way as when one has swallowed a heavy dose of opium, and cares not one cent for the heavens above, or the earth beneath, nor for those things that are in the waters under the earth. . . .

I have come to the startling conclusion that civilization is a cold and vapid humbug;—the tropics are the only living part of this dying planet. Seemed to me when I first saw them, that I had seen them before; I know I shall see them again,—think I shall spend a good deal of my life in them,—if it lasts. This is altogether divine.

A tan and healthy Lafcadio returned to New York City three months later, checked himself into a waterfront hotel at the corner of Water and Fulton streets, and speedily turned out a long travel essay entitled "A Midsummer Trip to the Tropics," featuring a Whitmanlike catalog of the dazzling, variegated blues of the Caribbean: vapory blue, spectral blue, foggy blue, limpid blue, gentian blue, pallid blue, tender blue, diaphanous blue.

Henry Alden, the renowned editor of *Harper's Magazine*, immediately bought the piece for $700. He also invited the writer to spend a few days at his family home in Metuchen, New Jersey, in order to get to know him better. During that time Alden assumed the role of Lafcadio's publishing patron and adviser—briefly taking over the position once held informally by Page Baker, whom Lafcadio by now retrospectively despised. As he wrote to Matas: "Page . . . was always willing to believe any chamber pot [designated by drawing of the same] who told him that what I wrote was scandalous or untrue or offensive to Jesus-C & Co. . . . Even now, while I have had some bad luck, I have the satisfaction of being my own master, and of being out of the sight and hearing of a great number of shitasses whom I was obliged to say 'Goodday' to in N.O. No: I will never set foot in N.O. any more—rather die."

Lafcadio felt right at home in the Aldens' country house with its large garden and extensive fields, and he especially enjoyed the company of the editor's young daughter, Annie, with whom he later corresponded. But winter was approaching, and he felt homesick for the sea and sun. From Metuchen he wrote his "Dear Old Dad": "I am going right back to the Tropics again, this time to stay. I have quit newspapering forever. Wish I could see you and chat with you before I go, but I cannot get a chance this time. . . . My conviction is that you and I would be well to spend our lives in the Antilles. All dreams of Paradise (even Mahomet's) are more than realized there by nature;—after returning, I find this world all colorless, all grey, and fearfully cold. I feel like an outcast from heaven."

On October 2, Lafcadio again boarded the S.S. *Barracouta* for Martinique. With him he brought one suitcase, a good supply of yellow writing paper, a cumbersome four-hundred-dollar camera he wanted to use to illustrate his travel sketches that Henry Alden had promised to "consider" publishing in *Harper's Magazine* and that Lafcadio hoped to collect into a book, and a bankroll of $300. He planned to remain in St. Pierre for a couple of months before moving on to another island; he stayed for a year and a half.

Lafcadio had fallen in love again.

From his small but comfortable room on Rue du Bois-Morin on a narrow street of St. Pierre, he could contemplate both the azure harbor below and the towering volcanic hills overshadowing this "delicious, divine, dreamy" West Indian town—"an idealized, tropicalized, glorified Old New Orleans," he reported to Rudolph Matas . . . and confessed to Elizabeth Bisland: "I love it as if it were a human being."

His first impressions of the port town were sensations of odor ("The smell of St. Pierre is a faint smell of Asparagus") and of intense color ("Yesterday at St. Pierre the water was a deep violet, full of naked brown boys swimming,—only the white soles of their feet making a gleam. Their bodies looked . . . a beautiful red in the water. As for greens! I can think of only two bright greens with us,—orange trees, young cane. Here there are about twenty thousand greens"). And he envisioned the inhabitants of the bright, narrow, palm-lined streets of St. Pierre as if they had just stepped off the walls of ancient Pompeii, as resplendent dancers with their unusual intermingling of African and Hellenic characteristics: "Radiance of costume—the semi-nudity of passing figures . . . the rounded outline of limbs yellow as tropic fruit—the grace of attitudes—the unconscious harmony of groupings—the gathering and folding and falling of light robes that oscillate with swaying of free hips—the sculptural symmetry of unshod feet. You look up and down the lemon-tinted streets—down to the dazzling azure brightness of meeting sky and sea; up to the perpetual verdure of mountain woods—wondering at the mellowness of tones, the sharpness of lines in the light, the diaphaneity of colored shadows; always asking memory: 'When? . . . where did I see all this . . . long ago?' . . ."

• • •

Lafcadio was thirty-seven years old, and he had finally reached the "enchanted abode *where summer never dies.*" Free of the daily newspaper grind ("with all its pettiness, cowardices, and selfishnesses") and fluent in the Martinique patois, he could now take time to observe intently, live the life of the islanders, and write at his own pace. As he remarked to Henry Alden: "The more I work, the more the conviction grows upon me that no study of life can be written in less than the actual time required to *live* the scenes described."

He spent weeks and months studying the racial diversity and complexity of the Martinique population, "ranging up from black or nearly black through bronze reds and coppery browns and fruit yellows to the dead ivory of the *sang-mêlé.*" Lafcadio discovered that "each individual of mixed race has his own particular color—discernible to Creole eyes only, not to the inexperienced eyes of a stranger," and that "the shadings and the intershadings of the social question are scarcely less multiple and complex than the differences of skin tint."

In spite of his deep attraction to black Creole women, Lafcadio came to the conclusion that "the greatest error of slavery was that which resulted in the creation of the mixed races—the illegitimate union between the white master and the African woman, whose offspring remained slaves by law. One might imagine that under any normal condition the offspring of union between a savage and a civilized race—even supposing both to be at war—would prove an element of reconciliation. But nothing more strongly reveals the abnormal character of slavery as a social institution in the West Indies, under the Code Noir, than the fact that everywhere the half-breed race sprang up as an all-powerful element of discord, and finally appeared in the role of an enemy of whites and blacks alike—forcing the parent races apart forever."

The old white Creole *békés*—engenderers of the island's colored children—were strongly opposed to race conciliation, and as Lafcadio noticed, they enforced upon their white daughters a monotonous, half-cloistered existence that prescribed endless rounds of wearisome social duties, mandatory church appearances in stifling, close-fitting black Parisian dresses, and arranged marriages. Such a life, Lafcadio commented, might have entrapped Josephine de la Pagerie, of Trois-Islets, if she had wedded a Martinique merchant or planter instead of the soldier who became the Emperor of France.

Meanwhile, living on the *mornes* and peaks of Martinique's interior, "the great black reserve, the mass of the old African element, always multiplying and strengthening . . . has learned its place and power in relation to the nature surrounding it; and it is satisfied to remain black and strong and free to speak its scorn of a yellow skin. In short it has returned to the condition of race consciousness; it is dreaming new dreams, and who may say in what manner those dreams may move it?"

Every morning Lafcadio got up at 5:00 A.M., had breakfast (a slice of custard apple and a cup of thick black coffee), and hurried down the stone terraces to the palm-lined beach for an hour's swim, then returned to his room and wrote for a couple of hours before the afternoon sun made his head feel "as if a heated feather pillow had been stuffed into your skull." He learned, nevertheless, to love Martinique enough "to be quite willing to abandon anything and everything to live in it. As in the old Sunday School hymn, 'Only man is vile': nature and Woman are unspeakably sweet."

Day after day he observed the island women—the *blanchisseuses* (washerwomen), *calendeuses* (women who specialized in painting yellow the madras squares used for *tignons*), and, in particular, the *porteuses* (carrier girls), whom he accompanied on several of their forty- to fifty-mile daily treks, as they carried hundred-pound loads on their heads over mountain ranges and through tropical forests:

The erect carriage and steady swift walk of the women who bear burdens is especially likely to impress the artistic observer: it is the sight of such passers-by which gives, above all, the antique tone and color to his first sensations;—and the larger part of the female population of mixed race are practiced carriers. Nearly all the transportation of light merchandise, as well as of meats, fruits, vegetables, and food stuffs—to and from the interior—is effected upon human heads. At some of the ports the regular local packets are loaded and unloaded by women and girls—able to carry any trunk or box to its destination. At Fort-de-France, the great steamers of the Compagnie Générale Transatlantique are entirely coaled by women, who carry the coal on their heads, singing as they come and go in processions of hundreds; and the work is done with incredible rapidity. Now, the Creole *porteuse*, or female carrier, is certainly one of the most remarkable physical types in the world; and whatever artistic enthusiasm her graceful port, lithe walk, or half-savage beauty may inspire you with, you can form no idea, if a total stranger, what a really wonderful being she is. . . . Let me tell you something about that highest type of professional female carrier, which is to the *charbonnière,* or coaling-girl, what the thoroughbred racer is to the draught-horse—the type of *porteuse* selected for swiftness and endurance to distribute goods in the interior parishes, or to sell on commission at long distances. To the same class naturally belong those country carriers able to act as *porteuses* of plantation produce, fruits, or vegetables—between the nearer ports and their own interior parishes. . . . Those who believe that great physical endurance and physical energy cannot exist in the tropics do not know the Creole carrier-girl.

*

At a very early age—perhaps at five years—she learns to carry small articles upon her head—a bowl of rice—a *dobanne,* or red earthen decanter, full of water—even an orange on a plate; and before long she is able to balance these perfectly without using her hands to steady them. (I have often seen children actually run with cans of water upon their heads, and never spill a drop.) At nine or ten she is able to carry thus a tolerably heavy basket, or a *trait* (a wooden tray with deep outward sloping sides) containing a weight of from twenty to thirty pounds; and is able to accompany her mother, sister, or cousin on long peddling journeys—walking barefoot twelve and fifteen miles a day. At sixteen or seventeen she is a tall robust girl—lithe, vigorous, tough—all tendon and hard flesh;—she carries a tray or a basket of the largest size, and a burden of one hundred and twenty to one hundred and fifty pounds weight;—she can now earn about thirty francs (about six dollars) a month, *by walking fifty miles a day,* as an itinerant seller.

Among her class there are figures to make you dream of Atalanta; —and all, whether ugly or attractive as to feature, are finely shapen as to body and limb. Brought into existence by extraordinary necessities of environment, the type is a peculiarly local one—a type of human thoroughbred representing the true secret of grace: economy of force. There are no corpulent *porteuses* for the long interior routes; all are built lightly and firmly as racers. There are no old *porteuses;*—to do the work even at forty signifies a constitution of astounding solidity. After the full force of youth and health is spent, the poor carrier must seek lighter labor;—she can no longer compete with the girls. For in this calling the young body is taxed to its utmost capacity of strength, endurance, and rapid motion.

As a general rule, the weight is such that no well-freighted *porteuse* can, unassisted, either "load" or "unload" (*châgé* or *déchâgé,* in Creole phrase);

the effort to do so would burst a blood vessel, wrench a nerve, rupture a muscle. She cannot even sit down under her burden without risk of breaking her neck: absolute perfection of the balance is necessary for self-preservation. A case came under my own observation of a woman rupturing a muscle in her arm through careless haste in the mere act of aiding another to unload.

And no one not a brute will ever refuse to aid a woman to lift or to relieve herself of her burden;—you may see the wealthiest merchant, the proudest planter, gladly do it;—the meanness of refusing, or of making any conditions for the performance of his little kindness has only been imagined in those strange Stories of Devils wherewith the oral and un-collected literature of the Creole abounds.

*

Preparing for her journey, the young *màchanne* (*marchande*) puts on the poorest and briefest chemise in her possession, and the most worn of her light calico robes. These are all she wears. The robe is drawn upward and forward, so as to reach a little below the knee, and is confined thus by a waist-string, or a long kerchief bound tightly round the loins. Instead of a Madras or painted turban-kerchief, she binds a plain *mouchoir* neatly and closely about her head; and if her hair be long, it is combed back and gathered into a loop behind. Then, with a second mouchoir of coarser quality she makes a pad, or, as she calls it, *tòche*, by winding the kerchief round her fingers as you would coil up a piece of string;—and the soft mass, flattened with a patting of the hand, is placed upon her head, over the coiffure. On this the great loaded *trait* is poised.

She wears no shoes! To wear shoes and do her work swiftly and well in such a land of mountains would be impossible. She must climb thousands and descend thousands of feet every day—march up and down slopes so steep that the horses of the country all break down after a few years of similar journeying. The girl invariably outlasts the horse—though carrying an equal weight. Shoes, unless extraordinarily well made, would shift place a little with every change from ascent to descent, or the reverse, during the march—would yield and loosen with the ever-varying strain—would compress the toes—produce corns, bunions, raw places by rubbing, and soon cripple the *porteuse*. Remember, she has to walk perhaps fifty miles between dawn and dark, under a sun to which a single hour's exposure, without the protection of an umbrella, is perilous to any European or American—the terrible sun of the tropics! Sandals are the only conceivable footgear suited to such a calling as hers; but she needs no sandals: the soles of her feet are toughened so as to feel no asperities, and present to sharp pebbles a surface at once yielding and resisting, like a cushion of solid *caoutchouc*.

Besides her load, she carries only a canvas purse tied to her girdle on the right side, and on the left a very small bottle of rum, or white *tafia*— usually the latter, because it is so cheap. . . . For she may not always find the Gouyave Water to drink—the cold clear pure stream conveyed to the fountains of Saint Pierre from the highest mountains by a beautiful and marvelous plan of hydraulic engineering: she will have to drink betimes the common spring-water of the bamboo-fountains on the remoter high-roads; and this may cause dysentery if swallowed without a spoonful of spirits. Therefore she never travels without a little liquor.

*

. . . So!—she is ready: *"Châgé moin, souplè, chè!"* she bends to lift the end of the heavy *trait:* some one takes the other—*yon!—dè!—toua!*—it is on her head. Perhaps she winces an instant;—the weight is not perfectly balanced; she settles it with her hands—gets it in the exact place. Then, all steady—lithe, light, half naked—away she moves with a long springy step. So even her walk that the burden never sways; yet so rapid her motion that however good a walker you may fancy yourself to be you will tire out after a sustained effort of fifteen minutes to follow her uphill. Fifteen minutes!—and she can keep up that pace without slackening— save for a minute to eat and drink at midday—for at least twelve hours and fifty-six minutes, the extreme length of a West Indian day. She starts before dawn; tries to reach her resting-place by sunset: after dark, like all her people, she is afraid of meeting zombis.

Let me give you some idea of her average speed under an average weight of one hundred and twenty-five pounds—estimates based partly upon my own observations, partly upon the declarations of the trustwor-thy merchants who employ her, and partly on the assertion of habitants of the burghs or cities named—all of which statements perfectly agree. From Saint Pierre to Basse-Pointe, by the national road, the distance is a trifle less than twenty-seven kilometres and three quarters. She makes the transit easily in three hours and a half; and returns in the afternoon, after an absence of scarcely more than eight hours. From Saint Pierre to Morne Rouge—two thousand feet up in the mountains (an ascent so abrupt that no one able to pay carriage-fare dreams of attempting to walk it)—the distance is seven kilometres and three quarters. She makes it in little more than an hour. But this represents only the beginning of her journey. She

passes on to Grande Anse, twenty-one and three-quarter kilometres away.
But she does not rest there: she returns at the same pace, and reaches
Saint Pierre before dark. From Saint Pierre to Gros-Morne the distance to
be twice traversed by her is more than thirty-two kilometres. A journey
of sixty-four kilometres—daily, perhaps—forty miles! And there are many
màchannes who make yet longer trips—trips of three or four days' duration;—these rest at villages upon their route. . . .

*

Forty to fifty miles a day, always under a weight of more than a hundred pounds—for when the *trait* has been emptied she puts in stones for
ballast;—carrying her employer's merchandise and money over the mountain ranges, beyond the peaks, across the ravines, through the tropical
forest, sometimes through by-ways haunted by the *fer-de-lance*—and this
in summer or winter, the season of rains or the season of heat, the time
of fevers or the time of hurricanes, at a franc a day! . . . How does she
live upon it?

There are twenty sous to the franc. The girl leaves Saint Pierre with
her load at early morning. At the second village, Morne Rouge, she halts
to buy one, two, or three biscuits at a sou apiece; and reaching Ajoupa-
Bouillon later in the forenoon, she may buy another biscuit or two. Altogether she may be expected to eat five sous of biscuit or bread before
reaching Grande Anse, where she probably has a meal waiting for her.
This ought to cost her ten sous—especially if there be meat in her *ragoût:*
which represents a total expense of fifteen sous for eatables. Then there
is the additional cost of the cheap liquor, which she must mix with her
drinking-water, as it would be more than dangerous to swallow pure cold
water in her heated condition; two or three sous more. This almost makes
the franc. But such a hasty and really erroneous estimate does not include
expenses of lodging and clothing;—she may sleep on the bare floor sometimes, and twenty francs a year may keep her in clothes; but she must
rent the floor and pay for the clothes out of that franc. As a matter of fact
she not only does all this upon her twenty sous a day, but can even
economize something which will enable her, when her youth and force
decline, to start in business for herself. And her economy will not seem
so wonderful when I assure you that thousands of men here—huge men
muscled like bulls and lions—live upon an average expenditure of five
sous a day. One sou of bread, two sous of manioc flour, one sou of dried
codfish, one sou of tafia: such is their meal.

There are women carriers who earn more than a franc a day—women with a particular talent for selling, who are paid on commission—from ten to fifteen per cent. These eventually make themselves independent in many instances;—they continue to sell and bargain in person, but hire a young girl to carry the goods.

*

. . . *"Ou 'lè màchanne!"* rings out a rich alto, resonant as the tone of a gong, from behind the balisiers that shut in our garden. There are two of them—no, three—Maiyotte, Chéchelle, and Rina. Maiyotte and Chéchelle have just arrived from Saint Pierre;—Rina comes from Gros-Morne with fruits and vegetables. Suppose we call them all in, and see what they have got. Maiyotte and Chéchelle sell on commission; Rina sells for her mother, who has a little garden at Gros-Morne.

. . . *"Bonjou', Maiyotte;—bonjou', Chéchelle! coument ou kallé, Rina, chè!"* . . . Throw open the folding-doors to let the great trays pass. . . . Now all three are unloaded by old Théréza and by young Adou;—all the packs are on the floor, and the waterproof wrappings are being uncorded, while Ah-Manmzell, the adopted child, brings the rum and water for the tall walkers.

. . . "Oh, what a medley, Maiyotte!" . . . Inkstands and wooden cows; purses and paper dogs and cats; dolls and cosmetics; pins and needles and soap and toothbrushes; candied fruits and smoking-caps; pelotes of thread, and tapes, and ribbons, and laces and Madeira wine; cuffs, and collars, and dancing-shoes, and tobacco sachets. . . . But what is in that little flat bundle? Presents for your *guêpe*, if you have one. . . . Jesis-Maïa!— the pretty foulards! Azure and yellow in checkerings; orange and crimson in stripes; rose and scarlet in plaidings; and bronze tints, and beetle-tints of black and green.

"Chéchelle, what a *bloucoutoum* if you should ever let that tray fall— *aïe yaïe yaïe!"* Here is a whole shop of crockeries and porcelains;—plates, dishes, cups—earthenware *canaris* and dobannes; and gift-mugs and cups bearing Creole girls' names—all names that end in *ine:* "Micheline," "Honorine," "Prospérine" [you will never sell that, Chéchelle: there is not a Prospérine this side of Saint Pierre], "Azaline," "Leontine," "Zéphyrine," "Albertine," "Chrysaline," "Florine," "Coralline," "Alexandrine." . . . And knives and forks, and cheap spoons, and tin coffee-pots, and tin rattles for babies, and tin flutes for horrid little boys—and pencils and note-paper and envelopes! . . .

. . . "Oh, Rina, what superb oranges!—fully twelve inches round! . . . and these, which look something like our mandarins, what do you call them?" *"Zorange-macaque!"* (monkey-oranges). And here are avocados—beauties!—guavas of three different kinds—tropical cherries (which have four seeds instead of one)—tropical raspberries, whereof the entire eatable portion comes off in one elastic piece, lined with something like white silk. . . . Here are fresh nutmegs: the thick green case splits in equal halves at a touch; and see the beautiful heart within—deep dark glossy red, all wrapped in a bright net-work of flat blood-colored fibre, spun over it like branching veins. . . . This big heavy red-and-yellow thing is a *pomme-cythère:* the smooth cuticle, bitter as gall, covers a sweet juicy pulp, interwoven with something that seems like cotton thread. . . . Here is a *pomme-cannelle:* inside its scaly covering is the most delicious yellow custard conceivable, with little black seeds floating in it. This larger *co-rossol* has almost as delicate an interior, only the custard is white instead of yellow. . . . Here are *christophines*—great pear-shaped things, white and green, according to kind, with a peel prickly and knobby as the skin of a horned toad; but they stew exquisitely. And *mélongènes,* or egg-plants; and *palmistepith,* and *chadèques,* and *pommes-d'Haïti*—and roots that at first sight look all alike, but they are not: there are *camanioc,* and *couscous,* and *choux-caraïbes,* and *zignames,* and various kinds of *patates* among them. Old Théréza's magic will transform these shapeless muddy things, before evening, into pyramids of smoking gold—into odorous porridges that will look like messes of molten amber and liquid pearl;—for Rina makes a good sale.

Then Chéchelle manages to dispose of a tin coffee-pot and a big canari. . . . And Maiyotte makes the best sale of all; for the sight of a funny *biscuit* doll has made Ah-Manmzell cry and smile so at the same time that I should feel unhappy for the rest of my life if I did not buy it for her. I know I ought to get some change out of that six francs;—and Maiyotte, who is black but comely as the tents of Kedar, and the curtains of Solomon, seems to be aware of the fact.

Oh, Maiyotte, how plaintive that pretty sphinx face of yours, now turned in profile;—as if you knew you looked beautiful thus—with the great gold circlets of your ears glittering and swaying as you bend! And why are you so long, so long untying that poor little canvas purse?—fumbling and fingering it?—is it because you want me to think of the weight of that *trait* and the sixty kilometres you must walk, and the heat and the dust, and all the disappointments? Ah, you are cunning, Maiyotte! No, I do not want the change!

*

. . . Traveling together, the *porteuses* often walk in silence for hours at a time;—this is when they feel weary. Sometimes they sing—most often when approaching their destination;—and when they chat, it is in a key so high-pitched that their voices can be heard to a great distance in this land of echoes and elevations.

But she who travels alone is rarely silent: she talks to herself or to inanimate things;—you may hear her talking to the trees, to the flowers—talking to the high clouds and the far peaks of changing color—talking to the setting sun!

Over the miles of the morning she sees, perchance, the mighty Piton Gélé, a cone of amethyst in the light; and she talks to it: *"Ou jojoll, oui!—moin ni envie monté assou ou, pou moin ouè bien, bien!"* ("Thou art pretty, pretty, aye!—I would I might climb thee, to see far, far off!")

By a great grove of palms she passes;—so thickly mustered they are that against the sun their intermingled heads form one unbroken awning of green. Many rise straight as masts; some bend at beautiful angles, seeming to intercross their long pale single limbs in a fantastic dance; others curve like bows: there is one that undulates from foot to crest, like a monster serpent poised upon its tail. She loves to look at that one—*joli-pié-bois-là!*—talks to it as she goes by—bids it good-day.

Or, looking back as she ascends, she sees the huge blue dream of the sea—the eternal haunter, that ever becomes larger as she mounts the road; and she talks to it: *"Mi lanmé ka gadé moin!"* ("There is the great sea looking at me!") *"Màché toujou deïé moin, lanmè!"* ("Walk after me, O Sea!")

Or she views the clouds of Pelée, spreading gray from the invisible summit, to shadow against the sun; and she fears the rain, and she talks to it: *"Pas mouillé moin, laplie-à! Quitté moin rivé avant mouillé moin!"* ("Do not wet me, O Rain! Let me get there before thou wettest me!")

Sometimes a dog barks at her, menaces her bare limbs; and she talks to the dog: *"Chien-a, pas mòdé moin, chien—anh! Moin pa fé ou arien, chien, pou ou mòdé moin!"* ("Do not bite, O Dog! Never did I anything to thee that thou shouldst bite me, O Dog! Do not bite me, dear! Do not bite me, *doudoux!*")

Sometimes she meets a laden sister traveling the opposite way. . . . *"Coument ou yé, chè?"* she cries. ("How art thou, dear?") And the other makes answer, *"Toutt douce chè—et ou?"* ("All sweetly, dear—and thou?") And each passes on without pausing: they have no time!

. . . It is perhaps the last human voice she will hear for many a mile.

After that only the whisper of the grasses—*graïe-gras, graïe-gras!*—and the gossip of the canes—*chououa, chououa!*—and the husky speech of the *pois-Angole, ka babillé conm yon vié fenme*—that babbles like an old woman;—and the murmur of the filao-trees, like the murmur of the River of the Washerwoman.   ("LES PORTEUSES")]

Two months after Lafcadio's arrival in Martinique, an epidemic of smallpox broke out in St. Pierre, so he decided to move temporarily up to the little cloud-covered village of Morne Rouge, where he rented a cottage overlooking "wild surges of purple and green mountains, all fissured and jagged, and stormy-looking: a volcanic sea of peaks and craters." Twenty-five hundred feet above sea level, Morne Rouge was an oasis of autumnal coolness and frequent showers, a relief from the unrelenting heat of St. Pierre. Lafcadio's landlady and her daughter taught him new *zombi* and ghost stories; and the landlady's son, Yébé, served as his guide into the mountains. It was here that he often encountered the *porteuses* on their eighteen-mile treks from St. Pierre to Grande Anse and back. The village baker, at whose shop the carrier-girls made brief stops, knew all the *porteuses* by name, and in response to Lafcadio's persistent questions about Grande Anse, where most of these beauties were from, told him: "I was never at Grande Anse, although I have been forty years in Martinique; but I know there is a fine class of young girls there: *il y a une jeunesse là, mon cher!*"

It was time for Lafcadio to see this paradisiacal realm for himself:

[Leaving Morne Rouge at about eight in the morning, my friend and I reached Grande Anse at half-past eleven. Everything had been arranged to make us comfortable. I was delighted with the airy corner room, commanding at once a view of the main street and of the sea—a very high room, all open to the trade-winds—which had been prepared to receive me. But after a long carriage ride in the heat of a tropical June day, one always feels the necessity of a little physical exercise. I lingered only a minute or two in the house, and went out to look at the little town and its surroundings.

As seen from the highroad, the burgh of Grande Anse makes a long patch of darkness between the green of the coast and the azure of the water: it is almost wholly black and gray—suited to inspire an etching. High slopes of cane and meadow rise behind it and on either side, undulating up and away to purple and gray tips of mountain ranges. North and south, to left and right, the land reaches out in two high promontories, mostly green, and about a mile apart—the Pointe du Rochet and the Pointe de Séguinau, or Croche-Mort, which latter name preserves the legend of an insurgent slave, a man of color, shot dead upon the cliff. These promontories form the semicircular bay of Grande Anse. All this Grande Anse, or "Great Creek," valley is an immense basin of basalt; and narrow as it is, no less than five streams water it, including the Rivière de la Grande Anse.

There are only three short streets in the town. The principal, or Grande Rue, is simply a continuation of the national road; there is a narrower one below, which used to be called the Rue de la Paille, because the cottages lining it were formerly all thatched with cane straw; and there is one above it, edging the cane-fields that billow away to the meeting of morne and sky. There is nothing of architectural interest, and all is sombre—walls and roofs and pavements. But after you pass through the city and follow the southern route that ascends the Séguinau promontory, you can obtain some lovely landscape views—a grand surging of rounded *mornes*, with farther violet peaks, truncated or horned, pushing up their heads in the horizon above the highest flutterings of cane; and looking back above the town, you may see Pelée all unclouded—not as you see it from the other coast, but an enormous ghostly silhouette, with steep sides and almost square summit, so pale as to seem transparent. Then if you cross the promontory southward, the same road will lead you into another beautiful valley, watered by a broad rocky torrent—the Valley of the Rivière du Lorrain. This clear stream rushes to the sea through a lofty opening in the hills; and looking westward between them, you will be charmed by the exquisite vista of green shapes piling and pushing up one behind another to reach a high blue ridge which forms the background—a vision of tooth-shaped and fantastical mountains—part of the great central chain running south and north through nearly the whole island. It is over those blue summits that the wonderful road called "La Trace" winds between primeval forest walls.

But the more you become familiar with the face of the little town itself, the more you are impressed by the strange swarthy tone it preserves in all this splendid expanse of radiant tinting. There are only two points of visible color in it—the church and hospital, built of stone, which have been painted yellow: as a mass in the landscape, lying between the dead-gold of the cane-clad hills and the delicious azure of the sea, it remains almost black under the prodigious blaze of light. The foundations of volcanic rock, three or four feet high, on which the frames of the wooden dwellings rest, are black; and the sea-wind appears to have the power of blackening all timber-work here through any coat of paint. Roofs and façades look as if they had been long exposed to coal-smoke, although probably no one in Grande Anse ever saw coal; and the pavements of pebbles and cement are of a deep ash-color, full of micaceous scintillation, and so hard as to feel disagreeable even to feet protected by good thick shoes. By and by you notice walls of black stone, bridges of black stone, and perceive that black forms an element of all the landscape about you. On the roads leading from the town you note from time to time masses of jagged rock or great boulders protruding through the green of the slopes, and dark as ink. These black surfaces also sparkle. The beds of all the neighboring rivers are filled with dark gray stones; and many of these, broken by those violent floods which dash rocks together—deluging the valleys, and strewing the soil of the bottom-lands (*fonds*) with dead serpents—display black cores. Bare crags projecting from the green cliffs here and there are soot-colored, and the outlying rocks of the coast offer a similar aspect. And the sand of the beach is funereally black—looks almost like powdered charcoal; and as you walk over it, sinking three or four inches every step, you are amazed by the multitude and brilliancy of minute flashes in it, like a subtle silver effervescence.

This extraordinary sand contains ninety per cent of natural steel, and efforts have been made to utilize it industrially. Some years ago a company was formed, and a machine invented to separate the metal from the pure sand—an immense revolving magnet, which, being set in motion under a sand shower, caught the ore upon it. When the covering thus formed by the adhesion of the steel became of a certain thickness, the simple interruption of an electric current precipitated the metal into appropriate receptacles. Fine bars were made from this volcanic steel, and excellent cutting tools manufactured from it: French metallurgists pronounced the product of peculiar excellence, and nevertheless the project of the company was abandoned. Political disorganization consequent upon the establishment of universal suffrage frightened capitalists who might have aided the undertaking under a better condition of affairs; and the lack of large means, coupled with the cost of freight to remote markets, ultimately baffled this creditable attempt to found a native industry.

Sometimes after great storms bright brown sand is flung up from the sea-depths; but the heavy black sand always reappears again to make the universal color of the beach.

*

Behind the roomy wooden house in which I occupied an apartment there was a small garden-plot surrounded with a hedge strengthened by bamboo fencing, and radiant with flowers of the *loseille-bois*—the Creole name for a sort of begonia, whose closed bud exactly resembles a pink and white dainty bivalve shell, and whose open blossom imitates the form of a butterfly. Here and there, on the grass, were nets drying, and nasses—curious fish-traps made of split bamboos interwoven and held in place with *mibi* stalks (the *mibi* is a liana heavy and tough as copper wire); and immediately behind the garden hedge appeared the white flashing of the surf. The most vivid recollection connected with my trip to Grande Anse is that of the first time that I went to the end of that garden, opened the little bamboo gate, and found myself overlooking the beach—an immense breadth of soot-black sand, with pale green patches and stripings here and there upon it—refuse of cane thatch, decomposing rubbish spread out by old tides. The one solitary boat owned in the community lay there before me, high and dry. It was the hot period of the afternoon; the town slept; there was no living creature in sight; and the booming of the surf drowned all other sounds; the scent of the warm strong sea-wind annihilated all other odors. Then, very suddenly, there came to me a sensation absolutely weird, while watching the strange wild sea roaring over its beach of black sand—the sensation of seeing something unreal, looking at something that had no more tangible existence than a memory! Whether suggested by the first white vision of the surf over the bamboo hedge—or by those old green tide-lines on the desolation of the black beach—or by some tone of the speaking of the sea—or something indefinable in the living touch of the wind—or by all of these, I cannot say;—but slowly there became defined within me the thought of having beheld just such a coast very long ago, I could not tell where—in those child years of which the recollections gradually become indistinguishable from dreams.

Soon as darkness comes upon Grande Anse the face of the clock in the church-tower is always lighted: you see it suddenly burst into yellow glow above the roofs and the cocoa-palms—just like a pharos. In my room I could not keep the candle lighted because of the seawind; but it never occurred to me to close the shutters of the great broad windows—sashless, of course, like all the glassless windows of Martinique;—the breeze was too delicious. It seemed full of something vitalizing that made one's blood warmer, and rendered one full of contentment—full of eagerness to believe life all sweetness. Likewise, I found it soporific—this pure, dry, warm wind. And I thought there could be no greater delight in existence than to lie down at night, with all the windows open—and the Cross of the South visible from my pillow—and the seawind pouring over the bed— and the tumultuous whispering and muttering of the surf in one's ears— to dream of that strange sapphire sea white-bursting over its beach of black sand. . . .

*

One whose ideas of the people of Grande Anse had been formed only by observing the young *porteuses* of the region on their way to the other side of the island, might expect on reaching this little town to find its population yellow as that of a Chinese city. But the dominant hue is much darker, although the mixed element is everywhere visible; and I was at first surprised by the scarcity of those clear bright skins I supposed to be so numerous. Some pretty children—notably a pair of twin-sisters, and perhaps a dozen school-girls from eight to ten years of age—displayed the same characteristics I have noted in the adult *porteuses* of Grande Anse; but within the town itself this brighter element is in the minority. The predominating race element of the whole commune is certainly colored (Grande Anse is even memorable because of the revolt of its *hommes de couleur* some fifty years ago);—but the colored population is not concentrated in the town; it belongs rather to the valleys and the heights surrounding the *chef-lieu*. Most of the *porteuses* are country girls, and I found that even those living in the village are seldom visible on the streets except when departing upon a trip or returning from one. An artist wishing to study the type might, however, pass a day at the bridge of the Rivière Falaise to advantage, as all the carrier-girls pass it at certain hours of the morning and evening.

But the best possible occasion on which to observe what my friend the baker called *la belle jeunesse,* is a confirmation day—when the bishop drives to Grande Anse over the mountains, and all the population turns out in holiday garb, and the bells are tapped like tam-tams, and triumphal arches—most awry to behold!—span the road-way, bearing in clumsiest lettering the welcome, *"Vive Monseigneur."* On that event, the long procession of young girls to be confirmed—all in white robes, white veils, and white satin slippers—is a numerical surprise. It is a moral surprise also—to the stranger at least; for it reveals the struggle of a poverty extraordinary with the self-imposed obligations of a costly ceremonialism.

No white children ever appear in these processions: there are not half a dozen white families in the whole urban population of about seven thousand souls; and those send their sons and daughters to Saint Pierre or Morne Rouge for their religious training and education. But many of the colored children look very charming in their costume of confirmation;—you could not easily recognize one of them as the same little *bonne* who brings your morning cup of coffee, or another as the daughter of a plantation *commandeur* (overseer's assistant)—a brown slip of a girl who will probably never wear shoes again. And many of those white shoes and white veils have been obtained only by the hardest physical labor and self-denial of poor parents and relatives: fathers, brothers, and mothers working with cutlass and hoe in the snake-swarming cane-fields; —sisters walking barefooted every day to Saint Pierre and back to earn a few francs a month. . . .

*

I thought Grande Anse the most sleepy place I had ever visited. I suspect it is one of the sleepiest in the whole world. The wind, which tans even a Creole of Saint Pierre to an unnatural brown within forty-eight hours of his sojourn in the village, has also a peculiarly somnolent effect. The moment one has nothing particular to do, and ventures to sit down idly with the breeze in one's face, slumber comes; and everybody who can spare the time takes a long nap in the afternoon, and little naps from hour to hour. For all that, the heat of the east coast is not enervating, like that of Saint Pierre; one can take a great deal of exercise in the sun without feeling much the worse. Hunting excursions, river fishing parties, surf-bathing, and visits to neighboring plantations are the only amusements; but these are enough to make existence very pleasant at Grande Anse. The most interesting of my own experiences were those of a day passed by invitation at one of the old colonial estates on the hills near the village.

It is not easy to describe the charm of a Creole interior, whether in the city or the country. The cool shadowy court, with its wonderful plants and fountain of sparkling mountain water, or the lawn, with its ancestral trees—the delicious welcome of the host, whose fraternal easy manner immediately makes you feel at home—the coming of the children to greet you, each holding up a velvety brown cheek to be kissed, after the old-time custom—the romance of the unconventional chat, over a cool drink, under the palms and the ceibas—the visible earnestness of all to please the guest, to inwrap him in a very atmosphere of quiet happiness— combine to make a memory which you will never forget. And maybe you enjoy all this upon some exquisite site, some volcanic summit, overlook- ing slopes of a hundred greens—mountains far winding in blue and pearly shadowing—rivers singing seaward behind curtains of arborescent reeds and bamboos—and perhaps, Pelée, in the horizon, dreaming violet dreams under her foulard of vapors—and, encircling all, the still sweep of the ocean's azure bending to the verge of day. . . .   ("LA GRANDE ANSE")]

Lafcadio returned to St. Pierre at the end of January 1888 to receive word that Henry Alden at *Harper's Magazine* had rejected a rambling, stylistically overheated novella the writer had worked on for two months (*Lys*)—the story of the disorienting effect of New York City on a simple Creole girl from the tropics. Lafcadio agreed with Alden's negative as- sessment of the manuscript ("I am convinced I have . . . no constructive ability for the manufacture of fiction," he told his editor). But having expected to sell *Lys*, Lafcadio was now almost out of funds and had to move to a small room on the Rue du Morne Mirail in one of the poorer quarters of town. He spent his days getting to know his neighbors— especially Manm-Robert, a woman who sold cigars to the *békés* and nursed her neighbors who had contracted smallpox, and Yzore, the abandoned ex-mistress of a white merchant, who became a *calendeuse* in order to support her three children, whom Lafcadio adored and often looked after while their mother was working.

The children were orphaned when Yzore suddenly died of smallpox, and soon thereafter, Lafcadio himself was a victim of typhoid fever. He lay, delirious, in bed with extreme fever for six weeks, during which time Manm-Robert brought him special herbs from the countryside to hasten his recovery. Several of Lafcadio's white Creole friends, hearing of his illness, came to see him, paid his long overdue rent and expenses, and eventually brought him up to Morne Rouge again to recuperate.

In May, fully recovered, Lafcadio returned to St. Pierre with the first series of articles he had written about Martinique. He sent them off to Alden, who thought them wonderful and who immediately sent the writer a check "by return steamer," with the promise of publication. Lafcadio now had enough money to "organize" his life—which meant he was able to afford a maid-*cum*-mistress (and to feed about thirty cats!).

"I keep house!" he announced to a surprised Matas. "It is the only earthly way of living comfortably here. No one thinks it scandalous, even if your housekeeper be young and pretty, and have a baby suspiciously like you. Fine folks come to visit you all the same: it is the custom! With me, however, there is no romance in the business as you might have suspected: I have just a good, plain, sensible little housekeeper who is really a *bonne,* and that's all!! You see, I could never do literary work, and have any nonsense going on in the house.—You believe all this,—don't you? Of course you do!" (His biographers Elizabeth Bisland and Elizabeth Stevenson would later and characteristically choose to take him at his word. Rudolph Matas knew how to interpret his friend's exclamation points.)

Lafcadio wrote a charming, affectionate portrait of his housekeeper ("*Ma Bonne*"), whose name was Cyrillia, who cooked and cleaned for him, looked after him, and slept with him. She also took issue with him, mostly to say that she thought it was sacrilegious to look at the moon and other works of the *Bon-Dié* (Good God) through a telescope, as Lafcadio would do from his balcony at night. Cyrillia, who kept a statue of the Virgin (to which she prayed) in a box-top *chapelle,* was shocked by Lafcadio's explanations that the stars pulsating in the night sky were really faraway suns. He was delighted by this gentle, credulous young woman, whom he would often find talking to the photograph of her daughter which he had taken and presented to her, and which she had then lovingly hung beside her little chapel.

And he would always listen to what she was saying.

In spite of his self-admitted shortcomings as a creator of fiction, Lafcadio began a novel shortly before he left St. Pierre entitled *Youma: The Story of a West-Indian Slave,* a rather prosaic and sentimental historical tale about a *da* (a black Creole nanny of a white Creole child) who remained loyal unto death to her charge during the 1848 slave revolt on Martinique.

The *da,* Lafcadio once pointed out, was the first person to teach a white Creole infant to say "*manman*" and "*papoute.*" Perhaps the writer may have sensed that his very own dark-eyed *manman* had also, in a way, been his *da.* When the heroine of *Youma,* therefore, remembers *her* dead mother—returning, in a trance, to the time of *her* infancy—Lafcadio imagines her doing so as if Youma's beloved mother were *his* beloved mother:

¶ But again a little while and her mind wakened to the fancy of a voice calling her name,—faintly, as from a great distance,—a voice remembered as in a dream one holds remembrance of dreams gone before.

Then she became aware of a face,—the face of a beautiful brown woman looking at her with black soft eyes,—smiling under the yellow folds of a *madras* turban,—and lighted by a light that came from nowhere,—that was only a memory of some long-dead morning. And through the dimness round about it a soft blue radiance grew,—the ghost of a day; and she knew the face and murmured to it:—*"Doudoux—manman. . . ."*

They two were walking somewhere she had been long ago, —somewhere among *mornes:* she felt the guiding of her mother's hand as when a child.

And before them as they went, something purple and vague and vast rose and spread,—the enormous spectre of the sea, rounding to the sky. . . .

"All my life," Lafcadio declared during his stay in Martinique, "I have suffered with cold—all kinds of cold!!!!—I *never* can resign myself to live in it!—I can't even think in it, and I would not be afraid of that Warm Place where sinners are supposed to go! Perhaps the G. A. [God Almighty] will sentence me to everlasting sojourn in an iceberg when I have ceased to sin." At other times, however, he spoke of "this stupid brutal never-varying heat" that enervated him and sapped his energy and demolished his will. "I find, worst of all," he admitted to Matas in one of his depressed moments, "there is no . . . psychological life, no aspiration, no self-sacrifice, no human effort . . . in the tropics." But a year later he asserted to another friend: "I am convinced now that most of our fashions are deformities; that grace is savage, or must be savage in order to be perfect; that man was never made to wear shoes; that in order to comprehend antiquity, the secret of Greek art, one must know the tropics a little. . . ."

For the sake of his vocation and work, however, Lafcadio sadly knew that it was getting time for him to take his leave of his tropical paradise which, for all its imperfections, would always haunt him with its "azure sea . . . turquoise sky . . . great palms . . . volcanic hills . . . and the beautiful brown women." Having never once regretted his departures from London, Cincinnati, or New Orleans, Lafcadio confessed: "I shall be much pained to leave Martinique,—which they call *Les Pays des Revenants*. I shall be a revenant, if I live."

When Lafcadio was about to leave Martinique, he wrote a letter to Dr. George M. Gould, a Philadelphia ophthalmologist and an admirer of the writer's collection of ghost stories entitled *Some Chinese Ghosts* (1887), with whom Lafcadio had corresponded since his last year in New Orleans. "I shall have to return to the States for a while," Lafcadio declared to Gould, "—a short while, probably;—but I do not think I will settle there. . . . You can comprehend how one becomes tired of the very stones of a place,—the odors, the colors, the shapes of Shadows, and tint of its sky;—and how small irritations become colossal and crushing by years of repetition;—yet perhaps you will not comprehend that one can actually become weary of a whole system of life, civilization, even with very limited experience. Such is exactly my present feeling,—an unutterable weariness of the aggressive characteristics of existence in a highly organized society. The higher the social development, the sharper the struggle. One feels this especially in America,—in the nervous centers of the world's activities."

CHAPTER 2

Nervous Centers

L AFCADIO arrived in New York City on May 8, 1889. After eighteen months in the tropics, he immediately contracted an acute case of culture shock. He also had trouble locating old friends: Elizabeth Bisland was nowhere to be found, nor was his ex-Cincinnati reporter friend Joseph Tunison, with whom he had hoped to stay for a few weeks, and to whom he now wrote a quick note:

This city drives me crazy, or, if you prefer, crazier; and I have no peace of mind or rest of body till I get out of it. Nobody can find anybody, nothing seems to be anywhere, everything seems to be mathematics and geometry and enigmatics and riddles and confusion worse confounded: architecture and mechanics run mad. One has to live by intuition and move by steam. I think an earthquake might produce some improvement. The so-called improvements in civilization have apparently resulted in making it impossible to see, hear, or find anything out. You are improving yourselves out of the natural world. I want to get back among the monkeys and the parrots, under a violet sky among green peaks and an eternally lilac and lukewarm sea,—where clothing is superfluous and reading too much of an exertion,—where everybody sleeps 14 hours out of the 24. This is frightful, nightmarish, devilish! Civilization is a hideous thing. Blessed is savagery! Surely a palm 200 feet high is a finer thing in the natural order than seventy times seven New Yorks. I came in by one door as you went out at the other. Now there are cubic miles of cut granite and iron fury between us. I shall at once find a hackman to take me away. I am sorry not to see you—but since you live in hell what can I do? I will try to find you again this summer.

Best affection,

L.H.   ]

In many of his letters, Dr. Gould had invited Lafcadio to spend five or six months with him and his wife as their guest. Six days after landing in New York, Lafcadio took a train to Philadelphia and found his way to the Gould residence on South Seventeenth Street, where the doctor welcomed him with open arms, somewhat to the dismay of Mrs. Gould.

With the exception of (or possibly *because* of) his own father, Lafcadio had always been drawn to doctors, especially those with a literary bent and curious, inquiring minds, like Rudolph Matas. Matas, especially, had had an unusually candid relationship with Lafcadio, who found him trustworthy, reassuring, and protective. At first, Dr. George Gould manifested these same qualities. He housed and fed Lafcadio (who, like a child, often referred to his protector as "Goolie") and provided the writer with a quiet room in which to complete *Youma* (published in 1890) and correct the proofs of his longest, most ambitious work to date, *Two Years in the French West Indies* (also 1890), consisting of twelve insightful sketches of Martinique life, one folktale, and the earlier article "A Midsummer Trip to the Tropics."

The doctor insisted on examining Lafcadio's right eye and observed that "he had about twenty-five diopters of myopia, to use the jargon of the oculist, and that consequently he knew little about the appearance of objects even a few feet away. . . ." (His attempt to make Lafcadio wear unusually thick-lensed glasses was rejected out of hand by his patient, firm in his belief that glasses strained his one functioning eye.) According to Gould, "intellect [was] largely, almost entirely, the product of vision," and he posited that everything about Lafcadio, both good and bad, was simply a function of his myopia.

Dr. Gould tried to minimize any possible important contributions to knowledge and awareness from the senses of touch, taste, sound, and smell. Lafcadio's articles and essays, however, are particularly sensitive to the odors of places (one thinks especially of his early newspaper report "Balm in Gilead") and people (the writer once told Dr. Matas that he could easily "smell" the difference between a blonde and a brunette!).

Indeed, Matas often declared that Lafcadio's supernormal olfactory sense was undoubtedly a compensation for his subnormal vision.

Like George Washington Cable, George Gould had had a strict puritanical upbringing (he had considered entering the ministry before deciding to become an ophthalmologist), and with his ineradicably preacherlike temperament he tried to persuade Lafcadio of the truth of his theories and to reform the writer's character, ideas, and way of life. He later asserted that he had singlehandedly taught his wayward boarder a sense of duty, and even claimed that he had given Lafcadio a "soul," having persuaded him that beauty was a "needless, harmful, and even impossible thing in a world of adamantine logic and necessity," as well as that "human beings are not always, and may never be wholly, the slaves of the senses and the dupes of desire."

Lafcadio, however, advanced the more subtle, Spencerian evolutionary notion he had once written in response to Henry James's criticisms of Pierre Loti—that "sensual perceptions must be sensitized and refined supernally,—fully evolved and built up *before* the moral ones, of which they are the physiological foundations, pedestals; . . . and that very sensuousness which at once delights and scandalizes James, rather seems to me a splendid augury of the higher sensitiveness to come, in some future age of writers and poets,—the finer 'sensibility of soul,' whose creative work will caress the nobler emotions more delicately than Loti's genius ever caressed the senses of color and form and odor."

For a while, a grateful Lafcadio submitted to his host's objurgations and pronouncements, as if Gould were now his teacher rather than a doctor and a friend. As he docilely remarked to Henry Alden: "How wonderfully a strong well-trained mind can expand a feebler and undisciplined one, when the teacher has pleasure and time to teach." (This from a remarkably disciplined and self-possessed writer!)

Perhaps Lafcadio's relaxed and guilt-free existence in Martinique forced him, upon his return, to confront once again his insecure sense of himself—"confessing" to Dr. Gould that he was truly a "small, puny, sickly, scrofulous" human being, and thereby laying himself open to victimization at the hands of a punitive autocrat and manipulative literary vampire.

Gould would later proudly proclaim, for instance, that a story Lafcadio wrote while staying with him—a second-rate work entitled "Karma" (about a guilty young man, a virtuous young lady, his abject confession, her compassionate forgiveness)—simply "incorporated" the author's "new spirit or soul," a result of the doctor's patient moral programming. "But

["Karma"] was only a *seeming* creation," Gould boasted. "It was only the telling, the coloring, that was [Lafcadio's], as in his other tales before or after. In our long walks and talks in the Park at night, *we* wrought out the title, the datum, and the whole trend of the story. *He rebelled,* but I held him to the task, which he finally executed with frank and artistic loyalty." (The italics are Gould's.)

Lafcadio trumpeted his admiration for Gould's literary and medical genius to Henry Alden and other magazine editors, announcing that the doctor's projected work on the "philosophy of spectacles" would be a *magnum opus.* He wrote an article for Gould—which the doctor published under his own name—assisted him in editing a medical dictionary, and placed an essay by him in a magazine called *Arena.* On taking leave of his mentor, however, and returning to New York, Lafcadio didn't take much time to discover that "Goolie" and "Mrs. Goolie" were more like ghouls than nurturers. Hearing that his benefactor had based a series of professional lectures on some private notebooks and manuscripts he had accidentally left behind in Philadelphia, Lafcadio wrote Gould an angry letter, asking him: "Are *you* a humbug, too!!" And upon receiving a testy note from Mrs. Gould demanding a formal "Thank You" from the writer for everything the couple had done for him, Lafcadio complied with a letter of dutiful beholdenness, and signed it: "Your horrid, horrid little friend, Lafcadio Hearn."

Back in New York in the fall of 1889, Lafcadio was invited to a dinner party on Central Park South, a rare event for the antisocial author. The party, given for him by Alice Wellington Rollins, a writer friend of Elizabeth Bisland's, was held in the Navarro Apartments whose 1882 architecture both fascinated and oppressed him. "Have you seen the Navarro buildings here," he asked Matas, "—a giant block of Moresque style, with interior courts deep as a mountain-canyon, with fountains of electric light instead of water? Fourteen stories each; with a mighty name,—'Cordova,' 'Grenada,' etc. Oh! the beauty of them! $5000 a year rent for a suite of apartments so lofty that men on the street look like flies;—yet, look up, five more stories beetle overhead! Twenty miles view from the gallery. No one climbs the splendid silent stairs that ascend to absolute dizziness. Elevators that move swift as thought, but noiselessly,—you feel, but do not hear the motion."

On his way to the Navarro, like a "savage" wandering half-blind through the "cyclopean streets" of New York, Lafcadio inevitably got lost amidst the "precipices of masonry" and the "thunder of tumult" all around him. So it was not surprising that an hour after the small, informal dinner party was supposed to have begun, Mrs. Rollins resigned herself to seating her guests in the dining room with the guest of honor's place remaining empty.

Meanwhile the wandering Lafcadio finally found his way to the grandiose Navarro façade, whereupon the doorman took one look at him and decided he was certainly not "carriage company." With a contumelious air, he directed him to the service elevator, out of which Lafcadio stumbled a few moments later into the Rollinses' kitchen pantry, and thence into the dining room where the astonished guests were seated, eating their salads. Greatly embarrassed, Lafcadio was shown his seat, and uttered not a word throughout the rest of the meal.

"He wore," one of the guests that night reported, "what we called 'spring-bottom' trousers which even then were out of date, a pea jacket, immaculate linen, and he carried a big, fawn-colored sombrero. . . . He sat off in a corner, rose as if in pain when introduced to anybody, and for the rest of the time he hugged his knees."

A sympathetic observer of this scene asked if he could liberate Lafcadio from his agony, to which Mrs. Rollins compassionately gave her assent. All too willing to make his getaway, Lafcadio found himself in a beer cellar in the West Fifties with another of those tall, broad-shouldered young men whom he had always found so compatible, this one a handsome twenty-eight-year-old bachelor named Ellwood Hendrick, a chemist by vocation who made his living as a successful insurance agent but who would years later become a lecturer in chemistry at Columbia University. "We discussed the ways of simple people," Hendrick said, recalling that night's inebriated conversation, "—of children, of dogs, of children with dogs, of what dogs knew and their point of view. We ventured over into philosophy and into abstractions and back again to human reactions, the sequelae of emotions—everything." Then at two in the morning the young man accompanied his slightly swaying new friend to his door, but woke him up late the next morning to continue their talk. They would talk a good part of that fall and winter, too, as this wryly cheerful scientist helped a grateful Lafcadio through many anxious New York evenings and became one of his few enduring, trusted friends.

Hendrick was the only person who could get Lafcadio to go almost anywhere, once accompanying him to meet Jay Gould's daughter Helen at the Gould mansion on Fifth Avenue. "I'm surprised you'll go to Jay

Gould's with me," the startled Hendrick remarked to his friend. Lafcadio simply said: "I'd go *anywhere* with you!" He was soon sorry he had been so complaisant, however. When the two men arrived at the mansion, the butler graciously let Hendrick enter but slammed the door on the shabby-looking fellow who had been standing shyly behind him in the shadows. Once allowed in, Lafcadio almost disappeared in an enormous chair in the gigantic drawing room. Even after being led to a more intimate sitting room by Miss Gould, who had been looking forward to meeting the renowned writer, Lafcadio made it perfectly clear to both Helen and Ellwood that it was already time for him to leave.

Lafcadio preferred going with Hendrick to call on Elizabeth Bisland, who he now found had "expanded mentally and physically into one of the most superb women you could wish to converse with. . . . It now seems to me as I had only seen the *chrysalis* of her before; this is the silkmoth!" Bisland, who had become the editor of *Cosmopolitan Magazine,* held court in her rooms above a candy shop on Fourth Avenue; and her salon was filled with rich and handsome suitors, each one attempting to outwit and outwait the others for a moment of privacy with this formidable woman. "She is a witch—turning heads everywhere," Lafcadio observed; "but some of her best admirers are afraid of her. One told me he felt as if he were playing with a beautiful dangerous leopard, which he loved for not biting him. As for me she is like hasheesh: I can't remember anything she says or anything I myself say after leaving the house; my head is all in a whirl, and I walk against people in the street, and get run over, and lose my way—my sense of orientation being grievously disturbed. But I am not in love at all,—no such foolishness as that: I am only experiencing the sensation produced upon—alas!—*hundreds* of finer men than I."

Years later, George Gould claimed it was he alone who first gave Lafcadio the idea to visit Japan and, furthermore, urged him to appreciate it with the proper "attitude of mind." Yet in his early days in New Orleans, Lafcadio was already writing to Henry Watkin: "Have also wild theories regarding Japan. Splendid field [for study] in Japan. . . . Climate just like England,—perhaps a little milder." In 1885, moreover, he contributed several articles to *Harper's Weekly* and *Harper's Bazaar* on the Japanese exhibit at the New Orleans Exposition of 1885.

The entrance to this impressive exhibit was through a highly decorated screenwork, inside which the enthralled writer came across large incense burners, delicate porcelain vases, tiny bronze gods, cotton crickets and cotton grasshoppers, embroidered silks, and breathtaking examples of ink-brush painting with its poetry of visible motion: "A flight of gulls sweeping through the gold light of a summer morning; a long line of cranes sailing against a vermilion sky; a swallow twirling its kite shape against the disk of the sun; the heavy, eccentric, velvety flight of bats under the moon; the fairy hoverings of moths or splendid butterflies. . . ."

Lafcadio returned many times to the exhibit with the same childlike delight and wonder he had felt when, as an eight-year-old, he viewed the Eastern bric-a-brac in the sea-captain's cottage in Carnarvon, Wales, and with the exhilaration he felt on reading Percival Lowell's *The Soul of the Far East*, a work that whetted his appetite to visit the Far East and one that he himself recommended to George Gould: "I have a book for you—an astounding book,—a godlike book. But I want you to promise to read every single word of it. Every word is dynamic. It is the finest book on the East ever written."

Lafcadio was frustrated with "trying to find the Orient at home," as he had once stated to Elizabeth Bisland. Now, having left Philadelphia, he realized that he would have either to look for a full-time, enslaving newspaper job in an unbearable city like New York or find a new world—preferably in the Orient—to explore and write about. So when William Patten, an art editor at *Harper's Magazine*, asked Lafcadio offhandedly one afternoon if he had ever thought of writing some articles about Japan, it was suddenly clear to him what he would do.

Ever since 1854, when Commodore Perry officially opened up imperial Japan ports to Western trade and influence, the American public longed for information about this enigmatic, mostly superficially described land. The arrival in New York harbor on June 16, 1860, of diplomat princes from Japan had further piqued the public's curiosity. Walt Whitman witnessed the procession up Broadway of these impassive and exotic envoys, riding in open barouches to the stares of "million footed Manhattan unpent." To Whitman, these princes' eastward voyage mirrored Columbus's westward journey; and looking westward to the East, the poet espied in the antipodes the place of mankind's origins:

> Inquiring, tireless, seeking that yet unfound,
> I, a child, very old, over waves toward the house
>   of maternity, the land of migrations, look afar,
> Look off the shores of my Western sea—having
>   arrived at last where I am—the circle
>   almost circled.

On November 28, 1889, Lafcadio sent Harper and Brothers a proposal for his next travel book: "In attempting a book upon a country so well trodden as Japan, I could not hope—nor would I consider it prudent attempting,—to discover totally new things, but only to consider things in a totally new way. . . . The studied aim would be to create, in the minds of the readers, a vivid impression of *living* in Japan,—not simply as an observer but as one taking part in the daily existence of the common people, and *thinking with their thoughts.*" Henry Alden agreed to publish such a book, but, nervous about the writer's "oversensitive" nature, offered him no contract and no advance.

Desperate for money to finance his journey, Lafcadio agreed to take on the job of translating Anatole France's novel *Le Crime de Sylvestre Bonnard,* which he completed in creditable fashion in two weeks for $115. He also rushed off a couple of articles for *Harper's Magazine* and garnered an assignment from the Canadian Pacific Railway to write about the transcontinental railway trip that would be the first leg of his journey to Japan. Then he gathered up some clothes, bought a larger than usual supply of yellow writing paper, and finally went about either saying fond good-byes or, as was his wont, breaking off the ties that bound him to his friends.

In a revelatory article he wrote for *Harper's Magazine* in December 1889 ("A Ghost"), Lafcadio discoursed on a certain type of person he designated as "the civilized nomad," whose peripatetic life displayed "irrational partings,—self-wreckings,—sudden isolations,—abrupt severances of attachment." Unannounced, he went to his old friend Krehbiel's apartment to pick up a pair of shoes he had remembered leaving there almost two years before. A new maid answered the bell, beheld a bizarre-looking stranger asking to be admitted to retrieve some shoes, and slammed the door in his face. Fuming, Lafcadio, who had felt increasingly less intimate with the increasingly stiff and conventional Krehbiel, sent a vitriolic note to his old friend, who replied: "Dear Hearn—You can go to Japan or you can go to hell."

He stopped by Elizabeth Bisland's apartment, knowing that she was away on a trip around the world representing *Cosmopolitan Magazine* in competition with a rival magazine's editor to see who could circle the planet first. (Lafcadio always played the tortoise to Elizabeth's hare.) "Did you often wish to stop somewhere," he wondered at the outset of her seventy-five-day dash, "and feel hearts beating about you, and see the faces of gods and dancing-girls? Or were you petted like the *Lady of the Aroostook* by officers and crews,—and British dignitaries eager to win one

Circe-smile,—and superb Indian Colonels of princely houses returning home,—that you had no chance to regret anything? I have been so afraid of never seeing you again, that I have been hating splendid imaginary foreigners in dreams,—which would have been quite wickedly selfish if I had been awake!"

Now, on the day he himself was to depart—and having said a heartfelt good-bye to his warm and loyal friend Ellwood Hendrick—Lafcadio quickly wrote a letter to his Lady of a Myriad Souls, and left it with her doorman for her return:

I must write you a line or two, before I finish packing—though it is the hour of ghosts, when writing is a grave imprudence. Something makes me write you nevertheless. . . .

I shall be very sorry not to see you again—and this time, you are not sorry to know I am going away as you were when I went South. Perhaps you are quite right. . . .

—But that is nothing. What I want to say is, that after looking at your portrait, I must tell you how sweet and infinitely good you . . . can be, and how much I like you, and how I like you—or at least *some* of those many who are one in you.

I might say love you—as we love those who are dead (the dead who still shape lives);—but which, or how many, of you I cannot say. One looks at me from your picture; but I have seen others, equally pleasing and less mysterious.

. . . Not when you were in evening dress, because you were then too beautiful; and what is thus beautiful is not that which is most charming in you. It only dazzles one, and constrains. . . . I like you best in the simple dark dress, when I can forget everything except all the souls of you. Turn by turn one or other floats up from the depth within and rushes to your face and transfigures it;—and that one which made you smile with pleasure like a child at something pretty we were both admiring is simply divine. . . . I do not think you really know how sacred you are; and yet you ought to know: it is because you do not know what is in you, *who* are in you, that you say such strangely material things. And you yourself, by being, utterly contradict them all.

It seems to me that all those mysterious lives within you—all the Me's that were—keep asking the Me that is, for something always refused;— that you keep saying to them: "But you are dead and cannot see—you can only feel; and *I* can see—and I will not open to you, because the world is all changed. You would not know it, and you would be angry with me were I to grant your wish. Go to your places, and sleep and wait and leave me in peace with myself." But they continue to wake up betimes, and quiver into momentary visibility to make you divine in spite of yourself—and as suddenly flit away again. I wish one would come—and stay: the one I saw that night when we were looking at . . . what was it?

Really, I can't remember what it was: the smile effaced the memory of it—just as a sun-ray blots the image from a dry-plate suddenly exposed. There was such a child-beauty in that smile. . . . Will you ever be *like that always* for any one being?

—I hope you will get my book [*Two Years in the French West Indies*]; it will be sent you Tuesday at latest, I think. I don't know whether you will like the paper; but you will only look for the "gnat of a soul" that belongs to me between the leaves.

—Forgive me all my horrid ways, my dear, sweet, ghostly sister.

Good-bye

Lafcadio Hearn

Lafcadio left New York City for Montreal on March 8, 1890; traveled by train across the Canadian plains and Rockies blanketed in snow; boarded the steamship *Abyssinia* in Vancouver on March 17; then, like Tennyson's Ulysses, he sailed "beyond the sunset, and the baths of all the western stars" toward the Country of Eight Islands.

Part

Four

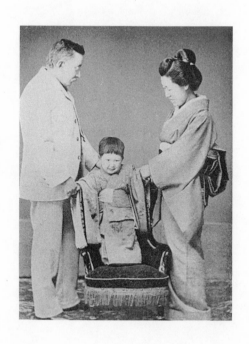

CHAPTER 1

In

Fairyland

C HILDHOOD remains within us a principle of deep life," the French philosopher Gaston Bachelard once stated, "of life always in harmony with the possibilities of new beginnings. Everything that begins in us with the distinctness of a beginning is a madness of life."

Whenever Lafcadio traveled somewhere for the first time, he did so with a kind of excitement, curiosity, and joy that was profoundly connected to his imagination and memory—as if he were reentering the realm of childhood itself.

It was in such a state that he arrived in Yokohama on April 12, 1890, and realized at once that the first charm of Japan was "intangible and volatile as a perfume." Fortunately he had a letter of introduction to the distinguished English professor Basil Hall Chamberlain, an expert in both spoken and written Japanese who taught Japanese literature at Tokyo Imperial University and who, at their first meeting, advised Lafcadio (perhaps redundantly): "Do not fail to write down your first impressions as soon as possible. They are evanescent, you know; they will never come to you again, once they have faded out; and yet of all the strange sensations you may receive in this country, you will feel none so charming as these."

It all began with his first *kuruma* ride out of the European quarter of the city into the Japanese town, where his myopic eyes allowed him to see in filmy mists of cherry petals and the gilded gleams of the lotus blossoms a "beauty of ghostly haze" that coincidentally mirrored the Japanese esthetic of ambiguous beauty:

It is with the delicious surprise of the first journey through Japanese streets—unable to make one's *kuruma*-runner understand anything but gestures, frantic gestures to roll on anywhere, everywhere, since all is unspeakably pleasurable, and new—that one first receives the real sensation of being in the Orient, in this Far East so much read of, so long dreamed of, yet, as the eyes bear witness, heretofore all unknown. There is a romance even in the first full consciousness of this rather commonplace fact; but for me this consciousness is transfigured inexpressibly by the divine beauty of the day. There is some charm unutterable in the morning air, cool with the coolness of Japanese spring and wind-waves from the snowy cone of Fuji; a charm perhaps due rather to softest lucidity than to any positive tone,—an atmospheric limpidity extraordinary, with only a suggestion of blue in it, through which the most distant objects appear focused with amazing sharpness. The sun is only pleasantly warm; the *jinrikisha,* or *kuruma,* is the most cosy little vehicle imaginable; and the street-vistas, as seen above the dancing white mushroom-shaped hat of my sandaled runner, have an allurement of which I fancy that I could never weary.

Elfish everything seems; for everything as well as everybody is small, and queer, and mysterious: the little houses under their blue roofs, the little shop-fronts hung with blue, and the smiling little people in their blue costumes. The illusion is only broken by the occasional passing of a tall foreigner, and by divers shop-signs bearing announcements in absurd attempts at English. Nevertheless such discords only serve to emphasize reality; they never materially lessen the fascination of the funny little streets.

'Tis at first a delightfully odd confusion only, as you look down one of them, through an interminable flutter of flags and swaying of dark blue drapery, all made beautiful and mysterious with Japanese or Chinese lettering. For there are no immediately discernible laws of construction or decoration: each building seems to have a fantastic prettiness of its own; nothing is exactly like anything else, and all is bewilderingly novel. But gradually, after an hour passed in the quarter, the eye begins to recognize in a vague way some general plan in the construction of these low, light, queerly-gabled wooden houses, mostly unpainted, with their first stories all open to the street, and thin strips of roofing sloping above each shop-front, like awnings, back to the miniature balconies of paper-screened second stories. You begin to understand the common plan of the tiny shops, with their matted floors well raised above the street level, and the general perpendicular arrangement of sign-lettering, whether undulating on drapery or glimmering on gilded and lacquered sign-boards. You observe that the same rich dark blue which dominates in popular costume rules also in shop draperies, though there is a sprinkling of other tints,— bright blue and white and red (no greens or yellows). And then you note also that the dresses of the laborers are lettered with the same wonderful lettering as the shop draperies. No arabesques could produce such an effect. As modified for decorative purposes, these ideographs have a speaking symmetry which no design without a meaning could possess. As they appear on the back of a workman's frock—pure white on dark blue—and large enough to be easily read at a great distance (indicating some guild or company of which the wearer is a member or employee), they give to the poor cheap garment a factitious appearance of splendor.

And finally, while you are still puzzling over the mystery of things, there will come to you like a revelation the knowledge that most of the amazing picturesqueness of these streets is simply due to the profusion of Chinese and Japanese characters in white, black, blue, or gold, decorating everything,—even surfaces of doorposts and paper screens. Perhaps, then, for one moment, you will imagine the effect of English lettering substituted for those magical characters; and the mere idea will give to whatever aesthetic sentiment you may possess a brutal shock, and you will become, as I have become, an enemy of the Romaji-Kwai,—that society founded for the ugly utilitarian purpose of introducing the use of English letters in writing Japanese.

*

An ideograph does not make upon the Japanese brain any impression similar to that created in the Occidental brain by a letter or combination of letters,—dull, inanimate symbols of vocal sounds. To the Japanese brain an ideograph is a vivid picture: it lives; it speaks; it gesticulates. And the whole space of a Japanese street is full of such living characters,—figures that cry out to the eyes, words that smile or grimace like faces.

What such lettering is, compared with our own lifeless types, can be understood only by those who have lived in the farther East. For even the printed characters of Japanese or Chinese imported texts give no suggestion of the possible beauty of the same characters as modified for decorative inscriptions, for sculptural use, or for the commonest advertising purposes. No rigid convention fetters the fancy of the calligrapher or designer: each strives to make his characters more beautiful than any others; and generations upon generations of artists have been toiling from

time immemorial with like emulation, so that through centuries and centuries of tireless effort and study, the primitive hieroglyph or ideograph
has been evolved into a thing of beauty indescribable. It consists only of
a certain number of brush-strokes; but in each stroke there is an undis-
coverable secret art of grace, proportion, imperceptible curve, which actually makes it seem alive, and bears witness that even during the
lightning-moment of its creation the artist felt with his brush for the ideal
shape of the stroke *equally along its entire length,* from head to tail. But
the art of the strokes is not all; the art of their combination is that which
produces the enchantment, often so as to astonish the Japanese themselves. It is not surprising, indeed, considering the strangely personal,
animate, esoteric aspect of Japanese lettering, that there should be wonderful legends of calligraphy, relating how words written by holy experts
became incarnate, and descended from their tablets to hold converse with
mankind.

*

My *kurumaya* calls himself "Cha." He has a white hat which looks like
the top of an enormous mushroom; a short blue wide-sleeved jacket;
blue drawers, close-fitting as "tights," and reaching to his ankles; and
light straw sandals bound upon his bare feet with cords of palmetto-fibre.
Doubtless he typifies all the patience, endurance, and insidious coaxing
powers of his class. He has already manifested his power to make me
give him more than the law allows; and I have been warned against him
in vain. For the first sensation of having a human being for a horse,
trotting between shafts, unwearyingly bobbing up and down before you
for hours, is alone enough to evoke a feeling of compassion. And when
this human being, thus trotting between shafts, with all his hopes, memories, sentiments, and comprehensions, happens to have the gentlest smile,
and the power to return the least favor by an apparent display of infinite
gratitude, this compassion becomes sympathy, and provokes unreasoning
impulses to self-sacrifice. I think the sight of the profuse perspiration has
also something to do with the feeling, for it makes one think of the cost
of heart-beats and muscle-contractions, likewise of chills, congestions,
and pleurisy. Cha's clothing is drenched; and he mops his face with a
small sky-blue towel, with figures of bamboo-sprays and sparrows in
white upon it, which towel he carries wrapped about his wrist as he runs.

That, however, which attracts me in Cha—Cha considered not as a motive
power at all, but as a personality—I am rapidly learning to discern in the

multitudes of faces turned toward us as we roll through these miniature streets. And perhaps the supremely pleasurable impression of this morning is that produced by the singular gentleness of popular scrutiny. Everybody looks at you curiously; but there is never anything disagreeable, much less hostile in the gaze: most commonly it is accompanied by a smile or half smile. And the ultimate consequence of all these kindly curious looks and smiles is that the stranger finds himself thinking of fairy-land. Hackneyed to the degree of provocation this statement no doubt is: everybody describing the sensations of his first Japanese day talks of the land as fairy-land, and of its people as fairy-folk. Yet there is a natural reason for this unanimity in choice of terms to describe what is almost impossible to describe more accurately at the first essay. To find one's self suddenly in a world where everything is upon a smaller and daintier scale than with us,—a world of lesser and seemingly kindlier beings, all smiling at you as if to wish you well,—a world where all movement is slow and soft, and voices are hushed,—a world where land, life, and sky are unlike all that one has known elsewhere,—this is surely the realization, for imaginations nourished with English folklore, of the old dream of a World of Elves.

*

The traveler who enters suddenly into a period of social change—especially change from a feudal past to a democratic present—is likely to regret the decay of things beautiful and the ugliness of things new. What of both I may yet discover in Japan I know not; but to-day, in these exotic streets, the old and the new mingle so well that one seems to set off the other. The line of tiny white telegraph poles carrying the world's news to papers printed in a mixture of Chinese and Japanese characters; an electric bell in some tea-house with an Oriental riddle of text pasted beside the ivory button; a shop of American sewing-machines next to the shop of a maker of Buddhist images; the establishment of a photographer beside the establishment of a manufacturer of straw sandals: all these present no striking incongruities, for each sample of Occidental innovation is set into an Oriental frame that seems adaptable to any picture. But on the first day, at least, the Old alone is new for the stranger, and suffices to absorb his attention. It then appears to him that everything Japanese is delicate, exquisite, admirable,—even a pair of common wooden chopsticks in a paper bag with a little drawing upon it; even a package of toothpicks of cherry-wood, bound with a paper wrapper wonderfully lettered in three different colors; even the little sky-blue towel, with designs of flying sparrows upon it, which the *jinrikisha* man uses to wipe his face. The bank bills, the commonest copper coins, are things of beauty. Even the piece of plaited colored string used by the shopkeeper in tying up your last purchase is a pretty curiosity. Curiosities and dainty objects bewilder you by their very multitude: on either side of you, wherever you turn your eyes, are countless wonderful things as yet incomprehensible.

But it is perilous to look at them. Every time you dare to look, something obliges you to buy it,—unless, as may often happen, the smiling vender invites your inspection of so many varieties of one article, each specially and all unspeakably desirable, that you flee away out of mere terror at your own impulses. The shopkeeper never asks you to buy; but his wares are enchanted, and if you once begin buying you are lost. Cheapness means only a temptation to commit bankruptcy; for the resources of irresistible artistic cheapness are inexhaustible. The largest steamer that crosses the Pacific could not contain what you wish to purchase. For, although you may not, perhaps, confess the fact to yourself, what you really want to buy is not the contents of a shop; you want the shop and the shopkeeper, and streets of shops with their draperies and their habitants, the whole city and the bay and the mountains begirdling it, and Fujiyama's white witchery overhanging it in the speckless sky, all Japan, in very truth, with its magical trees and luminous atmosphere, with all its cities and towns and temples, and forty millions of the most lovable people in the universe.

Now there comes to my mind something I once heard said by a practical American on hearing of a great fire in Japan: "Oh! those people can afford fires; their houses are so cheaply built." It is true that the frail wooden houses of the common people can be cheaply and quickly replaced; but that which was within them to make them beautiful cannot,—and every fire is an art tragedy. For this is the land of infinite hand-made variety; machinery has not yet been able to introduce sameness and utilitarian ugliness in cheap production (except in response to foreign demand for bad taste to suit vulgar markets), and each object made by the artist or artisan differs still from all others, even of his own making. And each time something beautiful perishes by fire, it is a something representing an individual idea.

Happily the art impulse itself, in this country of conflagrations, has a vitality which survives each generation of artists, and defies the flame that changes their labor to ashes or melts it to shapelessness. The idea whose symbol has perished will reappear again in other creations,—perhaps after the passing of a century,—modified, indeed, yet recognizably of kin to the thought of the past. And every artist is a ghostly worker. Not by years of groping and sacrifice does he find his highest expression; the sacrificial past is within him; his art is an inheritance; his fingers are guided by the dead in the delineation of a flying bird, of the vapors of mountains, of the colors of the morning and the evening, of the shape of branches and the spring burst of flowers: generations of skilled workmen have given him their cunning, and revive in the wonder of his drawing. What was conscious effort in the beginning became unconscious in later centuries,— becomes almost automatic in the living man,—becomes the art instinctive. Wherefore, one colored print by a Hokusai or Hiroshige, originally sold for less than a cent, may have more real art in it than many a Western painting valued at more than the worth of a whole Japanese street.

*

Here are Hokusai's own figures walking about in straw rain-coats, and immense mushroom-shaped hats of straw, and straw sandals,—bare-limbed peasants, deeply tanned by wind and sun; and patient-faced mothers with smiling bald babies on their backs, toddling by upon their *geta* (high, noisy, wooden clogs), and robed merchants squatting and smoking their little brass pipes among the countless riddles of their shops.

Then I notice how small and shapely the feet of the people are,— whether bare brown feet of peasants, or beautiful feet of children wearing tiny, tiny *geta*, or feet of young girls in snowy *tabi*. The *tabi*, the white digitated stocking, gives to a small light foot a mythological aspect,—the white cleft grace of the foot of a fauness. Clad or bare, the Japanese foot has the antique symmetry: it has not yet been distorted by the infamous foot-gear which has deformed the feet of Occidentals.

. . . Of every pair of Japanese wooden clogs, one makes in walking a slightly different sound from the other, as *kring* to *krang;* so that the echo of the walker's steps has an alternate rhythm of tones. On a pavement, such as that of a railway station, the sound obtains immense sonority; and a crowd will sometimes intentionally fall into step, with the drollest conceivable result of drawling wooden noise.

*

"*Tera e yuke!*" I have been obliged to return to the European hotel,— not because of the noon-meal, as I really begrudge myself the time necessary to eat it, but because I cannot make Cha understand that I want

to visit a Buddhist temple. Now Cha understands; my landlord has uttered the mystical words,—

"*Tera e yuke!*"

A few minutes of running along broad thoroughfares lined with gardens
and costly ugly European buildings; then passing the bridge of a canal
stocked with unpainted sharp-prowed craft of extraordinary construction,
we again plunge into narrow low bright pretty streets,—into another part
of the Japanese city. And Cha runs at the top of his speed between more
rows of little ark-shaped houses, narrower above than below; between
other unfamiliar lines of little open shops. And always over the shops
little strips of blue-tiled roof slope back to the paper-screened chamber
of upper floors; and from all the façades hang draperies dark blue, or
white, or crimson,—foot-breadths of texture covered with beautiful Japanese lettering, white on blue, red on black, black on white. But all this
flies by swiftly as a dream. Once more we cross a canal; we rush up a
narrow street rising to meet a hill; and Cha, halting suddenly before an
immense flight of broad stone steps, sets the shafts of his vehicle on the
ground that I may dismount, and, pointing to the steps, exclaims,—

"*Tera!*"

I dismount, and ascend them, and, reaching a broad terrace, find myself face to face with a wonderful gate, topped by a tilted, peaked, many-
cornered Chinese roof. It is all strangely carven, this gate. Dragons are
intertwined in a frieze above its open doors; and the panels of the doors
themselves are similarly sculptured; and there are gargoyles—grotesque
lion heads—protruding from the eaves. And the whole is gray, stone-
colored; to me, nevertheless, the carvings do not seem to have the fixity
of sculpture; all the snakeries and dragonries appear to undulate with a
swarming motion, elusively, in eddyings as of water.

I turn a moment to look back through the glorious light. Sea and sky
mingle in the same beautiful pale clear blue. Below me the billowing of
bluish roofs reaches to the verge of the unruffled bay on the right, and to
the feet of the green wooded hills flanking the city on two sides. Beyond
that semicircle of green hills rises a lofty range of serrated mountains,
indigo silhouettes. And enormously high above the line of them towers
an apparition indescribably lovely,—one solitary snowy cone, so filmily
exquisite, so spiritually white, that but for its immemorially familiar outline, one would surely deem it a shape of cloud. Invisible its base remains,
being the same delicious tint as the sky: only above the eternal snow-line
its dreamy cone appears, seeming to hang, the ghost of a peak, between

the luminous land and the luminous heaven,—the sacred and matchless mountain, Fujiyama.

And suddenly, a singular sensation comes upon me as I stand before this weirdly sculptured portal,—a sensation of dream and doubt. It seems to me that the steps, and the dragon-swarming gate, and the blue sky arching over the roofs of the town, and the ghostly beauty of Fuji, and the shadow of myself there stretching upon the gray masonry, must all vanish presently. Why such a feeling? Doubtless because the forms before me—the curved roofs, the coiling dragons, the Chinese grotesqueries of carving—do not really appear to me as things new, but as things dreamed: the sight of them must have stirred to life forgotten memories of picture-books. A moment, and the delusion vanishes; the romance of reality returns, with freshened consciousness of all that which is truly and deliciously new; the magical transparencies of distance, the wondrous delicacy of the tones of the living picture, the enormous height of the summer blue, and the white soft witchery of the Japanese sun.

*

I pass on and climb more steps to a second gate with similar gargoyles and swarming of dragons, and enter a court where graceful votive lanterns of stone stand like monuments. On my right and left two great grotesque stone lions are sitting,—the lions of Buddha, male and female. Beyond is a long low light building, with curved and gabled roof of blue tiles, and three wooden steps before its entrance. Its sides are simple wooden screens covered with thin white paper. This is the temple.

On the steps I take off my shoes; a young man slides aside the screens closing the entrance, and bows me a gracious welcome. And I go in, feeling under my feet a softness of matting thick as bedding. An immense square apartment is before me, full of an unfamiliar sweet smell—the scent of Japanese incense; but after the full blaze of the sun, the paper-filtered light here is dim as moonshine; for a minute or two I can see nothing but gleams of gilding in a soft gloom. Then, my eyes becoming accustomed to the obscurity, I perceive against the paper-paned screens surrounding the sanctuary on three sides shapes of enormous flowers cutting like silhouettes against the vague white light. I approach and find them to be paper flowers,—symbolic lotus-blossoms beautifully colored, with curling leaves gilded on the upper surface and bright green beneath. At the dark end of the apartment, facing the entrance, is the altar of Buddha, a rich and lofty altar, covered with bronzes and gilded utensils clustered to right and left of a shrine like a tiny gold temple. But I see no statue; only a mystery of unfamiliar shapes of burnished metal, relieved against darkness, a darkness behind the shrine and altar—whether recess or inner sanctuary I cannot distinguish.

The young attendant who ushered me into the temple now approaches, and, to my great surprise, exclaims in excellent English, pointing to a richly decorated gilded object between groups of candelabra on the altar:—

"That is the shrine of Buddha."

"And I would like to make an offering to Buddha," I respond.

"It is not necessary," he says, with a polite smile.

But I insist; and he places the little offering for me upon the altar. Then he invites me to his own room, in a wing of the building,—a large luminous room, without furniture, beautifully matted. And we sit down upon the floor and chat. He tells me he is a student in the temple. He learned English in Tōkyō, and speaks it with a curious accent, but with fine choice of words. Finally he asks me—

"Are you a Christian?"

And I answer truthfully:—

"No."

"Are you a Buddhist?"

"Not exactly."

"Why do you make offerings if you do not believe in Buddha?"

"I revere the beauty of his teaching, and the faith of those who follow it."

"Are there Buddhists in England and America?"

"There are, at least, a great many interested in Buddhist philosophy."

And he takes from an alcove a little book, and gives it to me to examine. It is an English copy of Olcott's *Buddhist Catechism.*

"Why is there no image of Buddha in your temple?" I ask.

"There is a small one in the shrine upon the altar," the student answers; "but the shrine is closed. And we have several large ones. But the image of Buddha is not exposed here every day—only upon festal days. And some images are exposed only once or twice a year.

From my place, I can see, between the open paper screens, men and women ascending the steps, to kneel and pray before the entrance of the temple. They kneel with such naïve reverence, so gracefully and so nat-

urally, that the kneeling of our Occidental devotees seems a clumsy stum-
bling by comparison. Some only join their hands; others clap them three
times loudly and slowly; then they bow their heads, pray silently for a
moment, and rise and depart. The shortness of the prayers impresses me
as something novel and interesting. From time to time I hear the clink
and rattle of brazen coin cast into the great wooden money-box at the
entrance.

I turn to the young student, and ask him:—
    "Why do they clap their hands three times before they pray?"
    He answers:—
    "Three times for the Sansai, the Three Powers: Heaven, Earth, Man."
    "But do they clap their hands to call the Gods, as Japanese clap their
hands to summon their attendants?"
    "Oh, no!" he replies. "The clapping of hands represents only the awak-
ening from the Dream of the Long Night." [Properly speaking, Buddhist
worshippers should not clap the hands, but only rub them softly together.
Shintō worshippers always clap their hands four times.]
    "What night? what dream?"
    He hesitates some moments before making answer:—
    "The Buddha said: All beings are only dreaming in this fleeting world
of unhappiness."
    "Then the clapping of hands signifies that in prayer the soul awakens
from such dreaming?"
    "Yes."
    "You understand what I mean by the word 'soul'?"
    "Oh, yes! Buddhists believe the soul always was, always will be."
    "Even in Nirvana?"
    "Yes."
    While we are thus chatting the Chief Priest of the temple enters,—a
very aged man,—accompanied by two young priests, and I am presented
to them; and the three bow very low, showing me the glossy crowns of
their smoothly-shaven heads, before seating themselves in the fashion of
gods upon the floor. I observe they do not smile; these are the first
Japanese I have seen who do not smile: their faces are impassive as the
faces of images. But their long eyes observe me very closely, while the
student interprets their questions, and while I attempt to tell them something about the translations of the Sutras in our *Sacred Books of the East*,
and about the labors of Beal and Burnouf and Feer and Davids and Kern,

and others. They listen without change of countenance, and utter no word in response to the young student's translation of my remarks. Tea, however, is brought in and set before me in a tiny cup, placed in a little brazen saucer, shaped like a lotus-leaf; and I am invited to partake of some little sugar-cakes (*kwashi*), stamped with a figure which I recognize as the Swastika, the ancient Indian symbol of the Wheel of the Law.

As I rise to go, all rise with me; and at the steps the student asks for my name and address.

"For," he adds, "you will not see me here again, as I am going to leave the temple. But I will visit you."

"And your name?" I ask.

"Call me Akira," he answers.

At the threshold I bow my good-bye; and they all bow very, very low,—one blue-black head, three glossy heads like balls of ivory. And as I go, only Akira smiles.

*

"*Tera?*" queries Cha, with his immense white hat in his hand, as I resume my seat in the *jinrikisha* at the foot of the steps. Which no doubt means, do I want to see any more temples? Most certainly I do: I have not yet seen Buddha.

"Yes, *tera*, Cha."

And again begins the long panorama of mysterious shops and tilted eaves, and fantastic riddles written over everything. I have no idea in what direction Cha is running. I only know that the streets seem to become always narrower as we go, and that some of the houses look like great wickerwork pigeon-cages only, and that we pass over several bridges before we halt again at the foot of another hill. There is a lofty flight of steps here also, and before them a structure which I know is both a gate and a symbol, imposing, yet in no manner resembling the great Buddhist gateway seen before. Astonishingly simple all the lines of it are: it has no carving, no coloring, no lettering upon it; yet it has a weird solemnity, an enigmatic beauty. It is a *torii*.

"*Miya*," observes Cha. Not a *tera* this time, but a shrine of the gods of the more ancient faith of the land,—a *miya*.

I am standing before a Shintō symbol; I see for the first time, out of a picture at least, a *torii*. How describe a *torii* to those who have never looked at one even in a photograph or engraving? Two lofty columns, like gate-pillars, supporting horizontally two cross-beams, the lower and lighter beam having its ends fitted into the columns a little distance below their summits; the uppermost and larger beam supported upon the tops of the columns, and projecting well beyond them to right and left. That is a *torii:* the construction varying little in design, whether made of stone, wood, or metal. But this description can give no correct idea of the appearance of a *torii,* of its majestic aspect, or its mystical suggestiveness as a gateway. The first time you see a noble one, you will imagine, perhaps, that you see the colossal model of some beautiful Chinese letter towering against the sky; for all the lines of the thing have the grace of an animated ideograph,—have the bold angles and curves of characters made with four sweeps of a master-brush.

Passing the *torii* I ascend a flight of perhaps one hundred stone steps, and find at their summit a second *torii,* from whose lower cross-beam hangs festooned the mystic *shimenawa.* It is in this case a hempen rope of perhaps two inches in diameter through its greater length, but tapering off at either end like a snake. Sometimes the *shimenawa* is made of bronze, when the *torii* itself is of bronze; but according to tradition it should be made of straw, and most commonly is. For it represents the straw rope which the deity Futo-tama-no-mikoto stretched behind the Sun-goddess, Ama-terasu-oho-mi-Kami, after Ame-no-ta-jikara-wo-no-Kami, the Heavenly-handstrength-god, had pulled her out, as is told in that ancient myth of Shintō which Professor Chamberlain has translated. And the *shimenawa,* in its commoner and simpler form, has pendent tufts of straw along its entire length, at regular intervals, because originally made, tradition declares, of grass pulled up by the roots which protruded from the twist of it.

Advancing beyond this *torii,* I find myself in a sort of park or pleasure-ground on the summit of the hill. There is a small temple on the right; it is all closed up; and I have read so much about the disappointing vacuity of Shintō temples that I do not regret the absence of its guardian. And I see before me what is infinitely more interesting,—a grove of cherry-trees covered with something unutterably beautiful,—a dazzling mist of snowy blossoms clinging like summer cloud-fleece about every branch and twig; and the ground beneath them, and the path before me, is white with the soft, thick, odorous snow of fallen petals.

Beyond this loveliness are flower-pots surrounding tiny shrines; and marvelous grotto-work, full of monsters,—dragons and mythologic beings chiseled in the rock; and miniature landscape work with tiny groves of dwarf trees, and lilliputian lakes, and microscopic brooks and bridges and cascades. Here, also, are swings for children. And here are belvederes, perched on the verge of the hill, wherefrom the whole fair city, and the whole smooth bay speckled with fishing-sails no bigger than pin-heads, and the far, faint, high promontories reaching into the sea, are all visible in one delicious view,—blue-penciled in a beauty of ghostly haze indescribable.

Why should the trees be so lovely in Japan? With us, a plum or cherry tree in flower is not an astonishing sight; but here it is a miracle of beauty so bewildering that, however much you may have previously read about it, the real spectacle strikes you dumb. You see no leaves,—only one great filmy mist of petals. Is it that the trees have been so long domesticated and caressed by man in this land of the Gods, that they have acquired souls, and strive to show their gratitude, like women loved, by making themselves more beautiful for man's sake? Assuredly they have mastered men's hearts by their loveliness, like beautiful slaves. That is to say, Japanese hearts. Apparently there have been some foreign tourists of the brutal class in this place, since it has been deemed necessary to set up inscriptions in English announcing that "IT IS FORBIDDEN TO INJURE THE TREES."

*

"Tera?"

"Yes, Cha, tera."

But only for a brief while do I traverse Japanese streets. The houses separate, become scattered along the feet of the hills: the city thins away through little valleys, and vanishes at last behind. And we follow a curving road overlooking the sea. Green hills slope steeply down to the edge of the way on the right; on the left, far below, spreads a vast stretch of dun sand and salty pools to a line of surf so distant that it is discernible only as a moving white thread. The tide is out; and thousands of cockle-gatherers are scattered over the sands, at such distances that their stooping figures, dotting the glimmering sea-bed, appear no larger than gnats. And some are coming along the road before us, returning from their search with well-filled baskets,—girls with faces almost as rosy as the faces of English girls.

As the jinrikisha rattles on, the hills dominating the road grow higher. All at once Cha halts again before the steepest and loftiest flight of temple steps I have yet seen.

I climb and climb and climb, halting perforce betimes, to ease the violent aching of my quadriceps muscles; reach the top completely out of breath; and find myself between two lions of stone; one showing his

fangs, the other with jaws closed. Before me stands the temple, at the
farther end of a small bare plateau surrounded on three sides by low
cliffs,—a small temple, looking very old and gray. From a rocky height to
the left of the building, a little cataract rumbles down into a pool, ringed
in by a palisade. The voice of the water drowns all other sounds. A sharp
wind is blowing from the ocean: the place is chill even in the sun, and
bleak, and desolate, as if no prayer had been uttered in it for a hundred
years.

Cha taps and calls, while I take off my shoes upon the worn wooden
steps of the temple; and after a minute of waiting, we hear a muffled step
approaching and a hollow cough behind the paper screens. They slide
open: and an old white-robed priest appears, and motions me, with a
low bow, to enter. He has a kindly face; and his smile of welcome seems
to me one of the most exquisite I have ever been greeted with. Then he
coughs again, so badly that I think if I ever come here another time, I
shall ask for him in vain.

I go in, feeling that soft, spotless, cushioned matting beneath my feet
with which the floors of all Japanese buildings are covered. I pass the
indispensable bell and lacquered reading-desk; and before me I see other
screens only, stretching from floor to ceiling. The old man, still coughing,
slides back one of these upon the right, and waves me into the dimness
of an inner sanctuary, haunted by faint odors of incense. A colossal bronze
lamp, with snarling gilded dragons coiled about its columnar stem, is the
first object I discern: and, in passing it, my shoulder sets ringing a festoon
of little bells suspended from the lotus-shaped summit of it. Then I reach
the altar, gropingly, unable yet to distinguish forms clearly. But the priest,
sliding back screen after screen, pours in light upon the gilded brasses
and the inscriptions; and I look for the image of the Deity or presiding
Spirit between the altar-groups of convoluted candelabra. And I see—only
a mirror, a round, pale disk of polished metal, and my own face therein,
and behind this mockery of me a phantom of the far sea.

Only a mirror! Symbolizing what? Illusion? or that the Universe exists
for us solely as the reflection of our own souls? or the old Chinese teaching that we must seek the Buddha only in our own hearts? Perhaps some
day I shall be able to find out all these things.

As I sit on the temple steps, putting on my shoes preparatory to going,
the kind old priest approaches me again, and, bowing, presents a bowl.
I hastily drop some coins in it, imagining it to be a Buddhist alms-
bowl, before discovering it to be full of hot water. But the old man's

beautiful courtesy saves me from feeling all the grossness of my mistake. Without a word, and still preserving his kindly smile, he takes the bowl away, and, returning presently with another bowl, empty, fills it with hot water from a little kettle, and makes a sign to me to drink.

Tea is most usually offered to visitors at temples; but this little shrine is very, very poor; and I have a suspicion that the old priest suffers betimes for want of what no fellow-creature should be permitted to need. As I descend the windy steps to the roadway I see him still looking after me, and I hear once more his hollow cough.

Then the mockery of the mirror recurs to me. I am beginning to wonder whether I shall ever be able to discover that which I seek—outside of myself! That is, outside of my own imagination.

*

"*Tera?*" once more queries Cha.

"*Tera*, no,—it is getting late. Hotel, Cha."

But Cha, turning the corner of a narrow street, on our homeward route, halts the *jinrikisha* before a shrine or tiny temple scarcely larger than the smallest of Japanese shops, yet more of a surprise to me than any of the larger sacred edifices already visited. For, on either side of the entrance, stand two monster-figures, nude, blood-red, demoniac, fearfully muscled, with feet like lions, and hands brandishing gilded thunderbolts, and eyes of delirious fury; the guardians of holy things, the Ni-Ō, or "Two Kings." And right between these crimson monsters a young girl stands looking at us; her slight figure, in robe of silver gray and girdle of iris-violet, relieved deliciously against the twilight darkness of the interior. Her face, impassive and curiously delicate, would charm wherever seen; but here, by strange contrast with the frightful grotesqueries on either side of her, it produces an effect unimaginable. Then I find myself wondering whether my feeling of repulsion toward those twin monstrosities be altogether just, seeing that so charming a maiden deems them worthy of veneration. And they even cease to seem ugly as I watch her standing there between them, dainty and slender as some splendid moth, and always naïvely gazing at the foreigner, utterly unconscious that they might have seemed to him both unholy and uncomely.

What are they? Artistically they are Buddhist transformations of Brahma and of Indra. Enveloped by the absorbing, all-transforming magical atmosphere of Buddhism, Indra can now wield his thunderbolts only in defense of the faith which has dethroned him: he has become a keeper of the temple gates; nay, has even become a servant of Bosatsu (*Bodhi-*

sattvas), for this is only a shrine of Kwannon, Goddess of Mercy, not yet
a Buddha.

"Hotel, Cha, hotel!" I cry out again, for the way is long, and the sun
sinking,—sinking in the softest imaginable glow of topazine light. I have
not seen Shaka (so the Japanese have transformed the name Sakya-Muni);
I have not looked upon the face of the Buddha. Perhaps I may be able to
find his image to-morrow, somewhere in this wilderness of wooden
streets, or upon the summit of some yet unvisited hill.

The sun is gone; the topaz-light is gone; and Cha stops to light his
lantern of paper; and we hurry on again, between two long lines of painted
paper lanterns suspended before the shops: so closely set, so level those
lines are, that they seem two interminable strings of pearls of fire. And
suddenly a sound—solemn, profound, mighty—peals to my ears over the
roofs of the town, the voice of the *tsurigane,* the great temple-bell of
Nungiyama.

All too short the day seemed. Yet my eyes have been so long dazzled
by the great white light, and so confused by the sorcery of that interminable maze of mysterious signs which made each street vista seem a
glimpse into some enormous *grimoire,* that they are now weary even of
the soft glowing of all these paper lanterns, likewise covered with characters that look like texts from a Book of Magic. And I feel at last the
coming of that drowsiness which always follows enchantment.

*

"Amma-kamishimo-go-hyakmon!"

A woman's voice ringing through the night, chanting in a tone of singular sweetness words of which each syllable comes through my open
window like a wavelet of flute-sound. My Japanese servant, who speaks
a little English, has told me what they mean, those words:—

"Amma-kamishimo-go-hyakmon!"

And always between these long, sweet calls I hear a plaintive whistle,
one long note first, then two short ones in another key. It is the whistle
of the *amma,* the poor blind woman who earns her living by shampooing
the sick or the weary, and whose whistle warns pedestrians and drivers
of vehicles to take heed for her sake, as she cannot see. And she sings
also that the weary and the sick may call her in.

"Amma-kamishimo-go-hyakmon!"

The saddest melody, but the sweetest voice. Her cry signifies that for
the sum of "five hundred mon" she will come and rub your weary body

"above and below," and make the weariness or the pain go away. Five hundred mon are the equivalent of five sen (Japanese cents); there are ten rin to a sen, and ten mon to one rin. The strange sweetness of the voice is haunting,—makes me even wish to have some pains, that I might pay five hundred mon to have them driven away.

I lie down to sleep, and I dream. I see Chinese texts—multitudinous, weird, mysterious—fleeing by me, all in one direction; ideographs white and dark, upon sign-boards, upon paper screens, upon backs of sandaled men. They seem to live, these ideographs, with conscious life; they are moving their parts, moving with a movement as of insects, monstrously, like *phasmidæ*. I am rolling always through low, narrow, luminous streets in a phantom *jinrikisha,* whose wheels make no sound. And always, always, I see the huge white mushroom-shaped hat of Cha dancing up and down before me as he runs.   ("MY FIRST DAY IN THE ORIENT")]

CHAPTER *2*

In the Province
of the Gods

H ERE I AM in the land of dreams," Lafcadio wrote to Henry Watkin, "—surrounded by strange Gods. I seem to have known and loved them before somewhere." To Elizabeth Bisland he wrote: "I feel indescribably toward Japan. Of course Nature here is not the Nature of the tropics, which is so splendid and savage and omnipotently beautiful that I feel at this very moment of writing the same pain in my heart I felt when leaving Martinique. This is a domesticated nature, which loves man, and makes itself beautiful for him in a quiet grey-and-blue way like the Japanese women, and the trees seem to know what people say about them—seem to have little human souls. What I love in Japan is the Japanese—the poor simple humanity of the country. It is divine. . . . And I believe that their art is as far in advance of our art as old Greek art was superior to that of the earliest European art-gropings."

On the island of Honshu—halfway across the earth from the island of Leucadia—Lafcadio felt the spirit of ancient Greece still alive. Like the Greeks, the Japanese worshipped their gods in shrines and groves. Unlike almost all other societies except the Greek, the Japanese cherished and felt compassion for insects. The music of the two societies, Lafcadio had read, used comparable scales. So, too, the poems of *The Greek Anthology* and the classic *haiku* and *tanka*—with their presentational immediacy of image and crystalline intensification of feeling and experience—shared a similar sensibility and method:

The moon has set,
And the Pleiades. It is
Midnight. Time passes.
I sleep alone.
(SAPPHO)

Someone passes,
And while I wonder
If it is he,
The midnight moon
Is covered with clouds.

(LADY MURASAKI SHIKIBU)

And as Guy Davenport declares, the ancient Greeks "decorated their houses and ships like Florentines and Japanese. . . . They dressed like Samurai; all was bronze, terra cotta, painted marble, dyed wool, and banquets." As Lafcadio remarked to his new mentor Basil Chamberlain: "[Percival Lowell's] observation . . . that the Japanese are the happiest people in the world, is superlatively true. It is the old Greek soul again. To escape out of Western civilization into Japanese life is like escaping from a pressure of ten atmospheres into a perfectly normal medium."

After living for two weeks in this "medium," Lafcadio had no desire to leave his "land of dreams." Still in Yokohama, he took up residence in a cheap waterfront hotel, run by a mulatto named Carey, with its "atmosphere of sailors and sealers and mates and masters of small craft—in a salty medium of water-dogs," which he used as a base for his expeditions to Kamakura, Enoshima, and other points of interest.

Lafcadio realized he would soon run out of money; but in a fit of characteristic pique, he decided it was time for him to make a clean break with Harper's for never having offered him a publishing contract, for having allowed his copy to be shoddily edited, and, Lafcadio claimed, for having cheated him of the sum of thirty-seven dollars! In a series of self-righteous, intemperate letters to Henry Alden, he accused his former literary patron of lying to him "for the purpose of duping me into the power of your brutal firm, which deals in books precisely as they might deal in pork or hay." And in response to Alden's annoyed but decorous attempts to defend his actions, Lafcadio lashed out with vigorous Irish mordancy and profanity: "Please to understand that your resentment has for me less than the value of a bottled fart, and your bank-account less consequence than a wooden shithouse struck by lightning."

The lightning struck, however, on his side of the world, and Lafcadio was left without a publisher or a current source of income. Unwilling and unable even to *consider* living as an aging vagabond on the docks of Yokohama—as he had done on the streets of Cincinnati and New Orleans—he cultivated the acquaintance of the two men to whom he had been given letters of introduction—Professor Chamberlain and Mitchell McDonald, the paymaster of the United States Navy in Yokohama. Lafcadio got on equally well with the scholar and the businessman, and they both took it upon themselves to see if they could find him a job.

While waiting for something to turn up, however, Lafcadio went broke. Desperate, he walked unannounced into the office of the headmaster of the English-language Victoria Public School . . . and walked out the official tutor of a handicapped fifteen-year-old student—the son of an English father and Japanese mother—who needed private remedial work in English. Lafcadio saw the boy, Edward Clarke, for a half-hour every weekday and an hour on Sunday. Years later, a grown-up Edward Clarke recalled one of Lafcadio's little heuristic tricks: "[He] would burst out in praise, as I fancied; but even as I was mentally patting myself on the back, he would come down with a crusher, and lay me out flat! This sort of thing: 'Aha, this is *very* good, ve-ry good, my boy! You have surpassed yourself! The words are well-chosen, the manner quite elegant, the grammar superb, but [a slight pause . . . then] *it is not English!*' "

When he arrived in Japan, Lafcadio submitted his *own* writing style to a rigorous self-examination, checking it for pleonasms, overwrought expressions, magniloquent phrases, purple prose, and examples of "gush," and concluded that he needed literary surgery. "I should like now," he declared, "to go through many paragraphs written years ago, and sober them down. . . . Ornamental luxurious work isn't the hardest. The hardest is perfect simplicity."

Much of Lafcadio's writing in New Orleans—*Chita, Fantastics,* "Torn Letters"—palpably displayed his habitual tendency toward overripeness; but in his Martinique sketches—portrayals of lives in a world of tropical abundance—Lafcadio returned to the clear, unadorned descriptive approach of many of his earliest newspaper articles ("Levee Life," "Gibbeted"), now conceived and executed with a new strength of form, technical control, and depth of perception that would characterize almost all of his work from then on. Lafcadio began to speak of his stylistic goals in Apollonian terms—"lucidity, sharpness, firm hard outline"—and of the "supreme artistic quality, self-restraint," with its attendant qualities of "concentration," "simplicity," "power."

"You can learn about the pine only from the pine," the seventeenth-century haiku-master Matsuo Bashō observed, "or about bamboo only from bamboo. When you see an object, you leave your subjective preoccupation with yourself; otherwise you impose yourself on the object, and do not learn." And this idea, along with Bashō's notions of "color," "tone," "scent," and "grace" as indispensable elements of a poem's "harmony of feeling," were affirmed by Lafcadio in his absorption of Japanese life, especially what he termed the *"Kokoro"* ["heart," "inner meaning"] of common people, common creatures, common things. For even before he had heard of Bashō, Lafcadio had followed the poet's counsel that "What is important is to keep your mind high in the world of true understanding and yet not to forget the value of that which is low. Seek always the truth of beauty, but always return to the world of common experience"—the world of dyers and well-cleaners, of ants and grasshoppers, of flowers and stones.

"In fact," Lafcadio stated, "I have not been able to convince myself that it is really an inestimable privilege to be reborn a human being. And if the thinking of this thought . . . must inevitably affect my next rebirth, then let me hope that the state to which I am destined will not be worse than that of a cicada or of a dragon-fly;—climbing the cryptomerias to clash my tiny cymbals in the sun—or haunting, with soundless flicker of amethyst and gold, some holy silence of lotus-pools."

In the 1890s, the United States witnessed a surge of imperialist expansion, extending its sway to Cuba, Puerto Rico, Hawaii, and the Philippines, and following an "Open Door" policy in the Far East, enforced by the American "Great White Fleet." Meanwhile, domestically—in spite of a major economic depression in 1893—the Gay Nineties was blazoning itself with multimillion-dollar mansions on Fifth Avenue, Palm Beach, Newport, and Long Island; and with hundreds of diverting *soirées* given by and for the rich and famous, in which monkeys dressed in formal attire were casually seated next to human dinner guests, black pearls were placed in diners' oysters, and loose cigarettes wrapped in hundred-dollar bills were available for smokers who had run out of their own. The automobile, the airplane, motion pictures, and the wireless had already made, or were soon to make, their world-altering appearances—along with the offering by the House of Morgan of the first billion-dollar trust (U.S. Steel).

Just twenty-two years since the demise (in 1868) of Japanese feudalism—occasioned by the overthrow of the anti-Western Shogun, the restoration of the power of the emperor, and the adoption of a modern constitution in 1869—Meiji Japan reflected on and considered what Teddy Roosevelt proudly spoke of as "the spread of the English-speaking peoples over the world's waste spaces." Indiana's Senator Albert Beveridge referred to this phenomenon as "God's great purpose made manifest in the instinct of our race, whose present phase is our personal profit, but whose far-off end is the redemption of the world and the Christianization of mankind." In the light of these sentiments Japan realized that it could either become subservient to the West or make an intense, concentrated attempt to industrialize and "modernize" itself, while trying to resist the Westernization of its culture and traditions. The Japanese chose the second course.

Because English was now a required subject in Japanese high schools and universities, Lafcadio, with the aid of Basil Chamberlain, was eventually offered a teaching job, for $100 a month, at the Middle and Normal Schools in the city of Matsue, 450 miles southwest of Tokyo, close to the Sea of Japan. With his interpreter—the student, named Akira Manabe, whom he had met at a Buddhist temple on his first day in Japan—Lafcadio began a strenuous journey, taking them by train to Okayama, then in two *kuruma* for four days over the mountains from the Pacific to the Sea of Japan, and, finally, in a small ship from Yonago to Matsue.

Far removed from the influence of foreigners, Matsue, with its samurai, merchant, and priestly quarters, was home to forty thousand persons living in a distinctly pre-Meiji world. It was fortuitous that the new English teacher (the new "Master" whom the students would politely refer to as *Herun-san)* was assigned to a community where festivals, rituals, and ceremonies were a part of everyday life.

On his first day of teaching, Lafcadio was introduced by the dean of the school, Sentarō Nishida, to the twelve- to sixteen-year-old students in their school uniforms, who stared unabashedly at a forty-year-old dark-complexioned man with graying hair ("gray as a beaver," as Lafcadio put it), blind in one eye, and small in stature like themselves (to Lafcadio's infinite joy). The boys thought him strange, not because Lafcadio himself looked strange to them but because every foreigner was considered strange.

Despite their curiosity, the students were courteous toward their new instructor, who spoke to them in clear, short English sentences in a gentle, melodious voice. Lafcadio wrote difficult and important words on a blackboard (one of which was Lafcadio's unvarying example of a "typical" English name—pronounced by students as *Aileesabbet Beeslan),* assigned them short essays to be written in English, and told them stories from Greek mythology and the Arthurian legends. He made them feel proud of their customs, traditions, and gods—unlike their previous teacher, a missionary who had continually spoken disparagingly of Japanese "heathenism" and tried to proselytize them. "Unconsciously," Lafcadio asserted, "the missionaries everywhere represent the edge—the *acies,* to use the Roman word—of Occidental aggression." ("I am practically a traitor to England," he remarked privately, "and a renegade. But in the eternal order of things, I know I am right." With regard to this subject, Robert Louis Stevenson, too, was a renegade. Writing from Samoa during this period, he declared that the changes of the natives' habits, instigated by missionaries as a result of conversions, were "bloodier than a bombardment.")

After his daily five hours of teaching, Lafcadio explored every quarter of Matsue. "I too must make divers pilgrimages," he stated, "for all about the city, beyond the waters or beyond the hills, lie holy places immemorially old."

He arranged a journey by boat from a fishing village north of Matsue along the coast to Kaka, where, in an enormous, dusky cavern by the sea, stood a famous stone *Jizō.* [A *jizō* is a stone or wooden statue of one of the most popular Bodhisattvas in Japanese Buddhism, generally dedicated to the divine protection of children.] Here, each night, it was said, the ghosts of little children piled up small heaps of pebbles and rocks before the statue, and in so doing left fresh prints of tiny feet in the sand, faint but perceptible by day. Like other pilgrims, Lafcadio brought a gift of small straw sandals (children's *zori*) and left them inside the grotto, hoping to prevent the infant ghosts from wounding their feet on the sharp rock-offerings. He also took the first of many trips to the village of Kitzuki (about twenty miles away) to visit the shrine of Izumo, the oldest and, after the shrine at Ise, the second-most sacred Shintō holy place in Japan, to which pilgrims have been journeying since at least the seventh century.

Shintō, the ancient nature religion of Japan, seemed to Lafcadio to be an "occult force . . . part of the Soul of the Race." In Shintō he found many resonances of his own belief in "ghostly presences," along with the notions that the world of the living is directly governed by the world of the dead; that every impulse, thought, or act is the work of a god; that all the dead become gods; and that the dead are not less real than the living. "When we become conscious," Lafcadio remarked, "that we owe whatever is wise or good or strong or beautiful in each one of us, not to one particular inner individuality, but to the struggles and sufferings and experiences of the whole unknown chain of human lives behind us, reaching back into mystery unthinkable,—the worship of ancestors seems an extremely righteous thing to do."

On each of his trips to Kitzuki, Lafcadio spent hours absorbing the atmosphere of the sacred place with its cedar and pine trees, its rocks, its extensive graveled enclosure, its majestic cross-beams. Then one day he was invited into the inner chambers of the shrine—the first Westerner ever to enter there—by the hereditary Guji of Taisha (the high priest, "a majestic bearded figure, strangely coiffed and robed all in white, seated upon the matted floor in hierophantic attitude"), who personally guided the renowned foreign writer to view the shrine's relics and permitted him to observe a dance by white-robed priests accompanied by flutes and drums.

Although Lafcadio's reception at Kitzuki distinguished him in the eyes of the Matsue elite, he carried on as always, without the appurtenances of status or honor. His dwelling was a tiny two-story house—he called it his "bird-cage"—at the edge of the Shinji Lake and just above a bridge spanning the nearby Ohashi River, from which he constantly heard the pattering sound of *geta* (wooden clogs) crossing from one side to another.

He wore *kimono, obi* (sash), and sandals when he came home from teaching; sat on a *zabuton* (square cushion) and smoked tobacco in a long-stemmed, carved Japanese pipe; slept on a *futon* on a matted floor; and ate Japanese food exclusively for a year, then broke down ("for a couple of days only!!!!" Lafcadio confessed); and, having discovered the one foreign cook in Matsue, reverted to gluttonous servings of beefsteak, fowl, sausages, bread, and Bass's Ale—"the fault of my ancestors . . . the ferocious, wolfish hereditary instincts and tendencies of boreal mankind. The sins of the father, etc." He was uncompromising, however, in his adoption of Japanese life's "interminable small etiquette, its everlasting round of interviews with people who have nothing to say but a few happy words, its Matsuri customs and household formalities. . . . I think it is only by this way, in the course of years, that I can get at the *Kokoro* of the common people,—which is my whole aim."

Lafcadio once formulated Pierre Loti's approach to descriptive writing: "On visiting a new country he always used to take notes of every fresh and powerful impression—a landscape,—a sunset-blaze,—a peculiar atmosphere,—a singular and typical face,—a moral trait,—an architectural eccentricity,—a bit of picturesqueness in custom. . . ." Lafcadio adopted this method, but expanded and deepened it, fusing pure description with folklore, ghost stories, legends, religious explications, personal narrative, and reverie into an expository assemblage that enabled him to become the perfect interpreter of Japan to the West. His literary voice was simply his own voice—enthusiastic, attentive, instructive—and with it he depicted, without prejudice or preconceptions, a world that inspired and spoke to him at every moment in his daily rounds spent "looking at curious things." Lafcadio's attentiveness was, he asserted, only that of the everyday person in Japan: "The faces of the people have an indescribable look of patient expectancy,—the air of waiting for something interesting to make its appearance." He listened to the "Pulse of the Land" in his beloved Matsue:

The first of the noises of Matsue day comes to the sleeper like the throbbing of a slow, enormous pulse exactly under his ear. It is a great, soft, dull buffet of sound—like a heartbeat in its regularity, in its muffled depth, in the way it quakes up through one's pillow so as to be felt rather than heard. It is simply the pounding of the ponderous pestle of the *kometsuki*, the cleaner of rice,—a sort of colossal wooden mallet with a handle about fifteen feet long horizontally balanced on a pivot. By treading with all his force on the end of the handle, the naked *kometsuki* elevates the pestle, which is then allowed to fall back by its own weight into the rice-tub. The measured muffled echoing of its fall seems to me the most pathetic of all sounds of Japanese life; it is the beating, indeed, of the Pulse of the Land.

Then the boom of the great bell of Tōkōji, the Zen-shu temple, shakes over the town; then come melancholy echoes of drumming from the tiny little temple of *Jizō* in the street Zaimokuchō, near by house, signaling the Buddhist hour of morning prayer. And finally the cries of the earliest itinerant vendors begin,—"*Daikoyai! kabuya-kabu!*"—the sellers of *daikon*, and other strange vegetables. "*Moyaya-moya!*"—the plaintive call of the women who sell little thin slips of kindling-wood for the lighting of charcoal fires.

*

Roused thus by these earliest sounds of the city's wakening life, I slide open my little Japanese paper window to look out upon the morning over a soft green cloud of spring foliage rising from the river-bounded garden below. Before me, tremulously mirroring everything upon its farther side, glimmers the broad glassy mouth of the Ōhashigawa, opening into the grand Shinji Lake, which spreads out broadly to the right in a dim gray frame of peaks. Just opposite to me, across the stream, the blue-pointed Japanese dwellings have their *to* [sliding wooden shutters] all closed; they are still shut up like boxes, for it is not yet sunrise, although it is day.

But oh, the charm of the vision,—those first ghostly love-colors of a morning steeped in mist soft as sleep itself resolved into a visible exhalation! Long reaches of faintly-tinted vapor cloud the far lake verge,—long nebulous bands, such as you may have seen in old Japanese picture-books, and must have deemed only artistic whimsicalities unless you had previously looked upon the real phenomena. All the bases of the mountains are veiled by them, and they stretch athwart the loftier peaks at different heights like immeasurable lengths of gauze (this singular appearance the Japanese term "shelving"), so that the lake appears incomparably larger than it really is, and not an actual lake, but a beautiful spectral sea of the same tint as the dawn-sky and mixing with it, while peak-tips rise like islands from the brume, and visionary strips of hill-ranges figure as league-long causeways stretching out of sight,—an exquisite chaos, ever changing aspect as the delicate fogs rise, slowly, very slowly. As the sun's yellow rim comes into sight, fine thin lines of warmer tone—spectral violets and opalines—shoot across the flood, treetops take tender fire, and the unpainted façades of high edifices across the water change their wood-color to vapory gold through the delicious haze.

Looking sunward, up the long Ōhashigawa, beyond the many-pillared wooden bridge, one high-pooped junk, just hoisting sail, seems to me the most fantastically beautiful craft I ever saw,—a dream of Orient seas, so idealized by the vapor is it; the ghost of a junk, but a ghost that catches the light as clouds do; a shape of gold mist, seemingly semi-diaphanous, and suspended in pale blue light.

*

And now from the river-front touching my garden there rises to me a sound of clapping of hands,—one, two, three, four claps,—but the owner of the hands is screened from view by the shrubbery. At the same time, however, I see men and women descending the stone steps of the wharves on the opposite side of the Ōhashigawa, all with little blue towels tucked into their girdles. They wash their faces and hands and rinse their mouths,—the customary ablution preliminary to Shintō prayer. Then they turn their faces to the sunrise and clap their hands four times and pray. From the long high white bridge come other clappings, like echoes, and others again from far light graceful craft, curved like new moons, —extraordinary boats, in which I see bare-limbed fishermen standing with

foreheads bowed to the golden East. Now the clappings multiply,
—multiply at last into an almost continuous volleying of sharp sounds.
For all the population are saluting the rising sun,—O-Hi-San, the Lady of
Fire,—Amaterasu-oho-mi-Kami, the Lady of the Great Light. *"Konnichi-Sama!*
Hail this day to thee, divinest Day-Maker! Thanks unutterable unto thee,
for this thy sweet light, making beautiful the world!" So, doubtless, the
thought, if not the utterance, of countless hearts. Some turn to the sun
only, clapping their hands; yet many turn also to the West, to holy Kitzuki, the immemorial shrine; and not a few turn their faces successively
to all the points of heaven, murmuring the names of a hundred gods; and
others, again, after having saluted the Lady of Fire, look toward high
Ichibata, toward the place of the great temple of Yakushi-Nyorai, who
giveth sight to the blind,—not clapping their hands as in Shintō worship,
but only rubbing the palms softly together after the Buddhist manner. But
all—for in this most antique province of Japan all Buddhists are Shintōists
likewise—utter the archaic words of Shintō prayer: *"Harai tamai kiyome
tamai to Kami imi tami."* . . .

*

"Ho—ke-kyō!"

My *uguisu* [Japanese bush warbler, often mistakenly translated as night-
ingale] is awake at last, and utters his morning prayer. You do not know
what an *uguisu* is? An *uguisu* is a holy little bird that professes Buddhism.
All *uguisu* have professed Buddhism from time immemorial; all *uguisu*
preach alike to men the excellence of the divine Sutra.

"Ho—ke-kyō!"

In the Japanese tongue, Ho-ke-kyō; in Sanscrit, Saddharma-Pundarika:
"The Sutra of the Lotus of the Good Law," the divine book of the Nichiren
sect. Very brief, indeed, is my little feathered Buddhist's confession of
faith,—only the sacred name reiterated over and over again like a litany,
with liquid bursts of twittering between.

"Ho—ke-kyō!"

Only this one phrase, but how deliciously he utters it! With what slow
amorous ecstasy he dwells upon its golden syllables!

It hath been written: "He who shall keep, read, teach, or write this
Sutra shall obtain eight hundred good qualities of the Eye. He shall see
the whole Triple Universe down to the great hell Aviki, and up to the
extremity of existence. He shall obtain twelve hundred good qualities of
the Ear. He shall hear all sounds in the Triple Universe,—sounds of gods,
goblins, demons, and beings not human."

"*Ho—ke-kyō!*"

A single word only. But it is also written: "He who shall joyfully accept but a single word from this Sutra, incalculably greater shall be his merit than the merit of one who should supply all beings in the four hundred thousand Asankhyeyas of worlds with all the necessaries for happiness."

"*Ho—ke-kyō!*"

Always he makes a reverent little pause after uttering it and before shrilling out his ecstatic warble,—his bird-hymn of praise. First the warble; then a pause of about five seconds; then a slow, sweet, solemn utterance of the holy name in a tone as of meditative wonder; then another pause; then another wild, rich, passionate warble. Could you see him, you would marvel how so powerful and penetrating a soprano could ripple from so minute a throat; for he is one of the very tiniest of all feathered singers, yet his chant can be heard far across the broad river, and children going to school pause daily on the bridge, a whole *cho* away, to listen to his song. And uncomely withal: a neutral-tinted mite, almost lost in his immense box-cage of *hinoki* wood, darkened with paper screens over its little wire-grated windows, for he loves the gloom. . . .

*

The clapping of hands has ceased; the toil of the day begins; continually louder and louder the pattering of *geta* over the bridge. It is a sound never to be forgotten, this pattering of *geta* over the Ōhashi,—rapid, merry, musical, like the sound of an enormous dance; and a dance it veritably is. The whole population is moving on tiptoe, and the multitudinous twinkling of feet over the verge of the sunlit roadway is an astonishment. All those feet are small, symmetrical,—light as the feet of figures painted on Greek vases,—and the step is always taken toes first; indeed, with *geta* it could be taken no other way; for the heel touches neither the *geta* nor the ground, and the foot is tilted forward by the wedge-shaped wooden sole. Merely to stand upon a pair of *geta* is difficult for one unaccustomed to their use, yet you see Japanese children running at full speed in *geta* with soles at least three inches high, held to the foot only by a forestrap fastened between the great toe and the other toes, and they never trip and the *geta* never falls off. Still more curious is the spectacle of men walking in *bokkuri* or *takageta*, a wooden sole with wooden supports at least five inches high fitted underneath it so as to make the whole structure seem the lacquered model of a wooden bench. But the wearers stride as freely as if they had nothing upon their feet.

Now children begin to appear, hurrying to school. The undulation of the wide sleeves of their pretty speckled robes, as they run, looks precisely like a fluttering of extraordinary butterflies. The junks spread their great white or yellow wings, and the funnels of the little streamers which have been slumbering all night by the wharves begin to smoke.

One of the tiny lake steamers lying at the opposite wharf has just opened its steam-throat to utter the most unimaginable, piercing, desperate, furious howl. When that cry is heard everybody laughs. The other little steamboats utter only plaintive mooings, but unto this particular vessel—newly built and launched by a rival company—there has been given a voice expressive to the most amazing degree of reckless hostility and savage defiance. The good people of Matsue, upon hearing its voice for the first time, gave it forthwith a new and just name,—Ōkami-Maru. "Maru" signifies a steamship. "Ōkami" signifies a wolf. . . .

*

The long white bridge with its pillars of iron is recognizably modern. It was, in fact, opened to the public only last spring with great ceremony. According to some most ancient custom, when a new bridge has been built the first persons to pass over it must be the happiest of the community. So the authorities of Matsue sought for the happiest folk, and selected two aged men who had both been married for more than half a century, and who had had not less than twelve children, and had never lost any of them. These good patriarchs first crossed the bridge, accompanied by their venerable wives, and followed by their grown-up children, grandchildren, and great-grandchildren, amidst a great clamor of rejoicing, the showering of fireworks, and the firing of cannon.

But the ancient bridge so recently replaced by this structure was much more picturesque, curving across the flood and supported upon multitudinous feet, like a long-legged centipede of the innocuous kind. For three hundred years it had stood over the stream firmly and well, and it had its particular tradition.

When Horiō Yoshiharu, the great general who became *daimyō* [feudal lord] of Izumo in the Keichō era, first undertook to put a bridge over the mouth of this river, the builders labored in vain; for there appeared to be no solid bottom for the pillars of the bridge to rest upon. Millions of great stones were cast into the river to no purpose, for the work constructed by day was swept away or swallowed up by night. Nevertheless, at last the bridge was built, but the pillars began to sink soon after it was finished; then a flood carried half of it away, and as often as it was repaired so often it was wrecked. Then a human sacrifice was made to appease the vexed spirits of the flood. A man was buried alive in the river-bed below the place of the middle pillar, where the current is most treacherous, and thereafter the bridge remained immovable for three hundred years.

This victim was one Gensuke, who had lived in the street Saikamachi; for it had been determined that the first man who should cross the bridge wearing *hakama* without a *machi* [a stiff piece of pasteboard or other material sewn into the waist of the *hakama* at the back, so as to keep the folds of the garment perpendicular and neat-looking] should be put under the bridge; and Gensuke sought to pass over not having a *machi* in his *hakama,* so they sacrificed him. Wherefore the midmost pillar of the bridge was for three hundred years called by his name,—Gensuke-bashira. It is averred that upon moonless nights a ghostly fire flitted about that pillar, —always in the dead watch hour between two and three; and the color of the light was red, though I am assured that in Japan, as in other lands, the fires of the dead are most often blue. . . .

*

The vapors have vanished, sharply revealing a beautiful little islet in the lake, lying scarcely half a mile away,—a low, narrow strip of land with a Shintō shrine upon it, shadowed by giant pines; not pines like ours, but huge, gnarled, shaggy, tortuous shapes, vast-reaching like ancient oaks. Through a glass one can easily discern a *torii,* and before it two symbolic lions of stone *(Kara-shishi),* one with its head broken off, doubtless by its having been overturned and dashed about by heavy waves during some great storm. This islet is sacred to Benten, the Goddess of Eloquence and Beauty, wherefore it is called Ben-ten-no-shima. But is it more commonly called Yome-ga-shima, or "The Island of the Young Wife," by reason of a legend. It is said that it arose in one night, noiselessly as a dream, bearing up from the depths of the lake the body of a drowned woman who had been very lovely, very pious, and very unhappy. The people, deeming this a sign from heaven, consecrated the islet to Benten, and thereon built a shrine unto her, planted trees about it, set a *torii* before it, and made a rampart about it with great curiously-shaped stones; and there they buried the drowned woman.

Now the sky is blue down to the horizon, the air is a caress of spring. I go forth to wander through the queer old city.

*

I perceive that upon the sliding doors, or immediately above the principal entrance of nearly every house, are pasted oblong white papers bearing ideographic inscriptions; and overhanging every threshold I see the sacred emblem of Shintō, the little rice-straw rope with its long fringe of pendent stalks. The white papers at once interest me; for they are *ofuda*, or holy texts and charms, of which I am a devout collector. Nearly all are from temples in Matsue or its vicinity; and the Buddhist ones indicate by the sacred words upon them to what particular *shū*, or sect, the family belongs,—for nearly every soul in this community professes some form of Buddhism as well as the all-dominant and more ancient faith of Shintō. And even one quite ignorant of Japanese ideographs can nearly always distinguish at a glance the formula of the great Nichiren sect from the peculiar appearance of the column of characters composing it, all bristling with long sharp points and banneret zigzags, like an army; the famous text *Namu-myō-hō-ren-ge-kyō*, inscribed of old upon the flag of the great captain Kato Kiyomasa, the extirpator of Spanish Christianity, the glorious *vir ter execrandus* of the Jesuits. Any pilgrim belonging to this sect has the right to call at whatever door bears the above formula and ask for alms or food.

But by far the greater number of the *ofuda* are Shintō. Upon almost every door there is one *ofuda* especially likely to attract the attention of a stranger, because at the foot of the column of ideographs composing its text there are two small figures of foxes, a black and a white fox, facing each other in a sitting posture, each with a little bunch of rice-straw in its mouth, instead of the more usual emblematic key. These *ofuda* are from the great Inari temple of Oshiroyama, within the castle grounds, and are charms against fire. They represent, indeed, the only form of assurance against fire yet known in Matsue,—so far, at least, as wooden dwellings are concerned. And although a single spark and a high wind are sufficient in combination to obliterate a larger city in one day, great fires are unknown in Matsue, and small ones are of rare occurrence.

The charm is peculiar to the city; and of the Inari in question this tradition exists:—

When Naomasu, the grandson of Iyeyasu, first came to Matsue to rule the province, there entered into his presence a beautiful boy, who said: "I came hither from the home of your august father in Echizen, to protect you from all harm. But I have no dwelling-place, and am staying therefore at the Buddhist temple of Fu-mon-in. Now if you will make for me a dwelling within the castle grounds, I will protect from fire the buildings there and the houses of the city, and your other residence likewise which is in the capital. For I am Inari Shinyemon." With these words he vanished from sight. Therefore Naomasu dedicated to him the great temple which still stands in the castle grounds, surrounded by one thousand foxes of stone.

*

I now turn into a narrow little street, which, although so ancient that its dwarfed two-story houses have the look of things grown up from the ground, is called the Street of the New Timber. New the timber may have been one hundred and fifty years ago; but the tints of the structures would ravish an artist,—the sombre ashen tones of the wood-work, the furry browns of old thatch, ribbed and patched and edged with the warm soft green of those velvety herbs and mosses which flourish upon Japanese roofs.

However, the perspective of the street frames in a vision more surprising than any details of its mouldering homes. Between very lofty bamboo poles, higher than any of the dwellings, and planted on both sides of the street in lines, extraordinary black nets are stretched, like prodigious cobwebs against the sky, evoking sudden memories of those monster spiders which figure in Japanese mythology and in the picture-books of the old artists. But these are only fishing-nets of silken thread; and this is the street of the fishermen. I take my way to the great bridge.

*

A stupendous ghost!

Looking eastward from the great bridge over those sharply beautiful mountains, green and blue, which tooth the horizon, I see a glorious spectre towering to the sky. Its base is effaced by far mists: out of the air the thing would seem to have shaped itself,—a phantom cone, diaphanously gray below, vaporously white above, with a dream of perpetual snow,—the mighty mountain of Daisen.

At the first approach of winter it will in one night become all blanched from foot to crest; and then its snowy pyramid so much resembles that Sacred Mountain, often compared by poets to a white inverted fan, half opened, hanging in the sky, that it is called Izumo-Fuji, "the Fuji of Izumo." But it is really in Hōki, not in Izumo, though it cannot be seen from any part of Hōki to such advantage as from here. It is the one sublime spectacle of this charming land; but it is visible only when the air is very pure. Many are the marvelous legends related concerning it, and somewhere upon its mysterious summit the Tengu are believed to dwell.

*

At the farther end of the bridge, close to the wharf where the little steamboats are, is a very small Jizō temple (*Jizō-dō*). Here are kept many bronze drags; and whenever any one has been drowned and the body not recovered, these are borrowed from the little temple and the river is dragged. If the body be thus found, a new drag must be presented to the temple.

From here, half a mile southward to the great Shintō temple of Tenjin, deity of scholarship and calligraphy, broadly stretches Tenjinmachi, the Street of the Rich Merchants, all draped on either side with dark blue hangings, over which undulate with every windy palpitation from the lake white wondrous ideographs, which are names and signs, while down the wide way, in white perspective, diminishes a long line of telegraph poles.

Beyond the temple of Tenjin the city is again divided by a river, the Shindotegawa, over which arches the bridge Tenjin-bashi. Again beyond this other large quarters extend to the hills and curve along the lake shore. But in the space between the two rivers is the richest and busiest life of the city, and also the vast and curious quarter of the temples. In this islanded district are likewise the theatres, and the place where wrestling-matches are held, and most of the resorts of pleasure.

Parallel with Tenjinmachi runs the great street of the Buddhist temples, or Teramachi, of which the eastern side is one unbroken succession of temples,—a solid front of court walls tile-capped, with imposing gateways at regular intervals. Above this long stretch of tile-capped wall rise the beautiful tilted massive lines of gray-blue temple roofs against the sky. Here all the sects dwell side by side in harmony,—Nichiren-shū, Shingon-shū, Zen-shū, Tendai-shū, even that Shin-shū, unpopular in Izumo because those who follow its teaching strictly must not worship the Kami. Behind each temple court there is a cemetery, or *hakaba;* and eastward beyond these are other temples, and beyond them yet others,—masses of Buddhist architecture mixed with shreds of gardens and miniature home-steads, a huge labyrinth of mouldering courts and fragments of streets.

To-day, as usual, I find I can pass a few hours very profitably in visiting the temples; in looking at the ancient images seated within the cups of golden lotus-flowers under their aureoles of gold; in buying curious *ma-mori;* in examining the sculptures of the cemeteries, where I can nearly always find some dreaming Kwannon or smiling Jizō well worth the visit.

The great courts of Buddhist temples are places of rare interest for one who loves to watch the life of the people; for these have been for unremembered centuries the playing-places of the children. Generations of happy infants have been amused in them. All the nurses, and little girls who carry tiny brothers or sisters upon their backs, go thither every morning that the sun shines; hundreds of children join them; and they play at strange, funny games,—"Onigokko," or the game of Devil, "Kage-Oni," which signifies the Shadow and the Demon, and "Mekusan-gokko," which is a sort of "blindman's buff."

Also, during the long summer evenings, these temples are wrestling-grounds, free to all who love wrestling; and in many of them there is a *dohyō-ba,* or wrestling-ring. Robust young laborers and sinewy artisans come to these courts to test their strength after the day's tasks are done, and here the fame of more than one now noted wrestler was first made. When a youth has shown himself able to overmatch at wrestling all others in his own district, he is challenged by champions of other districts; and if he can overcome these also, he may hope eventually to become a skilled and popular professional wrestler.

It is also in the temple courts that the sacred dances are performed and that public speeches are made. It is in the temple courts, too, that the most curious toys are sold, on the occasion of the great holidays, —toys most of which have a religious signification. There are grand old trees, and ponds full of tame fish, which put up their heads to beg for food when your shadow falls upon the water. The holy lotus is cultivated therein.

"Though growing in the foulest slime, the flower remains pure and undefiled.

"And the soul of him who remains ever pure in the midst of temptation is likened unto the lotus.

"Therefore is the lotus carven or painted upon the furniture of temples; therefore also does it appear in all the representations of our Lord Buddha.

"In Paradise the blessed shall sit at ease enthroned upon the cups of golden lotus-flowers." [From an English composition by one of Lafcadio's Japanese pupils.]

A bugle-call rings through the quaint street; and round the corner of the last temple come marching a troop of handsome young riflemen, uniformed somewhat like French light infantry, marching by fours so perfectly that all the gaitered legs move as if belonging to a single body, and every sword-bayonet catches the sun at exactly the same angle, as the column wheels into view. These are the students of the Shihan-Gakkō, the College of Teachers, performing their daily military exercises. Their professors give them lectures upon the microscopic study of cellular tissues, upon the segregation of developing nerve structure, upon spectrum analysis, upon the evolution of the color sense, and upon the cultivation of bacteria in glycerine infusions. And they are none the less modest and knightly in manner for all their modern knowledge, nor the less reverentially devoted to their dear old fathers and mothers whose ideas were shaped in the era of feudalism.

*

Here come a band of pilgrims, with yellow straw overcoats, "raincoats" (*mino*), and enormous yellow straw hats, mushroom-shaped, of which the down-curving rim partly hides the face. All carry staffs, and wear their robes well girded up so as to leave free the lower limbs, which are inclosed in white cotton leggings of a peculiar and indescribable kind. Precisely the same sort of costume was worn by the same class of travelers many centuries ago; and just as you now see them trooping by,—whole families wandering together, the pilgrim child clinging to the father's hand,—so may you see them pass in quaint procession across the faded pages of Japanese picturebooks a hundred years old.

At intervals they halt before some shop-front to look at the many curious things which they greatly enjoy seeing, but which they have no money to buy.

I myself have become so accustomed to surprises, to interesting or extraordinary sights, that when a day happens to pass during which nothing remarkable has been heard or seen I feel vaguely discontented. But such blank days are rare: they occur in my own case only when the weather is too detestable to permit of going out-of-doors. For with ever so little money one can always obtain the pleasure of looking at curious things. And this has been one of the chief pleasures of the people in Japan for centuries and centuries, for the nation has passed its generations of lives in making or seeking such things. To divert one's self seems, indeed, the main purpose of Japanese existence, beginning with the opening of the baby's wondering eyes. The faces of the people have an indescribable look of patient expectancy,—the air of waiting for something interesting to make its appearance. If it fail to appear, they will travel to find it: they are astonishing pedestrians and tireless pilgrims, and I think they make pilgrimages not more for the sake of pleasing the gods than of pleasing themselves by the sight of rare and pretty things. For every temple is a museum, and every hill and valley throughout the land has its temple and its wonders.

Even the poorest farmer, one so poor that he cannot afford to eat a grain of his own rice, can afford to make a pilgrimage of a month's duration; and during that season when the growing rice needs least attention hundreds of thousands of the poorest go on pilgrimages. This is possible, because from ancient times it has been the custom for everybody to help pilgrims a little; and they can always find rest and shelter at particular inns (*kichinyado*) which receive pilgrims only, and where they are charged merely the cost of the wood used to cook their food.

But multitudes of the poor undertake pilgrimages requiring much more than a month to perform, such as the pilgrimage to the thirty-three great temples of Kwannon, or that to the eighty-eight temples of Kōbōdaishi; and these, though years be needed to accomplish them, are as nothing compared to the enormous Sengaji, the pilgrimage to the thousand temples of the Nichiren sect. The time of a generation may pass ere this can be made. One may begin it in early youth, and complete it only when youth is long past. Yet there are several in Matsue, men and women, who have made this tremendous pilgrimage, seeing all Japan, and supporting themselves not merely by begging, but by some kinds of itinerant peddling.

The pilgrim who desires to perform this pilgrimage carries on his shoulders a small box, shaped like a Buddhist shrine, in which he keeps his spare clothes and food. He also carries a little brazen gong, which he constantly sounds while passing through a city or village, at the same time chanting the *Namu-myō-hō-ren-ge-kyō;* and he always bears with him a little blank book, in which the priest of every temple visited stamps the temple seal in red ink. The pilgrimage over, this book with its one thousand seal impressions becomes an heirloom in the family of the pilgrim. . . .

*

. . . The city [Matsue] can be definitely divided into three architectural quarters: the district of the merchants and shop-keepers, forming the heart of the settlement, where all the houses are two stories high; the district of the temples, including nearly the whole southeastern part of the town; and the district or districts of the *shizoku* (formerly called samurai), comprising a vast number of large, roomy, garden-girt, one-story dwellings. From these elegant homes, in feudal days, could be summoned at a moment's notice five thousand "two-sworded men" with their armed retainers, making a fighting total for the city alone of probably not less than thirteen thousand warriors. More than one third of all the city buildings were then samurai homes; for Matsue was the military center of the most ancient province of Japan. At both ends of the town, which curves in a crescent along the lake shore, were the two main settlements of samurai; but just as some of the most important temples are situated outside of the temple district, so were many of the finest homesteads of this knightly caste situated in other quarters. They mustered most thickly, however, about the castle, which stands today on the summit of its citadel hill—the Oshiroyama—solid as when first built long centuries ago, a vast and sinister shape, all iron-gray, rising against the sky from a cyclopean foundation of stone. Fantastically grim the thing is, and grotesquely complex in detail; looking somewhat like a huge pagoda, of which the second, third, and fourth stories have been squeezed down and telescoped into one another by their own weight. Crested at its summit, like a feudal helmet, with two colossal fishes of bronze lifting their curved bodies skyward from either angle of the roof, and bristling with horned gables and gargoyled eaves and tilted puzzles of tiled roofing at every story, the creation is a veritable architectural dragon, made up of magnificent monstrosities,—a dragon, moreover, full of eyes set at all conceivable angles, above, below, and on every side. From under the black scowl of the loftiest eaves, looking east and south, the whole city can be seen at a single glance, as in the vision of a soaring hawk; and from the northern angle the view plunges down three hundred feet to the castle road, where walking figures of men appear no larger than flies.

*

The grim castle has its legend.

It is related that, in accordance with some primitive and barbarous custom, precisely like that of which so terrible a souvenir has been preserved for us in the most pathetic of Serbian ballads, "The Foundation of Skadra," a maiden of Matsue was interred alive under the walls of the castle at the time of its erection, as a sacrifice to some forgotten gods. Her name has never been recorded; nothing concerning her is remembered except that she was beautiful and very fond of dancing.

Now after the castle had been built, it is said that a law had to be passed forbidding that any girl should dance in the streets of Matsue. For whenever any maiden danced the hill Oshiroyama would shudder, and the great castle quiver from basement to summit. . . .

*

Over the Tenjin-bashi, or Bridge of Tenjin, and through small streets and narrow of densely populated districts, and past many a tenantless and mouldering feudal homestead, I make my way to the extreme south-western end of the city, to watch the sunset from a little *sobaya* [an inn where soba is sold] facing the lake. For to see the sun sink from this *sobaya* is one of the delights of Matsue.

There are no such sunsets in Japan as in the tropics: the light is gentle as a light of dreams; there are no furies of color; there are no chromatic violences in nature in this Orient. All in sea or sky is tint rather than color, and tint vapor-toned. I think that the exquisite taste of the race in the matter of colors and of tints, as exemplified in the dyes of their wonderful textures, is largely attributable to the sober and delicate beauty of nature's tones in this all-temperate world where nothing is garish.

Before me the fair vast lake sleeps, softly luminous, far-ringed with chains of blue volcanic hills shaped like a sierra. On my right, at its eastern end, the most ancient quarter of the city spreads its roofs of blue-gray tile; the houses crowd thickly down to the shore, to dip their wooden feet into the flood. With a glass I can see my own windows and the far-spreading of the roofs beyond, and above all else the green citadel with its grim castle, grotesquely peaked. The sun begins to set, and exquisite astonishments of tinting appear in water and sky.

Dead rich purples cloud broadly behind and above the indigo black-ness of the serrated hills—mist purples, fading upward smokily into faint vermilions and dim gold, which again melt up through ghostliest greens into the blue. The deeper waters of the lake, far away, take a tender violet indescribable, and the silhouette of the pine-shadowed island seems to float in that sea of soft sweet color. But the shallower and nearer is cut from the deeper water by the current as sharply as by a line drawn, and all the surface on this side of that line is a shimmering bronze,—old rich ruddy gold-bronze.

All the fainter colors change every five minutes,—wonderously change and shift like tones and shades of fine shot-silks.

*

Often in the streets at night, especially on the nights of sacred festivals (*matsuri*), one's attention will be attracted to some small booth by the spectacle of an admiring and perfectly silent crowd pressing before it. As soon as one can get a chance to look one finds there is nothing to look at but a few vases containing sprays of flowers, or perhaps some light gracious branches freshly cut from a blossoming tree. It is simply a little flower-show, or, more correctly, a free exhibition of master skill in the arrangement of flowers. For the Japanese do not brutally chop off flower-heads to work them up into meaningless masses of color, as we barbarians do: they love nature too well for that; they know how much the natural charm of the flower depends upon its setting and mounting, its relation to leaf and stem, and they select a single graceful branch or spray just as nature made it. At first you will not, as a Western stranger, comprehend such an exhibition at all: you are yet a savage in such matters compared with the commonest coolies about you. But even while you are still wondering at popular interest in this simple little show, the charm of it will begin to grow upon you, will become a revelation to you; and, despite your Occidental idea of self-superiority, you will feel humbled by the discovery that all flower displays you have ever seen abroad were only monstrosities in comparison with the natural beauty of those few simple sprays. You will also observe how much the white or pale blue screen behind the flowers enhances the effect by lamp or lantern light. For the screen has been arranged with the special purpose of showing the exquisiteness of plant shadows: and the sharp silhouettes of sprays and blossoms cast thereon are beautiful beyond the imagining of any Western decorative artist.

*

It is still the season of mists in this land whose most ancient name signifies the Place of the Issuing of Clouds. With the passing of twilight a faint ghostly brume rises over lake and landscape, spectrally veiling surfaces, slowly obliterating distances. As I lean over the parapet of the Tenjin-bashi, on my homeward way, to take one last look eastward, I find that the mountains have already been effaced. Before me there is only a shadowy flood far vanishing into vagueness without a horizon—the phantom of a sea. And I become suddenly aware that little white things are fluttering slowly down into it from the fingers of a woman standing upon the bridge beside me, and murmuring something in a low sweet voice. She is praying for her dead child. Each of those little papers she is dropping into the current bears a tiny picture of Jizō, and perhaps a little inscription. For when a child dies the mother buys a small woodcut (*hanko*) of Jizō, and with it prints the image of the divinity upon one hundred little papers. And she sometimes also writes upon the papers words signifying "For the sake of . . . ,"—inscribing never the living, but the *kaimyō* or soul-name only; which the Buddhist priest has given to the dead, and which is written also upon the little commemorative tablet kept within the Buddhist household shrine, or *butsuma*. Then, upon a fixed day (most commonly the forty-ninth day after the burial), she goes to some place of running water and drops the little papers therein one by one; repeating, as each slips through her fingers, the holy invocation, *"Namu Jizō, Dai Bosatsu!"*

Doubtless this pious little woman, praying beside me in the dusk, is very poor. Were she not, she would hire a boat and scatter her tiny papers far away upon the bosom of the lake. (It is now only after dark that this may be done; for the police—I know not why—have been instructed to prevent the pretty rite, just as in the open ports they have been instructed to prohibit the launching of the little straw boats of the dead, the *shōr-yōbune*).

But why should the papers be cast into running water? A good old Tendai priest tells me that originally the rite was only for the souls of the drowned. But now these gentle hearts believe that all waters flow downward to the Shadow-world and through the Sai-no-Kawara, where Jizō is.

*

At home again, I slide open once more my little paper window, and look out upon the night. I see the paper lanterns flitting over the bridge, like a long shimmering of fireflies. I see the spectres of a hundred lights trembling upon the black flood. I see the broad *shōji* of dwellings beyond the river suffused with the soft yellow radiance of invisible lamps; and upon those lighted spaces I can discern slender moving shadows, silhouettes of graceful women. Devoutly do I pray that glass may never become universally adopted in Japan,—there would be no more delicious shadows.

I listen to the voices of the city awhile. I hear the great bell of Tōkōji rolling its soft Buddhist thunder across the dark, and the songs of the night-walkers whose hearts have been made merry with wine, and the long sonorous chanting of the night-peddlers.

"U-mu-don-yai-soba-yai!" It is the seller of hot *soba*, Japanese buckwheat, making his last round.

"Umai handan, machibito endan, usemono ninsō kasō kichikyō no urainai!" The cry of the itinerant fortune-teller.

"Ame-yu!" The musical cry of the seller of *midzuame*, the sweet amber syrup which children love.

"Amai!" The shrilling call of the seller of *amazake*, sweet rice wine.

"Kawachi-no-kuni-hiotan-yama-koi-no-tsuji-ura!" The peddler of love-papers, of divining-papers, pretty tinted things with little shadowy pictures upon them. When held near a fire or a lamp, words written upon them with invisible ink begin to appear. These are always about sweet-

hearts, and sometimes tell one what he does not wish to know. The fortunate ones who read them believe themselves still more fortunate; the unlucky abandon all hope; the jealous become even more jealous than they were before.

From all over the city there rises into the night a sound like the bubbling and booming of great frogs in a marsh,—the echoing of the tiny drums of the dancing-girls, of the charming geisha. Like the rolling of a waterfall continually reverberates the multitudinous pattering of *geta* upon the bridge. A new light rises in the east; the moon is wheeling up from behind the peaks, very large and weird and wan through the white vapors. Again I hear the sounds of the clapping of many hands. For the wayfarers are paying obeisance to O-Tsuki-San: from the long bridge they are saluting the coming of the White Moon-Lady.

I sleep, to dream of little children, in some mouldering mossy temple court, playing at the game of Shadows and of Demons.

("THE CHIEF CITY OF THE PROVINCE OF THE GODS")

CHAPTER *3*

A Wedding
in Matsue

IN HIS HOUSE of paper and wood, Lafcadio felt the dreaded winter coming on, as fierce winds from the Asian coast blew across the Sea of Japan, depositing five feet of snow around his defenseless dwelling. Warmed solely by a charcoal-burning *hibachi* and a *kotasu* (a small, heated fireplace beneath a quilt-covered table)—"mere shadow of heat . . . ghosts, illusions," Lafcadio called them—he shivered continuously both inside and outside his home, and soon developed a debilitating respiratory infection. "My first serious discouragement," he told Chamberlain, "came with this check to my enthusiasm; I fear a few more winters of this kind will put me underground." He began dreaming about Martinique, considered traveling on to the Philippines, and wondered whether it was truly possible to cultivate Buddhist sentiments if one were freezing: "Cold compels painful notions of solidity; cold sharpens the delusion of personality; cold quickens egotism; cold numbs thought, and shrivels up the little wings of dreams."

Sentarō Nishida, who visited Lafcadio during his illness and observed clearly that his colleague could not take care of himself, came to Lafcadio one day with a simple and unusual solution to his plight—marriage to a young Japanese woman, who would not only keep him warmer than a *kotasu* but would also make his life easier by ordering his affairs and providing for his domestic needs in his new country. Professor Nishida had, moreover, just the girl for him, a twenty-two-year-old named Setsu (or Setsuko—meaning "true" or "virtuous"), the daughter of the Koizumi family that had once belonged to the now-functionless and impoverished samurai caste. Setsu's marriage to *Herun-san,* Nisihda explained, while certainly unconventional, would be considered an act of compassion toward her family, to whom she owed her primary duty; for Lafcadio, of course, as a good husband, would be expected to assume financial responsibility for all of his in-laws.

The forty-year-old Lafcadio thought about the matter, and calmly made up his mind. In January 1891—the twenty-fourth year of Meiji—he and Setsu Koizumi celebrated their nuptials with an exchange of rice wine in the presence of Lafcadio's friends from Matsue and the members of his new family—and with the marriage duly noted by the local authorities.

Lafcadio had arrived in America homeless and an orphan, and had created a family for himself in the persons of the fatherly Henry Watkin, the motherly Mrs. Courtney, Elizabeth Bisland (his "Fairy Sister"), and Henry Krehbiel, Rudolph Matas, and Ellwood Hendrick (his intellectual brothers). But now Lafcadio became part of a preexisting family that was willing to accept him as one of its own. There was, however, in the eyes of Japanese law, only one legal way to marry a Japanese woman, and that was to be adopted into her family, thereby becoming a Japanese citizen. Although he avoided this step at that time, Lafcadio nevertheless considered himself "morally, and according to public opinion, fast married."

In his autobiographical novel *Madame Chrysanthème* (1888), Pierre Loti confesses to his "childish" Japanese bride: "I took you to amuse me; you have not perhaps succeeded very well, but after all you have done what you could: given me your little face, your little curtseys, your little music; in short, you have been pleasant enough in your Japanese way." And as the narrator also remarks: "What a pity this little Chrysanthème cannot always be asleep; she is really extremely decorative seen in this manner,— and like this, at least, she does not bore me. Who knows what may perchance be going on in that little head and heart! If I only had the means of finding out! But strange to say, since we have kept house together, instead of pushing my studies in the Japanese language further, I have neglected them, so much have I felt the utter impossibility of ever interesting myself in the subject."

Loti's callous, amoral attitude toward his marriage, along with his shallow-minded description of Japan as "little, finical, affected," was the antithesis of the view of Lafcadio, who now bitterly remarked about his literary mentor: "To me Loti seems for a space to have looked into nature's whole splendid burning fulgurant soul. . . . He was young. Then the color and the light faded, and only the worn-out *blasé* nerves remained; and the poet became,—a little morbid modern affected French-man."

Many persons have wondered how Lafcadio could have so readily considered embracing an arranged marriage with a traditional, utterly plain, conventional, non-English-speaking woman . . . and with respon-sibilities for most of her family members thrown in for good measure. Apparently from the beginning, Lafcadio had every intention of remaining with Setsu and raising a family according to traditional norms of Japanese behavior, rather than simply "taking off" after a while à la Loti or Madama Butterfly's Lieutenant Pinkerton.

Lafcadio had confessed to Julia Wetherall, years before, "that he would not care for intellectual companionship in a wife, but would prefer some simple, quiet creature who would look after his domestic comfort and stay meekly outside of his realm of thought." In this regard, Setsu Koizumi was literally his ideal wife because, not speaking or reading a word of English, she had no choice but to stay outside his intellectual world. (For their everyday communications they created between themselves some-thing they called the Hearn San Kotoba, or "Hearnian dialect," a combi-nation Japanese-English baby talk that only they could understand.)

"How diamond-hard," he declared (in a veiled and surprisingly harsh reference to Elizabeth Bisland), "the character of the American woman becomes under the idolatry of which she is the subject. In the eternal order of things, which is the highest being,—the childish, confiding, sweet Japanese girl,—or the superb, calculating, penetrating Occidental Circe of our more artificial society, with her enormous power for evil, and her limited capacity for good?"

Lafcadio had deep feelings for his "intellectual" sister Elizabeth. But in characteristic Victorian fashion, he also felt afraid of and unsettled by the cool, heartbreakingly seductive, ambitious aspects of her personality—as he felt about all women who strove for positions of power in what he viewed as a corrupting society. "Only nature and Woman are unspeak-ably sweet," he maintained. So a woman who became a woman-in-society was, to him, someone who had fallen from grace.

Setsu was a traditional, submissive Japanese housewife who handed her husband his clothing every morning—garment by garment—and, as she had similarly been trained to do, walked several paces behind Laf-cadio when they went out together. If he wasn't "in love" with Setsu in the way he had been erotically attached to Mattie or Cyrillia or obsessed by the young Basque girl Marie, he felt secure with his wife, admired her sensible ways, and grew to cherish and depend completely on her. So instead of taking off on the first boat to Hong Kong, Manila, or Tahiti, he made a decision, even in the midst of his periodic depressions, to stay put.

Lafcadio consciously resolved to exorcise his "hunger" for the "curse and delusion" of the Eternal Feminine ("the Woman thou shalt never know!"). As he confided to Hendrick: "Marriage seems to me the certain destruction of all that emotion and suffering,—so that one afterwards looks back at the old times with wonder. One cannot dream or desire anything more after love is transmuted into the friendship of marriage. It is like a haven from which you can see the dangerous sea-currents, running like violet bands beyond you out of sight."

Occasionally, Lafcadio was invited by his academic colleagues to dine with them at banquets with geishas in attendance: "A band of beautiful girls come in to wait upon you, with exquisite voices, and beautiful voices. . . . After a while they dance. If you wish to fall in love with them, you may." Or he would be sent a book by one of his Western friends, such as a novel by William Mallock recommended by Ellwood Hendrick, in which he would identify with the married hero's passion for the heroine:

[I asked myself: "If it was I?" . . . And conscience answered: "If it was you, in spite of love and duty and honor and hellfire staring you in the face you would have gone after her—and tried to console yourself by considering the Law of Attraction of Bodies and Souls in the incomprehensible cosmical order of things, which is older than the gods." And I was very much inclined to demur; but conscience repeated: "Oh! don't be such a liar and quibbler;—you know you would! . . . Your ancestors were not religious people; you lack constitutional morality. That's why you are poor, and unsuccessful, and void of mental balance, and an exile in Japan. You know you cannot be happy in an English moral community. You are a fraud—a vile Latin—a vicious French-hearted scalawag.]

Gradually, however, Lafcadio attended fewer functions with "bands of beautiful girls," and fell in love less frequently with the heroines of romantic Western novels. "The magnetism of another faith about you," he realized, "necessarily polarizes that loose-quivering needle of desire in a man that seeks source or attraction in spite of synthetic philosophy. The general belief in an infinite past and future interpenetrates one somehow."

From the perspective of evolutionary philosophy, one could say that Lafcadio's "physical sensations" were being refined into "more complex moral susceptibilities." From a more mundane point of view, one might say that Lafcadio was getting older, was dissatisfied with temporary relationships with women, was tired of living alone, was anxious to have children (he once confessed that at the age of thirty-five he began to feel that "no man died so utterly as the man without children"), and, more than ever before, was feeling a compulsion to concentrate on his work (his *raison d'être*). Finally, on a spiritual plane, the "magnetic" implications of a conversation Lafcadio had had with a Buddhist monk, in a tiny temple behind a street of small shops during his first weeks in Japan, was gradually polarizing him in the depths of his being:

❮ . . . Presently appeared an aged nun, who welcomed us [to the temple] and bade us enter; her smoothly shaven head shining like a moon at every reverence. We doffed our footgear, and followed her behind the screen, into a little room that opened upon a garden; and we saw the old priest seated upon a cushion, and writing at a very low table. He laid aside his brush to greet us; and we also took our places on cushions before him. Very pleasant his face was to look upon: all wrinkles written there by the ebb of life spake of that which was good.

The nun brought us tea, and sweetmeats stamped with the Wheel of the Law; the red cat curled itself up beside me; and the priest talked to us. His voice was deep and gentle; there were bronze tones in it, like the rich murmurings which follow each peal of a temple bell. We coaxed him to tell us about himself. He was eighty-eight years of age, and his eyes and ears were still as those of a young man; but he could not walk because of chronic rheumatism. For twenty years he had been occupied in writing a religious history of Japan, to be completed in three hundred volumes; and he had already completed two hundred and thirty. The rest he hoped to write during the coming year. I saw on a small book-shelf behind him the imposing array of neatly bound MSS.

"But the plan upon which he works," said my student interpreter, "is quite wrong. His history will never be published; it is full of impossible stories—miracles and fairytales."

(I thought I should like to read the stories.)

"For one who has reached such an age," I said, "you seem very strong."

"The signs are that I shall live some years longer," replied the old man, "though I wish to live only long enough to finish my history. Then, as I am helpless and cannot move about, I want to die so as to get a new body. I suppose I must have committed some fault in a former life, to be crippled as I am. But I am glad to feel that I am nearing the Shore."

"He means the shore of the Sea of Death and Birth," says my interpreter. "The ship whereby we cross, you know, is the Ship of the Good Law; and the farthest shore is Nehan,—Nirvana."

"Are all our bodily weaknesses and misfortunes," I asked, "the results of errors committed in other births?"

"That which we are," the old man answered, "is the consequence of that which we have been. We say in Japan the consequence of *mangō* and *ingō,*—the two classes of actions."

"Evil and good?" I queried.

"Greater and lesser. There are no perfect actions. Every act contains both inerit and demerit, just as even the best painting has defects and excellences. But when the sum of good in any action exceeds the sum of evil, just as in a good painting the merits outweigh the faults, then the result is progress. And gradually by such progress will all evil be eliminated."

"But how," I asked, "can the result of actions affect the physical conditions? The child follows the way of his fathers, inherits their strength or their weakness; yet not from them does he receive his soul."

"The chain of causes and effects is not easy to explain in a few words. To understand all you should study the Dai-jō or Greater Vehicle; also the Shō-jō, or Lesser Vehicle. There you will learn that the world itself exists only because of acts. Even as one learning to write, at first writes only with great difficulty, but afterward, becoming skillful, writes without knowledge of any effort, so the tendency of acts continually repeated is to form habit. And such tendencies persist far beyond this life."

"Can any man obtain the power to remember his former births?"

"That is very rare," the old man answered, shaking his head. "To have such memory one should first become a Bosatsu [*Bodhissattva*]."

"Is it not possible to become a Bosatsu?"

"Not in this age. This is the Period of Corruption. First there was the Period of True Doctrine, when life was long; and after it came the Period of Images, during which men departed from the highest truth; and now the world is degenerate. It is not now possible by good deeds to become a Buddha, because the world is too corrupt and life is too short. But devout persons may attain the *Gokuraku* [Paradise] by virtue of merit, and by constantly repeating the Nembutsu; and in the *Gokuraku,* they may be able to practice the true doctrine. For the days are longer there, and life also is very long."

"I have read in our translations of the Sutras," I said, "that by virtue of good deeds men may be reborn in happier and yet happier conditions successively, each time obtaining more perfect faculties, each time surrounded by higher joys. Riches are spoken of, and strength and beauty, and graceful women, and all that people desire in this temporary world. Wherefore I cannot help thinking that the way of progress must continually grow more difficult the further one proceeds. For if these texts be true, the more one succeeds in detaching one's self from the things of the senses, the more powerful become the temptations to return to them. So that the reward of virtue would seem itself to be made an obstacle in the path."

"Not so!" replied the old man. "They, who by self-mastery reach such conditions of temporary happiness, have gained spiritual force also, and some knowledge of truth. Their strength to conquer themselves increases more and more with every triumph, until they reach at last that world of Apparitional Birth, in which the lower forms of temptation have no existence."

The red cat stirred uneasily at a sound of *geta,* then went to the entrance, followed by the nun. There were some visitors waiting; and the priest begged us to excuse him a little while, that he might attend to their spiritual wants. We made place quickly for them, and they came in, —poor pleasant folk, who saluted us kindly: a mother bereaved, desiring to have prayers said for the happiness of her little dead boy; a young wife to obtain the pity of the Buddha for her ailing husband; a father and daughter to seek divine help for somebody that had gone very far away. The priest spoke caressingly to all, giving to the mother some little prints of Jizō, giving a paper of blest rice to the wife, and on behalf of the father and daughter, preparing some holy texts. Involuntarily there came to me the idea of all the countless innocent prayers thus being daily made in countless temples; the idea of all the fears and hopes and heartaches of simple love; the idea of all the humble sorrows unheard by any save the gods. The student began to examine the old man's books, and I began to think of the unthinkable.

•   •   •

Life—life as unity, uncreated, without beginning,—of which we know the luminous shadows only;—life forever striving against death, and always conquered yet always surviving—what is it?—why is it? A myriad times the universe is dissipated,—a myriad times again evolved; and the same life vanishes with every vanishing, only to reappear in another cycling. The Cosmos becomes a nebula, the nebula a Cosmos: eternally the swarms of suns and worlds are born; eternally they die. But after each tremendous integration the flaming spheres cool down and ripen into life; and the life ripens into Thought. The ghost in each one of us must have passed through the burning of a million suns,—must survive the awful vanishing of countless future universes. May not Memory somehow and somewhere also survive? Are we sure that in ways and forms unknowable it does not? as infinite vision,—remembrance of the Future in the Past? Perhaps in the Night-without-end, as in deeps of Nirvana, dreams of all that has ever been, of all that can ever be, are being perpetually dreamed.

The parishioners uttered their thanks, made their little offerings to Jizō, and retired, saluting us as they went. We resumed our former places beside the little writing-table, and the old man said:—

"It is the priest, perhaps, who among all men best knows what sorrow is in the world. I have heard that in the countries of the West there is also much suffering, although the Western nations are so rich."

"Yes," I made answer; "and I think that in Western countries there is more unhappiness than in Japan. For the rich there are larger pleasures, but for the poor greater pains. Our life is much more difficult to live; and, perhaps for that reason, our thoughts are more troubled by the mystery of the world."

The priest seemed interested, but said nothing. With the interpreter's help, I continued:—

"There are three great questions by which the minds of many men in the Western countries are perpetually tormented. These questions we call 'the Whence, the Whither, and the Why,' meaning, Whence Life? Whither does it go? Why does it exist and suffer? Our highest Western Science declares them riddles impossible to solve, yet confesses at the same time that the heart of man can find no peace till they are solved. All religions have attempted explanations; and all their explanations are different. I have searched Buddhist books for answers to these questions, and I found answers which seemed to me better than any others. Still, they did not satisfy me, being incomplete. From your own lips I hope to obtain some answers to the first and the third questions at least. I do not ask for proof or for arguments of any kind: I ask only to know doctrine. Was the beginning of all things in universal Mind?"

To this question I really expected no definite answer, having, in the Sutra called *Sabbâsava,* read about "those things which ought not to be considered," and about the Six Absurd Notions, and the words of the rebuke to such as debate within themselves: *"This is a being: whence did it come? whither will it go?"* But the answer came, measured and musical, like a chant:—

"All things considered as individuals have come into being, through forms innumerable of development and reproduction, out of the universal Mind. Potentially within that mind they had existed from eternity. But between that we call Mind and that we call Substance there is no difference of essence. What we name Substance is only the sum of our own sensations and perceptions; and these themselves are but phenomena of Mind. Of Substance-in-itself we have not any knowledge. We know nothing beyond the phases of our mind, and these phases are wrought in it by outer influence or power, to which we give the name Substance. But Substance and Mind in themselves are only two phases of one infinite Entity."

"There are Western teachers also," I said, "who teach a like doctrine; and the most profound researches of our modern science seem to demonstrate that what we term Matter has no absolute existence. But concerning that infinite Entity of which you speak, is there any Buddhist teaching as to when and how It first produced those two forms which in name we still distinguish as Mind and Substance?"

"Buddhism," the old priest answered, "does not teach, as other religions do, that things have been produced by creation. The one and only Reality is the universal Mind, called in Japanese *Shinnyo,*—the Reality-in-its-very-self, infinite and eternal. Now this infinite Mind within Itself beheld Its own sentiency. And, even as one who in hallucination assumes apparitions to be actualities, so the universal Entity took for external existences that which It beheld only within Itself. We call this illusion *Mumyo,* signifying 'without radiance,' or 'void of illumination.' "

"The word has been translated by some Western scholars," I observed, "as 'Ignorance.' "

"So I have been told. But the idea conveyed by the word we use is not the idea expressed by the term 'ignorance.' It is rather the idea of enlightenment misdirected, or of illusion."

"And what has been taught," I asked, "concerning the time of that illusion?"

"The time of the primal illusion is said to be Mu-shi, 'beyond beginning,' in the incalculable past. From *Shinnyo* emanated the first distinction of the Self and the Not-Self, whence have arisen all individual existences, whether of Spirit or of Substance, and all those passions and desires, likewise, which influence the conditions of being through countless births. Thus the universe is the emanation of the infinite Entity; yet it cannot be said that we are the creations of that Entity. The original Self of each of us is the universal Mind; and within each of us the universal Self exists, together with the effects of the primal illusion. And this state of the original Self enwrapped in the results of illusion, we call Nyōrai-zō, or the Womb of the Buddha. The end for which we should all strive is simply our return to the infinite Original Self, which is the essence of Buddha."

"There is another subject of doubt," I said, "about which I much desire to know the teaching of Buddhism. Our Western science declares that the visible universe has been evolved and dissolved successively innumerable times during the infinite past, and must also vanish and reappear through countless cycles in the infinite future. In our translations of the ancient Indian philosophy, and of the sacred texts of the Buddhists, the same thing is declared. But is it not also taught that there shall come at last for all things a time of ultimate vanishing and of perpetual rest?"

He answered: "The Shō-jō indeed teaches that the universe has appeared and disappeared over and over again, times beyond reckoning in the past, and that it must continue to be alternately dissolved and reformed through unimaginable eternities to come. But we are also taught that all things shall enter finally and forever, into the state of *Nehan* [Nirvana]."

An irreverent yet irrepressible fancy suddenly arose within me. I could not help thinking of Absolute Rest as expressed by the scientific formula of two hundred and seventy-four degrees (centigrade) below zero, or $-525°.2$ Fahrenheit. But I only said:—

"For the Western mind it is difficult to think of absolute rest as a condition of bliss. Does the Buddhist idea of *Nehan* include the idea of infinite stillness, of universal immobility?"

"No," replied the priest. "*Nehan* is the condition of Absolute Self-sufficiency, the state of all-knowing, all-perceiving. We do not suppose it a state of total inaction, but the supreme condition of freedom from all restraint. It is true that we cannot imagine a bodiless condition of perception or knowledge; because all our ideas and sensations belong to the condition of the body. But we believe that *Nehan* is the state of infinite vision and infinite wisdom and infinite spiritual peace."

The red cat leaped upon the priest's knees, and there curled itself into a posture of lazy comfort. The old man caressed it; and my companion observed, with a little laugh:—

"See how fat it is! Perhaps it may have performed some good deeds in a previous life."

"Do the conditions of animals," I asked, "also depend upon merit and demerit in previous existences?"

The priest answered me seriously:—

"All conditions of being depend upon conditions preëxisting, and Life is One. To be born into the world of men is fortunate; there we have some enlightenment, and chances of gaining merit. But the state of an animal is a state of obscurity of mind, deserving our pity and benevolence. No animal can be considered truly fortunate; yet even in the life of animals there are countless differences of condition."

A little silence followed,—softly broken by the purring of the cat. I looked at the picture of Adelaide Neilson [English actress—1848–1880—known for her impersonations of Shakespearean heroines], just visible above the top of the screen; and I thought of Juliet, and wondered what the priest would say about Shakespeare's wondrous story of passion and sorrow, were I able to relate it worthily in Japanese. Then suddenly, like an answer to that wonder, came a memory of the two hundred and fifteenth verse of the *Dhammapada*: *"From love comes grief; from grief comes fear: one who is free from love knows neither grief nor fear."*

"Does Buddhism," I asked, "teach that all sexual love ought to be suppressed? Is such love of necessity a hindrance to enlightenment? I know that Buddhist priests, excepting those of the Shin-shū, are forbidden to marry; but I do not know what is the teaching concerning celibacy and marriage among the laity."

"Marriage may be either a hindrance or a help on the Path," the old man said, "according to conditions. All depends upon conditions. If the love of wife and child should cause a man to become too much attached to the temporary advantages of this unhappy world, then such love would be a hindrance. But, on the contrary, if the love of wife and child should enable a man to live more purely and more unselfishly than he could do in a state of celibacy, then marriage would be a very great help to him in the Perfect Way. Many are the dangers of marriage for the wise; but for those of little understanding the dangers of celibacy are greater. And even the illusion of passion may sometimes lead noble natures to the higher knowledge. There is a story of this. Dai-Mokukenren, whom the people call Mokuren, was a disciple of Shaka [the Japanese rendering of Sakyamuni]. He was a very comely man; and a girl became enamored of him. As he belonged already to the Order, she despaired of being ever able to have him for her husband; and she grieved in secret. But at last she found courage to go to the Lord Buddha, and to speak all her heart to him. Even while she was speaking, he cast a deep sleep upon her; and she dreamed she was the happy wife of Mokuren. Years of contentment seemed to pass in her dream; and after them years of joy and sorrow mingled; and suddenly her husband was taken away from her by death. Then she knew such sorrow that she wondered how she could live; and she awoke in that pain, and saw the Buddha smile. And he said to her: 'Little Sister, thou hast seen. Choose now as thou wilt,—either to be the bride of Mokuren, or to seek the higher Way upon which he has entered.' Then she cut off her hair, and became a nun, and in aftertime attained to the condition of one never to be reborn."

For a moment it seemed to me that the story did not show how love's illusion could lead to self-conquest; that the girl's conversion was only the direct result of painful knowledge forced upon her, not a consequence of her love. But presently I reflected that the vision accorded her could have produced no high result in a selfish or unworthy soul. I thought of disadvantages unspeakable which the possession of foreknowledge might involve in the present order of life; and felt it was a blessed thing for most of us that the future shaped itself behind a veil. Then I dreamed that the power to lift that veil might be evolved or won, just so soon as such a faculty should be of real benefit to men, but not before; and I asked:—

"Can the power to see the Future be obtained through enlightenment?"

The priest answered:—

"Yes. When we reach that state of enlightenment in which we obtain the *Roku-Jindzū,* or Six Mysterious Faculties, then we can see the Future as well as the Past. Such power comes at the same time as the power of remembering former births. But to attain that condition of knowledge, in the present age of the world, is very difficult."

• • •

My companion made me a stealthy sign that it was time to say goodbye.
We had stayed rather long—even by the measure of Japanese etiquette,
which is generous to a fault in these matters. I thanked the master of the
temple for his kindness in replying to my fantastic questions, and ventured to add:—

"There are a hundred other things about which I should like to ask
you, but to-day I have taken too much of your time. May I come again?"

"It will make me very happy," he said. "Be pleased to come again as
soon as you desire. I hope you will not fail to ask about all things which
are still obscure to you. It is by earnest inquiry that truth may be known
and illusions dispelled. Nay, come often—that I may speak to you of the
Shō-jō. And these I pray you to accept."

He gave me two little packages. One contained white sand—sand from
the holy temple of Zenkōji, whither all good souls make pilgrimage after
death. The other contained a very small white stone, said to be a *shari*,
or relic of the body of a Buddha.

I hoped to visit the kind old man many times again. But a school contract
took me out of the city and over the mountains; and I saw him no more.

("IN YOKOHAMA")]

After six months of teaching, Lafcadio had saved $200, and was re-
ceiving occasional royalty checks from Harper and Brothers for books like
Chita, Youma, and *Two Years in the French West Indies.* So in June 1891,
he, Setsu, a maid, and a cat moved into a more spacious and secluded
ex-samurai house (a *yashiki*) called Kitabori, situated between the castle
hill and a neighboring wood. Setsu took care of all domestic matters and
oversaw her maid's culinary responsibilities—feeding Lafcadio three meals
a day, including one Western repast, so that he soon gained twenty
pounds—and provided him with the time he needed to write undisturbed.

It wasn't long into their marriage that Setsu discovered that Lafcadio
was somewhat strange, and possibly a bit mad. "He wept when alone,"
she stated in her memoirs, "and he was irritated or elated in an abnormal
degree." When enmeshed in writing, he often seemed to be in a trance—
his face drained of color, crying and moaning as his pen flew over his
yellow paper, totally unaware of where he was. "One night about eleven
o'clock," Setsu recalled, "I opened the *shoji* [sliding paper window] and
smelt dense smoke from the oil lamp. To my astonishment I found that

the wick of the lamp was way up and that the room was dark with smoke. Hearn was almost suffocating, but he was writing so enthusiastically that he noticed nothing, although he had a very sensitive nose for odors. I hurriedly opened the *shoji* and let in the air, and said, 'Papa-san! how dangerous it was that you did not know the lamp was on fire!' He exclaimed, 'Why was I so stupid!' "

Disturbed by his behavior, Setsu went to see Professor Sentarō to ask whether her husband might have lost one of his souls. But the scholar gently explained to her that "this enthusiasm in thought and writing" was common to certain writers, and that she should not be overly concerned. Setsu did not at all understand, however, why her husband shared his food with a pet snake. "I give the food so that he will not eat the frogs," Lafcadio told her. "He had more delicate and kindly sentiments than a girl," his wife later commented. With time she got used to his moods, habits, manners, and tastes, and eventually came to admire and feel deep affection for the eccentric *gakusha* (scholar) she had dutifully married.

In their beautiful home, each bare, wooden room with its sliding walls contained a graceful vase in an alcove, one *kakemono* (a hanging picture painted on silk), and an *hibachi* encircled by kneeling cushions. From every room, sliding panels opened onto one of the three gardens surrounding the *yashiki,* with their raked gravel plots, lotus ponds, miniature lakes and hills, tiny islands, and moss, stones, ferns, shrubs, trees, plants, and flowers—all attended to by a full-time gardener, who graciously spent hours telling his master the Japanese names of every object and creature in this exquisite, cultivated little world. Dressed in his *yukata* and smoking a pipe, Lafcadio squatted on the veranda overlooking the gardens, and silently followed the comings and goings of various insects and reptiles through his pocket telescope, remaining in this position for a long while and becoming part of everything he saw:

I have already become a little too fond of my dwelling-place. Each day, after returning from my college duties, and exchanging my teacher's uniform for the infinitely more comfortable Japanese robe, I find more than compensation for the weariness of five class-hours in the simple pleasure of squatting on the shaded veranda overlooking the gardens. Those antique garden walls, high-mossed below their ruined coping of tiles, seem to shut out even the murmur of the city's life. There are no sounds but the voices of birds, the shrilling of *semi* [cicadae], or, at long, lazy intervals, the solitary plash of a diving frog. Nay, those walls seclude me from much

more than city streets. Outside them hums the changed Japan of tele-
graphs and newspapers and steamships; within dwell the all-reposing
peace of nature and the dreams of the sixteenth century. There is a charm
of quaintness in the very air, a faint sense of something viewless and
sweet all about one; perhaps the gentle haunting of dead ladies who
looked like the ladies of the old picture-books, and who lived here when
all this was new. Even in the summer light—touching the gray strange
shapes of stone, thrilling through the foliage of the long-loved trees—there
is the tenderness of a phantom caress. These are the gardens of the past.
The future will know them only as dreams, creations of a forgotten art,
whose charm no genius may reproduce.

Of the human tenants here no creature seems to be afraid. The little
frogs resting upon the lotus-leaves scarcely shrink from my touch; the
lizards sun themselves within easy reach of my hand; the water-snakes
glide across my shadow without fear; bands of *semi* establish their deaf-
ening orchestra on a plum branch just above my head, and a praying
mantis insolently poses on my knee. Swallows and sparrows not only
build their nests on my roof, but even enter my rooms without concern,
—one swallow has actually built its nest in the ceiling of the bath-room,—
and the weasel purloins fish under my very eyes without any scruples of
conscience. A wild *uguisu* perches on a cedar by the window, and in a
burst of savage sweetness challenges my caged pet to a contest in song;
and always through the golden air, from the green twilight of the mountain pines, there purls to me the plaintive, caressing, delicious call of the
yamabato:—

> *Tété*
> > *poppō,*
> *Kaka*
> > *poppō,*
> *Tété*
> > *poppō,*
> *Kaka*
> > *poppō,*
> *Tété* . . .

No European dove has such a cry. He who can hear, for the first time,
the voice of the *yamabato* without feeling a new sensation at his heart
little deserves to dwell in this happy world.

Yet all this—the old *katchiū-yashiki* and its gardens—will doubtless have vanished forever before many years. Already a multitude of gardens, more spacious and more beautiful than mine, have been converted into rice-fields or bamboo groves; and the quaint Izumo city, touched at last by some long-projected railway line,—perhaps even within the present de-cade,—will swell, and change, and grow commonplace, and demand these grounds for the building of factories and mills. Not from here alone, but from all the land the ancient peace and the ancient charm seem doomed to pass away. For impermanency is the nature of things, more particularly in Japan; and the changes and the changers shall also be changed until there is found no place for them,—and regret is vanity. The dead art that made the beauty of this place was the art, also, of that faith to which belongs the all-consoling text, *"Verily, even plants and trees, rocks and stones, all shall enter into Nirvana."* ("IN A JAPANESE GARDEN") ‖

CHAPTER 4

Little Spring, Eight Clouds

I T W A S a sweltering summer day in July 1893—the twenty-sixth year of Meiji. Pulled in his open *kuruma* by a straw-sandaled *kurumaya* along the curving and rolling Japanese shoreline from the town of Misumi to the southern city of Kumamoto, Lafcadio stared, as if in a trance, at the infinite blazing blue light of sea, cliffs, and sky, broken only by a few radiant and motionless white clouds.

Glancing down drowsily at his hands, he saw the paper fan, given to him that morning at breakfast as a keepsake by his beautiful innkeeper—a fan depicting the white rush of an enormous breaking wave on a beach, with seabirds flying exaltedly through the blue skies overhead.

"Now we will go to my father's palace, the Dragon Palace, under the waves of the South."

"No, I must go home to Kumamoto;—I have telegraphed, you see."

Having fallen asleep in the hundred-degree heat of the day, and dreaming of his favorite Japanese fairy tale—the story of Urashima—Lafcadio woke up to the sound of peasants beating ritual drums to invoke the rain for their parched lands. Passing through a village of a dozen or so thatched cottages clustered about a rocky pool, shaded by pines, the exhausted, perspiring *kurumaya* pulled over to quench his thirst and to rest for a short while in the shade; and Lafcadio, too, got out of the *kuruma* to sit by the pool:

[. . . It was evidently a favorite halting-place, judging by the number of *kuruma* and of people resting. There were benches under the trees; and, after having allayed thirst, I sat down to smoke and to look at the women washing clothes and the travelers refreshing themselves at the pool—while my *kurumaya* stripped, and proceeded to dash buckets of cold water over his body. Then tea was brought me by a young man with a baby on his back; and I tried to play with the baby, which said "Ah, bah!"

Such are the first sounds uttered by a Japanese babe. But they are purely Oriental; and in Romaji should be written *Aba*. And, as an utterance untaught, *Aba* is interesting. It is in Japanese child-speech the word for "good-bye"—precisely the last we would expect an infant to pronounce on entering into this world of illusion. To whom or to what is the little soul saying good-bye?—to friends in a previous state of existence still freshly remembered?—to comrades of its shadowy journey from nobody-knows-where? Such theorizing is tolerably safe, from a pious point of view, since the child can never decide for us. What its thoughts were at the mysterious moment of first speech, it will have forgotten long before it has become able to answer questions.

Unexpectedly, a queer recollection came to me—resurrected, perhaps, by the sight of the young man with the baby, perhaps by the song of the water in the cliff: the recollection of a story:

Long, long ago there lived somewhere among the mountains a poor woodcutter and his wife. They were very old, and had no children. Every day the husband went alone to the forest to cut wood, while the wife sat weaving at home.

One day the old man went farther into the forest than was his custom, to seek a certain kind of wood; and he suddenly found himself at the edge of a little spring he had never seen before. The water was strangely clear and cold, and he was thirsty; for the day was hot, and he had been working hard. So he doffed his great straw hat, knelt down, and took a long drink. That water seemed to refresh him in a most extraordinary way. Then he caught sight of his own face in the spring, and started back. It was certainly his own face, but not at all as he was accustomed to see it in the old mirror at home. It was the face of a very young man! He could not believe his eyes. He put up both hands to his head, which had been quite bald only a moment before. It was covered with thick black hair. And his face had become smooth as a boy's; every wrinkle was gone. At the same moment he discovered himself full of new strength. He stared in astonishment at the limbs that had been so long withered by age; they were now shapely and hard with dense young muscle. Unknowingly he had drunk at the Fountain of Youth; and that draught had transformed him.

First, he leaped high and shouted for joy; then he ran home faster than he had ever run before in his life. When he entered his house his wife was frightened—because she took him for a stranger; and when he told her the wonder, she could not at once believe him. But after a long time he was able to convince her that the young man she now saw before her was really her husband; and he told her where the spring was, and asked her to go there with him.

Then she said: "You have become so handsome and so young that you cannot continue to love an old woman; so I must drink some of that water immediately. But it will never do for both of us to be away from the house at the same time. Do you wait here while I go." And she ran to the woods all by herself.

She found the spring and knelt down, and began to drink. Oh! how cool and sweet that water was! She drank and drank and drank, and stopped for breath only to begin again.

Her husband waited for her impatiently; he expected to see her come back changed into a pretty slender girl. But she did not come back at all. He got anxious, shut up the house, and went to look for her.

When he reached the spring, he could not see her. He was just on the point of returning when he heard a little wail in the high grass near the spring. He searched there and discovered his wife's clothes and a baby—a very small baby, perhaps six months old!

For the old woman had drunk too deeply of the magical water; she had drunk herself far back beyond the time of youth into the period of speechless infancy.

He took up the child in his arms. It looked at him in a sad, wondering way. He carried it home—murmuring to it—thinking strange, melancholy thoughts.   ("THE DREAM OF A SUMMER DAY")

On November 17, 1893, in the city of Kumamoto, at one o'clock in the morning—with an indefatigable Lafcadio kneeling next to his wife throughout her labor, importuning: "Come into this world with good eyes!"—Setsu Koizumi gave birth to Leopold Kazuo Koizumi, a child with perfect eyes. The next day the amazed father proclaimed the news in letters to several of his American friends:

⟦ Last night my child was born,—a very strong boy, with large black eyes; he looks more like a Japanese, however, than a foreign boy. He has my nose, but his mother's features in some other respects, curiously blended with mine. There is no fault with him; and the physicians say, from the form of his little bones, that he promises to become very tall. A cross between European and Japanese is nearly always an improvement when both parents are in good condition; and happily the old military caste to which my wife belongs is a strong one. . . .

"If ever you [Ellwood Hendrick] become a father, I think the strangest and strongest sensation of your life will be hearing for the first time the thin cry of your own child. For a moment you have the strange feeling of being double; but there is something more, quite impossible to analyze—perhaps the echo in a man's heart of all the sensations felt by all the fathers and mothers of his race at a similar instant in the past. It is a very tender, but also a very ghostly feeling. . . .

No man can possibly know what life means, what the world means, what anything means, until he has a child and loves it. And then the whole universe changes—and nothing will ever again seem exactly as it seemed before. ⟧

Ironically, the child's first name, like his father's before him, was dropped; and Kazuo (a name meaning "the first of the excellent," "the best of the peerless") was never referred to or called by his "Christian" name ever again. (Lafcadio playfully called him Kaji-wo or Kajio.)

The Koizumi clan was now residing in Kumamoto (about a thousand miles south of Yokohama), where at the end of 1891, Lafcadio had been invited to teach Latin and English at a large government college for a salary of $200 a month. Lafcadio had dreaded the idea of leaving Matsue, but Setsu preferred living in a larger city, and the promise of warmer weather on this southernmost Japanese island of Kyushu, facing Formosa and the Chinese coast, was an advantage, as was the larger salary for a growing family.

Lafcadio, however, was immediately depressed by this "straggling, dull, unsightly," half-Europeanized garrison town brimming with soldiers, by the antiseptic red-bricked buildings of the Government College (built after the 1877 Saigo Rebellion had destroyed most of the old city), and by the promise of an oncoming winter almost as chilling as the one in Matsue. Then he knew *he* had opened Urashima's box and had permanently lost his enchanted abode in the palace of the Dragon King, that he would now have to grow old and suffer the "sorrows of the nineteenth century." He said: "I wish I could fly out of Meiji forever, back against the stream of Time, into Tempō [the end of the Tokugawa Period], or into the age of the Mikado Yūriaku,—fourteen hundred years ago. The life of the old fans, the old *byōbu* [screens], the tiny villages—that is the *real* Japan I love. Somehow or other, Kumamoto doesn't seem to me Japan at all. I hate it."

Lafcadio taught twenty-seven hours a week to mostly unprepared and unresponsive students, and made only one friend among his impersonal colleagues, who preferred beer and cigars to saké and pipes ("Their brains seem to have shrivelled up like kernels in roasted nuts," Lafcadio said of them). His only moments of "redemption" occurred during his one-hour lunch breaks when he climbed up a small hill behind the college grounds to a moldering old village cemetery, sat down on the pedestal of a stone Buddha, ate his meal of rice, fried fish, pickles, and beans, and contemplated eternal landscapes:

❡ On the ridge of the hill behind the Government College,—above a succession of tiny farm fields ascending the slope by terraces,—there is an ancient village cemetery. It is no longer used: the people of Kurogamimura now bury their dead in a more secluded spot; and I think their fields are beginning already to encroach upon the limits of the old graveyard.

Having an idle hour to pass between two classes, I resolve to pay the ridge a visit. Harmless thin black snakes wiggle across the way as I climb; and immense grasshoppers, exactly the color of parched leaves, whirr away from my shadow. The little field path vanishes altogether under coarse grass before reaching the broken steps at the cemetery gate; and in the cemetery itself there is no path at all—only weeds and stones. But there is a fine view from the ridge: the vast green Plain of Higo, and beyond it bright blue hills in a half-ring against the horizon light, and even beyond them the cone of Aso smoking forever.

Below me, as in a bird's-eye view, appears the college, like a miniature modern town, with its long ranges of many-windowed buildings, all of the year 1887. They represent the purely utilitarian architecture of the nineteenth century: they might be situated equally well in Kent or in Auckland or in New Hampshire without appearing in the least out of tone with the age. But the terraced fields above and the figures toiling in them might be of the fifth century. The language cut upon the *haka* [gravestone] whereon I lean is transliterated Sanskrit. And there is a Buddha beside me, sitting upon his lotus of stone just as he sat in the days of Kato Kiyomasa. His meditative gaze slants down between his half-closed eyelids upon the Government College and its tumultuous life; and he smiles the smile of one who has received an injury not to be resented. This is not the expression wrought by the sculptor: moss and scurf have distorted it. I also observe that his hands are broken. I am sorry, and try to scrape the moss away from the little symbolic protuberance on his forehead, remembering the ancient text of the "Lotus of the Good Law:"—

There issued a ray of light from the circle of hair between the brows of the Lord. It extended over eighteen hundred thousand Buddha fields, so that all those Buddha fields appeared wholly illuminated by its radiance, down to the great hell Aviki, and up to the limit of existence. And all the beings in each of the Six States of existence became visible,—all without exception. Even the Lord Buddhas in those Buddha fields who had reached final Nirvana, all became visible."

*

The sun is high behind me; the landscape before me as in an old Japanese picture-book. In old Japanese color-prints there are, as a rule, no shadows. And the Plain of Higo, all shadowless, broadens greenly to the horizon, where the blue spectres of the peaks seem to float in the enormous glow. But the vast level presents no uniform hue: it is banded and seamed by all tones of green, intercrossed as if laid on by long strokes of a brush. In this again the vision resembles some scene from a Japanese picture-book.

Open such a book for the first time, and you receive a peculiarly startling impression, a sensation of surprise, which causes you to think: "How strangely, how curiously, these people feel and see Nature!" The wonder of it grows upon you, and you ask: "Can it be possible their senses are so utterly different from ours?" Yes, it is quite possible; but look a little more. You do so, and there defines a third and ultimate idea, confirming the previous two. You feel the picture is more true to Nature than any Western painting of the same scene would be,—that it produces sensations of Nature no Western picture could give. And indeed there are contained within it whole ranges of discoveries for you to make. Before making them, however, you will ask yourself another riddle, somewhat thus: "All this is magically vivid; the inexplicable color is Nature's own. *But why does the thing seem so ghostly?*"

Well, chiefly because of the absence of shadows. What prevents you from missing them at once is the astounding skill in the recognition and use of color-values. The scene, however, is not depicted as if illumined from one side, but as if throughout suffused with light. Now there are really moments when landscapes do wear this aspect; but our artists rarely study them.

Be it nevertheless observed that the old Japanese loved shadows made by the moon, and painted the same, because these were weird and did not interfere with color. But they had no admiration for shadows that blacken and break the charm of the world under the sun. When their noon-day landscapes are flecked by shadows at all, 'tis by very thin ones only,—mere deepenings of tone, like those fugitive half-glooms which run before a summer cloud. And the inner as well as the outer world was luminous for them. Psychologically also they saw life without shadows.

Then the West burst into their Buddhist peace, and saw their art, and bought it up till an Imperial law was issued to preserve the best of what was left. And when there was nothing more to be bought, and it seemed possible that fresh creation might reduce the market price of what had been bought already, then the West said: "Oh, come now! you mustn't go on drawing and seeing things that way, you know! It isn't Art! You must really learn to see shadows, you know,—and pay me to teach you."

So Japan paid to learn how to see shadows in Nature, in life, and in thought. And the West taught her that the sole business of the divine sun was the making of the cheaper kind of shadows. And the West taught her that the higher-priced shadows were the sole product of Western civilization, and bade her admire and adopt. Then Japan wondered at the shadows of machinery and chimneys and telegraph-poles; and at the shadows of mines and of factories, and the shadows in the hearts of those who worked there; and at the shadows of houses twenty stories high, and of hunger begging under them; and shadows of enormous charities that multiplied poverty; and shadows of social reforms that multiplied vice; and shadows of shams and hypocrisies and swallow-tail coats; and the shadow of a foreign God, said to have created mankind for the pur- pose of an *auto-da-fé*. Whereat Japan became rather serious, and refused to study any more silhouettes. Fortunately for the world, she returned to her first matchless art; and, fortunately for herself, returned to her own beautiful faith. But some of the shadows still clung to her life; and she cannot possibly get rid of them. Never again can the world seem to her quite so beautiful as it did before.   ("THE STONE BUDDHA")]

Lafcadio's home, two miles from the college, was spacious but characterless, and his garden was a stunted version of his *yashiki* paradise in Matsue. He soon, however, had glass *shoji* installed in his study (replacing the usual paper shutters), along with an unsightly but efficient American Franklin stove (replacing the *hibachi*), allowing him to write in comfort. "My folks say I have never said a cross word since I had a warm room. Heat thus appears as a moral force. Just think how holy I should be could I live forever under the equator."

He kept in touch with three of his best students from Matsue (Otani, Adzukizawa, and Tanabe), and they were soon working as his paid informants, reporting on rural folk customs and Shintō practices—though Lafcadio insisted that they "never try to translate a Japanese idiom by an English idiom. That would be no use to me. Simply translate the words *exactly*,—however funny it seems."

Lafcadio was quick to reject almost all the "educated modernized" Japanese who knocked on his door, considering them "a soft reflection of Latin types, without the Latin force and brilliancy and passion— somewhat as in dreams the memory of people we have known become smilingly aerial and imponderable." On the other hand, he had the pleasure of occasional visits to his home by the kind of common working people who always fascinated him:

❦ *July 25.* Three extraordinary visits have been made to my house this week.

The first was that of the professional well-cleaners. For once every year all wells must be emptied and cleansed, lest the God of Wells, Suijin-Sama, be wroth. On this occasion I learned some things relating to Japanese wells and the tutelar deity of them, who has two names, being also called Mizuha-nome-no-mikoto.

Suijin-Sama protects all wells, keeping their water sweet and cool, provided that house-owners observe his laws of cleanliness, which are rigid. To those who break them sickness comes, and death. Rarely the god manifests himself, taking the form of a serpent. I have never seen any temple dedicated to him. But once each month a Shintō priest visits the homes of pious families having wells, and he repeats certain ancient prayers to the Well-God, and plants *nobori,* little paper flags, which are symbols, at the edge of the well. After the well has been cleaned, also, this is done. Then the first bucket of the new water must be drawn up by a man; for if a woman first draw water, the well will always thereafter remain muddy.

The god has little servants to help him in his work. These are the small fishes the Japanese call *funa* [a kind of small silver carp]. One or two *funa* are kept in every well, to clear the water of larvæ. When a well is cleaned, great care is taken of the little fish. It was on the occasion of the coming of the well-cleaners that I first learned of the existence of a pair of *funa* in my own well. They were placed in a tub of cool water while the well was refilling, and thereafter were replunged into their solitude.

The water of my well is clear and ice-cold. But now I can never drink it without a thought of those two small white lives circling always in darkness, and startled through untold years by the descent of plashing buckets.

The second curious visit was that of the district firemen, in full costume, with their hand-engines. According to ancient custom, they make a round of all their district once a year during the dry spell, and throw water over the hot roofs, and receive some small perquisite from each wealthy householder. There is a belief that when it has not rained for a long time roofs may be ignited by the mere heat of the sun. The firemen played with their hose upon my roofs, trees, and garden, producing considerable refreshment; and in return I bestowed on them wherewith to buy saké.

The third visit was that of a deputation of children asking for some help to celebrate fittingly the festival of Jizō, who has a shrine on the other side of the street, exactly opposite my house. I was very glad to contribute to their fund, for I love the gentle god, and I knew the festival would be delightful. Early next morning, I saw that the shrine had already been decked with flowers and votive lanterns. A new bib had been put about Jizō's neck, and a Buddhist repast set before him. Later on, carpenters constructed a dancing-platform in the temple court for the children to dance upon; and before sundown the toy-sellers had erected and stocked a small street of booths inside the precincts. After dark I went out into a great glory of lantern fires to see the children dance; and I found, perched before my gate, an enormous dragonfly more than three feet long. It was a token of the children's gratitude for the little help I had given them,—a *kazari*, a decoration. I was startled for the moment by the realism of the thing; but upon close examination I discovered that the body was a pine branch wrapped with colored paper, the four wings were four fire-shovels, and the gleaming head was a little teapot. The whole was lighted by a candle so placed as to make extraordinary shadows, which formed part of the design. It was a wonderful instance of art sense working without a speck of artistic material, yet it was all the labor of a poor little child only eight years old!

*

July 30. The next house to mine, on the south side,—a low, dingy structure,—is that of a dyer. You can always tell where a Japanese dyer is by the long pieces of silk or cotton stretched between bamboo poles before his door to dry in the sun,—broad bands of rich azure, of purple, of rose, pale blue, pearl gray. Yesterday my neighbor coaxed me to pay the family a visit; and after having been led through the front part of their little dwelling, I was surprised to find myself looking from a rear veranda at a garden worthy of some old Kyōto palace. There was a dainty landscape in miniature, and a pond of clear water peopled by goldfish having wonderfully compound tails.

When I had enjoyed this spectacle awhile, the dyer led me to a small room fitted up as a Buddhist chapel. Though everything had had to be made on a reduced scale, I did not remember to have seen a more artistic display in any temple. He told me it had cost him about fifteen hundred yen. I did not understand how even that sum could have sufficed. There were three elaborately carven altars,—a triple blaze of gold lacquer-work; a number of charming Buddhist images; many exquisite vessels; an ebony reading-desk; a *mokugyō* [dolphin's-head-shaped, percussive wooden block], two fine bells,—in short, all the paraphernalia of a temple in miniature. My host had studied at a Buddhist temple in his youth, and knew the sutras, of which he had all that are used by the Jōdo sect. He told me that he could celebrate any of the ordinary services. Daily, at a fixed hour, the whole family assembled in the chapel for prayers; and he generally read the Kyō [sutra] for them. But on extraordinary occasions a Buddhist priest from the neighboring temple would come to officiate.

He told me a queer story about robbers. Dyers are peculiarly liable to be visited by robbers; partly by reason of the value of the silks intrusted to them, and also because the business is known to be lucrative. One evening the family were robbed. The master was out of the city; his old mother, his wife, and a female servant were the only persons in the house at the time. Three men, having their faces masked and carrying long swords, entered the door. One asked the servant whether any of the apprentices were still in the building; and she, hoping to frighten the invaders away, answered that the young men were still at work. But the robbers were not disturbed by this assurance. One posted himself at the entrance, the other two strode into the sleeping-apartment. The women started up in alarm, and the wife asked, "Why do you wish to kill us?" He who seemed to be the leader answered, "We do not wish to kill you; we want money only. But if we do not get it, then it will be this"—striking his sword into the matting. The old mother said, "Be so kind as not to frighten my daughter-in-law, and I will give you whatever money there is in the house. But you ought to know there cannot be much, as my son has gone to Kyōto." She handed them the money-drawer and her own purse. There were just twenty-seven yen and eighty-four sen. The head robber counted it, and said, quite gently, "We do not want to frighten you. We know you are a very devout believer in Buddhism, and we think you would not tell a lie. Is this all?" "Yes, it is all," she answered. "I am, as you say, a believer in the teaching of the Buddha, and if you come to rob me now, I believe it is only because I myself, in some former life, once robbed you. This is my punishment for that fault, and so, instead of wishing to deceive you, I feel grateful at this opportunity to atone for the wrong which I did to you in my previous state of existence." The robber laughed, and said, "You are a good old woman, and we believe you. If you were poor, we would not rob you at all. Now we only want a couple of *kimono* and this,"—laying his hand on a very fine silk overdress. The old woman replied, "All my son's *kimono* I can give you, but I beg you will not take that, for it does not belong to my son, and was confided to us only for dyeing. What is ours I can give, but I cannot give what belongs to another." "That is quite right," approved the robber, "and we shall not take it."

After receiving a few robes, the robbers said good-night, very politely, but ordered the women not to look after them. The old servant was still near the door. As the chief robber passed her, he said, "You told us a lie,—so take that!"—and struck her senseless. None of the robbers were ever caught.

*

September 13. A letter from Matsue, Izumo, tells me that the old man who used to supply me with pipestems is dead. (A Japanese pipe, you must know, consists of three pieces, usually,—a metal bowl large enough to hold a pea, a metal mouthpiece, and a bamboo stem which is renewed at regular intervals.) He used to stain his pipestems very prettily: some looked like porcupine quills, and some like cylinders of snakeskin. He lived in a queer narrow little street at the verge of the city. I know the street because in it there is a famous statue of Jizō called Shiroko-Jizō,—"White-Child-Jizō,"—which I once went to see. They whiten its face, like the face of a dancing-girl, for some reason which I have never been able to find out.

The old man had a daughter, O-Masu, about whom a story is told. O-Masu is still alive. She has been a happy wife for many years; but she is dumb. Long ago, an angry mob sacked and destroyed the dwelling and the storehouses of a rice speculator in the city. His money, including a quantity of gold coin (*koban*), was scattered through the street. The rioters—rude, honest peasants—did not want it: they wished to destroy, not to steal. But O-Masu's father, the same evening, picked up a *koban* from the mud, and took it home. Later on a neighbor denounced him, and secured his arrest. The judge before whom he was summoned tried to obtain certain evidence by cross-questioning O-Masu, then a shy girl of fifteen. She felt that if she continued to answer she would be made, in spite of herself, to give testimony unfavorable to her father; that she was in the presence of a trained inquisitor, capable, without effort, of forcing her to acknowledge everything she knew. She ceased to speak, and a stream of blood gushed from her mouth. She had silenced herself forever by simply biting off her tongue. Her father was acquitted. A merchant who admired the act demanded her in marriage, and supported her father in his old age.

*

October 10. There is said to be one day—only one—in the life of a child during which it can remember and speak of its former birth.

On the very day that it becomes exactly two years old, the child is taken by its mother into the most quiet part of the house, and is placed in a *mi*, or rice-winnowing basket. The child sits down in the *mi*. Then the mother says, calling the child by name, *"Omae no zensé wa, nande attakane?—iute, gōran"* ("Thy previous life as for,—what was it? Honorably look [or, *please look*] and tell"). Then the child always answers in one word. For some mysterious reason, no more lengthy reply is ever given. Often the answer is so enigmatic that some priest or fortune-teller must be asked to interpret it. For instance, yesterday, the little son of a coppersmith living near us answered only "Umé" to the magical question. Now *umé* might mean a plum-flower, a plum, or a girl's name,—"Flower-of-the-Plum." Could it mean that the boy remembered having been a girl? Or that he had been a plum-tree? "Souls of men do not enter plum-trees," said a neighbor. A fortune-teller this morning declared, on being questioned about the riddle, that the boy had probably been a scholar, poet, or statesman, because the plum-tree is the symbol of Tenjin, patron of scholars, statesmen, and men of letters.

*

November 17. The scientific problem of the origin of the Japanese has never yet been solved. But sometimes it seems to me that those who argue in favor of a partly Malay origin have some psychological evidence in their favor. Under the submissive sweetness of the gentlest Japanese woman—a sweetness of which the Occidental can scarcely form any idea— there exist possibilities of hardness absolutely inconceivable without ocular evidence. A thousand times she can forgive, can sacrifice herself in a thousand ways unutterably touching; but let one particular soul-nerve be stung, and fire shall forgive sooner than she. Then there may suddenly appear in that frail-seeming woman an incredible courage, an appalling, measured, tireless purpose of honest vengeance. Under all the amazing self-control and patience of the man there exists an adamantine something very dangerous to reach. Touch it wantonly, and there can be no pardon. But resentment is seldom likely to be excited by mere hazard. Motives are keenly judged. An error can be forgiven; deliberate malice never.

In the house of any rich family the guest is likely to be shown some of the heirlooms. Among these are almost sure to be certain articles belonging to those elaborate tea ceremonies peculiar to Japan. A pretty little box, perhaps, will be set before you. Opening it, you see only a beautiful silk bag, closed with a silk running-cord decked with tiny tassels. Very soft and choice the silk is, and elaborately figured. What marvel can be hidden under such a covering? You open the bag, and see within another bag, of a different quality of silk, but very fine. Open that, and lo! a third, which contains a fourth, which contains a fifth, which contains a sixth, which contains a seventh bag, which contains the strangest, roughest, hardest vessel of Chinese clay that you ever beheld. Yet it is not only curious but precious: it may be more than a thousand years old.

Even thus have centuries of the highest social culture wrapped the Japanese character about with many priceless soft coverings of courtesy, of delicacy, of patience, of sweetness, of moral sentiment. But underneath these charming multiple coverings there remains the primitive clay, hard as iron;—kneaded perhaps with all the mettle of the Mongol,—all the dangerous suppleness of the Malay.

*

December 28. Beyond the high fence inclosing my garden in the rear rise the thatched roofs of some very small houses occupied by families of the poorest class. From one of these little dwellings there continually issues a sound of groaning,—the deep groaning of a man in pain. I have heard it for more than a week, both night and day, but latterly the sounds have been growing longer and louder, as if every breath were an agony. "Somebody there is very sick," says Manyemon, my old interpreter, with an expression of extreme sympathy.

The sounds have begun to make me nervous. I reply, rather brutally, "I think it would be better for all concerned if that somebody were dead." . . .

It is a positive relief, later in the morning, to hear the moaning drowned by the beating of a little Buddhist drum in the sick man's room, and the chanting of the *Namu myō ho renge kyō* by a multitude of voices. Evidently there is a gathering of priests and relatives in the house. "Somebody is going to die," Manyemon says. And he also repeats the holy words of praise to the Lotus of the Good Law.

The chanting and the tapping of the drum continue for several hours. As they cease, the groaning is heard again. Every breath a groan! Toward evening it grows worse—horrible. Then it suddenly stops. There is a dead silence of minutes. And then we hear a passionate burst of weeping,—the weeping of a woman,—and voices calling a name. "Ah! somebody is dead!" Manyemon says.

We hold council. Manyemon has found out that the people are miserably poor; and I, because my conscience smites me, propose to send them the amount of the funeral expenses, a very small sum. Manyemon thinks I wish to do this out of pure benevolence, and says pretty things. We send the servant with a kind message, and instructions to learn if possible the history of the dead man. I cannot help suspecting some sort of tragedy; and a Japanese tragedy is generally interesting.

*

December 29. As I had surmised, the story of the dead man was worth learning. The family consisted of four,—the father and mother, both very old and feeble, and two sons. It was the eldest son, a man of thirty-four, who had died. He had been sick for seven years. The younger brother, a *kurumaya*, had been the sole support of the whole family. He had no vehicle of his own, but hired one, paying five sen a day for the use of it. Though strong and a swift runner, he could earn little: there is in these days too much competition for the business to be profitable. It taxed all his powers to support his parents and his ailing brother; nor could he have done it without unfailing self-denial. He never indulged himself even to the extent of a cup of saké; he remained unmarried; he lived only for his filial and fraternal duty.

This was the story of the dead brother: When about twenty years of age, and following the occupation of a fish-seller, he had fallen in love with a pretty servant at an inn. The girl returned his affection. They pledged themselves to each other. But difficulties arose in the way of their marriage. The girl was pretty enough to have attracted the attention of a man of some means, who demanded her hand in the customary way. She disliked him; but the conditions he was able to offer decided her parents in his favor. Despairing of union, the two lovers resolved to perform jōshi. Somewhere or other they met at night, renewed their pledge in wine, and bade farewell to the world. The young man then killed his sweetheart with one blow of a sword, and immediately afterward cut his own throat with the same weapon. But people rushed into the room before he had expired, took away the sword, sent for the police, and summoned a military surgeon from the garrison. The would-be suicide was removed to the hospital, skillfully nursed back to health, and after some months of convalescence was put on trial for murder.

What sentence was passed I could not fully learn. In those days, Japanese judges used a good deal of personal discretion when dealing with emotional crime; and their exercise of pity had not yet been restricted by codes framed upon Western models. Perhaps in this case they thought that to have survived a jōshi was in itself severe punishment. Public opinion is less merciful, in such instances, than law. After a term of imprisonment the miserable man was allowed to return to his family, but was placed under perpetual police surveillance. The people shrank from him. He made the mistake of living on. Only his parents and brother remained to him. And soon he became a victim of unspeakable physical suffering; yet he clung to life.

The old wound in his throat, although treated at the time as skillfully as circumstances permitted, began to cause terrible pain. After its apparent healing, some slow cancerous growth commenced to spread from it, reaching into the breathing-passages above and below where the sword-blade had passed. The surgeon's knife, the torture of the cautery, could only delay the end. But the man lingered through seven years of continually increasing agony. There are dark beliefs about the results of betraying the dead,—of breaking the mutual promise to travel together to the *Meido* [the underworld, the realm of the Shades]. Men said that the hand of the murdered girl always reopened the wound,—undid by night all that the surgeon could accomplish by day. For at night the pain invariably increased, becoming most terrible at the precise hour of the attempted *shinjū!*

Meanwhile, through abstemiousness and extraordinary self-denial, the family found means to pay for medicines, for attendance, and for more nourishing food than they themselves ever indulged in. They prolonged by all possible means the life that was their shame, their poverty, their burden. And now that death has taken away that burden, they weep!

Perhaps all of us learn to love that which we train ourselves to make sacrifices for, whatever pain it may cause. Indeed, the question might be asked whether we do not love most that which causes us most pain.

("BITS OF LIFE AND DEATH")

His general disappointment with Kumamoto notwithstanding, Lafcadio knew that his sole reason for being there was to earn enough money to allow him the freedom to write, as well as to support his sizable family. Even before the birth of Kazuo, the paterfamilias noted to Ellwood Hendrick: "I have nine lives depending on my work—wife, wife's mother, wife's father, wife's adopted mother, wife's father's father, and then servants, and a Buddhist student. . . . You can't let a little world grow up around you, to depend on you, and then break it all up—not if you are a respectable person. And I indulge in the luxury of 'filial piety'—a virtue of which the good and evil results are only known to us Orientals."

Lafcadio was particularly fond of Setsu's father's father, whom he called "Grandfather"—the eccentric, hard-of-hearing eighty-four-year-old ex-tutor to the family of the *daimyō* of Matsue, who, in his mind, imagined he was still living in pre-Meiji times. His "grandson" admired his old-fashioned values and manners, and loved to hear him recount the old stories, legends, and history of a world that had disappeared in just one generation.

In Kumamoto, Grandfather wandered around the streets in his wooden clogs like an *enfant sauvage*, determining his whereabouts by the path of the sun or the light and shadows on the peaks of nearby Mount Aso. Occasionally miscalculating, he would realize he was lost in a strange, unfamiliar city with peculiar inhabitants. Then he would enter a shop, sit down on the matted floor, light his pipe, and wait for his grandson or a servant to come bring him back home. Like the other "old men" of Japan, Grandfather, according to Lafcadio, was "divine. . . . I do not know any other word to express what they are." And he loved, and tried to live, the kind of lives they had once led.

To Chamberlain he warily entrusted a detailed description of a typical day in the domestic routine of the Koizumi clan—a description, he feared, that if published, would shock his Christian, Occidental friends, some of whom thought of the Japanese as the Cincinnati whites thought of the inhabitants of Bucktown:

October 11, 1893.

Dear Chamberlain,—I am thinking it is time to write you—though there is no news. Suppose I write you of one day of my life as a sample. I don't see why I shouldn't—though I would not write it to anybody else on either side of the world.

Morning, 6 A.M.—The little alarm clock rings. Wife rises and wakes me,—with the salutation *de rigueur* of old Samurai days. I get myself into a squatting posture, draw the never-extinguished *hibachi* to the side of the *futons,* and begin to smoke. The servants enter, prostrate themselves, and say good morning to the *danna-sama* [master of the house], and proceed to open the *tō* [sliding wooden shutter]. Meanwhile in the other chambers the little oil lamps have been lighted before the tablets of the ancestors, and the Buddhist (not the Shintō) deities—and prayers are being said, and offerings to the ancestors made. (Spirits are not supposed to eat *the food* offered them,—only to absorb some of its living essence. Therefore the offerings are very small.) Already the old men are in the garden, saluting the rising sun, and clapping their hands, and murmuring the Izumo prayers. I stop smoking, and make my toilet on the *Engawa* [covered outdoor veranda facing the garden].

7 A.M.—Breakfast. Very light—eggs and toast. Lemonade with a spoonful of whiskey in it; and black coffee. Wife serves; and I always make her eat a little with me. But she eats sparingly,—as she must afterward put in an appearance at the regular family breakfast. Then *kurumaya* comes. I begin to put on my *yofuku* [Western clothes]. I did not at first like the Japanese custom,—that the wife should give each piece of clothing in regular order, see to the pockets, etc.;—I thought it encouraged laziness

in a man. But when I tried to oppose it, I found I was giving offence and spoiling pleasure. So I submit to the ancient rule.

7.30 A.M.—All gather at the door to say *Sayonara;* but the servants stand outside,—according to the new custom requiring the servants to stand when the master is in *yofuku.* I light a cigar,—kiss a hand extended to me (this is the only imported custom), and pass to the school.

(Blank of 4 to 5 hours.)

Returning, at the call of the *kurumaya,*—all come to the door again as before, to greet me with the O-Kaeri; and I have to submit to aid in undressing, and in putting on the *kimono, obi,* etc. The kneeling-cushion and *hibachi* are ready. There is a letter from Chamberlain San, or Mason San. Dinner.

The rest eat only when I am finished. . . . The principle is that the family supporter's wants are first to be considered,—though in other matters he does not rank first. For instance, the place of honor when sitting together is always by age and parentage. I then take the fourth place, and wife the fifth. And the old man is always then served the first.

During the repast there is a sort of understanding that the rest of the family and the servants are not to be disturbed without necessity. There is no rule; but the custom I respect. So I never go into that part of the house unnecessarily till they are finished. There is also some etiquette about favorite places,—which is strictly observed.

3 P.M. 4.—If very hot, everybody sleeps,—the servants sleeping by turns. If cool and pleasant, all work. The women make clothes. The men do all kinds of little things in the garden and elsewhere. Children come to play. The *Asahi Shimbun* [Asahi newspaper] arrives.

6 P.M.—Bath hour.

6.30—7.30.—Supper.

8 P.M.—Everybody squats round the *hako-hibachi* to hear the *Asahi Shimbun* read, or to tell stories. Sometimes the paper does not come,— then curious games are played, in which the girls join. The mother sews at intervals. One game is very original. A piece of string is tied in a large loop, and a number of little loops and ends are made with short pieces of string. Then the large loop is spread on a velvet *zabaton* [square cushion], so as to form the outline of the face of Otafuku [caricature of moon-faced female head]. Blindfolded, then, the players must put the other loose ends and bits of string inside the circle, so as to make the rest of the face. But this is hard to do, and every mistake produces extraordinary comicalities. But if the night is very fine, we sometimes go out—always taking

turns so that the girls get their share of the outing. Sometimes the theatre is the attraction. Sometimes there are guests. I think the greatest joy, though, is the discovery and purchase of odd or pretty things in some lamp-lit shop at night. It is brought home in great triumph, and all sit round it in a circle to admire. My own evening, however, is generally passed in writing. If guests come for me, the rest of the family remains invisible till they go away,—except wife,—that is, if the guests are important. Then she sees to their comfort. Ordinary guests are served only by the girls.

As evening wanes, the turn of the *Kami-sama* [spirits of the dead, the "upper ones" in the Shintō tradition] comes. During the day, they receive their usual offerings; but it is at night the special prayers are made. The little lamps are lighted; and each of the family in turn, except myself, say the prayers and pay reverence. These prayers are always said standing, but those to the *hotoke* [spirits of the dead in the Buddhist tradition] are said kneeling. Some of the prayers are said for me. I was never asked to pray but once—when there was grief in the house; and then I prayed to the Gods, repeating the Japanese words one by one as they were told to me. The little lamps of the *Kami* are left to burn themselves out.

All wait for me to give the signal of bed-time,—unless I should become so absorbed in writing as to forget the hour. Then I am asked if I am not working too hard. The girls spread the futons in the various rooms; and the *hibachi* are replenished, so that we—i.e., I and the men only—may smoke during the night if we wish. Then the girls prostrate themselves with an *o-yasumi!* [good night!] and all becomes quiet.

Sometimes I read till I fall asleep. Sometimes I keep on writing—with a pencil in bed—but always, according to ancient custom, the little wife asks *pardon for being the first to go to sleep.* I once tried to stop the habit—thinking it too humble. But after all it is pretty,—and is so set into the soul that it could not be stopped. And this is an ordinary day in outline. Then we sleep.

Ever since his marriage, Lafcadio had lived the life of a thoroughly traditional Japanese husband. So it was not surprising that in 1895 he finally decided to *become* one by giving up his British citizenship (he had, surprisingly, never thought of becoming an American, even though many of his critics, then as well as now, assumed him to be an "American expatriate" writer), knowing he would suffer the loss of his foreign status that accorded him an appreciably higher wage than what he might receive as a "Japanese" professor. Conversely, he knew that if Setsu became an English citizen—and Lafcadio considered that possibility—she would lose all native property rights and be forced to live among the Europeanized Japanese in Open Port cities.

The solution seemed clear as he wrote to Chamberlain: "The Japanese are still the best people in the world to live among;—therefore why wish ever to live elsewhere? No one will ever, or could ever, love me any more than those about me now love me;—and that is the most precious consideration in life aside from the mere capacity to live."

To become a Japanese citizen, Lafcadio had to be adopted by a Japanese family. He was therefore obliged to take "Koizumi" (meaning "little spring" or "little source") as his family name. For his own name he chose "Yakumo" (meaning "eight clouds"), which was the first word in the "most ancient poem extant in the Japanese language," as well as an alternative name for Izumo, "my beloved province, the Place of the Issuing of Clouds." After bureaucratic delays, the government finally informed Lafcadio in February 1896 that he was now the Japanese citizen Koizumi Yakumo (or Y. Koizumi, as he often signed his letters).

Throughout his life, Lafcadio had flouted societal and religious conventions; yet he had now become a citizen of one of the most socially adhesive, coercive, and unindividualistic countries in the world, whose subjects conformed to "the despotism of collective opinion." (As a Japanese proverb says: "The nail that sticks out shall be hammered down.") Though citizens in the New Japan were made directly accountable to the law, and the household relieved from its ancient responsibility for the acts of its members, in practice, the family, with its patriarchal organization and ancestor-cult, remained the basic social unit: young people were not at liberty to marry at will or free to consider themselves unencumbered by family authority, nor would children or wives dream of attempting to claim recently granted legal rights in opposition to family and public opinion.

In New Orleans, Lafcadio told Mrs. Courtney that he considered the morality of the ant "far higher than that of the human," because ants worked for the common good of their community and were willing to sacrifice their lives to the general welfare. Lafcadio's Japanese experience confirmed for him what he had always felt—that "properly . . . there is no such thing as an individual, but only a combination,—one balance of an infinite sum. The charm of a very superior man or woman is the ghostliest of all conceivable experiences." (The more "individual," the more ghostly; the more "ghostly," the more truly individual.)

To Lafcadio, the "pure aggressive selfishness" that went under the name of "personality and individuality" was "intensely repellent"; yet he understood that "the highly selfish and cunning, as well as the unselfish and frank qualities of man are necessary to the preservation of society and its development." And he recognized that inflexible subserviency to an enforced social consensus would lead to social, psychological, and moral stagnation, mediocrity, impersonal dependence, as well as to madness—a legendary case (almost half a century after Lafcadio's time) being that of the Japanese soldier Soichi Yokoi who, faithful to the military code that prohibited surrender, hid out for twenty-eight years after World War II on the island of Guam and, once discovered and returned to Japan, apologized for disgracing the Emperor.

The West saw and defined the East in its own terms and with its own values; the East rarely defined itself to the West, as it saw itself. Lafcadio was able to perceive both realms from a double perspective, and in his story of a samurai's son who is born into one world (a feudal town like pre-Meiji Matsue) and is to another bound (a Westernized Japan) he depicted the European spirit through the eye of Koizumi Yakumo, and the Japanese spirit through the eye of Lafcadio Hearn. Describing the samurai's son's conversion to, followed by his renunciation of, Christianity, Lafcadio writes of his young hero (obviously his alter ego) going off to see the West:

During those years he saw Western civilization as few Japanese ever saw it; for he wandered through Europe and America, living in many cities, and toiling in many capacities,—sometimes with his brain, oftener with his hands,—and so was able to study the highest and the lowest, the best and the worst of the life about him. But he saw with the eyes of the Far East; and the ways of his judgments were not as our ways. For even as the Occident regards the Far East, so does the Far East regard the Occident,—only with this difference: that what each most esteems in itself is least likely to be esteemed by the other. And both are partly right and partly wrong; and there never has been, and never can be, perfect mutual comprehension.

Larger than all anticipation the West appeared to him,—a world of giants; and that which depresses even the boldest Occidental who finds

himself, without means or friends, alone in a great city, must often have
depressed the Oriental exile: that vague uneasiness aroused by the sense
of being invisible to hurrying millions; by the ceaseless roar of traffic
drowning voices; by monstrosities of architecture without a soul; by the
dynamic display of wealth forcing mind and hand, as mere cheap machinery, to the uttermost limits of the possible. Perhaps he saw such cities
as Doré saw London: sullen majesty of arched glooms, and granite deeps
opening into granite deeps beyond range of vision, and mountains of
masonry with seas of labor in turmoil at their base, and monumental
spaces displaying the grimness of ordered power slow-gathering through
centuries. Of beauty there was nothing to make appeal to him between
those endless cliffs of stone which walled out the sunrise and the sunset,
the sky and the wind. All that which draws us to great cities repelled or
oppressed him; even luminous Paris soon filled him with weariness. It
was the first foreign city in which he made a long sojourn. French art, as
reflecting the æsthetic thought of the most gifted of European races, surprised him much, but charmed him not at all. What surprised him especially were its studies of the nude, in which he recognized only an
open confession of the one human weakness which, next to disloyalty or
cowardice, his stoical training had taught him to most despise. Modern
French literature gave him other reasons for astonishment. He could little
comprehend the amazing art of the story-teller; the worth of the workmanship in itself was not visible to him; and if he could have been made
to understand it as a European understands, he would have remained
none the less convinced that such application of genius to production
signified social depravity. And gradually, in the luxurious life of the capital
itself, he found proof for the belief suggested to him by the art and the
literature of the period. He visited the pleasure-resorts, the theatres, the
opera; he saw with the eyes of an ascetic and a soldier, and wondered
why the Western conception of the worth of life differed so little from
the Far-Eastern conception of folly and of effeminacy. He saw fashionable
balls, and exposures *de rigueur* intolerable to the Far-Eastern sense of
modesty,—artistically calculated to suggest what would cause a Japanese
woman to die of shame: and he wondered at criticisms he had heard
about the natural, modest, healthy half-nudity of Japanese toiling under a
summer sun. He saw cathedrals and churches in vast number, and near
to them the palaces of vice, and establishments enriched by the stealthy
sale of artistic obscenities. He listened to sermons by great preachers; and
he heard blasphemies against all faith and love by priest-haters. He saw

the circles of wealth, and the circles of poverty, and the abysses under-
lying both. The "restraining influence" of religion he did not see. That
world had no faith. It was a world of mockery and masquerade and
pleasure-seeking selfishness, ruled not by religion, but by police; a world
into which it were not good that a man should be born.

England, more sombre, more imposing, more formidable, furnished
him with other problems to consider. He studied her wealth, forever
growing, and the nightmares of squalor forever multiplying in the shadow
of it. He saw the vast ports gorged with the riches of a hundred lands,
mostly plunder; and knew the English still like their forefathers, a race of
prey; and thought of the fate of her millions if she should find herself for
even a single month unable to compel other races to feed them. He saw
the harlotry and drunkenness that make night hideous in the world's
greatest city; and he marveled at the conventional hypocrisy that pretends
not to see, and at the religion that utters thanks for existing conditions,
and at the ignorance that sends missionaries where they are not needed,
and at the enormous charities that help disease and vice to propagate
their kind. He saw also the declaration of a great Englishman [Alfred
Russel Wallace] who had traveled in many countries that one tenth of
the population of England were professional criminals or paupers. And
this in spite of the myriads of churches, and the incomparable multipli-
cation of laws! Certainly English civilization showed less than any other
the pretended power of that religion which he had been taught to believe
the inspiration of progress. English streets told him another story: there
were no such sights to be seen in the streets of Buddhist cities. No: this
civilization signified a perpetual wicked struggle between the simple and
the cunning, the feeble and the strong; force and craft combining to thrust
weakness into a yawning and visible hell. Never in Japan had there been
even the sick dream of such conditions. Yet the merely material and
intellectual results of those conditions he could not but confess to be
astonishing; and though he saw evil beyond all he could have imagined
possible, he also saw much good, among both poor and rich. The stupendous riddle of it all, the countless contradictions, were above his powers of interpretation.

He liked the English people better than the people of other countries
he had visited; and the manners of the English gentry impressed him as
not unlike those of the Japanese samurai. Behind their formal coldness
he could discern immense capacities of friendship and enduring kindness,—kindness he experienced more than once; the depth of emotional

power rarely wasted; and the high courage that had won the dominion of half a world. But ere he left England for America, to study a still vaster field of human achievement, mere differences of nationality had ceased to interest him: they were blurred out of visibility in his growing perception of Occidental civilization as one amazing whole, everywhere displaying—whether through imperial, monarchical, or democratic forms—the working of the like merciless necessities with the like astounding results, and everywhere based on ideas totally the reverse of Far-Eastern ideas. Such civilization he could estimate only as one having no single emotion in harmony with it,—as one finding nothing to love while dwelling in its midst, and nothing to regret in the hour of leaving it forever. It was as far away from his soul as the life of another planet under another sun. But he could understand its cost in terms of human pain, feel the menace of its weight, and divine the prodigious range of its intellectual power. And he hated it,—hated its tremendous and perfectly calculated mechanism; hated its utilitarian stability; hated its conventions, its greed, its blind cruelty, its huge hypocrisy, the foulness of its want and the insolence of its wealth. Morally, it was monstrous; conventionally, it was brutal. Depths of degradation unfathomable it had shown him, but no ideals equal to the ideals of his youth. It was all one great wolfish struggle;—and that so much real goodness as he had found in it could exist, seemed to him scarcely less than miraculous. The real sublimities of the Occident were intellectual only; far steep cold heights of pure knowledge, below whose perpetual snow-line emotional ideals die. Surely the old Japanese civilization of benevolence and duty was incomparably better in its comprehension of happiness, in its moral ambitions, its larger faith, its joyous courage, its simplicity and unselfishness, its sobriety and contentment. Western superiority was *not* ethical. It lay in forces of intellect developed through suffering incalculable, and used for the destruction of the weak by the strong.

And, nevertheless, that Western science whose logic he knew to be irrefutable assured him of the larger and larger expansion of the power of that civilization, as of an irresistible, inevitable, measureless inundation of world-pain. Japan would have to learn the new forms of action, to master the new forms of thought, or to perish utterly. There was no other alternative. And then the doubt of all doubts came to him, the question which all the sages have had to face: *Is the universe moral?* To that question Buddhism had given the deepest answer.

But whether moral or immoral the cosmic process, as measured by

infinitesimal human emotion, one conviction remained with him that no
logic could impair: the certainty that man should pursue the highest moral
ideal with all his power to the unknown end, even though the suns in
their courses should fight against him. The necessities of Japan would
oblige her to master foreign science, to adopt much from the material
civilization of her enemies; but the same necessities could not compel
her to cast bodily away her ideas of right and wrong, of duty and of
honor. Slowly a purpose shaped itself in his mind,—a purpose which was
to make him in after years a leader and a teacher: to strive with all his
strength for the conservation of all that was best in the ancient life, and
to fearlessly oppose further introduction of anything not essential to national self-preservation, or helpful to national self-development. Fail he
well might, and without shame; but he could hope at least to save something of worth from the drift of wreckage. The wastefulness of Western
life had impressed him more than its greed of pleasure and its capacity
for pain: in the clean poverty of his own land he saw strength; in her
unselfish thrift, the sole chance of competing with the Occident. Foreign
civilization had taught him to understand, as he could never otherwise
have understood, the worth and the beauty of his own; and he longed
for the hour of permission to return to the country of his birth.

*

It was through the transparent darkness of a cloudless April morning,
a little before sunrise, that he saw again the mountains of his native
land,—far lofty sharpening sierras, towering violet-black out of the circle
of an inky sea. Behind the steamer which was bearing him back from
exile the horizon was slowly filling with rosy flame. There were some
foreigners already on deck, eager to obtain the first and fairest view of
Fuji from the Pacific;—for the first sight of Fuji at dawn is not to be
forgotten in this life or the next. They watched the long procession of the
ranges, and looked over the jagged looming into the deep night, where
stars were faintly burning still,—and they could not see Fuji. "Ah!" laughed
an officer they questioned, "you are looking too low! higher up—much
higher!" Then they looked up, up, up into the heart of the sky, and saw
the mighty summit pinkening like a wondrous phantom lotos-bud in the
flush of the coming day: a spectacle that smote them dumb. Swiftly the
eternal snow yellowed into gold, then whitened as the sun reached out
beams to it over the curve of the world, over the shadowy ranges, over
the very stars, it seemed; for the giant base remained viewless. And the
night fled utterly; and soft blue light bathed all the hollow heaven; and

colors awoke from sleep;—and before the gazers there opened the luminous bay of Yokohama, with the sacred peak, its base ever invisible, hanging above all like a snowy ghost in the arch of the infinite day.

Still in the wanderer's ears the words rang, *"Ah! you are looking too low!—higher up—much higher!"*—making vague rhythm with an immense, irresistible emotion swelling at his heart. Then everything dimmed: he saw neither Fuji above, nor the nearing hills below, changing their vapory blue to green; nor the crowding of the ships in the bay; nor anything of the modern Japan; he saw the Old. The land-wind, delicately scented with odors of spring, rushed to him, touched his blood, and startled from long-closed cells of memory the shades of all that he had once abandoned and striven to forget. He saw the faces of his dead: he knew their voices over the graves of the years. Again he was a very little boy in his father's *yashiki*, wandering from luminous room to room, playing in sunned spaces where leaf-shadows trembled on the matting, or gazing into the soft green dreamy peace of the landscape garden. Once more he felt the light touch of his mother's hand guiding his little steps to the place of morning worship, before the household shrine, before the tablets of the ancestors; and the lips of the man murmured again, with sudden new-found meaning, the simple prayer of the child.　　　　　("A CONSERVATIVE")]

As early as his days in Matsue, Lafcadio felt the ideological pull of the samurai son's quest for the highest moral ideals, national self-respect, and the preservation of Japanese traditions. As a teacher, he gave his seventy-two boys, as a subject for composition, the question: "What would you most like in this world?" Nine of the compositions, Lafcadio reported to Chamberlain, "contained in substance this answer: 'To die for our Sacred Emperor.' That is Shintō. Isn't it grand and beautiful? and do you wonder that I love it after that?"

Lafcadio, who hated to kill a fly or an ant, wrote enthusiastically to Chamberlain from Kumamoto about that "old military spirit. Oh! What pains should be taken to preserve it!" And when the professor expressed some astonishment at these sentiments, Lafcadio replied that he had only meant to contrast "the insincere and artificial character of the teaching of the national feeling" in Kumamoto with "the sincere heart-rooted character of loyalty" in Izumo.

In the countryside, Lafcadio had often been mistaken for an *Ainoku* (half-Japanese), which pleased him greatly. With the increase of anti-Western feeling in the years just before the Russo-Japanese War (1904), however, he was frequently taunted in the city streets by little boys shouting *"gaijin!"* ("foreigner") behind his back. He understood the reasons for this anger; but he also knew, as his street hecklers did not, that he was in fact a Japanese citizen and, as such, a proud Japanese patriot. And as a writer, moreover, he penned polemical defenses of the Japanese military during the war with Russia: "a struggle for national existence," Lafcadio called it, "against an empire capable of threatening simultaneously the civilizations of the East and the West—a medieval power that, unless vigorously checked, seems destined to absorb Scandinavia and to dominate China." It was a contest between a Goliath from the West and a David from the East, and Lafcadio did not care for Occidental giants. "Japan is doing well without us," he wrote to his half-sister Minnie Atkinson; "and we have not been kind enough to her to win her love. We have persecuted her with hordes of fanatical missionaries, robbed her by unjust treaties, forced her to pay monstrous indemnities for trifling wrongs;—we have forced her to become strong, and she is going to do without us presently, the future is dark."

Meanwhile, in the Koizumi dining room after supper, fearless, heroic Lafcadio, in *yukata* and *obi,* commenced marching mock-seriously around the table with his family, maids, and visiting students, as, for an hour, they all shouted out, *"Teikoku banzai!"* and sang patriotic war songs (like *Kampira, funé, funé*) and the Japanese national anthem (*Kimigayo*).

After dismissing the troops, Lafcadio (whose own father, of course, had also been a military man) sat down exhausted, and announced to his wife, "You see, I have nothing Western about me." To which Setsu mischievously remarked, "You may have nothing Western about you, but look at your nose!" And her husband glanced up at her unhappily and said, "Oh, what can I do with my nose? Pity me because of my nose, for I, Koizumi Yakumo, truly love Japan more than any Japanese!"

CHAPTER 5

The
Path

IN OCTOBER 1894, Lafcadio, his wife, son, father- and mother-in-law, two female servants, and one of Setsu's male relatives set out, by train and steamer, from Kumamoto to the port city of Kobe on the island of Honshu. Depressed by the prospect of teaching for another year at the Fifth National College, Lafcadio had decided earlier in July to accept—in spite of his previous vow never again to work as a newspaper journalist— a full-time job as editorial writer for the English-language *Kobe Chronicle*.

His first book on his adopted country *(Glimpses of Unfamiliar Japan)* was about to be published in America and England (and shortly thereafter in France and Germany), and his essays were now appearing on a regular basis in the *Atlantic Monthly*—the same magazine, he reminded an aging Henry Watkin in a letter, that the callow youth Lafcadio had used to read aloud to the printer almost twenty-five years before:

⟦ Dear Old Dad: It delighted me to get that kindest double letter from yourself and sweet-hearted little daughter [Effie Watkin],—or rather delighted us. My wife speaks no English, but I translated it for her. She will send a letter in Japanese, which Miss Effie will not be able to read, but which she will keep as a curiosity perhaps. Our love to you both.

How often I have thought of you, and wondered about you, and wished I could pass with you more of the old-fashioned evenings, reading ancient volumes of the *Atlantic Monthly,*—so much better a magazine in those days than in these, when I am regularly advertised as one of its contributors.

I often wonder now at your infinite patience with the extraordinary, superhuman foolishness and wickedness of the worst pet you ever had in your life. When I think of all the naughty, mean, absurd, detestable things I did to vex you and to scandalize you, I can't for the life of me understand why you didn't want to kill me,—as a sacrifice to the Gods. What an idiot I was!—and how could you be so good?—and why do men change so? I think of my old self as of something which ought not to have been allowed to exist on the face of the earth,—and yet, in my present self, I sometimes feel ghostly reminders that the old self was very real indeed. Well, I wish I were near you to love you and make up for all old troubles.

I have a son. He is my torment and my pride. He is not like me or his mother. He has chestnut hair and blue eyes, and is enormously strong,— the old Gothic blood came out uppermost. I am, of course, very anxious about him. He *can't* become a Japanese,—his soul is all English, and his looks. I must educate him abroad. Head all above the ears,—promises to be intelligent. I shall never have another child. I feel too heavily the tremendous responsibility of the thing. But the boy is there,—intensely alive; and I must devote the rest of my existence to him. One thing I hope for is that he will never be capable of doing such foolish things as his daddy used to do. His name is Kaji-wo or Kajio. He does not cry, and has a tremendous capacity for growing. And he gives me the greatest variety of anxiety about his future.

When you hear that I have been able to save between thirty-five hundred and four thousand dollars, you will not think I have made no progress. But I have put all, or all that I could reasonably do, in my wife's name. The future looks very black. The reaction against foreign influence is strong; and I feel more and more every day that I shall have to leave Japan eventually, at least for some years. When I first met you I was— nineteen. I am now forty-four! Well, I suppose I must have lots more trouble before I go to Nirvana.

Effie says you do not see my writings. My book will be out by the time you get this letter,—that is, my first book on Japan. Effie can read bits of it to you. And I figure in the *Atlantic* every few months. Cheap fame;—the amazing fortune I once expected doesn't turn up at all. I have been obliged to learn the fact that I am not a genius, and that I must be content with the crumbs from the tables of Dives.

But this is all Egotism. I am guilty of it only because you asked for a small quantity. About yourself and all who love you my letter rather ought to be. . . . Do you remember the long walks over the Ohio, in the evening, among the fireflies and grasshoppers, to hear lectures upon spiritual things? If I were near you now, I could saturate you with Oriental spiritualism,—Buddhism,—everything you would like, but after a totally novel fashion. When one has lived alone five years in a Buddhist atmosphere, one naturally becomes penetrated by the thoughts that hover in it; my whole thinking, I must acknowledge, has been changed, in spite of my long studies of Spencer and of Schopenhauer. I do not mean that I am a Buddhist, but I mean that the inherited ancestral feelings about the universe—the Occidental ideas every Englishman has—have been totally transformed.

There is yet no fixity, however: the changes continue,—and I really do not know how I shall feel about the universe later on. What a pity that Western education and Western ideas only corrupt and spoil the Japanese,—and that the Japanese peasant is now superior to the Japanese noble! . . .

I wish we could be together somewhere for a pleasant evening chat, hearing in the intervals the office clock, like the sound of a long-legged walker. I wish we could talk over all the hopes and dreams of ideal societies, and the reasons of the failure to realize them. I wish I could tell you about the ideas of Western civilization which are produced by a long sojourn in the Orient. How pleasant to take country walks again! that is, if there be any country left around Cincinnati. How pleasant to read to you strange stories and theories from the Far East! Still, I have become so accustomed to Japanese life that a return to Western ways would not be altogether easy at first. What a pity I did not reach Japan ten years sooner!

Tell me, if you write again, all pleasant news about old friends. Love to you always, and believe me ever,

Your extremely bad and ungrateful

  Grey-headed boy,

    Lafcadio Hearn

In Kobe, for a monthly salary of 100 yen, Lafcadio was responsible for writing daily *Chronicle* editorials which, except for fervent attacks on missionaries, were mostly bland, dry commentaries on subjects such as "The Labor Problem in America," "Japanese Emigration to the West Indies,"

"Patriotism and Education," "Are Englishmen Angels?," and other matters of supposed interest to Kobe's enclave of foreign bankers, traders, merchants, shippers, military personnel, and tourists.

Three months into his job, Lafcadio's right eye became severely inflamed from neuritis, and a doctor advised him to leave the newspaper and to rest in a darkened room for a month if he ever intended to work again. At the same time, Lafcadio was undergoing a personal writing crisis that had begun in Kumamoto, where he felt himself drained of "sensations—dreams—glimpses. . . . I can only grind, grind all the time." This writing block was the consequence of the end of his romance with the "fairy tale" of Japan. Now in his darkened room in Kobe he reflected: "My conclusion is that the charm of Japanese life is largely the charm of childhood, and that the most beautiful of all race childhoods is passing into an adolescence which threatens to prove repulsive."

It was the sense of childhood, not adolescence, that always connected Lafcadio to the mysterious processes of creativity and imagination. Now, in a depressed mood, he began feeling homesick for the West ("I saw myself among giants. Everything seemed huge, full of force, dignity, massive potentialities divined but vaguely") and he fantasized about going off for the winter to Manila, Java, Pondicherry, or Samoa. (Having just read R. L. Stevenson's recently published accounts of his life in Samoa, Lafcadio swore that if he were still a bachelor, he would have already been on his way to the South Pacific, or "should fly to savage lands and live upon bananas and guava jelly.")

In earlier times, a dispirited Lafcadio would have packed a bag and taken his leave of Japan forever. But he had a family, and Setsu—his protestations to Watkin to the contrary—was pregnant with Lafcadio's second son (Iwao). *This* father was not about to abandon wife and children as his own father had done. He willed himself to be who he wanted to be.

The decision to remain where he was and to confront and accept the reality that he was getting older surprisingly mitigated his creative stagnation, leading him to follow the advice he had once given Leona Queyrouze about searching within one's own "psychical depths." To Chamberlain he declared: "I really think I have stored away in me somewhere powers larger than those I have yet been able to use. Of course I don't mean that I have any hidden wisdom, or anything of that sort; but I believe I have some power to reach the public emotionally, if conditions allow. . . .

"Composition becomes difficult only when it becomes work,—that is

literary labor without a strong inspirational impulse or an emotional feeling behind it. Now, in Japan, after the first experiences are over,—I can't
imagine anybody having either an inspiration or a strong emotion. The
atmosphere is soporific, grey, without electricity. There work has to be
forced. I never work without painfully forcing myself to do it."

For Lafcadio there were two ways to "force" work: one, "to force
thought by concentration"—something he found too fatiguing to do; and
two, "to force the *work* only, and let the thought develop itself." By means
of four to five rewritings and two final copies, "the whole thought re-
shapes itself, and the whole style is changed and fixed. The work has
done itself, developed, grown; it would have been very different had I
trusted to the first thought. But I let the thought define and crystallize
itself." Or, as he also put it: "All the best work is done the way ants do
things—by tiny but tireless and regular additions. I wouldn't recommend
introspection,—except in commentary. You *must* see interesting life. Of
course only in flashes and patches. But preserve in writing the memory
of these. In a year you will be astounded to find them self-arranging,
kaleidoscopically, into something symmetrical,—and trying to live. Then
play God, and breathe into the nostrils,—and be astonished and pleased."

"I think that on the whole," Lafcadio commented to Ellwood Hendrick,
"I am gaining a little in the path; but I have regular fits of despondency
and disgust about my work, of course. One day I think I have done well;
the next that I am a hideous ass and fool." His path was his work, his
work his way of being in the world, and his writing was an act of self-
criticism as well as an instrument for monitoring the disappearance of
things. "I long for the primitive west coast," he said, "where speech is
ruder and ways simpler and nothing can be had to eat,—but where the
ancient Gods live still in hearts." The Japanese gods were dying, as in
ancient Greece before them, but the act of writing kept them alive in his
heart and work. "What is there, after all," he asked with characteristic
Japanese regret, "to love in Japan, except what is passing away?" And in
the process of asking, Lafcadio accepted and moved forward on his path
as a writer and as a transient creature of this world.

It was therefore with a sense of renewal, not of resignation, that Lafcadio
visited Yokohama in the spring of 1895 and paid a second visit to the
small Buddhist temple in a remembered back street of the city:

⟨ Five years, all spent far away from treaty ports, slowly flitted by before I
saw the Jizō-Dō again. Many changes had taken place both without and

within me during that time. The beautiful illusion of Japan, the almost weird charm that comes with one's first entrance into her magical atmosphere, had, indeed, stayed with me very long, but had totally faded out at last. I had learned to see the Far East without its glamour. And I had mourned not a little for the sensations of the past.

But one day they all came back to me—just for a moment. I was in Yokohama, gazing once more from the Bluff at the divine spectre of Fuji haunting the April morning. In that enormous spring blaze of blue light, the feeling of my first Japanese day returned, the feeling of my first delighted wonder in the radiance of an unknown fairy-world full of beautiful riddles,—an Elf-land having a special sun and a tinted atmosphere of its own. Again I knew myself steeped in a dream of luminous peace; again all visible things assumed for me a delicious immateriality. Again the Orient heaven—flecked only with thinnest white ghosts of cloud, all shadowless as Souls entering into Nirvana—became for me the very sky of Buddha; and the colors of the morning seemed deepening into those of the traditional hour of His birth, when trees long dead burst into blossom, and winds were perfumed, and all creatures living found themselves possessed of loving hearts. The air seemed pregnant with even such a vague sweetness, as if the Teacher were about to come again; and all faces passing seemed to smile with premonition of the celestial advent.

Then the ghostliness went away, and things looked earthly; and I thought of all the illusions I had known, and of the illusions of the world as Life, and of the universe itself as illusion. Whereupon the name Mu-myo returned to memory; and I was moved immediately to seek the ancient thinker of the Jizō-Dō.

The quarter had been much changed: old houses had vanished, and new ones dovetailed wondrously together. I discovered the court at last nevertheless, and saw the little temple just as I had remembered it. Before the entrance women were standing; and a young priest I had never seen before was playing with a baby; and the small brown hands of the infant were stroking his shaven face. It was a kindly face, and intelligent, with very long eyes.

"Five years ago," I said to him, in clumsy Japanese, "I visited this temple. In that time there was an aged bonsan here."

The young bonsan gave the baby into the arms of one who seemed to be its mother, and responded:—

"Yes. He died—that old priest; and I am now in his place. Honorably please to enter."

I entered. The little sanctuary no longer looked interesting: all its innocent prettiness was gone. Jizō still smiled over his bib; but the other divinities had disappeared, and likewise many votive offerings—including the picture of Adelaide Neilson. The priest tried to make me comfortable in the chamber where the old man used to write, and set a smoking-box before me. I looked for the books in the corner; they also had vanished. Everything seemed to have been changed.

I asked:—

"When did he die?"

"Only last winter," replied the incumbent, "in the Period of Greatest Cold. As he could not move his feet, he suffered much from the cold. This is his *ihai*."

He went to an alcove containing shelves incumbered with a bewilderment of objects indescribable,—old wrecks, perhaps, of sacred things,—and opened the doors of a very small *butsudan*, placed between glass jars full of flowers. Inside I saw the mortuary tablet,—fresh black lacquer and gold. He lighted a lamplet before it, set a rod of incense smouldering, and said:—

"Pardon my rude absence a little while; for there are parishioners waiting."

So left alone, I looked at the *ihai* and watched the steady flame of the tiny lamp and the blue, slow, upcurlings of incense,—wondering if the spirit of the old priest was there. After a moment I felt as if he really were, and spoke to him without words. Then I noticed that the flower vases on either side of the *butsudan* still bore the name of Toussaint Cosnard of Bordeaux, and that the incense-box maintained its familiar legend of richly flavored cigarettes. Looking about the room I also perceived the red cat, fast asleep in a sunny corner. I went to it, and stroked it; but it knew me not, and scarcely opened its drowsy eyes. It was sleeker than ever, and seemed happy. Near the entrance I heard a plaintive murmuring; then the voice of the priest, reiterating sympathetically some half-comprehended answer to his queries: "*A woman of nineteen, yes. And a man of twenty-seven,—is it?*" Then I rose to go.

"Pardon," said the priest, looking up from his writing, while the poor women saluted me, "yet one little moment more!"

"Nay," I answered; "I would not interrupt you. I came only to see the old man, and I have seen his *ihai*. This, my little offering, was for him. Please to accept it for yourself."

"Will you not wait a moment, that I may know your name?"

"Perhaps I shall come again," I said evasively. "Is the old nun also dead?"

"Oh no! she is still taking care of the temple. She has gone out, but will presently return. Will you not wait? Do you wish nothing?"

"Only a prayer," I answered. "My name makes no difference. A man of forty-four. Pray that he may obtain whatever is best for him."

The priest wrote something down. Certainly that which I had bidden him pray for was not the wish of my "heart of hearts." But I knew the Lord Buddha would never hearken to any foolish prayer for the return of lost illusions.

("IN YOKOHAMA")

CHAPTER 6

Tokyo Story

IN DECEMBER 1895, Lafcadio was offered the Chair of English
Language and Literature at Tokyo Imperial University. To any ambitious
educator, moving up from an instructorship at the Middle School in Matsue to a professorship at Japan's most important university would have
been an extraordinary and unprecedented professional accomplishment.
To Lafcadio, it was a miserable prospect. Tokyo was "the most horrible
place in Japan." There was no Japan in Tokyo, he declared,—only "dirty
shoes,—absurd fashions,—wickedly expensive living,—airs,—vanities,—
gossip." Lafcadio's "simple, sweet-hearted country girl," however, was
overjoyed at the news. "In spite of all I say," Lafcadio remarked, "Setsu
thinks of Tokyo just as a French lady thinks of Paris."

Acceding to his wife's wishes, he and the family settled in the Tokyo
suburb of Ushigome. In front of the nondescript, utilitarian house, the
road was being torn up and ditches for water pipes dug—signs of Japan's
capital city's inevitable expansion. Lafcadio only looked the other way,
out back, where a large untended field rose gradually to become a hill,
covered with interlacing pines, cedars, oaks, and cypress trees under
which was a dark, wooded terrain of thorn hedges, bush clover, sorrel,
vines, spear flowers, and stripped bamboos. Owls, pheasants, rabbits, and
foxes made their home here, as did a Buddhist temple of the Tendai sect
built in 1643. Commonly known as Kobudera (which means the "gnarled"
or "knobby" temple), it was hidden among the hillside's dense covering
of trees and thick moss. Lafcadio soon made friends with the temple's
aging abbot, who was happy to allow his respectful neighbor to spend as

much time as he wished in the desolate garden, the small cemetery overgrown with weeds and surrounded by a grove of pines, and the temple
compound filled with Buddhist sculpture.

Kobudera made life in the "dead waste and muddle" of Tokyo almost
bearable for Lafcadio, who visited the temple every morning and evening
with his wife. As Setsu recalled:

> Many times while out walking, he said, "Mamma-san, is it hard to get
> into a temple? Isn't there any way by which I could live in the temple?"
>
> I replied, "You are not a priest, so perhaps you cannot very well do
> so."
>
> "I should prefer to be a priest," Hearn said; "and how pleased I should
> be if I could be one."
>
> "If you should become a priest, how funny you would look with your
> large eyes and high nose—a fine priest!" I remarked.
>
> "You could become a nun at the same time, and Kazuo [our eldest
> son] a novice. How cute he would look! Every day we should read the
> scriptures and take care of the graves. That would be true happiness!"
>
> "Pray that you may be born a priest in the next world!"
>
> "That is my wish," replied Hearn.

When Lafcadio talked about his "path" of writing, he might just as
well have been referring to the deep affinity with Buddhist thought and
practice that he had expressed since his days in New Orleans. Now, when
his creative inspiration began to wane in Japan, Lafcadio reflected: "I can
imagine no means of consoling myself except by plunging into the study
of Buddhism. . . . What is . . . the use of the life of a solar system—
evolution, dissolution,—re-evolution, re-dissolution, forever more? Really,
Buddhism alone gives us any consolatory ideas on the subject; but it is
now vulgar to mention Buddhism to the Japanese." For, in their rush to
modernize, the Japanese, Lafcadio realized, were turning away from doc-
trinaire and often ignorant and corrupt Buddhist sects, and paying little
attention to those pedantic Buddhist scholars with "lukewarm souls."

In "A Conservative," Lafcadio contended that "a Buddhism strongly
fortified by Western science will meet the future needs of the race." (Here
he was referring to the Japanese race; at other times he extended this
view to the *human* race.)

He began writing challenging, theoretical essays about Mahayana Buddhist doctrines and about concepts such as Nirvana, Karma, and the idea
of preexistence—essays sometimes said to be overly influenced by Spen-

cerian ideas, though orthodox Spencerians often accused Lafcadio of seeing Spencer as a kind of crypto-Buddhist. (For all his talk about "previous"
and "future" lives, Lafcadio ultimately believed that since "there is no
escape through death from the supreme necessity of self-conquest [the
overcoming of ego and its demands]" what was "reincarnated" was not
one's personality or permanent individual soul but rather one's particular
karma.)

Most of all, Lafcadio was a tireless investigator of the ways in which
Buddhism was expressed in daily life—in the common people's proverbs,
children's riddles, toys, burial customs, legends, festivals, rituals, and
charming oddities like the Yuki-Daruma snowman:

The young folks are delighted, because last night a heavy fall of snow
made for us what the Japanese poets so prettily call "a silver world." . . .
Really these poets have been guilty of no extravagance in their charming
praises of winter. For in Japan winter is beautiful—fantastically beautiful.
It bestirs no melancholy imaginings about "the death of Nature"—
inasmuch as Nature remains most visibly alive during even the Period of
Greatest Cold.

It does not afflict the aesthetic eye with the spectacle of "skeleton-
woods"—for the woods largely consist of evergreens. And the snow—
heaping softly upon the needles of the pines, or forcing the bamboos to
display their bending grace under its momentary weight—never suggests
to Far-Eastern poet the dismal fancy of a winding-sheet. Indeed the singular charm of Japanese winter is made by this snow—lumping itself into
grostesqueries unimaginable above the constant verdure of woods and
gardens.

This morning my two students, Aki and Niimi, have been amusing themselves and the children by making a Yuki-Daruma; and I have been amusing myself by watching them. The rules for making a Yuki-Daruma are
ancient and simple. You first compose a huge snowball—between three
and four feet in diameter, if possible—which is to represent the squatting
body of Daruma. Then you make a smaller snowball, about two feet in
diameter, to represent his head; and you put this smaller ball on top of
the other—packing snow around the under-parts of both, so as to fix
them in place. Two round lumps of charcoal serve to make eyes for
Daruma; and some irregular fragments of the same material will suffice to

indicate his nose and mouth. Finally, you must scoop out a hollow in the great belly of him, to represent a navel, and stick a lighted candle inside. The warmth of the candle gradually enlarges the opening. . . .

But I forgot to explain the term Yuki-Daruma, or Snow-Daruma. "Daruma" is an abbreviation of the name Bodai-Daruma—Japanese rendering of the Sanskrit "Bodhidharma." . . .

Now of the many legends about Daruma, the most famous is the story that he once remained for nine years in uninterrupted meditation, during which time his legs fell off. Wherefore images of him are made without legs.

Certainly Daruma has large claims to re-spect. But the artists and the toymakers of the Far East have never allowed these claims to interfere with the indulgence of their sense of humor—originally bestirred, no doubt, by the story of the loss of his legs. For centuries this legendary mishap has been made the subject of comical drawings and comical carvings; and generations of Japanese children have amused themselves with a certain toy-image of Daruma so contrived that, however the little figure be thrown down, it will always bob up again into a squatting posture. This still popular toy, called *Okiagari-Koboshi* (The Getting-up Little Priest), may have been originally modeled, or re-modeled, after a Chinese toy made upon the same principle, and called *Puh-Tau-Ung* (The Not-falling-down Old Man). Mention is made of the *Okiagari-Koboshi* in a Japanese play called *Manjū-Kui,* known to have been composed in the fourteenth century. But the earlier forms of the toy do not seem to have been representations of Daruma. There is, however, a children's-song, dating from the seventeenth century, which proves that the Daruma-toy was popular more than two hundred years ago:

> *Hi ni! fu ni!*
> *Fundan Daruma ga*
> *Akai zukin kaburi sunmaita!*

("Once! twice! . . . Ever the red-hooded Daruma heedlessly sits up again!")

From this little song it would seem that the form of the toy has not been much changed since the seventeenth century; Daruma still wears his hood, and is still painted red—all of him except his face.

Besides the Snow-Daruma already described, and the toy-Daruma (usually made of papier-mâché), there are countless comical varieties of Daruma: figures moulded or carved in almost every kind of material, and ranging in size from the tiny metal Daruma, half-an-inch long, designed for a pouch-clasp, to the big wooden Daruma, two or three feet high, which the Japanese tobacconist has adopted for a shop-sign. . . . Thus profanely does popular art deride the holy legend of the nine years' meditation.

*

Now that Yuki-Daruma in my garden reminds me of a very peculiar Daruma which I discovered several years ago, at a certain fishing-village on the eastern coast where I passed a happy summer. There was no hotel in the place; but a good man called Otokichi, who kept a fish-shop, used to let me occupy the upper part of his house, and fed me with fish cooked in a wonderful variety of ways.

One morning he called me into his shop to show me a very fine *hōbō*. . . . I wonder if you ever saw anything resembling a *hōbō*. It looks so much like a gigantic butterfly or moth, that you must examine it closely to make sure that it is not an insect, but a fish—a sort of gurnard. It has four fins arranged like pairs of wings—the upper pair dark, with bright spots of sky-blue; the lower pair deep red. It seems also to have legs like a butterfly—slender legs upon which it runs about quickly. . . .

"Is it good to eat?" I asked.

"*Hé!*" answered Otokichi: "this shall be prepared for the Honorable Dinner."

[To any question asked of him—even a question requiring answer in the negative—Otokichi would begin his reply with the exclamation "*Hé*" (Yes)—uttered in such a tone of sympathy and good-will as to make the hearer immediately forget all the tribulations of existence.]

Then I wandered back into the shop, looking at things. On one side were rows of shelves supporting boxes of dried fish, and packages of edible seaweed, and bundles of straw sandals, and gourds for holding saké, and bottles of lemonade! On the opposite side, high up, I perceived the *kamidana*—the Shelf of the Gods; and I noticed, under the *kamidana*, a smaller shelf occupied by a red image of Daruma. Evidently the image was not a toy: there were offerings in front of it. I was not surprised to find Daruma accepted as a household divinity—because I knew that in many parts of Japan prayers were addressed to him on behalf of children attacked by smallpox. But I was rather startled by the peculiar aspect of Otokichi's Daruma, which had only one eye—a large and formidable eye that seemed to glare through the dusk of the shop like the eye of a great owl. It was the right eye, and was made of glazed paper. The socket of the left eye was a white void.

Therefore I called to Otokichi:

"Otokichi San!—did the children knock out the left eye of Daruma Sama?"

"*Hé, hé!*" sympathetically chuckled Otokichi—lifting a superb *katsuo* to the cutting-bench—"he never had a left eye."

"Was he made that way?" I asked.

"*Hé!*" responded Otokichi—as he swept his long knife soundlessly through the argent body— "the folk here make only blind Darumas. When I got that Daruma, he had no eyes at all. I made the right eye for him last year—after a day of great fishing."

"But why not have given him both eyes?" I queried; "he looks so unhappy with only one eye!"

"*Hé, hé!*" replied Otokichi—skillfully ranging the slices of pink-and-silver flesh upon a little mat of glass rods—"when we have another day of great good fortune, then he shall be given the other eye."

Then I walked about the streets of the village, peeping into the houses and shops; and I discovered various other Darumas in different stages of development—some without eyes, some with only one, and some with two. I remembered that in Izumo it was especially Hotei—the big-bellied God of Comfort—who used to be practically rewarded for his favors. As soon as the worshiper found reason for gratitude, Hotei's recumbent image was put upon a soft cushion; and for each additional grace bestowed the god would be given an additional cushion. But it occurred to me that Daruma could not be given more than two eyes: three would change him into the sort of goblin called "Mitsumé-Kozō." . . . I learned, upon inquiry, that when a Daruma has been presented with a pair of eyes, and with sundry small offerings, he is put away to make room for an eyeless successor. The blind Daruma can be expected to do wonderful things, because he has to work for his eyes.

*

There are many such funny little deities in Japan—so many that it would need a very big book to describe them; and I have found that the people who worship these queer little gods are, for the most part, pathetically honest. Indeed my own experience would almost justify the belief that the more artless the god, the more honest the man—though I do not want my reader to make any hasty deductions. I do not wish to imply, for example, that the superlative point of honesty might begin at the vanishing point of the god. Only this much I would venture: Faith in very small gods—toy-gods—belongs to that simplicity of heart which, in this wicked world, makes the nearest possible approach to pure goodness.

On the evening before I left the village, Otokichi brought me his bill—representing the cost of two months' good cheer;—and the amount proved to be unreasonably small. Of course a present was expected, according to the kindly Japanese custom; but, even taking that fact into consideration, the bill was absurdly honest. The least that I could do to show my appreciation of many things was to double the payment requested; and Otokichi's satisfaction, because perfectly natural and at the same time properly dignified, was something beautiful to see.

I was up and dressed by half-past three the next morning, in order to take an early express-train; but even at that ghostly hour I found a warm breakfast awaiting me downstairs, and Otokichi's little brown daughter ready to serve me. . . . As I swallowed the final bowl of warm tea, my gaze involuntarily wandered in the direction of the household gods, whose tiny lamps were still glowing. Then I noticed that a light was burning also in front of Daruma; and almost in the same instant I perceived that Daruma was looking straight at me—with two eyes! . . .   ("OTOKICHI'S DARUMA")]

During the years Lafcadio and Setsu lived in Tokyo, she gave birth to three more children—two boys (Iwao, Kiyoshi) and one girl (Suzuko)—but it was his sensitive, first-born son, Kazuo, with his increasingly pronounced Western features, with whom Lafcadio was most deeply involved. "Two of the boys are all Japanese," he commented, "—sturdy and not likely to cause anxiety. But the eldest is almost altogether of another race—with brown hair and eyes of the fairy-color—and a tendency to pronounce with a queer little Irish accent the words of old English poems which he has to learn by heart. He is not very strong; and I must give the rest of my life to looking after him." Lafcadio recognized what he took to be "Hearnian" elements in his son, and was therefore all the more anxious to do for Kazuo what Charles Hearn had never done for *him*. "I do not think a father," he asserted, "should leave his son alone in a foreign school, if it can be helped; he ought to be always near him, until manhood." Lafcadio added, with a kind of amazed credulity: "[Kazuo] says, by the way, that he was a doctor in his former birth. It is quite possible, for he has my father's eyes."

Years later, Kazuo remembered a "very loving but very severe" parent who, from the time Kazuo was five years old, taught him the English alphabet, English grammar, English conversation, as well as geography, arithmetic, swimming, and gymnastics, for three hours every day. In order to get his son to pronounce English correctly, Lafcadio made him stand with his feet straight, toes out, chin up, head high, and chest out, explaining: "In every country, soldiers all stand in this manner. In reading and writing, if the position is bad, we get sick or injure the eyes, so correct position is very important." He insisted on making Kazuo take lessons on Sundays and holidays because, as he frequently insisted, "Time won't wait, Papa's life will not wait," and, after a poor recitation of a fable from Aesop or a poem from *A Child's Garden of Verses,* he would shout, "What a useless child!" and slap his son several times, saying: "Every little boy must cry when he begins to learn." He was compulsive about Kazuo's keeping his hands clean at all times, dirty hands (even during play) being an occasion for strong admonition. When a family friend suggested sending the boy to a French Catholic school, he exclaimed, "Before I send Kazuo to such a place, I would first cut off his head!" He was in the habit of sleeping with an "old fashioned big pistol" under his pillow, yet would convince his son to set free in the evening all the grasshoppers and cicadas he had caught in the field during the day, and demanded that Kazuo, engaged in no matter what, come immediately outdoors to observe a procession of ants, a toad swallowing mosquitoes, a larva on a tree branch, or "to look in the direction where Paradise is supposed to be and admire the beauty of the setting sun." Lafcadio would say unhappily to his wife, "There is no feeling so bad as after spanking the children. Everytime I scold them, my life is shortened." He celebrated with enthusiasm (and refreshments all around) the Japanese navy's routing of the Vladivostok fleet—a small Oriental country's first defeat of a large Occidental one—and described the victory as a "killing off of the devils!" He refused to translate into English a play by the famous dramatist Chikamatsu because it concerned a husband who abandoned his wife and child to elope with another woman, and he believed that a man guilty of a major crime "should be made to repent or resort to forced suicide, even if he be one's own child or kinsman." He called Kazuo's mother "Little Mamma" or "Small Mamma," even though she was "quite plump," and overlooked what Kazuo reports were her "hysterical" outbursts and "selfish" demands. He sometimes had to be convinced he hadn't yet eaten dinner when he imagined that he had (*"Papa-san,* it is about time I should ask you to wake up from your dream," his wife would gently say to him), and when finally seated at the table—still in a trance—he would put sugar in his soup and pepper in his coffee. When walking with his son past a crematorium, he would always point to the tall chimney and say, "Very soon I, too, will become smoke and rise from that chimney into the sky." Then Kazuo, who loved his father ("His severity made him the more endearing," he said), would offer wordless prayers in his heart, "asking God to let father live for a long time."

At ten years old, Kazuo entered the fourth-year class at a local primary school. One day, Lafcadio asked his young scholar whether he now preferred Japanese or English. Kazuo replied, "English has so many tongue-twisting sounds, hard and difficult, but Japanese is easy and refined." Lafcadio laughed, but offered some advice: "Surely Japan is most advanced in customs and manners, but I regret to say that in this world we cannot get by only on ease and refinement. You may not like it, but it is better in every way to learn practical English, which is used all over the world."

So Kazuo decided, like his father, to become a writer of English. He asked for, and received, a little notebook, and, again like his father, noted down his observations, perceptions, and sensations, as well as his explanations of curious events and phenomena:

> Last night the snow fell; and this morning the trees were white with snow. In the garden the snow was deep; and the bamboos were bending under the weight of the snow. I played with the snow; I made nine snowballs, and I painted them like cakes. Then I made a target of paper, and threw snowballs at it.

> Today I was very naughty and disobedient, and so my father set me to taking dictation as follows:—

"Can you write Japanese?" "Only a little." "Can you write a Japanese letter as well as Nakamura? [a *rikisha*-man]." "No, I cannot." "Can you read a Japanese newspaper?" "No." "Can you read a Japanese letter?" "No." "Can you write or read or speak English well?" "No." "Have you learned any trade?" "No." "When papa is dead, how will you make some money?" "I do not know." "If you do not know, this house will be taken and sold—you will have no home—and your mamma and grandmamma will be dead—and you will have no friend. Then you will find how cruel people are in this world."

Today Papa went to the University; and while he was away, I translated into Japanese the poem entitled "The Moon"—from *A Child's Garden of Verses*. It was very easy. This afternoon there is a great wind, which is scattering the petals of the plum-flowers over the garden—so that the ground seems as if covered with snow.

Today is a holiday,—the holiday called *Shokonsha;* so the school closed early, early, early. Today all the soldiers are in full-dress uniform.

"To beleaguer"—to surround a place with soldiers. "Vague"—dim, not clearly seen. "Host"—an army. "Spectre"—a ghost. "Marvellous"—wonderful. "Legend"—an old story.

This afternoon Papa called me into the garden; a queer caterpillar was crawling over the stepping-stones, and he wanted me to see it. It was very hairy, and of different colors, and it moved very fast. In our garden there are many extraordinary caterpillars,—some are so strange that even to see them makes you afraid.

Dear Papa took me to Yaidzu on the tenth day of this month. We stayed there nineteen days,—swimming, diving, eating, drinking, sleeping, boating, fishing, catching dragonflies and crabs and grasshoppers. We all got sunburnt—especially Iwao. He became as brown as any Yaidzu boy; and some Yaidzu boys are so brown they seem to be black.

The five senses are (1) Sight, (2) Hearing, (3) Smell, (4) Taste, and (5) Touch.

The word "sense," in the singular, also means intelligence—natural power to understand. Intelligence, or common sense, is very different from the knowledge that we get from books.

Suzuko is my baby sister. She is eleven months old; and she is very tender and small and plump. Though she is so young, she likes to laugh and crow and play.

When she laughs, she jumps up and down, and waves her little hands. She cannot talk yet; but she can say "Bo," "Ah, bah," and "Ah."

Today I saw many lizards—I think there must have been at least ten. They were basking on the ground, in the bamboo-grove. They were of beautiful changing colors;—when they moved the colors changed. Sometimes they appeared to be purple, sometimes red, sometimes green, sometimes brown like the ground, and sometimes black.

Now the cicadas are crying with all their might, because the autumn has come, and they will not have much longer to sing.

Soon there will be frost; and when the frost comes, they will all die. Now the crape-myrtle, which the Japanese call *sarusuberi,* is blossoming.

Kazuo clearly remembered his father getting ready every morning for his university classes, as he wrapped several books for the day's lectures, along with a boxed lunch, in his blue *furoshiki* (a large muslin scarf), and then stepped into his open *kuruma* for the three-mile trip—a broad-brimmed, soft gray hat on his head, several small cigars in his hand (which he only smoked when traveling), and his invariable parting words ("Goodbye, darlings!").

The students at Tokyo Imperial University, where Lafcadio taught twelve hours of classes a week, were known for their obstreperousness, disrupting or walking out of lectures whenever they felt like it. They were, moreover, ill prepared for a survey of English literature, about which Lafcadio himself claimed imperfect knowledge, having spent most of his life dazzled by the literature of France. It was nevertheless a challenge for him to see whether he could introduce to his recalcitrant students representative examples of great English poetry and prose and somehow convince them of the emotional and intellectual power of these works, as well as the moral consciousness they inspired. Lafcadio had, furthermore, to do so in the clearest and simplest English, without the aid of any notes or prepared remarks.

Skeptical at first of their unconventional new professor, Lafcadio's students were soon not only attentive but inspired. One student later remarked: "His lectures were revelations to us, at once poignant and lucid," and another said: "It often seemed to us as if we were actually leaning out from the bar of Heaven beside Rossetti's Blessed Damozel or walking along the corridors of the Palace of Art, till the bell for the recess broke the spell." One of Lafcadio's colleagues happened to enter his class one day, and described the scene: "I opened the door and went in. The first two or three rows of his students . . . were all in tears. I do not know what it was all about. It is a rare event for a Japanese to be in tears; even a coolie is ashamed of it, and with men of higher rank it is much more striking than it would be in England. Hearn had been reading some very simple English poem; and there was the effect."

Lafcadio's opinions about English writers were personal and heterodox. William Blake to him was like a great Zen teacher who "suggested questions without giving answers; you must think of the answers for yourself." Wordsworth was a poet who produced "an astonishing amount of nonsense" and had no sense of humor . . . but his love of children, family, country, and friends "found in his verse the most beautiful expression which English poetry can offer." Coleridge "was able to influence the intellectual life of England in matters of religious feeling" and also "infused . . . something ghostly and supernatural into poetry." Byron, on the other hand, "infused the whole of European literature for a time with the Satanic spirit, a spirit which signified a vague recognition of another law than that of pure morality—the law of struggle, the law of battle, and the splendor of strength even in a bad or cruel cause." Wilkie Collins was "the greatest inventor of plots we have ever had." Charlotte Brontë expressed "her own experiences of love, despair, and struggle, but this with the very highest art of the novel-writer, with a skill of grouping incident and of communicating vividness to the least detail, rarely found in English." Sir Thomas Browne was "the first great English writer to create an original classic style." Kipling was simply "the greatest writer of short stories in English: he is all mind and eye . . . sensitiveness extraordinary."

What were Lafcadio's lectures like? A number of his students took down what he said word for word in Japanese; and with the translation into English after his death of many of these notebooks, Lafcadio's approaches to his subjects are made clear. His extemporaneous discussion of "The Value of the Supernatural in Fiction," for instance, was one that went to the heart of his own work:

. . . Now let me speak to you about this word "ghostly"; it is a much bigger word, perhaps, than some of you imagine. The old English had no other word for "spiritual" or "supernatural"—which two terms, you know, are not English but Latin. Everything that religion today calls divine, holy, miraculous, was sufficiently explained for the old Anglo-Saxons by the term ghostly. They spoke of a man's ghost, instead of speaking of his spirit or soul; and everything relating to religious knowledge they called ghostly. In the modern formula of the Catholic confession, which has remained almost unchanged for nearly two thousand years, you will find that the priest is always called a "ghostly" father—which means that his business is to take care of the ghosts or souls of men as a father does. In addressing the priest, the penitent really calls him "Father of my ghost." You will see, therefore, that a very large meaning really attaches to the adjective. It means everything relating to the supernatural. It means to the Christian even God himself, for the Giver of Life is always called in English the Holy Ghost.

Accepting the evolutional philosophy which teaches that the modern idea of God as held by western nations is really but a development from the primitive belief in a shadow-soul, the term ghost in its reference to the Supreme Being certainly could not be found fault with. On the contrary, there is a weirdness about this use of the word which adds greatly to its solemnity. But whatever belief we have, or have not, as regards religious creeds, one thing that modern science has done for us, is to prove beyond all question that everything which we used to consider material and solid is essentially ghostly, as is any ghost. If we do not believe in old-fashioned stories and theories about ghosts, we are nevertheless obliged to recognize today that we are ghosts of ourselves—and utterly incomprehensible. The mystery of the universe is now weighing upon us, becoming heavier and heavier, more and more awful, as our knowledge expands, and it is especially a ghostly mystery. All great art reminds us in some way of this universal riddle; that is why I say that all great art has something ghostly in it. It touches something within us which relates to infinity. When you read a very great thought, when you see a wonderful picture or statue or building, and when you hear certain kinds of music, you feel a thrill in the heart and mind much like the thrill which in all times men felt when they thought they saw a ghost or a god. Only the modern thrill is incomparably larger and longer and deeper. And this is why, in spite of all knowledge, the world still finds pleasure in the literature of the supernatural, and will continue to find pleasure in it for hundreds of years to come. The ghostly represents always some shadow of truth, and no amount of disbelief in what used to be called ghosts can ever diminish human interest in what relates to that truth.

So you will see that the subject is not altogether trifling. Certainly it is of very great moment in relation to great literature. The poet or the story-teller who cannot give the reader a little ghostly pleasure at times never can be either a really great writer or a great thinker. I have already said

that I know of no exception to this rule in the whole of English literature.
Take, for instance, Macaulay, the most practical, hard-headed, logical writer
of the century, the last man in whom you would expect to find the least
trace of superstition. Had you read only certain of his essays, you would
scarcely think him capable of touching the chords of the supernatural.
But he has done this in a masterly way in several of the *Lays of Ancient
Rome*—for example, in speaking of the apparition of the Twin Brethren at
the battle of Lake Regillus, and of Tarquin haunted by the phantom of
his victim Lucretia. Both of these passages give the ghostly thrill in a
strong way; and there is a fainter thrill of the same sort to be experienced
from the reading of parts of the "Prophecy of Capys." It is because Macaulay had this power, though using it sparingly, that his work is so great.
If he had not been able to write these lines of poetry which I referred to,
he could not even have made his history of England the living history
that it is. A man who has no ghostly feeling cannot make anything alive,
not even a page of history or a page of oratory. To touch men's souls,
you must know all that those souls can be made to feel by words; and
to know that, you must yourself have a "ghost" in you that can be touched
in the same way.

Now leaving the theoretical for the practical part of the theme, let us
turn to the subject of the relation between ghosts and dreams.

No good writer—no great writer—ever makes a study of the supernatural according to anything which has been done before by other writers.
This is one of those subjects upon which you cannot get real help from
books. It is not from books, nor from traditions, nor from legends, nor
from anything of that kind that you can learn how to give your reader a
ghostly thrill. I do not mean that it is of no use for you to read what has
been written upon the subject, so far as mere methods of expression,
mere effects of literary workmanship, are concerned. On the contrary, it
is very important that you should read all you can of what is good in
literature upon these subjects; you will learn from them a great deal about
curious values of words, about compactness and power of sentences,
about peculiarities of beliefs and of terrors relating to those beliefs. But
you must never try to use another man's ideas or feelings, taken from a
book, in order to make a supernatural effect. If you do, the work will
never be sincere, and will never make a thrill. You must use your own
ideas and feelings only, under all possible circumstances. And where are
you to get these ideas and feelings from, if you do not believe in ghosts?
From your dreams. Whether you believe in ghosts or not, all the artistic

elements of ghostly literature exist in your dreams, and form a veritable treasury of literary material for the man that knows how to use them.

All the great effects obtained by poets and story writers, and even by religious teachers, in the treatment of supernatural fear or mystery, have been obtained; directly or indirectly, through dreams. Study any great ghost story in any literature, and you will find that no matter how surprising or unfamiliar the incidents seem, a little patient examination will prove to you that every one of them has occurred, at different times, in different combinations, in dreams of your own. They give you a thrill. But why? Because they remind you of experiences, imaginative or emotional, which you had forgotten. There can be no exception to this rule—absolutely none. I was speaking to you the other day about a short story by Bulwer Lytton ["The Haunted and the Haunters"] as being the best ghost story in the English language. The reason why it is the best story of this kind is simply because it represents with astonishing faithfulness the experiences of nightmare. The terror of all great stories of the supernatural is really the terror of nightmare, projected into waking consciousness. And the beauty or tenderness of other ghost stories or fairy-stories, or even of certain famous and delightful religious legends, is the tenderness and beauty of dreams of a happier kind, dreams inspired by love or hope or regret. But in all cases where the supernatural is well treated in literature, dream experience is the source of the treatment. I know that I am now speaking to an audience acquainted with literature of which I know practically nothing. But I believe that there can be no exception to these rules even in the literature of the Far East. I do not mean to say that there may not be in Chinese and in Japanese literature many ghost stories which are not derived from dream-experience. But I will say that if there are any of this kind, they are not worth reading, and cannot belong to any good class of literature. I have read translations of a number of Chinese ghost stories in French, also a wonderful English translation of ghostly Chinese stories in two volumes, entitled *Strange Stories from a Chinese Studio* by Herbert Giles. These stories, translated by a great scholar, are very wonderful; but I noticed that in every successful treatment of a supernatural subject, the incidents of the story invariably correspond with the phenomena of dreams. Therefore I think that I cannot be mistaken in my judgment of the matter. Such Japanese stories as I could get translations of, obeyed the same rule. The other day, in a story which I read for the first time, I was very much interested to find an exact parallel between the treatment of a supernatural idea by the Japanese author, and by the best English author of dream studies. The story was about a picture, painted upon a screen, representing a river and a landscape. In the Japanese story (perhaps it has a Chinese origin) the painter makes a sign to the screen; and a little boat begins to sail down the river, and sails out of the picture into the room, and the room becomes full of water, and the painter, or magician, or whoever he is, gets into the boat and sails away into the picture again, and disappears forever. This is exactly, in every detail, a dream story, and the excellence of it is in its truth to dream experience. The same phenomena you will find, under another form, in *Alice in Wonderland* and *Through the Looking Glass*.

But to return to the point where we left off. I was saying that all successful treatment of the ghostly or the impossible must be made to correspond as much as possible with the truth of dream experience, and that Bulwer Lytton's story of the haunted house illustrates the rule. Let us now consider especially the literary value of nightmare. Nightmare, the most awful form of dream, is also one of the most peculiar. It has probably furnished all the important elements of religious and supernatural terror which are to be found in really great literature. It is a mysterious thing in itself; and scientific psychology has not yet been able to explain many facts in regard to it. We can take the phenomena of nightmare separately, one by one, and show their curious relation to various kinds of superstitious fear and supernatural belief.

The first remarkable fact in nightmare is the beginning of it. It begins with a kind of suspicion, usually. You feel afraid without knowing why. Then you have the impression that something is acting upon you from a distance—something like fascination, yet not exactly fascination, for there may be no visible fascinator. But feeling uneasy, you wish to escape, to get away from the influence that is making you afraid. Then you find it is not easy to escape. You move with great difficulty. Presently the difficulty increases—you cannot move at all. You want to cry out, and you cannot; you have lost your voice. You are actually in a state of trance— seeing, hearing, feeling, but unable to move or speak. This is the beginning. It forms one of the most terrible emotions from which a man can suffer. If it continued more than a certain length of time, the mere fear might kill. Nightmare does sometimes kill, in cases where the health has been very much affected by other causes.

Of course we have nothing in ordinary waking life of such experience— the feeling of being deprived of will and held fast from a great distance by some viewless power. This is the real experience of magnetism, mesmerism; and it is the origin of certain horrible beliefs of the Middle Ages in regard to magical power. Suppose we call it supernatural mesmerism, for want of a better word. It is not true mesmerism, because in real hypnotic conditions, the patient does not feel or think or act mentally according to his own personality; he acts by the will of another. In nightmare the will is only suspended, and the personal consciousness remains; this is what makes the horror of it. So we shall call the first stage supernatural mesmerism, only with the above qualification. Now let us see how Bulwer Lytton uses this experience in his story.

A man is sitting in a chair, with a lamp on the table beside him, and is reading Macaulay's essays, when he suddenly becomes uneasy. A shadow falls upon the page. He rises, and tries to call; but he cannot raise his voice above a whisper. He tries to move; and he cannot stir hand or foot. The spell is already upon him. This is the first part of nightmare.

The second stage of the phenomenon, which sometimes mingles with the first stage, is the experience of terrible and unnatural appearances. There is always a darkening of the visible, sometimes a disappearance or dimming of the light. In Bulwer Lytton's story there is a fire burning in the room, and a very bright lamp. Gradually both lamp and fire become dimmer and dimmer; at last all light completely vanishes, and the room becomes absolutely dark, except for spectral and unnatural luminosities that begin to make their appearance. This also is a very good study of dream experience. The third stage of nightmare, the final struggle, is chiefly characterized by impossible occurrences, which bring to the dreamer the extreme form of horror, while convincing him of his own impotence. For example, you try to fire a pistol or to use a steel weapon. If a pistol, the bullet will not project itself more than a few inches from the muzzle; then it drops down limply, and there is no report. If a sword or dagger, the blade becomes soft, like cotton or paper. Terrible appearances, monstrous or unnatural figures, reach out hands to touch; if human figures they will grow to the ceiling, and bend themselves fantastically as they approach. There is one more stage, which is not often reached—the climax of the horror. That is when you are caught or touched. The touch in nightmare is a very peculiar sensation, almost like an electric shock, but unnaturally prolonged. It is not pain, but something worse than pain, an experience never felt in waking hours.

The third and fourth stages have been artistically mixed together by Bulwer Lytton. The phantom towers from floor to ceiling, vague and threatening; the man attempts to use a weapon, and at the same time

receives a touch or shock that renders him absolutely powerless. He describes the feeling as resembling the sensation of some ghostly electricity.
The study is exactly true to dream-experience. I need not here mention
this story further, since from this point a great many other elements enter
into it which, though not altogether foreign to our subject, do not illustrate
that subject so well as some of the stories of Poe. Poe has given us other
peculiar details of nightmare-experience, such as horrible sounds. Often
we hear in such dreams terrible muffled noises, as of steps coming. This
you will find very well studied in the story called "The Fall of the House
of Usher." Again in these dreams inanimate objects either become alive,
or suggest to use, by their motion, the hiding of some horrible life behind
them—curtains, for example, doors left half open, alcoves imperfectly
closed. Poe has studied these in "Eleonora" and in some other sketches.

Dreams of the terrible have beyond question had a good deal to do
with the inspiration both of religious and of superstitious literature. The
returning of the dead, visions of heavenly or infernal beings,—these, when
well described, are almost always exact reproductions of dream-
experience. But occasionally we find an element of waking fear mixed
with them—for example, in one of the oldest ghost stories of the world,
the story in The Book of Job. The poet speaks of feeling intense cold, and
feeling the hairs of his head stand up with fear. These experiences are
absolutely true, and they belong to waking life. The sensation of cold and
the sensation of horror are not sensations of dreams. They come from
extraordinary terror felt in active existence, while we are awake. You will
observe the very same signs of fear in a horse, a dog, or a cat—and there
is reason to suppose that in these animal cases, also, supernatural fear is
sometimes a cause. I have seen a dog—a brave dog, too—terribly frightened by seeing a mass of paper moved by a slight current of air. This
slight wind did not reach the place where the dog was lying; he could
not therefore associate the motion of the paper with a motion of the wind;
he did not understand what was moving the paper; the mystery alarmed
him, and the hair on his back stood up with fear. But the mingling of
such sensations of waking fear with dream sensations of fear, in a story
or poem, may be very effectually managed, so as to give to the story an
air of reality, of actuality, which could not be obtained in any other way.
A great many of our old fairy ballads and goblin stories mixed the two
experiences together with the most excellent results. I should say that the
fine German story of "Undine" is a good example of this kind. The sight
of the faces in the water of the river, the changing of waterfalls and

cataracts into ghostly people, the rising from the closed well of the form of Undine herself, the rising of the flood behind her, and the way in which she "weeps her lover to death"—all this is pure dream; and it seems real because most of us have had some such experiences of fancy in our own dreams. But the other part of the story dealing with human emotions, fears, passions—these are of waking life, and the mixture is accomplished in a most artistic way. Speaking of Undine obliges me also to speak of Undine's predecessors in medieval literature—the medieval spirits, the *succubae* and *incubi,* the sylphs and salamanders or salamandrines, the whole wonderful goblin population of water, air, forest, and fire. All the good stories about them are really dream studies. And coming down to the most romantic literature of our own day, the same thing must be said of those strange and delightful stories by Gautier, *"La Morte Amoureuse," "Arria Marcella," "Le Pied de Momie."* The most remarkable is perhaps *"La Morte Amoureuse";* but there is in this a study of double personality, which complicates it too much for purposes of present illustration. I shall therefore speak of *"Arria Marcella"* instead. Some young students visit the city of Pompeii, to study the ruins and the curiosities preserved in the museum of Naples, nearby. All of them are familiar with classic literature and classic history; moreover, they are artists, able to appreciate the beauty of what they see. At the time of the eruption, which occurred nearly two thousand years ago, many people perished by being smothered under the rain of ashes; but their bodies were encased in the deposit so that the form was perfectly preserved as in a mould. Some of these moulds are to be seen in the museum mentioned; and one is the mould of the body of a beautiful young woman. The youngest of the three students sees this mould, and romantically wishes that he could see and love the real person, so many centuries dead. That night, while his companions are asleep, he leaves his room and wanders into the ruined city, for the pleasure of thinking all by himself. But presently, as he turns the corner of a street, he finds that the city looks quite different from what it had appeared by day; the houses seem to have grown taller; they look new, bright, clean. While he is thus wandering, suddenly the sun rises, and the streets fill with people—not the people of today, but the people of two thousand years ago, all dressed in the old Greek and Roman costumes. After a time a young Greek comes up to the student and speaks to him in Latin. He has learned enough Latin at the university to be able to answer, and a conversation begins, of which the result is that he is invited to the theatre of Pompeii to see the gladiators and other amusements of the time. While in this theatre, he suddenly sees the woman that he wanted to see, the woman whose figure was preserved in the Naples museum. After the theatre, he is invited to her house; and everything is very delightful until suddenly the girl's father appears on the scene. The old man is a Christian, and he is very angry that the ghost of his daughter should receive a young man in this manner. He makes a sign of the cross, and immediately poor Arria crumbles into dust, and the young man finds himself alone in the ruins of Pompeii. Very beautiful this story is; but every detail in it is dream study. I have given so much mention to it only because it seems to me the very finest French example of this artistic use of dream experience. But how many other romances belong to the same category? I need only mention among others Irving's "The Adalantado of the Seven Cities," which is pure dream, so realistically told that it gives the reader the sensation of being asleep. Although such romances as "The Seven Sleepers," "Rip Van Winkle," and "Urashima" are not, on the other hand, pure dreams, yet the charm of them is just in that part where dream experience is used. The true romance in all is in the old man's dream of being young, and waking up to cold and grave realities. By the way, in the old French lays of Marie de France, there is an almost precisely similar story to the Japanese one—similar, at least, at all points except the story of the tortoise. It is utterly impossible that the oriental and the occidental story-tellers could have, either of them, borrowed from the other; more probably each story is a spontaneous growth. But it is curious to find the legend substantially the same in other literatures—Indian and Arabian and Javanese. In all of the versions the one romantic truth is ever the same—a dream truth.

Now besides the artistic elements of terror and of romance, dreams certainly furnish us with the most penetrating and beautiful qualities of ghostly tenderness that literature contains. For the dead people that we loved all come back to us occasionally in dreams, and look and talk as if they were actually alive, and become to us everything that we could have wished them to be. In a dream-meeting with the dead, you must have observed how everything is gentle and beautiful, and yet how real, how true it seems. From the most ancient times such visions of the dead have furnished literature with the most touching and the most exquisite passages of unselfish affection. We find this experience in nearly all the ancient ballad-literature of Europe; we find it in all the world's epics; we find it in every kind of superior poetry; and modern literature draws from it more and more as the years go by. Even in such strange compositions as the *Kalevala* of the Finns, an epic totally unlike any other ever written in this world, the one really beautiful passage in an emotional sense is the coming back of the dead mother to comfort the wicked son, which is a dream study, though not so represented in the poem.

Yet one thing more. Our dreams of heaven, what are they in literature but reflections in us of the more beautiful class of dreams? In the world of sleep all the dead people we loved meet us again; the father recovers his long-buried child, the husband his lost wife, separated lovers find the union that was impossible in this world, those whom we lost sight of in early years—dead sisters, brothers, friends—all come back to us just as they were then, just as loving, and as young, and perhaps even more beautiful than they could really have been. In the world of sleep there is no growing old; there is immortality, there is everlasting youth. And again how soft, how happy everything is; even the persons unkind to us in waking life become affectionate to us in dreams. Well, what is heaven but this? Religion in painting perfect happiness for the good, only describes the best of our dream-life, which is also the best of our waking life; and I think you will find that the closer religion has kept to dream experience in these descriptions, the happier has been the result. Perhaps you will say that I have forgotten how religion teaches the apparition of supernatural powers of a very peculiar kind. But I think that you will find the suggestion for these powers also in dream-life. Do we not pass through the air in dreams, pass through solid substances, perform all kinds of miracles, achieve all sorts of impossible things? I think we do. At all events, I am certain that when, as men-of-letters, you have to deal with any form of supernatural subject—whether terrible, or tender, or pathetic, or splendid—you will do well, if you have a good imagination, not to trust to books for your inspiration. Trust to your own dream-life; study it carefully, and draw your inspiration from that. For dreams are the primary source of almost everything that is beautiful in the literature which treats of what lies beyond mere daily experience.

Meanwhile, on quiet evenings back at home, Setsu would lower the wicks of all the lamps and begin to tell her husband ghost stories she remembered from her childhood. Years later, Setsu recalled these occasions:

> . . . Hearn would ask questions with bated breath, and would listen to
> my tales with a terrified air. I naturally emphasized the exciting parts of

the stories when I saw him so moved. At those times our house seemed as if it were haunted. I often had horrid dreams and nightmares. Hearn would say, "We will stop talking about such things for a while"; and we would do so. He was pleased when I told a story he liked.

When I told him the old tales, I always first gave the plot roughly; and wherever he found an interesting place, he made a note of it. Then he would ask me to give the details, and often to repeat them. If I told him the story by reading it from a book, he would say, "There is no use of your reading it from the book. I prefer your own words and phrases—all from your own thought. Otherwise, it won't do." Therefore I had to assimilate the story before telling it. That made me dream. He would become so eager when I reached an interesting point of a story! His facial expression would change and his eyes would burn intensely. This change was extraordinary. . . .

While we were working on the story of "Mimi-Nashi-Hōïchi," night fell, but we lighted no lamp. I went into the adjoining room, and called out in a small voice, *"Yoshi-ichi! Yoshi-ichi!"*

"Yes," Hearn answered, playing the part, "I am blind. Who are you?" and remained silent. In this way he worked and became absorbed in it.

One day at that time, when I came home from a walk, I brought a *miyagé* (gift) of a little clay figure, a blind musician playing a *biwa* (a native four-stringed lute), and, without saying a word, I left it on his desk. Hearn, as soon as he noticed it, was delighted, and exclaimed, "Oh!" as if he saw some one whom he was expecting to meet. And sometimes when he heard during the night the swish of the bamboo leaves in the wind near his study, he would say, "Ah! there goes a Heiké!" And when he heard the wind, he listened to it earnestly, and said, "That is the waves of the Dan-no-ura!"

And sometimes I would ask him, "Have you written "The Story of Mimi-Nashi-Hōïchi" yet?" . . .

⌊ More than seven hundred years ago, at Dan-no-ura, in the Straits or Shi-monoséki, was fought the last battle of the long contest between the Heiké, or Taira clan, and the Genji, or Minamoto clan. There the Heiké perished utterly, with their women and children, and their infant emperor likewise—now remembered as Antoku Tennō. And that sea and shore have been haunted for seven hundred years. . . . Elsewhere I told you about the strange crabs found there, called *Heiké* crabs, which have human faces on their backs, and are said to be the spirits of Heiké warriors. But there are many strange things to be seen and heard along that coast. On dark nights thousands of ghostly fires hover about the beach, or flit above the waves—pale lights which the fishermen call *Oni-bi*, or demon-fires; and, whenever the winds are up, a sound of great shouting comes from that sea, like a clamor of battle.

In former years the Heiké were much more restless than they now are. They would rise about ships passing in the night, and try to sink them; and at all times they would watch for swimmers, to pull them down. It was in order to appease those dead that the Buddhist temple, Amidaji, was built at Akamagaséki. A cemetery also was made close by, near the beach; and within it were set up monuments inscribed with names of the drowned emperor and of his great vassals; and Buddhist services were regularly performed there, on behalf of the spirits of them. After the temple had been built, and the tombs erected, the Heiké gave less trouble than before; but they continued to do queer things at intervals—proving that they had not found the perfect peace.

Some centuries ago there lived at Akamagaséki a blind man named Hōï-chi, who was famed for his skill in recitation and in playing upon the *biwa*. From childhood he had been trained to recite and to play; and while yet a lad he had surpassed his teachers. As a professional *biwa-hōshi* he became famous chiefly by his recitations of the history of the Heiké and the Genji; and it is said that when he sang the song of the battle of Dan-no-ura "even the goblins (*kijin*) could not refrain from tears."

At the outset of his career, Hōïchi was very poor; but he found a good friend to help him. The priest of the Amidaji was fond of poetry and music; and he often invited Hōïchi to the temple, to play and recite. Afterwards, being much impressed by the wonderful skill of the lad, the priest proposed that Hōïchi should make the temple his home; and this offer was gratefully accepted. Hōïchi was given a room in the temple-building; and, in return for food and lodging, he was required only to gratify the priest with a musical performance on certain evenings, when otherwise disengaged.

One summer night the priest was called away, to perform a Buddhist service at the house of a dead parishioner; and he went there with his acolyte, leaving Hōïchi alone in the temple. It was a hot night; and the blind man sought to cool himself on the verandah before his sleeping-room. The verandah overlooked a small garden in the rear of the Amidaji. There Hōïchi waited for the priest's return and tried to relieve his solitude by practicing upon his *biwa*. Midnight passed; and the priest did not appear. But the atmosphere was still too warm for comfort within doors; and Hōïchi remained outside. At last he heard steps approaching from the backgate. Somebody crossed the garden, advanced to the verandah, and halted directly in front of him—but it was not the priest. A deep voice called the blind man's name—abruptly and unceremoniously in the manner of a samurai summoning an inferior:

"Hōïchi!"

Hōïchi was too much startled, for the moment, to respond; and the voice called again, in a tone of harsh command:

"Hōïchi!"

"Hai!" answered the blind man, frightened by the menace in the voice—"I am blind!—I cannot know who calls!"

"There is nothing to fear," the stranger exclaimed, speaking more gently. "I am stopping near this temple, and have been sent to you with a message. My present lord, a person of exceedingly high rank, is now staying in Akamagaséki, with many noble attendants. He wished to view the scene of the battle of Dan-no-ura; and to-day he visited that place. Having heard of your skill in reciting the story of the battle, he now desires to hear your performance; so you will take your *biwa* and come with me at once to the house where the august assembly is waiting."

In those times, the order of a samurai was not to be lightly disobeyed. Hōïchi donned sandals, took his *biwa*, and went away with the stranger, who guided him deftly, but obliged him to walk very fast. The hand that guided was iron; and the clank of the warrior's stride proved him fully armed—probably some palace-guard on duty. Hōïchi's first alarm was over: he began to imagine himself in good luck;—for, remembering the retainer's assurance about a "person of exceedingly high rank," he thought that the lord who wished to hear the recitation could not be less than a *daimyō* of the first class. Presently the samurai halted; and Hōïchi became aware that they had arrived at a large gateway;—and he wondered, for he could not remember any large gate in that part of the town, except the main gate of the Amidaji. *"Kaimon!"* the samurai called—and there was a sound of unbarring; and the twain passed on. They traversed a space of garden, and halted again before some entrance; and the retainer cried in a loud voice, "Within there! I have brought Hōïchi." Then came sounds of feet hurrying, and screens sliding, and rain-doors opening, and voices of women in converse. By the language of the women Hōïchi knew them to be domestics in some noble household; but he could not imagine to what place he had been conducted. Little time was allowed him for conjecture. After he had been helped to mount several stone steps, upon the last of which he was told to leave his sandals, a woman's hand guided him along interminable reaches of polished planking, and round pillared angles too many to remember, and over widths amazing of matted floor, —into the middle of some vast apartment. There he thought that many great people were assembled: the sound of the rustling of silk was like the sound of leaves in a forest. He heard also a great humming of voices— talking undertones; and the speech was the speech of courts.

Hōïchi was told to put himself at ease, and he found a kneeling-cushion ready for him. After having taken his place upon it, and tuned his instrument, the voice of a woman—whom he divined to be the *Rōjo*, or matron in charge of the female service—addressed him, saying:

"It is now required that the history of the Heiké be recited, to the accompaniment of the *biwa*."

Now the entire recital would have required a time of many nights: therefore Hōïchi ventured a question:

"As the whole of the story is not soon told, what portion is it augustly desired that I now recite?"

The woman's voice made answer:

"Recite the story of the battle at Dan-no-ura—for the pity of it is the most deep."

Then Hōïchi lifted up his voice, and chanted the chant of the fight on the bitter sea—wonderfully making his *biwa* to sound like the straining of oars and the rushing of ships, the whirr and the hissing of arrows, the shouting and trampling of men, the crashing of steel upon helmets, the plunging of slain in the flood. And to left and right of him, in the pauses of his playing, he could hear voices murmuring praise: "How marvelous an artist!"—"Never in our own province was playing heard like this!" —"Not in all the empire is there another singer like Hōïchi!" Then fresh courage came to him, and he played and sang yet better than before; and a hush of wonder deepened about him. But when at last he came to tell the fate of the fair and helpless—the piteous perishing of the women and children—and the death-leap of Nii-no-Ama, with the imperial infant in her arms—then all the listeners uttered together one long, long shuddering cry of anguish; and thereafter they wept and wailed so loudly and so wildly that the blind man was frightened by the violence of the grief that he had made. For much time the sobbing and the wailing continued. But gradually the sounds of lamentation died away; and again, in the great stillness that followed, Hōïchi heard the voice of the woman whom he supposed to be the Rōjo.

She said:

"Although we had been assured that you were a very skillful player upon the *biwa,* and without an equal in recitative, we did not know that any one could be so skillful as you have proved yourself tonight. Our lord has been pleased to say that he intends to bestow upon you a fitting reward. But he desires that you shall perform before him once every night for the next six nights—after which time he will probably make his august return-journey. To-morrow night, therefore, you are to come here at the same hour. The retainer who to-night conducted you will be sent for you. . . . There is another matter about which I have been ordered to inform you. It is required that you shall speak to no one of your visits here, during the time of our lord's august sojourn at Akamagaséki. As he is traveling incognito, he commands that no mention of these things be made. . . . You are now free to go back to your temple."

After Hōïchi had duly expressed his thanks, a woman's hand conducted him to the entrance of the house, where the same retainer, who had before guided him, was waiting to take him home. The retainer led him to the verandah at the rear of the temple, and there bade him farewell.

It was almost dawn when Hōïchi returned; but his absence from the temple had not been observed—as the priest, coming back at a very late hour, had supposed him asleep. During the day Hōïchi was able to take some rest; and he said nothing about his strange adventure. In the middle of the following night the samurai again came for him, and led him to the august assembly, where he gave another recitation with the same success that had attended his previous performance. But during this second visit his absence from the temple was accidentally discovered; and after his return in the morning he was summoned to the presence of the priest, who said to him, in a tone of kindly reproach:

"We have been very anxious about you, friend Hōïchi. To go out, blind and alone, at so late an hour, is dangerous. Why did you go without telling us? I could have ordered a servant to accompany you. And where have you been?"

Hōïchi answered, evasively:

"Pardon me, kind friend! I had to attend to some private business; and I could not arrange the matter at any other hour."

The priest was surprised, rather than pained, by Hōïchi's reticence: he felt it to be unnatural, and suspected something wrong. He feared that the blind lad had been bewitched or deluded by some evil spirits. He did not ask any more questions; but he privately instructed men-servants of the temple to keep watch upon Hōïchi's movements, and to follow him in case that he should again leave the temple after dark.

On the very next night, Hōïchi was seen to leave the temple; and the servants immediately lighted their lanterns, and followed after him. But it was a rainy night, and very dark; and before the temple-folks could get to the roadway, Hōïchi had disappeared. Evidently he had walked very fast—a strange thing, considering his blindness; for the road was in a bad condition. The men hurried through the streets, making inquiries at every house which Hōïchi was accustomed to visit; but nobody could give them any news of him. At last, as they were returning to the temple by way of the shore, they were startled by the sound of a *biwa*, furiously played, in the cemetery of the Amidaji. Except for some ghostly fires—such as usually flitted there on dark nights—all was blackness in that direction. But the men at once hastened to the cemetery; and there, by the help of their lanterns, they discovered Hōïchi—sitting alone in the rain before the memorial tomb of Antoku Tennō, making his *biwa* resound, and loudly chanting the chant of the battle of Dan-no-ura. And behind him, and about him, and everywhere above the tombs, the fires of the dead were burning, like candles. Never before had so great a host of Oni-bi appeared in the sight of mortal man. . . .

"Hōïchi San!—Hōïchi San!" the servants cried—"you are bewitched! . . . Hōïchi San!"

But the blind man did not seem to hear. Strenuously he made his *biwa* to rattle and ring and clang;—more and more wildly he chanted the chant of the battle of Dan-no-ura. They caught hold of him;—they shouted into his ear:

"Hōïchi San!—Hōïchi San!—come home with us at once!"

Reprovingly he spoke to them:

"To interrupt me in such a manner, before this august assembly, will not be tolerated."

Whereat, in spite of the weirdness of the thing, the servants could not help laughing. Sure that he had been bewitched, they now seized him, and pulled him up on his feet, and by main force hurried him back to the temple—where he was immediately relieved of his wet clothes, by order of the priest, and reclad, and made to eat and drink. Then the priest insisted upon a full explanation of his friend's astonishing behavior.

Hōïchi long hesitated to speak. But at last, finding that his conduct had really alarmed and angered the good priest, he decided to abandon his reserve; and he related everything that had happened from the time of the first visit of the samurai.

The priest said:

"Hōïchi, my poor friend, you are now in great danger! How unfortunate that you did not tell me all this before! Your wonderful skill in music has indeed brought you into strange trouble. By this time you must be aware that you have not been visiting any house whatever, but have been passing your nights in the cemetery, among the tombs of the Heiké;—and it was before the memorial-tomb of Antoku Tennō that our people tonight found you, sitting in the rain. All that you have been imagining was illusion—except the calling of the dead. By once obeying them, you have put yourself in their power. If you obey them again, after what has already occurred, they will tear you in pieces. But they would have destroyed you, sooner or later, in any event. . . . Now I shall not be able to remain with you tonight: I am called to perform another service. But, before I go, it will be necessary to protect your body by writing holy texts upon it."

Before sundown the priest and his acolyte stripped Hōïchi: then, with their writing-brushes, they traced upon his breast and back, head and face and neck, limbs and hands and feet—even upon the soles of his feet, and upon all parts of his body—the text of the holy sutra called *Hannya-Shin-Kyō*. When this had been done, the priest instructed Hōïchi, saying:

"To-night, as soon as I go away, you must seat yourself on the verandah, and wait. You will be called. But, whatever may happen, do not answer, and do not move. Say nothing, and sit still—as if meditating. If you stir, or make any noise, you will be torn asunder. Do not get frightened; and do not think of calling for help—because no help could save you. If you do exactly as I tell you, the danger will pass, and you will have nothing more to fear."

After dark the priest and the acolyte went away; and Hōïchi seated himself on the verandah, according to the instructions given him. He laid his *biwa* on the planking beside him, and, assuming the attitude of meditation, remained quite still—taking care not to cough, or to breathe audibly. For hours he stayed thus.

Then, from the roadway, he heard the steps coming. They passed the gate, crossed the garden, approached the verandah, stopped—directly in front of him.

"Hōïchi!" the deep voice called. But the blind man held his breath, and sat motionless.

"Hōïchi!" grimly called the voice a second time. Then a third time—savagely:

"Hōïchi!"

Hōïchi remained as still as a stone—and the voice grumbled:

"No answer!—that won't do! . . . Must see where the fellow is." . . .

There was a noise of heavy feet mounting upon the verandah. The feet approached deliberately—halted beside him. Then, for long minutes—during which Hōïchi felt his whole body shake to the beating of his heart—there was dead silence.

At last the gruff voice muttered close to him:

"Here is the *biwa;* but of the *biwa*-player I see—only two ears! . . . So that explains why he did not answer: he had no mouth to answer with—there is nothing left of him but his ears. . . . Now to my lord those ears I will take—in proof that the august commands have been obeyed, so far as was possible." . . .

At that instant Hōïchi felt his ears gripped by fingers of iron, and torn off. Great as the pain was, he gave no cry. The heavy footfalls receded along the verandah—descended into the garden—passed out to the road-way—ceased. From either side of his head, the blind man felt a thick warm trickling; but he dared not lift his hands. . . .

Before sunrise the priest came back. He hastened at once to the veran-dah in the rear, stepped and slipped upon something clammy, and uttered a cry of horror;—for he saw, by the light of his lantern, that the clammi-ness was blood. But he perceived Hōïchi sitting there, in the attitude of meditation—with the blood still oozing from his wounds.

"My poor Hōïchi!" cried the startled priest—"what is this? . . . You have been hurt?" . . .

At the sound of his friend's voice, the blind man felt safe. He burst out sobbing, and tearfully told his adventure of the night.

"Poor, poor Hōïchi!" the priest exclaimed—"all my fault!—my very grievous fault! . . . Everywhere upon your body the holy texts had been written—except upon your ears! I trusted my acolyte to do that part of the work; and it was very, very wrong of me not to have made sure that he had done it! . . . Well, the matter cannot now be helped;—we can only try to heal your hurts as soon as possible. . . . Cheer up, friend! —the danger is now well over. You will never again be troubled by those visitors."

With the aid of a good doctor, Hōïchi soon recovered from his injuries. The story of his strange adventure spread far and wide, and soon made him famous. Many noble persons went to Akamagaséki to hear him recite; and large presents of money were given to him—so that he became a wealthy man. . . . But from the time of his adventure, he was known only by the appellation of "Mimi-nashi-Hōïchi": Hōïchi-the-Earless.

("THE STORY OF MIMI-NASHI-HŌÏCHI")]

In writing a fairy tale, a romance, a legend, or a ghost story like "The Story of Mimi-nashi-Hōïchi," Lafcadio drew on numerous old and new versions, oral and written, of a work, and particularly on Setsu's reenactments, then allowed himself to be possessed by it. Often, his children heard him pacing up and down the veranda, moaning, weeping, his face pale, his good eye shining eerily as a story took him over. Then he wrote it down, transforming it—adding, subtracting, rearranging, clarifying, simplifying, intensifying. His literary model was Hans Christian Andersen, whose works he had requested from his publisher in 1895. "They [Houghton Mifflin Company] sent me four volumes, [and] the old charm comes back with tenfold force, and makes me despair," he admitted. "How great the art of the man!—the immense volume of fancy,—the magical simplicity—the astounding force of compression! This isn't mere literary art; it is a soul photographed and phonographed and put, like electricity, in storage. To write like Andersen, one must be Andersen. But the fountain of his inspiration is unexhausted, and I hope to gain by drinking from it. I read, and let the result set up disturbances interiorly."

That he did exactly this is made clear in "Oshidori," a brief, astonishing version of a Japanese tale about a grown-up duckling and its ultimate sacrifice:

There was a falconer and hunter, named Sonjō, who lived in the district called Tamura-no-Gō, of the province of Mutsu. One day he went out hunting, and could not find any game. But on his way home, at a place called Akanuma, he perceived a pair of oshidori (mandarin-ducks), swimming together in a river that he was about to cross. To kill *oshidori* is not good; but Sonjō happened to be very hungry, and he shot at the pair. His arrow pierced the male: the female escaped into the rushes of the farther shore, and disappeared. Sonjō took the dead bird home, and cooked it.

That night he dreamed a dreary dream. It seemed to him that a beautiful woman came into his room, and stood by his pillow, and began to weep. So bitterly did she weep that Sonjō felt as if his heart were being torn out while he listened. And the woman cried to him: "Why—oh! why did you kill him?—of what wrong was he guilty? . . . At Akanuma we were so happy together—and you killed him! . . . What harm did he ever do you? Do you even know what you have done?—oh! do you know what a cruel, what a wicked thing you have done? . . . Me too you have killed—for I will not live without my husband! . . . Only to tell you this I came." . . . Then again she wept aloud—so bitterly that the voice of her crying pierced into the marrow of the listener's bones;—and she sobbed out the words of this poem:

> Hi kururéba
> Sasoëshi mono wo—
> Akanuma no
> Makomo no kuré no
> Hitori-né zo uki!

"At the coming of twilight I invited him to return with me—! Now to sleep alone in the shadow of the rushes of Akanuma—ah! what misery unspeakable!"

And after having uttered these verses she exclaimed: "Ah, you do not know—you cannot know what you have done! But to-morrow, when you go to Akanuma, you will see—you will see. . . ." So saying, and weeping very piteously, she went away.

When Sonjō awoke in the morning, this dream remained so vivid in his mind that he was greatly troubled. He remembered the words: "But to-morrow, when you go to Akanuma, you will see—you will see." And he resolved to go there at once, that he might learn whether his dream was anything more than dream.

So he went to Akanuma; and there, when he came to the river-bank, he saw the female *oshidori* swimming alone. In the same moment the bird perceived Sonjō; but, instead of trying to escape, she swam straight toward him, looking at him the while in a strange fixed way. Then, with her beak, she suddenly tore open her own body, and died before the hunter's eyes. . . .

Sonjō shaved his head, and became a priest.   ]

At the end of 1901, three years before Chekhov published *The Cherry Orchard*, Lafcadio and Setsu took their customary walk to the neighboring Kobudera temple, and saw to their dismay that three giant trees had been cut down in the temple's cedar grove. The parishioners had decided to sell the woods to property developers, and the abbot was to be transferred to another temple in Tokyo. Within weeks, the hill was bare, and lots on the hillside were being sold for homes.

Lafcadio thought the family should move immediately to the Oki Islands or back to Matsue. Setsu waited a day for her husband's impetuosity to pass, then suggested that they finally build their own home, and convinced Lafcadio that a house in Nishi-Okubo—known as the Gardeners' Quarter of Tokyo—would be suitable for raising the children and, at the same time, meet Lafcadio's needs. "Well, do as you please," he said with resignation. He had only one request: "If you're going to build me a study, make it light and warm."

On her own, Setsu made designs for a house in Japanese style, and dealt with carpenters, masons, and cabinetmakers. A year later—March 1902—the house was completed, and Lafcadio was cajoled into attending the roof-raising ceremony (*tatemaé*). His name, Koizumi Yakumo, was written in Chinese characters on the main beam; and, in Shintō tradition, the carpenters chanted, clapped their hands, and raised high the roof-beam.

From the garden, the fragrant scent of plum blossom welcomed the family, as did the song of an *uguisu* perching in the bamboo grove. Setsu found the bush warbler's presence auspicious, and was overjoyed. Her husband said, "It hurts my heart. It is too pleasant to last. . . . I wonder if I can live to hear it more than three springs." Setsu replied, "My, how foolish!"

"My home will always have its atmosphere of thousands of years ago," Lafcadio declared. "But in the raw light outside, the changings are ugly and sad." In these later years he hated going out or taking a trip, since it distracted him from his writing, and when he did—to be given dinner in Yokohama, for instance, by his friend Mitchell McDonald ("That whiskey! Those cigars! That wonderful beefsteak!")—he regretted it afterward. "One thing sure," he told McDonald, "is that I shall not go down to the Grand Hotel [of which McDonald was the principal owner] again for ages to come—I wish I could venture to say 'never'—nevermore. It is one more nail in my literary coffin every time I go down."

Only once was he happy in his "detestable Tokyo," and then by accident, when he got lost one night in a labyrinth of the city's crooked streets that led serendipitously to a temple festival (*en-nichi*) with its booths of toys and representations of gods and demons. Under the light of thirty-foot lanterns, Lafcadio suddenly stopped in astonishment before the stall of a vendor of singing insects in their wooden cages, and for hours he studied and listened to the music of scores of short-lived, enchanting night singers such as grass larks, bell insects, and night crickets, in particular, the noisy *kutsuwamushi* ("the bridle-bit insect," with its green back and a yellowish-white abdomen), whose "recital" Lafcadio described: "The sound begins with a thin sharp whizzing, as of leaking steam, and slowly strengthens; then to the whizzing is suddenly added a quick dry clatter, as of castanets; and then, as the whole machinery rushes into operation, you hear, high above the whizzing and the clatter, a torrent of rapid ringing tones like the tapping of a gong. These, the last to begin, are also the first to cease; then the castanets stop; and finally the whizzing dies."

At home, Lafcadio paid little attention to the busy life of the Koizumi household. He summarily rejected appointments and overtures from foreign tourists who had read his articles and books, academic colleagues, representatives of writers' societies, and the like ("Attentions numb, paralyze, destroy every vestige of inspiration")—accepting visits only from "his" people—*natto*-sellers, street singers, pilgrims, craftsmen, and former students. He also decided, in one of his corrosive moods (in mid-1897), to leave his American publisher, Houghton Mifflin Company, accusing it of having invaded his privacy by printing, without his permission, a short biography of him as an advertisement. Six months later he signed a contract with Little, Brown and Company instead.

"I am pretty much in the position," he now reflected after leaving Houghton Mifflin, "of a book-keeper known to have once embezzled, or of a man who has been in prison, or of a prostitute who has been on the street. These are, none of them . . . *important* persons. But what keeps them in their holes? Society, Church, and public opinion—the Press. No man is too small to get the whole world's attention *if* he does certain things. Talent signifies nothing. Talent starves in the streets, and dies in the ginhouse. Talent helps no one not in some way independent of society. *Temporarily, I am* thus independent."

CHAPTER *7*

"Almost"
Japanese

IN SEVERAL SENSES, Lafcadio "died" to his former self ("debauchée," "disreputable ex-reporter") in order to become Koizumi Yakumo. He paid grateful and reverential homage to his new family's ancestors, and attempted in his daily life to embody the virtues of filial piety, loyalty, family love, and patriotism. To the race-conscious Japanese, however, even to his most respectful admirers and the members of his family, he would always be "almost" Japanese (just as he had never been entirely Greek, Irish, English, French, or American).

In his informal letters to Basil Chamberlain, Ellwood Hendrick, Mitchell McDonald, and several other friends, Lafcadio revealed that part of himself where contradictions and ambivalences coexisted and conversed. As Lafcadio once said, in a particularly Whitmanesque mood: "The largest thought accepts all, surrounds all, absorbs all,—like light itself. The ugly and the beautiful, the ignorant and the wise, the virtuous and the vile, —all come within its recognition. . . ."

In Japan, some important oppositions in Lafcadio's personal and ideological makeup actually intersected or overlapped to an extent that one could speak of him as a Western Easterner (or an Eastern Westerner) and a radical conservative (or a conservative radical). But in much of his behavior as a family man, profoundly committed to traditional ways, Lafcadio accepted a world of antinomies: Old Japan/New Japan, prudery/ sensuality, moralism/tolerance, married love/passion, creative isolation/ sociability, commitment/escape.

When Lafcadio designed his family crest for his Tokyo University identity card, he chose the emblem of a white heron with its wings down. (The original Northumberland Hearn clan spelled its name *Heron;* and the crest of the Irish Protestant branch of Lafcadio's family was also a heron: its motto, "The Heron Seeks the Heights.") In both Chinese and Japanese traditions, the heron is linked and associated with the black crow (black as a raven!) as yin is to yang, solar to lunar, light to darkness—the heron serious and silent, the crow mischievous and chattering. And in the Oriental Buddhist tradition, the heron is connected with the crane—a messenger of the gods, a sacred bird able to enter into higher states of consciousness. (In ancient Greece, moreover, the heron was sacred to Apollo as a herald of spring and light.)

Lafcadio once stated to his brother James that he always felt as if he had "two souls, each pulling a different way." In Japan, however, they seem to have been *ultimately* subsumed in his awareness that "there is no permanent individual, no constant personality: there is only phantom-self, and phantom succeeds to phantom, as undulation to undulation, over the ghostly Sea of Birth and Death." "For thousands of years," he asserted, "we have been thinking inside-out and upside-down. The only reality is One;—all that we have taken for Substance is only Shadow;—the physical is the unreal;—*and the outer-man is the ghost.*"

"You write most delightful letters," he said to Chamberlain's friend W. B. Mason, "but I haven't the faintest idea who you are. I don't know whether I ought even to try to find out. It is more charming to know one's friends as amiable ghosts thus."

In the thousands of pages of letters Lafcadio wrote in Japan to various "amiable ghosts," he displayed his multifaceted personality, ever-varying moods, and unpredictable opinions, many of which reiterated, modified, or even reversed those antinomies accepted by Koizumi Yakumo. As always, though, Lafcadio's letters served as a kind of "unconscious auto-biography," revealing the directness, moodiness, enthusiasms, willfulness, and intellectual strength of this most substantial of ghosts:

TO BASIL HALL CHAMBERLAIN. DECEMBER 1892. KUMAMOTO
I wonder if you ever heard of a strange old superstition that a *miko* [medium], or even the wife of a *Kannushi* [Shintō priest], cannot rest in the grave, but is eaten by a goblin wolf after death. The goblin comes to the grave and howls, and the corpse then rises up to be devoured, just as Southey's Old Woman of Berkeley gets up when the devil calls. It is a

superstition of the Izumo peasantry. Please don't mention my name in connection with it if you happen to speak of it to anybody else. I can't afford to write about many things in connection with rustic Shintō, which is a totally different thing from the majestic and dignified Izumo Taisha. The peasant's *Kannushi* does queer things;—primitive things—extraordinary things. But why should the peasants have so ghastly a fancy about a faith which they respect most profoundly otherwise? The origin of such a hideous story cannot be in Shintō itself, which has always respected woman. And it cannot be naturally in Buddhism which vindicates the holiness of womanhood so magnificently in the *Saddharma Pundarika*—a passage finer by far than that of Christ and the adulteress, not in its humanity, but in its spirituality. Perhaps there survives an older belief than any form of either religion we know of, attaching an idea of evil to the assumption of any sacerdotal function by women—an idea going back to that remoter age in which a priestess could exist only as a witch? What do you think?

TO ELLWOOD HENDRICK. APRIL 1893. KUMAMOTO

I think civilization is a fraud, because I don't like the hopeless struggle. If I were very rich I should perhaps think quite differently—or, what would be still more rational, try not to think at all about it. Religion under an empire preaches the divinity of autocracy; under a monarchy, the divinity of aristocracy. In this industrial epoch it is the servant of the monster business, and is paid to declare that religion is governed by God, and business by religion—"whoever says the contrary, let him be anathema!" Business has its fixed standard of hypocrisy; everything above or below that is to be denounced by the ministers of the gospel of God and business. Hence the howl about Jay Gould, who, with splendid brutal frankness, exposed to the entire universe the real laws of business— without any preaching at all—and overrode society and law and became supreme. Wherefore I hold that a statue should be erected to him. Here we have been having a newspaper fight. All the missionaries are down on "that anonymous writer" as usual. I wrote an article to prove that Gould was the grandest moral teacher of the century. Even sermons were preached in Tōkyō denouncing the writer of that article. I was accused of declaring that the end justified the means. I had not said so; but I quoted American authorities to show Gould had created and made effective the railroad-transportation system of the West; and then I quoted English financial authorities to prove that that very transportation system alone was now saving the United States from bankruptcy. The facts were unanswerable (at least by the clerics); and they proved that in order to get power to save a whole nation from ruin—Gould had to ruin a few thousand people. Wherefore I am called "immoral, low, beastly." Nobody *knows* it is I; but some suspect. I am already deemed the "moral plaguespot" of Japan by the dear missionaries. Next week I'll try them with an article on "The Abomination of Civilization." . . .

TO CHAMBERLAIN. JANUARY 1893. KUMAMOTO

I should find living away from all Europeans rather hard, if it were not for the little world I have made around me. Some of it lingers in Matsue; but there are nearly twelve here to whom I am Life and Food and other things. However intolerable anything else is, at home I enter into my little smiling world of old ways and thoughts and courtesies;—where all is soft and gentle as something seen in sleep. It is so soft, so intangibly gentle and lovable and artless, that sometimes it seems a dream only; and then a fear comes that it might vanish away. It has become Me. When I am pleased, it laughs; when I don't feel jolly, everything is silent. Thus, light and vapory as its force seems, it is a moral force, perpetually appealing to conscience. I cannot imagine what I should do away from it. It is better to enter some old Buddhist cemetery here, than moulder anywhere else. For one may at least vaguely hope the realization of the old Buddhist saying: "The relation of father and child is but one life only; yet that of husband and wife is for two, and that of master and servant for three." You know the verse, of course.

TO CHAMBERLAIN. JUNE 1893. KUMAMOTO

I see you and the Editor of the *Atlantic* are at one in condemning my use of Japanese words. Now, I can't entirely agree with either of you. As to the practical side of the question, I do. But as to the artistic, the romantic side, I don't. For me words have color, form, character; they have faces, ports, manners, gesticulations; they have moods, humours, eccentricities;—they have tints, tones, personalities. That they are unintelligible makes no difference at all. Whether you are able to speak to a stranger or not, you can't help being impressed by his appearance sometimes—by his dress—by his air—by his exotic look. He is also unintelligible, but not a whit less interesting. Nay! he is interesting BECAUSE he is unintelligible. I won't cite other writers who have felt the same way about African, Chinese, Arabian, Hebrew, Tartar, Indian, and Basque words—I mean novelists and sketch writers.

To such it has been justly observed: "The readers do not feel as you do about words. They can't be supposed to know that you think the letter A is blush-crimson, and the letter E pale sky-blue. They can't be supposed to know that you think KH wears a beard and a turban; that initial X is a mature Greek with wrinkles;—or that '—no—' has an innocent, lovable, and childlike aspect." All this is true from the critic's standpoint.

But from ours, the standpoint of—

The dreamer of dreams
To whom what is and what seems
Is often one and the same—

To us the idea is thus:

"Because people cannot see the color of words, the tints of words, the secret ghostly motions of words:

"Because they cannot hear the whispering of words, the rustling of the procession of letters, the dream-flutes and dream-drums which are thinly and weirdly played by words:

"Because they cannot perceive the pouting of words, the frowning and fuming of words, the weeping, the raging and racketing and rioting of words:

"Because they are insensible to the phosphorescing of words, the fragrance of words, the noisomeness of words, the tenderness or hardness, the dryness or juiciness of words—the interchange of values in the gold, the silver, the brass and the copper of words:

"Is that any reason why we should not try to make them hear, to make them see, to make them feel? Surely one who has never heard Wagner, cannot appreciate Wagner without study! Why should the people not be forcibly introduced to foreign words, as they were introduced to tea and coffee and tobacco?"

Unto which, the friendly reply is—"Because they won't buy your book, and you won't make any money."

And I say: "Surely I have never yet made, and never expect to make any money. Neither do I expect to write ever for the multitude. I write for beloved friends who can see color in words, can smell the perfume of syllables in blossom, can be shocked with the fine elfish electricity of words. And in the eternal order of things, words will eventually have their rights recognized by the people."

All this is heresy. But a bad reason, you will grant, is better than—etc.

Why am I writing this letter? Well, just because a new idea came to me somewhat definitely. The Japanese problem is such a huge one, that I am venturesome enough to believe you have time to listen to any ideas about it not already worn out. The idea I refer to was given me by the sight of the American newspaper of which I used to be literary editor. It comes to me filled with columns headed "Feminine Gossip," "New Fashions," "Woman in Art," "Clara Belle's Letter about Small Feet," etc., all accompanied by small outline woodcuts, representing wonderful women in wonderful dresses. The original poetry is all about love and despair. The stories are tales about enamored swains and cruel beauties. The whole thing is now nauseating to me—yet I used to think it rather refined compared with other papers. At all events it is a type of several hundred. As a type it is suggestive.

"Teacher," cry my students, "why are English novels all about love and marriage? That seems to us very strange." They say "strange." They think "indecent." Then I try to explain: "My dear lads, the world of the West is not as the world of the East. In the West, Society is not, as you know, constituted upon the same plan. A man must make his own family; the family does not make him. What you do not know, is that for the average educated man without money, life is a bitter and terrible fight—a battle in which no quarter is given. And what is the simplest and most natural thing of all in Japan—to get married—is in the West extremely difficult and dangerous. Yet all a man's life turns upon that effort. Without a wife he has no home. He seeks success, in order to be rich enough to get married. Success in life means success in marriage. And the obstacles are many and wonderful." . . . (I explain.) "Therefore English novels treat of love and marriage above all things; because these mean everything in life for the English middle classes at least; and the middle classes like these books, and make the men rich who write them well, because they sympathize with the imaginary sufferings of the lovers.—Which you don't—because you can't—and I guess you're just about right on that score."

But I know my explanation is very partial. Still, without endangering my reputation, I can't go into further particulars. The further particulars might be furnished by the American newspaper already referred to—as a type of newspaper. England has countless kindred papers. But the supreme art of the business is French—the *Charivari*, the *Figaro*, the *Petit Journal pour Rire*, etc.

What do they tell us? I think it is this: That the Western Civilization is steeped in an atmosphere of artificially created . . . passionalism. That all art and all literature open to common comprehension are directed to the Eternal Feminine. That our pleasures, the theatre, the opera, the marvels of sculpture and painting, the new musical faculty—all are shapen with a view to the stimulation of sexual idealism. Nay, the luxury of it—the voluptuousness—betrays itself in the smallest details of business or invention—from the portrait of an actress or ballet-dancer on a package of cigarettes, to the frescoes of a Government building; from a child's toy, to the bronze lamp upheld by a splendid nude at the foot of a palace stairway. If the God of the West is Money, it is only because money is the Pandarus that holds Cressida's key. In education, indeed, our object is to delay puberty and its emotions as long as possible—so as to store up force in the individual. We lie, dupe, conceal, play hypocrite for a good purpose. But when the children become men and women, they are suddenly plunged into an atmosphere full of the Eternal Feminine, and for the rest of life they can escape it only by fleeing to some less civilized country. Of the evils thus produced, nothing need be here said. They are only the accidents;—they don't explain matters.

Now your Japanese thinks it indecent even to talk about his wife, and at least impolite to talk about his children. This doesn't mean he is without affection at all. The affection is all right—but the mere mention of it, he thinks, suggests other matters—unfortunate necessities of existence. He introduces his wife to a European, simply because he has heard it is the strange and barbarous Western custom to do such things; but otherwise his women live in shadow, by themselves. They are used to it—would be unhappy or awkward if pulled out of it. He does not mention his marriage, except to a few intimates invited to the wedding; and still more rarely the birth of his child—for obvious reasons. An English novel (of the Trollope sort) would seem to him a monstrous morbid piece of nonsense. A Parisian ballet would seem to him worse than ever any Methodist minister deemed it. And he would hold at sight any Japanese *Jorō* [prostitute] more modest than the Society belle who shows her shoulders above the lace-fringe of an evening dress. His atmosphere is cool and without illusion. His artists succeed best with nature and least with man. We are all opposite. Which is the best condition for future intellectual expansion?

(I am only hazarding all this.) At present the condition of passional thought in the West does seem to me morbid, exasperating. But I think it does more than evil. It is a creative force in the highest sense. I think so. The process is slow, and accompanied with ugly accidents. But the results will perhaps be vast. All this woman-worship and sex-worship is tending to develop to a high degree certain moral qualities. As the pleasure of color has been developed out of perceptions created by appetite, so out of vague sense of physical charm a sense of spiritual charm is being evolved. The result must be rather elevating and refining at last, than gross and selfish. It seems the latter to one who looks—say at that American newspaper. But just as uncultivated minds like the force of raw bright colors, and care nothing for delicate tints—so imperfectly cultivated minds need strong coarse impulses to bestir them in emotional directions. I think the general direction is one of gentleness, nervous sympathy, generosity. There is surely a vast reserve of tenderness in even our roughest Western natures, that comes out only in the shocks of life, as fire from flint. By tenderness I don't mean simple woman-loving, sexual inclination, but something higher developed out of that more primitive loving, etc.— sensibility, comprehension, readiness to do for the weak on impulse. I can't see this in the Orient—except among the women. Did you not say that the Japanese woman preserved the purity and grace of the native tongue? Well, I think she has preserved also the whole capacity of the race for goodness—all locked up within her. . . .

And here my pessimistic epistle shall close.

TO HENDRICK. APRIL 1893. KUMAMOTO

To return to Japan and Japanese life. What do you think of the following? It happened near Kumamoto. A peasant went to consult an astrologer what to do for his mother's eyes: she had become blind. The astrologer said that she would get her sight back if she could eat a little human liver,—taken fresh and from a young body. The peasant went home crying, and told his wife. She said: "We have only one boy. He is beautiful. You can get another wife as good, or better than I, very easily, but might never be able to get another son. Therefore, you must kill me instead of the son, and give my liver to your mother." They embraced; and the husband killed her with a sword, and cut out the liver and began to cook it, when the child awoke and screamed. Neighbors and police came. In the police court, the peasant told his tale with childish frankness and cited stories from the Buddhist scriptures. The judges were moved to tears. They did not condemn the man to death;—they gave only nine years in prison. Really the man who ought to have been killed was the astrologer. And this but a few miles off from where they are teaching integral calculus, trigonometry, and Herbert Spencer! yet Western science and religion could never inspire that idolatrous self-devotion to a mother which the old ignorant peasant and his wife had. She thought it her sacred duty to die for her mother-in-law. . . .

TO CHAMBERLAIN. DECEMBER 1893. KUMAMOTO

The awful melancholy of that book of Pearson's [Charles Henry Pearson, English historian, 1830–1894] may be summed up in this, I think—"The Aspirational has passed forever out of life." It is horribly true. What made the aspirational in life? Ghosts. Some were called Gods, some Demons, some Angels;—they changed the world for man; they gave him courage and purpose and the awe of Nature that slowly changed into love;—they filled all things with a sense and motion of invisible life—they made both terror and beauty.

There are no ghosts, no angels and demons and gods: all are dead. The world of electricity, steam, mathematics, is blank and cold and void. No man can even write about it. Who can find a speck of romance in it? What are our novelists doing? Crawford must write of Italy or India or ancient Persia;—Kipling of India;—Black of remote Scotch country life;—James lives only as a marvellous psychologist, and he has to live and make his characters live on the Continent;—Howells portrays the ugliest and harshest commonplaces of a transient democracy. What great man is writing, or can write of fashionable society anything worth reading, or of modern middle life—or of the poor of cities—unless after the style of *Ginx's Baby* [1871 novel by Edward Jenkins]? No! those who write must seek their material in those parts of the world where ghosts still linger—in Italy, in Spain, in Russia, in the old atmosphere of Catholicism. The Protestant world has become bald and cold as a meeting-house. The ghosts are gone; and the results of their departure prove how real they were. The Cossacking of Europe might have one good result—that of bringing back the ghosts—with that Wind of the Spirit which moves the ocean of Russian peasant life for the gathering storm.

Sometimes I think of writing a paper to be called "The Vanishing of the Gods."

TO CHAMBERLAIN. OCTOBER 1893. KUMAMOTO

The more I read Kipling's "Rhyme of the Three Sealers," the more I am astonished at the immense power of the thing. It gains with every reading. And how little of the world's modern fiction and poetry does this! It is the sign of *true* genius,—the perfect imagination that reaches its goal by unknown methods. There is, indeed, the trouble you spoke of long ago, —that it is written in a dialect, so to speak, which may change rapidly. Still, I doubt if our rough speech changes much more rapidly than does our refined tongue. The English of the eighteenth century is not the English of today, though we understand and admire it. Kipling must last, anyhow, a hundred years,—that will make his best work classic.

But what are "sheer strakes," "chocks," "bends and butts," "cleats," and "topping-lifts"? You will confess that, though mysterious to the land-lubber, there is a blocky, bumping, raking force, even in the sound of them that tells. Yet again, *what*—oh what is a holluschickie? Is it a kite?— a *pi-yoro-yoro?* Weird and funny at once—isn't it?

And we'll go up to the wrath of God as the holluschickie *goes.*
But he'll lie down on the killing-grounds where the holluschickie *go.*

But it seems to me that, leaving the descriptive art of the thing out of the question as above all praise, Kipling reaches his supreme art in the two simple lines,—

And west you'll turn and south again, beyond the sea-fog's rim,
And tell the Yoshiwara girls to burn a stick for him. . . .

It is, of course, the very first time that any Western writer ever succeeded in making infinite poetry with that much befouled word;—there is more art in that one line than in all [Loti's] *Madame Chrysanthème.* But that isn't the wonder alone: the wonder is, that with that simplest touch, a whole world of pathos,—the whole romance and better nature of the rough sailor appears,—his rude tenderness,—his superstition,—his isola-tion,—his vague empiric education by travel, teaching him that one faith may be good as another,—his consciousness of no hope from his own by the breaking of every law, human and divine,—and fifty other things! That is sheer magic. One word more would have spoiled the effect. One word less would have rendered it impossible. And no genius—not Victor Hugo— could even have changed a word without ruining the perfect balance of the whole infinitely pathetic utterance,—the moral of it,—the poetry of it,—"the pity of it."

I won't try to praise the rest of the astonishing study,—the sudden change of feeling from anger to kindness,—the change of the *modern* man, wicked only for a reason, for a profit,—good underneath all. But one could write a book on the thing.

We were chatting about the morality of business. Now let me tell you how the question strikes an intelligent Japanese student.

"Sir, what was your opinion when you first came to our country about the old-fashioned Japanese? Please be frank with me."

"You mean the old men, who still preserve the old customs and courtesy,—men like Mr. Akizuki, the Chinese teacher?"

"Yes."

"I think they were much better men than the Japanese of today. They seemed to me like the ideals of their own gods realized. They seemed to me all that was good and noble."

"And do you still think as well of them?"

"I think better of them, if anything. The more I see the Japanese of the new generation, the more I admire the men of the old."

"But you must have, as a foreigner, also observed their defects."

"What defects?"

"Such weaknesses or faults as foreigners would observe."

"No. According as a man is more or less perfectly adapted to the society to which he belongs, so is he to be judged as a citizen and as a man. To judge a man by the standards of a society totally different to his own would not be just."

"That is true."

"Well, judged by that standard, the old-fashioned Japanese were perfect men. They represented fully all the virtues of their society. And that society was morally better than ours."

"In what respect?"

"In kindness, in benevolence, in generosity, in courtesy, in heroism, in self-sacrifice, in simple faith, in loyalty, in self-control,—in the capacity to be contented with a little,—in filial piety."

"But would those qualities you admire in the old Japanese suffice for success in Western life—practical success?"

"Why, no."

"The qualities required for practical success in a Western country are just those qualities which the old Japanese did not possess, are they not?"

"I am sorry to say they are."

"And the old Japanese society cultivated those qualities of un-

selfishness and courtesy and benevolence which you admire at the sacrifice of the individual. But Western society cultivates the individual by
a competition in mere powers—intellectual power, power of calculating
and of acting?"

"Yes."

"But in order that Japan may be able to keep her place among nations,
she *must* adopt the industrial and financial methods of the West. Her
future depends upon industry and commerce; and these cannot be developed if we continue to follow our ancient morals and manners."

"Why?"

"Not to be able to compete with the West means ruin; yet in order to
compete with the West, we must follow the methods of the West,—and
these are contrary to the old morality."

"Perhaps—"

"I do not think there is any 'perhaps.' To do any business on a large
scale, we must not be checked by the idea that we should never take any
advantage if another be injured by it. Those who are checked by emotional feeling, where no check is placed upon competition, must fail. The
law of what you call the struggle for existence is that the strong and clever
succeed, and the weak and foolish fail. But the old morality condemned
such competition."

"That is true."

"Then, sir, no matter how good the old morality may seem to be, we
can neither make any great progress in industry or commerce or finance,
nor even preserve our national independence, by following it. We must
forsake our past, and substitute law for morality."

"But it is not a good substitute."

"It seems to me that it has proved a good substitute in Western countries—England especially—if we are to judge by material progress. We will
have to learn to be moral by reason, not by emotion. Knowledge of law,
and the reasons for obeying law, must teach a rational morality of some
sort at last."

Pretty good reasoning for a Japanese boy, wasn't it? He goes to the
university next month. . . .

TO CHAMBERLAIN. MARCH 1894. KUMAMOTO

. . . I found in *Wilhelm Meister's Travels* one of these marvellous little
stories by Goethe which have a hundred different meanings. Perhaps you
know "The New Mélusine." . . . I repeat some of the facts only to suggest

one application. There was a man a fairy loved;—and she told him she must either say good-bye, or that he must become little like herself, and go to dwell with her in her father's kingdom. She made him very, very, very small, by putting a gold ring upon his finger. Then they entered into their tiny world. Everything in the palace of the fairy king was unimaginably pretty, and the man was petted greatly by the fairy-people, and had everything given to him which he could desire. He had a pretty child, too; and the old king was good to him. After a time, however, being ungrateful and selfish, he got tired of all this; he dreamed of having been a giant. He supplied himself with gold for a journey, and then managed to file the ring off his finger—which made him big again—and he ran away to spend the gold in riotous living. He did other horrible things, which you may remember. The character of the fairy was altogether Japanese—don't you think so? And the man was certainly a detestable fellow. . . .

TO CHAMBERLAIN. MARCH 1894. KUMAMOTO

Well, I read Loti all through in bed last night—and dropped asleep at last to dream of the *Venise fantasque et tremblotante.*

Before talking of the book especially I want to utter my heterodoxies and monstrosities in your ear. You will not be pleased, I fear; but truth is truth, however far it be from accepted standards.

To me the Japanese eye has a beauty which I think Western eyes have not. I have read nasty things written about Japanese eyes until I am tired of reading them. Now let me defend my seemingly monstrous proposition.

Miss Bird [Isabella Bird (1831–1904) English travel writer, author of *Unbeaten Tracks in Japan* (1880)] has well said that when one remains long in Japan, one finds one's standard of beauty changing; and the fact is true of other countries than Japan. Any *real* traveller can give similar experiences. When I show beautiful European engravings of young girls or children to Japanese, what do they say? I have done it fifty times, and whenever I was able to get a criticism, it was always the same: "The faces are nice—all but the eyes: the eyes are too big—the eyes are monstrous." We judge by our conventions. The Orient judges by its own. Who is right?

There are eyes and eyes, in all countries—ugly and beautiful. To make comparisons of beauty we must take the most beautiful types of the West and East. If we do this, I think we find the Orient is right. The most beautiful pair of eyes I ever saw—a pair that fascinated me a great deal too much, and caused me to do some foolish things in old bachelor days—were Japanese. They were not small, but very characteristically racial; the lashes were very long, and the opening also of the lids;—and the feeling they gave one was that of the eyes of a great wonderful bird of prey. There are wonderful eyes in Japan for those who can see.

The eyelid is so very peculiar that I think its form decides—more than any other characteristic of the Far Eastern races—the existence of two entirely distinct original varieties of mankind. The muscular attachments are quite different, and the lines of the lashes—indeed the whole outer anatomy.

One might ask mockingly whether to Japanese eyelids could be applied the Greek term *"charitoblepharos"* [with eyelids like the graces]. I think it could. There is a beauty of the Japanese eyelid, quite rare, but very singular—in which the lid-edge seems double, or at least marvellously grooved—and the effect is a softness and shadowiness difficult to describe.

However, it seems to me that the chief beauty of a beautiful Japanese eye is in the peculiar anatomical arrangement which characterizes it. The ball of the eye is *not* shown—the setting is totally hidden. The brown smooth skin opens quite suddenly and strangely over a moving jewel. Now in the most beautiful Western eyes the set of the ball into the skull is visible—the whole orbed form, and the whole line of the bone-socket— except in special cases. The mechanism is visible. I think that from a perfectly artistic point of view, the veiling of the mechanism is a greater feat on Nature's part. (I have seen a most beautiful pair of Chinese eyes— that I will *never* forget.)

I don't mean to make any sweeping general rule. I only mean this: "Compare the most beautiful Japanese, or Chinese eye with the most beautiful European eye, and see which suffers by comparison." I believe the true artist would say "neither." But that which least shows the *machinery behind it*—the osteological and nervous machinery—now appears to me to have the greater charm. I dare say such eyes as I speak of are not common; but beautiful eyes are common in no country that I have ever visited. . . .

TO CHAMBERLAIN. MAY 1894. KUMAMOTO
I forgot to tell you:

Today I spent an hour in reading over part of the notes taken on my first arrival, and during the first six months of 1890. Result, I asked myself: "How came you to go mad?—absolutely mad?" It was the same kind of madness as the first love of a boy.

I find I described horrible places as gardens of paradise, and horrid people as angels and divinities. How happy I must have been without knowing it! There are all my illusions facing me—on faded yellow paper. I feel my face tingle as I study some of them. Happily I had the judgment not to print many lines from them.

But—I ask myself—am I the only fool in the world? Or was I a fool at all? Or is everybody, however wise, at first deluded more or less by unfamiliar conditions when these are agreeable, the idea always being the son of the wish?

Perhaps I was right in one way. For that moment Japan was really for *me* what I thought it. To the child the world is blue and green; to the old man grey—both are right.

So with all things. Relations alone exist. The writer's danger is that of describing his own, as if they were common or permanent. Perhaps the man who comes to Japan full of hate for all things Oriental may get nearer to truth at once—though, of course, he will also make a kindred mistake.

TO CHAMBERLAIN. JULY 1894. KUMAMOTO

How touching Tolstoi is! Still, the fault of the beautiful religion of the man is simply that it is unsuited to the real order of things. Resentment, as Spencer has not hesitated to point out, is not only essential to self-preservation, but is often a moral duty. Altruistic characters may be regulated by Buddhist or Christian codes of action—but what about anti-altruistic characters, the Ape-souls and tiger-souls whose pleasure is in malice or destruction? The number is few;—but which of us has not met some, and recognized their capacity for evil? I believe the mass of humanity is good. I think every man must so think who has suffered much, and reached middle life. Nevertheless the sum of this goodness is not so preponderant that we can practically adopt either Tolstoiism or Buddhism to our Western civilization. Indeed no general course of action will suit. The dynamics of ethics must be varied according to class and time. The great fault of all religious systems is their application of a single code to many widely different conditions.—For all that, Tolstoi is certainly a light of the world,—a practical Christ in his own life. Curious that in Russia and England, in the same generation, two poets, Ruskin and Tolstoi, should have attempted to follow in practice the teaching, "Sell all thou hast, and give it to the poor." The most religious men of the nineteenth century are the infidels—the "atheists and blasphemers."

I wish you could get Minnie Hauk to sing you a *Habanera*, or the *Seguidilla* (seducing word!) from *Carmen*. I heard her sing it, and the little eddies it made in my soul still thrill.—I cannot tell how glad I was to find that Mason had not read Prosper Mérimée's *Carmen*. The opera, lovely as it is, does not give the awful poignancy of the tale—simple and clear beyond description. I am going to send it up to you, with a bundle of other things, as soon as I get back.

This reminds me of a dream I had a few months ago. I was sleeping, after reading *Carmen* for the fifth time, I think—quite a tropical afternoon it was. I entered a patio,—between lemon-colored walls,—there was a crowd and music. I saw no face in the crowd—only felt people were there;—all my eyes and soul were for a gypsy dancing in the midst:—poising, hovering, balancing, tantalizing with eyes and gestures,—and every click of the castanets went into my blood. I woke up and found the clicking of the castanets was only the ticking of the little clock,—strangely exaggerated in the heated silence of the afternoon. . . .

TO CHAMBERLAIN. SEPTEMBER 1894. KUMAMOTO

In the whole United States there is now not one single publication of the first-class entirely under liberal control. Is the case any better in England—when Frederic Harrison must write side by side with the Right Reverend Jack-in-the-Box—and an essay by Spencer must be controverted by His Grace the Archbishop of Croquemitaine—and the Gladstone Skeleton must be dragged into utterance as a respectable denunciation of Huxley's common-sense? Is the whole world going back into the dark ages again—through the mere demoralizing effect of that centralization of wealth and of conventionalism following upon the solidification or stratification of society? How much better seems to me the wild days of Mormon evan-gelization in America—of the Freelove phalansteries—of Brook Farm and the Oneida Community—of Hepworth Dixon's "Spiritual Wives"! Hum-bug, of course, but what a finely fluid aspirational condition of society the whole thing meant—even with "Mr. Sludge, the Medium" thrown in! Anything is better than the crystallization of ideas, the hardening of con-ventions, the recognized despair of thinkers to oppose the enormous weight and power of Philistinism. *"You!"*—said a Jew to me long ago (a Jew with Heine's soul, and therefore now dead and double-damned)— *"You* fight society. Oh, you fly! the elephant's foot will crush you *without feeling you."* What matter! In those days being supremely an ass as well as a fly, I thought I could overturn the universe. I was a new Archimedes: the lever was enthusiasm! all radicals were my brothers, and had I been in Russia I might have tried to blow up the Czar. . . .

Thinking over the matter, I cannot help admiring the damned Jesuits. There race-feeling is trampled out of a man's soul;—there the conventions of society are subjected utterly to one spiritual though fanatical idea; —there is religious democracy—equality—fraternity;—there no moral question is caught up as a hypocrite's mask for race-hate. I almost wish I could believe, and hie me to a monastery, or preach Rome on the banks of the Amazon.

Oh! this is a blue letter—and you have been so kind—sending telegrams and everything! Never mind, I'll try to make it up to you some day. I am going to try to flee soon.

TO CHAMBERLAIN. OCTOBER 1894. KUMAMOTO

What a book I could NOW write about a Roman Catholic country, like Mexico, after having lived in Japan. In order to write well about Catholicism, one must have studied paganism *outside of it.* The whole poetry of the thing then appears. Who can really feel the poetry of the Bible except the man who is not a Christian? Well, isn't it the same way with other matters? Roman Catholicism in some Latin countries—with its vast world of ghosts, saints, evil and good spirits at each man's elbow—its visions, its miracles, its skulls and bones enshrined in silver and gold—its cruelties and consolations—its lust-exasperating asceticisms that create temptations—surely to understand it all one must have felt either the life of the pagan or polytheistic Orient, or understand profoundly the polytheism of the antique West. A book on Latin life—studied through polytheistic feeling, sympathetic feeling—would certainly be a novelty. Strange sensations might be evoked—new even to the nineteenth century.

TO CHAMBERLAIN. NOVEMBER 1894. KOBE

I am glad you agree about the Italian and French character—the depth, subtlety, and amazing latent power of the former; the Greek cast of the latter. Yes, I don't think we should disagree much—except as to my firm conviction of the artistic and moral value of sensuality. You know in this nineteenth century we are beginning to make war upon even intellectual sensuality, the pleasure in emotional music, the pleasure in physical grace as a study, the pleasure in colored language and musical periods. I doubt if this is right. The puritanism of intellect is cultivated to the gain of certain degrees of power, but also to the hardening of character,— ultimately tending to absolute selfishness and fixity of mental habit. Too deeply fixed in the cause of life are the pleasures of sense to be weeded out without injury to the life-centres themselves and to all the emotions springing from them. We cannot attack the physical without attacking the moral; for evolutionally all the higher intellectual faculties have their origin in the development of the physical. . . .

TO CHAMBERLAIN. MARCH 1895. KOBE

I had a sensation the other day, though, which I want to talk to you about. I felt as if I hated Japan unspeakably, and the whole world seemed not worth living in, when there came two women to the house, to sell ballads. One took her *samisen* [banjolike instrument] and sang; and people crowded into the tiny yard to hear. Never did I listen to anything sweeter. All the sorrow and beauty, all the pain and the sweetness of life thrilled and quivered in that voice; and the old first love of Japan and of things Japanese came back, and a great tenderness seemed to fill the place like a haunting. I looked at the people, and I saw they were nearly all weeping, and snuffing; and though I could not understand the words, I could feel the pathos and the beauty of things. Then, too, for the first time, I noticed that the singer was blind. Both women were almost surprisingly ugly, but the voice of the one that sang was indescribably beautiful; and she sang as peasants and birds and *semi* sing, which is nature and is divine. They were wanderers both. I called them in, and treated them well, and heard their story. It was not romantic at all,—small-pox, blindness, a sick husband (paralyzed) and children to care for. I got two copies of the ballad, and enclose one. . . .

TO CHAMBERLAIN. SEPTEMBER 1895. KOBE

Work with me is a pain—no pleasure till it is done. It is not voluntary; it is not agreeable. It is forced by necessity. The necessity is a curious one. The mind, in my case, eats itself when unemployed. Reading, you might suggest, would employ it. No: my thoughts wander, and the gnawing goes on just the same. What kind of gnawing? Vexation and anger and imaginings and recollections of unpleasant things said or done. *Unless somebody does or says something horribly mean to me, I can't do certain kinds of work,*—the tiresome kinds, that compel a great deal of thinking. The exact force of a hurt I can measure at the time of receiving it: "This will be over in six months," "This I shall have to fight for two years," "This will be remembered longer." When I begin to think about the matter afterwards, then I rush to work. I write page after page of vagaries, metaphysical, emotional, romantic,—throw them aside. Then next day, I go to work rewriting them. I rewrite and rewrite them till they begin to define and arrange themselves into a whole,—and the result is an essay; and the editor of the *Atlantic* writes, "It is a veritable illumination,"—and no mortal man knows why, or how it was written,—not even I myself,—or what it cost to write it. Pain is therefore to me of exceeding value betimes; and everybody who does me a wrong indirectly does me as right. I wonder if anybody else works on this plan. The benefit of it is that a *habit* is forming,—a habit of studying and thinking in a way I should otherwise have been too lazy-minded to do. But whenever I begin to forget one burn, new caustic from some unexpected quarter is poured into my brain: then the new pain forces other work. It strikes me as being possibly a peculiar morbid condition. If it is, I trust that some day the power will come to do something really extraordinary—I mean very unique. What is the good of having a morbid sensitive spot, if it cannot be utilized to some purpose worth achieving?

There was a funny suicide here the other day. A boy of seventeen threw himself on the railroad track and was cut to pieces by a train. He left a letter to his employer, saying that the death of the employer's little son had made the world dark for him. The child would have nobody to play with: so, he said, "I shall go to play with him. But I have a little sister of six;—I pray you to take care of her."

TO ERNEST FENOLLOSA. DECEMBER 1898. TOKYO

My Dear Professor [Ernest Fenollosa (1853–1908), American art historian, poet, curator, professor at Tokyo University]—I have been meditating, and after the meditation I came to the conclusion not to visit your charming new home again—not at least before the year 1900. I suppose that I am a beast and an ape; but I nevertheless hope to make you understand.

The situation makes me think of Béranger's burthen,—*Vive nos amis les ennemis!* My friends are much more dangerous than my enemies. These latter—with infinite subtlety—spin webs to keep me out of places where I hate to go,—and tell stories of me to people whom it would be vanity and vexation to meet;—and they help me so much by their unconscious aid that I almost love them. They help me to maintain the isolation indispensable to quiet regularity of work, and the solitude which is absolutely essential to thinking upon such subjects as I am now engaged on. Blessed be my enemies, and forever honored all them that hate me!

But my friends!—ah! my friends! They speak so beautifully of my work; they *believe* in it; they say they want more of it,—and yet they would destroy it! They do not know what it costs,—and they would break the wings and scatter the featherdust, even as the child that only wanted to caress the butterfly. And they speak of communion and converse and sympathy and friendship,—all of which are indeed precious things to others, but mortally deadly to me,—representing the breaking-up of habits of industry, and the sin of disobedience to the Holy Ghost,—against whom sin shall not be forgiven,—either in this life, or in the life to come.

And they say,—Only a day,—just an afternoon or an evening. But *each* of them says this thing. And the sum of the days in these holidays—the days inevitable—are somewhat more than a week in addition. A week of work dropped forever into the Abyss of what might-have-been! Therefore I wish rather that I were lost upon the mountains, or cast away upon a rock, than in this alarming city of Tōkyō,—where a visit, and the forced labour of the university, are made by distance even as one and the same thing.

Now if I were to go down to your delightful little house, with my boy, —and see him kindly treated,—and chat with you about eternal things,— and yield to the charm of old days (when I must confess that you fascinated me not a little),—there is no saying what the consequences to me might eventually become. Alas! I can afford friends only on paper,—I can occasionally write,—I can get letters that give me joy; but visiting is out of the possible. I must not even *think* about other people's kind words and kind faces, but work,—work,—work,—while the Scythe is sharpening within vision. Blessed again, I say, are those that don't like me, for they do not fill my memory with thoughts and wishes contrary to the purpose of the æons and the Eternities!

When a day passes in which I have not written—much is my torment. Enjoyment is not for me,—excepting in the completion of work. But I have not been the loser by my visits to you both—did I not get that wonderful story? And so I have given you more time than any other person or persons in Tōkyō. But now—through the seasons—I must again disappear. Perhaps *le jeu ne vaudra pas la chandelle;* nevertheless I have some faith as to ultimate results.

Faithfully, with every most grateful and kindly sentiment,

Lafcadio Hearn

TO ERNEST CROSBY. AUGUST 1904. TOKYO

Dear Mr. Crosby [Ernest Crosby, American university student]—A namesake of yours, a young lieutenant in the United States Army, first taught me, about twenty years ago, how to study Herbert Spencer. To that Crosby I shall always feel a very reverence of gratitude; and I shall always find myself inclined to seek the good opinion of any man bearing the name of Crosby.

I received recently a copy of *The Whim* [a university journal] containing some strictures upon the use of the word "regeneration," in one of my articles, as applied to the invigorating and developing effects of militancy in the history of human societies. I am inclined to agree with you that the word was ill-chosen; but it seems to me that your general attitude upon the matter is not in accordance with evolutional truth. . . .

The history of social evolution, I think, amply proves that the higher conditions of civilization have been reached, and could have been reached, only through the discipline of militancy. Until human nature becomes much more developed than it is now, and the sympathies incomparably more evolved, wars will probably continue; and however much we may detest and condemn war as moral crime, it will be scarcely reasonable to declare that its results are purely evil,—certainly not more reasonable than to assert that to knock down a robber is equally injurious to the moral feelings of the robber and to the personal interest of the striker. As for "re-generation"—the Reformation, the development of European Protestantism and of intellectual liberty, the French Revolution, the Independence of the United States (to mention only a few instances of progress), were rendered possible only by war. As for Japan—immediately after her social organization had been dislocated by outside pressure,—and at a time when serious disintegrations seemed likely,—the results of the war with China were certainly invigorating. National self-confidence was strengthened, national discords extinguished, social disintegrations checked, the sentiment of patriotism immensely developed. To understand these things, of course, it is necessary to understand the Japanese social organization. What holds true of one form of society, as regards the evil of war, does not necessarily hold true of another.

Yours faithfully,

Lafcadio Hearn.

I have reopened the envelope to acknowledge your interesting sketch of Edward Carpenter [English poet, disciple of Walt Whitman, advocate of "The New Thought"]. . . . What an attractive personality.

But I fear that I must shock you by my declaration of non-sympathy with much of the work of contemporary would-be reformers. They are toiling for socialism; and socialism will come. It will come very quietly and gently, and tighten about nations as lightly as a spider's web; and then there will be revolutions! Not sympathy and fraternity and justice—but a Terror in which no man will dare to lift his voice.

No higher condition of human freedom ever existed than what America enjoyed between—let us say, 1870 and 1885. To effect higher conditions, a higher development of human nature would have been necessary. Where have American liberties now gone? A free press has ceased to exist. Within another generation publishers' syndicates will decide what the public shall be allowed to read. A man can still print his thoughts in a book, though not in any periodical of influence; within another twenty years he will write only what he is told to write. It is a pleasure to read the brave good things sometimes uttered in prints like the *Conservator* or *The Whim;* but those papers are but the candlesticks in which free thought now makes its last flickering. In the so-called land of freedom men and women are burnt at the stake in the presence of Christian churches—for the crime of belonging to another race. The stake reëstablished for the vengeance of race-hatred today, may tomorrow be maintained for the vengeance of religious hate—mocking itself, of course, under some guise of moral zeal. Competition will soon be a thing of the past; and the future will be to your stock-companies, trusts, and syndicates. The rule of the many will be about as merciful as a calculating-machine, and as moral as a lawn-mower. What socialism means really no one seems to know or care. It will mean the most insufferable oppression that ever weighed upon mankind.

Here are gloomy thoughts for you! You see that I cannot sympathize with the Whitmanesque ideal of democracy. That ideal was the heart-felt expression of a free state that has gone by. It was in itself a generous dream. But social tendencies, inevitable and irresistible, are now impelling the dreamers to self-destruction. The pleasure that in other times one could find in the literature of humanity, of brotherhood, of pity, is numbed to-day by perception of the irresistible drift of things.

TO SETSU. JULY-AUGUST 1904. YAIZU

[Although Lafcadio had not mastered Japanese well enough to read a Japanese newspaper, he had learned enough of the *kana* sound syllabary to write simple notes and letters to his wife.]

Little Mamma—Today we have not much sunlight, but I and Kazuo swam as usual. Kazuo played a torpedo in the water. [Lafcadio is referring to Kazuo's pulling his legs from under the water while swimming.] He is growing clever in swimming, to my delight. We had a long walk yesterday. We bought a little ball and bell for the cat whose life I had saved and brought home. The stone-cutter is showing me his design of the Jizō's face. Shall I let him carve the name of Kazuo Koizumi somewhere on the idol? I can see how glad the Yaizu [fishing village on Suruga Bay where members of the Koizumi family spent several summers] people would be to see the new idol.

We have too many fleas here. Please, bring some flea-powder when you come. But this little delightful cat makes us forget the fleas. She is really funny. We call her Hinoko.

Plenty of kisses to Suzuko and Kiyoshi from

                    Papa

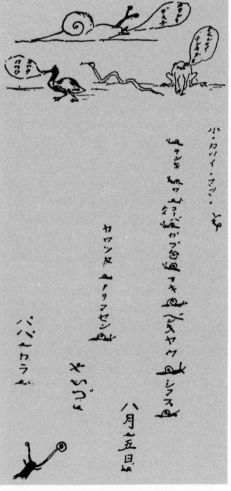

AN EXAMPLE OF HEARN'S
LETTER-WRITING TO HIS WIFE

Little Mamma,—Yesterday it was so hot; the thermometer rose to ninety-one degrees. However, the winds blew from the sea at night. And this morning the waves are so high, I only take a walk. Otoyo gave the boys plenty of pears. Last evening, Kazuo and Iwao went to a shooting gallery for fun. We drank soda and ginger ale, and also ate ice.

Iwao has finished his first reader; it seems that learning is not hard for his little head at all. He studied a great deal here. And he is learning from Mr. Niimi how to write Japanese characters.

Just this moment I received your big letter. I am very glad to hear how you treated the snake you mentioned. You were right not allowing the girls to kill it. They only fear, as they don't understand that it never does any harm. I believe it must be a friend of Kami-sama in our bamboo bush.

Mr. Papa and others wish to see Mamma's sweet face. Good words to everybody at home.

Yakumo

Little Mamma,—Your welcome letter at hand. It reached me this morning to my delight, and I can explain my joy with it in my Japanese. You must never think of any danger which might occur to your boy; I hope you do not worry about him. I haven't gone to the sea at night this year yet. Otokichi [Lafcadio's landlord in Yaizu] and Niimi [one of Lafcadio's live-in students] take good care of Kazuo. He is perfectly safe, although he often swims in deep water. He is so afraid of the jelly-fishes this summer, but he swims and plays all the same. It was such a lovely thing, this charm of the Narita temple. I feel lonely sometimes; I wish I could see your sweet face. It is difficult to sleep on account of the thick fleas. But as I have a delightful swim in the morning, I usually forget the misery of the night. I take a little hand bath in a ridiculously little tub for the last two or three evenings.

Good words to everybody at home from

Papa

Little Mamma,—Yesterday we went to Wada, where we had our lunch; and there I taught Kazuo. He was delighted to catch the crabs. Iwao is beginning to learn how to swim. The house at Wada has been mended a little. The tea we had there is always good; and I am told that the tea is homemade, which might be the reason of its excellence. Fuji was seen clearly last evening. We cannot swim this morning, as the sea is so high.

It was so hot last night we could not shut the doors. But the weather is always good. Iwao let his crabs walk on the roofs of Otokichi's house; and they walked and walked. During the night those crabs tried to bite into the box of our soap, but it was beyond their power to open the tin cover. How sorry! From

Papa

Little Mamma Sama,—Your lovely letter to hand. I am glad to hear that the carpenters and masons are at work. This morning the sea was very rough, and I could not go for swimming. So we intend to take walk to Wada with Otokichi.

Do you remember that little lame girl in this village? What a pity it was to see her! She has now much grown up. Then the boy in our next-door neighbor has become as big as I was and goes to school. He learns very well. It is two years since. Isn't it wonderfully rapid that all young people grow up?

Iwao will finish his first English book very soon; there but remain *4 or 5 pages* more to be studied. I have ordered Kazuo to write these underlined letters.

I am giving just a moderate work to Kazuo and he does it well. It is just the reviewing, not the new lesson. When we return to Tokyo, I shall give him new lessons. At present he is diligent in penmanship, letter-writing, writing his diary, and English reading, so I do not press upon him. Nor do I force Iwao, for he does his half an hour's study very well. It is simply lovely to see them learn well.

We have collected a great number of pebbles and put them on our window-sill. Every day Papa's pocket in the sleeve is filled with pebbles. What lovely, innocent, and pitiable creatures the children are!

Good-bye! and looking forward to the time of seeing Mamma's lovely face,

Koizumi Yakumo

Little Mamma,—*Gomen, gomen:* [Forgive me] I thought only to give a little joy as I hoped. The Jizō I wrote you about is not the thing you will find in the graveyards; but it is the Jizō who shall guard and pacify the seas. It is not a sad kind; but you do not like my idea, so I have given up my project. It was only Papa's foolish thought. However, poor Jizō-sama wept bitterly when it heard of your answer to me. I said to it, "I cannot help it, as Mamma San doubted your real nature, and thinks that you are a graveyard keeper. I know that you are the savior of seas and sailors." The Jizō is crying even now.

Gomen, gomen:
"The Jizō idol is shedding stone-tears."

Papa]

CHAPTER 8

Restless
Ghost

A T T H E E N D of 1902, Lafcadio suffered a hemorrhage from a burst blood vessel in his throat. He had previously come down with severe bronchitis, and experienced mild outbreaks of malaria, and he had been told by a doctor that he had a serious case of hardening of the arteries—news which he had kept from his family. At fifty-two, Lafcadio found his years of hard living on the streets of London, Cincinnati, and New Orleans were taking their toll. He recovered from his hemorrhage, but he now walked more slowly and with a slight stoop, was overweight and out of condition, and his gray hair and mustache were beginning to turn white. "In other words," he informed "Dad" Watkin, "I'm getting down the shady side of the hill,—and the horizon before me is already darkening, and the winds blowing out of it, cold."

On March 5, 1903, he was forced out of Tokyo University on the grounds that as a Japanese citizen, he was not entitled to a "foreigner's salary." (In fact, the new president of the university, a nationalist, wanted to rid the institution of foreigners.) His unhappy students protested, but to no avail. He then asked for at least the paid sabbatical year that was due him after his service of seven years. The request was denied. To Lafcadio, Japanese bureaucrats and officials had "no souls." As he had once commented to Chamberlain: "Imagine people having no sentiment of light—of blue—of infinity!"

Now he began to recall his childhood, writing a series of reminiscences about his years in Dublin and his summer vacations in Ireland and Wales. After a silence of almost eight years, he renewed a correspondence with

Elizabeth Bisland, informing her that he often dreamt of seeing her again, "—even for a moment; and to hear you speak (in some one of the Myriad Voices), would be such a memory for me. And you would let me 'walk about gently, touching things'?" And sometimes he thought of his long-lost mother:

⟦ It has been said that men fear death much as the child cries at entering the world, being unable to know what loving hands are waiting to receive it. Certainly this comparison will not bear scientific examination. But as a happy fancy it is beautiful, even for those to whom it can make no religious appeal whatever,—those who must believe that the individual mind dissolves with the body, and that an eternal continuance of person-ality could only prove an eternal misfortune. It is beautiful, I think, be-cause it suggests, in so intimate a way, the hope that to larger knowledge the Absolute will reveal itself as mother-love made infinite. The imagining is Oriental rather than Occidental; yet it accords with a sentiment vaguely defined in most of our Western creeds. Through ancient grim conceptions of the Absolute as Father, there has gradually been infused some later and brighter dream of infinite tenderness—some all-transfiguring hope created by the memory of Woman as Mother; and the more that races evolve toward higher things, the more Feminine becomes their idea of a God.

Conversely, this suggestion must remind even the least believing that we know of nothing else, in all the range of human experience, so sacred as mother-love,—nothing so well deserving the name of divine. Mother-love alone could have enabled the delicate life of thought to unfold and to endure upon the rind of this wretched little planet: only through that supreme unselfishness could the nobler emotions ever have found strength to blossom in the brain of man;—only by help of mother-love could the higher forms of trust in the Unseen ever have been called into existence.

But musings of this kind naturally lead us to ask ourselves emotional questions about the mysteries of Whither and Whence. Must the evolu-tionist think of mother-love as a merely necessary result of material affin-ities,—the attraction of the atom for the atom? Or can he venture to assert, with ancient thinkers of the East, that all atomic tendencies are shapen by one eternal moral law, and that some are in themselves divine, being manifestations of the Four Infinite Feelings? . . . What wisdom can decide for us? And of what avail to know our highest emotions divine,—since the race itself is doomed to perish? When mother-love shall have wrought its uttermost for humanity, will not even that uttermost have been in vain?

At first thought, indeed, the inevitable dissolution must appear the blackest of imaginable tragedies,—tragedy made infinite! Eventually our planet must die: its azure ghost of air will shrink and pass, its seas dry up, its very soil perish utterly, leaving only a universal waste of sand and stone—the withered corpse of a world. Still for a time this mummy will turn about the sun, but only as the dead moon wheels now across our nights,—one face forever in scorching blaze, the other in icy darkness. So will it circle, blank and bald as a skull; and like a skull will it bleach and crack and crumble, ever drawing nearer and yet more near to the face of its flaming parent, to vanish suddenly at last in the cyclonic lightning of his breath. One by one the remaining planets must follow. Then will the mighty star himself begin to fail—to flicker with ghastly changing colors—to crimson toward his death. And finally the monstrous fissured cinder of him, hurled into some colossal sun-pyre, will be dissipated into vapor more tenuous than the dream of the dream of a ghost. . . .

What, then, will have availed the labor of the life that was,—the life effaced without one sign to mark the place of its disparition in the illimitable abyss? What, then, the worth of mother-love, the whole dead world of human tenderness, with its sacrifices, hopes, memories,—its divine delights and diviner pains,—its smiles and tears and sacred caresses,—its countless passionate prayers to countless vanished gods?

Such doubts and fears do not trouble the thinker of the East. Us they disturb chiefly because of old wrong habits of thought, and the consequent blind fear of knowing that what we have so long called Soul belongs, not to Essence, but to Form. . . . Forms appear and vanish in perpetual succession; but the Essence alone is Real. Nothing real can be lost, even in the dissipation of a million universes. Utter destruction, everlasting death,—all such terms of fear have no correspondence to any truth but the eternal law of change. Even forms can perish only as waves pass and break: they melt but to swell anew,—nothing can be lost. . . .

In the nebulous haze of our dissolution will survive the essence of all that has ever been in human life,—the units of every existence that was or is, with all their affinities, all their tendencies, all their inheritance of forces making for good or evil, all the powers amassed through myriad generations, all energies that ever shaped the strength of races;—and times innumerable will these again be orbed into life and thought. Transmutations there may be; changes also made by augmentation or diminution of affinities, by subtraction or addition of tendencies; for the dust of us will then have been mingled with the dust of other countless worlds and of their peoples. But nothing essential can be lost. We shall inevitably bequeath our part to the making of the future cosmos—to the substance out of which another intelligence will slowly be evolved. Even as we must have inherited something of our psychic being out of numberless worlds dissolved, so will future humanities inherit, not from us alone, but from millions of planets still existing.

For the vanishing of our world can represent, in the disparition of a universe, but one infinitesimal detail of the quenching of thought: the peopled spheres that must share our doom will exceed for multitudes the visible lights of heaven.

Yet those countless solar fires, with their viewless millions of living planets, must somehow reappear: again the wondrous Cosmos, self-born as self-consumed, must resume its sidereal whirl over the deeps of the eternities. And the love that strives forever with death shall rise again, through fresh infinitudes of pain, to renew the everlasting battle.

The light of the mother's smile will survive our sun;—the thrill of her kiss will last beyond the thrilling of stars;—the sweetness of her lullaby will endure in the cradle-songs of worlds yet unevolved;—the tenderness of her faith will quicken the fervor of prayers to be made to the hosts of another heaven,—to the gods of a time beyond Time. And the nectar of her breasts can never fail: that snowy stream will still flow on, to nourish the life of some humanity more perfect than our own, when the Milky Way that spans our night shall have vanished forever out of Space.

("REVERY")]

Feeling insecure about his position in Japan, Lafcadio considered, with trepidation, accepting lecturing offers from Cornell University and the University of London. Neither worked out, but he managed to live off the royalties of his twelve books on Japan, which were being published in America and Europe. He also accepted, with gratitude but little enthusiasm, a teaching position at the privately endowed Waseda University. For the first time, he stopped reading newspapers ("so that my soul find rest from fury"), and he avoided almost all social contacts. He even disconnected his friendship with Basil Chamberlain over a slighting comment by Chamberlain about Herbert Spencer and Chamberlain's passing remark on another occasion that Lafcadio could "never be a ladies' man," which the latter took as a disparaging reference to his physical appearance.

Lafcadio concentrated his diminishing energies on his work. Apart from completing an essay or a story, his only joys were watching his children grow up, observing the snakes, toads, and other creatures in his garden, and in particular listening to the song of a beloved insect musician he had bought for twelve cents in the market:

His cage is exactly two Japanese inches high and one inch and a half wide: its tiny wooden door, turning upon a pivot, will scarcely admit the tip of my little finger. But he has plenty of room in that cage,—room to walk, and jump, and fly; for he is so small that you must look very carefully through the brown-gauze sides of it in order to catch a glimpse of him. I have always to turn the cage round and round, several times, in a good light, before I can discover his whereabouts; and then I usually find him resting in one of the upper corners,—clinging, upside down, to his ceiling of gauze.

Imagine a cricket about the size of an ordinary mosquito,—with a pair of antennae much longer than his own body, and so fine that you can distinguish them only against the light. *Kusa-Hibari*, or "Grass-Lark," is the Japanese name of him; and he is worth in the market exactly twelve cents: that is to say, very much more than his weight in gold. Twelve cents for such a gnat-like thing! . . .

By day he sleeps or meditates, except while occupied with the slice of fresh egg-plant or cucumber which must be poked into his cage every morning. . . . To keep him clean and well fed is somewhat troublesome: could you see him, you would think it absurd to take any pains for the sake of a creature so ridiculously small.

But always at sunset the infinitesimal soul of him awakens: then the room begins to fill with a delicate and ghostly music of indescribable sweetness,—a thin, thin silvery rippling and trilling as of tiniest electric bells. As the darkness deepens, the sound becomes sweeter,—sometimes swelling till the whole house seems to vibrate with the elfish resonance,— sometimes thinning down into the faintest imaginable thread of a voice. But loud or low, it keeps a penetrating quality that is weird. . . . All night the atomy thus sings: he ceases only when the temple bell proclaims the hour of dawn.

Now this tiny song is a song of love,—vague love of the unseen and unknown. It is quite impossible that he should ever have seen or known, in this present existence of his. Not even his ancestors, for many generations back, could have known anything of the night-life of the fields, or the amorous value of song. They were born of eggs hatched in a jar of clay, in the shop of some insect-merchant; and they dwelt thereafter only in cages. But he sings the song of his race as it was sung a myriad years ago, and as faultlessly as if he understood the exact significance of every note. Of course he did not learn the song. It is a song of organic memory,—deep, dim memory of other quintillions of lives, when the ghost of him shrilled at night from the dewy grasses of the hills. Then that song brought him love—and death. He has forgotten all about death; but he remembers the love. And therefore he sings now—for the bride that will never come.

So that his longing is unconsciously retrospective: he cries to the dust of the past,—he calls to the silence and the gods for the return of time. . . . Human lovers do very much the same thing without knowing it. They call their illusion an Ideal; and their Ideal is, after all, a mere shadowing of race-experience, a phantom of organic memory. The living present has very little to do with it. . . . Perhaps this atomy also has an ideal, or at least the rudiment of an ideal; but, in any event, the tiny desire must utter its plaint in vain.

The fault is not altogether mine. I had been warned that if the creature were mated, he would cease to sing and would speedily die. But, night after night, the plaintive, sweet, unanswered trilling touched me like a reproach,—became at last an obsession, an affliction, a torment of conscience; and I tried to buy a female. It was too late in the season; there were no more *kusa-hibari* for sale,—either males or females. The insect-merchant laughed and said, "He ought to have died about the twentieth day of the ninth month." (It was already the second day of the tenth month.) But the insect-merchant did not know that I have a good stove in my study, and keep the temperature at above 75° F. Wherefore my grass-lark still sings at the close of the eleventh month, and I hope to keep him alive until the Period of Greatest Cold. However, the rest of his generation are probably dead: neither for love nor money could I now find him a mate. And were I to set him free in order that he might make the search for himself, he could not possibly live through a single night, even if fortunate enough to escape by day the multitude of his natural enemies in the garden,—ants, centipedes, and ghastly earth-spiders.

Last evening—the twenty-ninth of the eleventh month—an odd feeling came to me as I sat at my desk: a sense of emptiness in the room. Then I became aware that my grass-lark was silent, contrary to his wont. I went to the silent cage, and found him lying dead beside a dried-up lump of egg-plant as gray and hard as a stone. Evidently he had not been fed for three or four days; but only the night before his death he had been singing wonderfully,—so that I foolishly imagined him to be more than usually contented. My student, Aki, who loves insects, used to feed him; but Aki had gone into the country for a week's holiday, and the duty of caring for the grass-lark had developed upon Hana, the housemaid. She is not sympathetic, Hana the housemaid. She says that she did not forget the mite,—but there was no more egg-plant. And she had never thought of substituting a slice of onion or of cucumber! . . . I spoke words of reproof to Hana the housemaid, and she dutifully expressed contrition. But the fairy-music has stopped; and the stillness reproaches; and the room is cold, in spite of the stove.

Absurd! . . . I have made a good girl unhappy because of an insect half the size of a barley grain! The quenching of that infinitesimal life troubles me more than I could have believed possible. . . . Of course, the mere habit of thinking about a creature's wants—even the wants of a cricket— may create, by insensible degrees, an imaginative interest, an attachment of which one becomes conscious only when the relation is broken. Be-sides, I had felt so much, in the hush of the night, the charm of the delicate voice,—telling of one minute existence dependent upon my will and selfish pleasure, as upon the favor of a god,—telling me also that the atom of ghost in the tiny cage, and the atom of ghost within myself, were forever but one and the same in the deeps of the Vast of being. . . . And then to think of the little creature hungering and thirsting, night after night, and day after day, while the thoughts of his guardian deity were turned to the weaving of dreams! . . . How bravely, nevertheless, he sang on to the very end,—an atrocious end, for he had eaten his own legs! . . . May the gods forgive us all,—especially Hana the housemaid!

Yet, after all, to devour one's own legs for hunger is not the worst that can happen to a being cursed with the gift of song. There are human crickets who must eat their own hearts in order to sing.

("KUSA-HIBARI")]

On September 19, 1904, Setsu entered her husband's study to find him walking around the room with his hands on his chest.

"Are you not well?" she asked him.

"I have a new kind of sickness," he said.

"What kind?"

"Sickness of heart, I think."

"I think you worry too much," Setsu told him. "You had better rest quietly."

But she immediately sent a *kuruma* for the family physician, then went back to minister to her husband. Lying down, Lafcadio looked at her and declared: "If I die, do not weep. Buy a little urn; you can find one for three or four *sen*. Put my bones in it, and bury it near a quiet temple in the country. I shall not like it if you cry. Amuse the children and play cards with them—how much better I shall enjoy that!"

Setsu begged that he not say such sad things.

"I am very serious. Honestly, from my heart," he told her.

Then, after a few minutes, he stood up and said his pain was completely gone and that he wanted a glass of whiskey, which he raised to his lips and cheerily proclaimed: "I shall not die."

The doctor arrived, examined the patient, said there was nothing to worry about, and exchanged some jokes with the *Sensei*, who, his wife observed, was being uncharacteristically sociable.

At half-past six on the morning of September 26, Setsu greeted her husband in the study. "I had a very unusual dream last night," he told her in a peculiar and soft tone of voice, as if he were still in a dream. "I traveled for a very long distance . . . not a journey in Europe or in Japan—it was a strange place."

Kazuo, who was then ten years old, entered the study. "I went to father as usual," he later recalled, "to say, 'Papa, now I am going to school—goodbye'; but this time, without knowing what I was saying, I said instead, 'Good night, pleasant dreams.' Father replied, 'The same to you, darling, good night.' . . . Mother, hearing us, scolded and said, 'Why, it's morning.' Father and I looked at each other and laughed."

That evening after supper, Lafcadio confided to Setsu that the "trouble" was beginning again. He walked around with his hands on his chest; then, at her suggestion, he lay down on his *futon* and said to her, *"Ah, byōki no tamé"* (Ah, on account of sickness). He closed his eyes, and his ghost departed.

Setsu Koizumi once remarked: "I may name again some things that Hearn liked extremely—sunsets, summer, the sea, swimming, banana trees, cryptomerias (the *sugi,* the Japanese cedar), lonely cemeteries, insects, *Kwaidan* (ghostly tales), Urashima, and *Horai* (songs). . . . He was fond of beefsteak and plum-pudding, and enjoyed smoking. He disliked liars, abuse of the weak, Prince Albert coats, white shirts, the City of New York, and many other things."

Lafcadio's widow decided to hold the funeral at the Kobudera temple, in its now suburban setting. The old abbot, wearing gold brocade and a cap, returned to officiate at the Buddhist burial service. In attendance were forty professors, a hundred students, several foreign admirers of the writer's work, and a white-robed Setsu and her children—a multitude that would have *immediately* sent a living Lafcadio into the afterlife!

Eight Buddhist priests chanted from the chapter of Kannon in the *Hokkekyo.* Kazuo was the first to offer incense to his father's spirit, and a group of former students presented a laurel wreath to his memory. After the service, Otokichi, Lafcadio's summer landlord in the village of Yaizu, was given permission to assist with the gathering of the bones after the cremation of the *Sensei*'s body. "While muttering Buddhist prayers," Kazuo noted with an unflinching sense of grotesque detail that would have delighted the onetime journalist from Cincinnati, "and picking up father's bones (two persons picking up the same bone with unmated chopsticks), Otokichi suddenly remarked, 'Here is something like the cover of *sazae* (top-shell), round and flat. What is it?' he asked of the crematory man. 'That is the knee-cap—commonly called *hiza hozo.*' When Otokichi heard this, 'He-he-i, is that so? Then with this, *Sensei-sama* moved his leg and swam in our sea until just a little while ago—eh?' So saying, he wiped his eyes with his blue towel to brush away the tears."

"Had there been a cemetery with walls overgrown with weeds," Setsu remarked, "it would have been an ideal resting-place for Hearn's body. But such a place was hard to find quickly." Lafcadio's bones were therefore buried in the Zoshigaya Cemetery, with its conventional straight graveled paths and formal plots, in the northern part of Tokyo.

Today, under maple and plane trees and sheltered by evergreens transplanted from Setsu's garden, the grave site (still kept up by one of Lafcadio's descendants) contains a tombstone and an upright granite slab. On it is inscribed his name and dates: KOIZUMI YAKUMO—1850–1904 . . . and also his *kaimyō,* or Buddhist name given to the spirit of the dead: BELIEVING-MAN SIMILAR TO PURE FLOWER BLOOMING LIKE EIGHT RISING CLOUDS, WHO DWELLS IN THE MANSION OF RIGHT ENLIGHTENMENT.

At the family's little Buddhist shrine in the study of the Koizumi home, none of Lafcadio's four children ever went to bed before saying, "Good night, happy dreams, *Papa-san,*" to his commemorative tablet, in front of which stood a lighted lamp, burning incense rods, tiny lacquered bowls containing tiny portions of their father's favorite food, two vases of artificial iris shoots, a photograph of Papa (his face, as always, looking down and off to the left), and one of his writing pens in a bronze stand. Here, Koizumi Yakumo was still alive.

Lafcadio Hearn once put it another way: "*I* an individual—an individual soul! Nay, I am a population—a population unthinkable for multitude, even by groups of a thousand millions! Generations of generations I am, æons of æons! Countless times the concourse now making me has been scattered, and mixed with other scatterings. Of what concern, then, the next disintegration? Perhaps, after trillions of ages of burning in different dynasties of suns, the very best of me may come together again."

Although traces of Lafcadio Hearn's world can occasionally be glimpsed today in Cincinnati's Over-the-Rhine district, in New Orleans's Vieux Carré, in the northern rural areas of Martinique, and in remote Japanese mountain villages, the places the writer lived in and described have, for the most part, been transformed beyond recognition or have simply vanished. Not one warehouse, roustabout dive, or frame building from Cincinnati's Bucktown or the Levee exists any longer. The city of St. Pierre on Martinique was totally destroyed by an eruption of Mont Pelée on May 8, 1902. Lafcadio's beloved island of Grand Isle in the Gulf of Mexico was inundated in 1893 by a tidal wave that washed away most of the island's houses and fishing shacks, as well as Krantz's Hotel. And on the island of Levkas, the three-story wooden house in which Hearn was born was decimated by an earthquake on June 30, 1948. Only the city of Matsue, Japan, has preserved one of Lafcadio's homes and kept his memory alive with a memorial museum.

In attempting to reconstruct and explain the significance of Lafcadio Hearn's life, one is therefore obliged to examine his articles, essays, novels, and letters, and then to read with some skepticism the often distorted and inaccurate writings about him. Even *The Cambridge Guide to Literature in English* (1988) makes no mention of Lafcadio's years in Cincinnati, and thus erroneously states that his "first successful newspaper articles" were written in New Orleans. The *Guide* also introduces its entry on Hearn by listing him as "Hearn, (Patricio) Lafcadio (Tessima Carlos)"—undoubtedly following the English biographer Nina Kennard's misreading, in an old Hearn family Bible, of "Tessima" for "Cassimati" in Romaic.

Since 1906, five major biographies of Lafcadio Hearn have, in various ways, contributed substantially to our knowledge of the writer's life: Elizabeth Bisland's *Life and Letters of Lafcadio Hearn;* Nina H. Kennard's *Lafcadio Hearn: Containing Some Letters from Lafcadio Hearn to His Half-Sister, Mrs. Atkinson;* Edward L. Tinker's *Lafcadio Hearn's American Days;* O. W. Frost's *Young Hearn;* and Elizabeth Stevenson's *Lafcadio Hearn.* Nevertheless, in these works as well, errors enter. Readers of Kennard's book, in particular (New York: D. Appleton and Co., 1912), should be on constant alert. For this biographer gives the wrong date of Hearn's birth, states incorrectly that Lafcadio's mother, Rosa, for whom Kennard continually expresses her distaste, had Maltese blood, and neglects to mention her marriage to Charles Hearn. Nina Kennard also declares her high-toned disgust at Hearn's "Tanyard Murder" stories for the Cincinnati *Enquirer,* and gives us a supercilious description of a Japanese meal she shared with Lafcadio's wife in Tokyo several years after the writer's death: "That any sane people," Kennard comments, "should eat a succession of horrible concoctions made up of raw fish, lotus roots, bamboo shoots, and sweets that tasted of Pears' soap, whisked into a lather, with a little sugar added as an afterthought, eaten Japanese fashion, was worse than the judgment passed on Nebuchadnezzar; and with the beasts of the field Nebuchadnezzar, at least, had no appearance to keep up, whereas we had to respond to a courtesy that was agonizing in the exquisiteness of its delicacy."

Elizabeth Bisland and Elizabeth Stevenson, Hearn's first and most recent biographers, respectively, are happily free of such inane and patronizing outbursts. Bisland is still the most ardent of Hearn's explainers, if a prudish and protective one—freely admitting that her portrait of her lifelong friend might justifiably be accused of lacking "the veracity of shadow" (two volumes, Boston: Houghton Mifflin Co., 1906); while Stevenson is the most diligent and thorough detailer of Lafcadio's entire life, particularly of his years in Japan (New York: The Macmillan Company, 1961). As balanced and cool as Bisland is biased and impassioned, Stevenson is still clearly not at home in the Hearnian universe, and her estimation of her subject's work tends to be lukewarm ("A bias of his mind organized his vivid impressions into a shape of some significance"). Edward L. Tinker's *Lafcadio Hearn's American Days* provides lively, unconstrained reminiscences of many of Lafcadio's comrades and associates in New Orleans (New York: Dodd, Mead and Co., Inc., 1924); and O. W. Frost's *Young Hearn* is the only work that accurately depicts Lafcadio's and his mother's life in the town of Santa Maura on the island of Levkas, as well as the author's childhood in Ireland, France, and England (Tokyo: Hokuseido Press, 1958).

In addition to these basic works about Hearn, there are a number of biographies (by, among others, Edward Thomas, Jean Temple, Joseph de Smet, Kenneth Kirkwood, Vera McWilliams, Marcel Robert, and Ryuji Tanebe) that are heavily dependent on Bisland's and Kennard's often-inaccurate works. Also valuable are scores of personal memoirs, especially the overly rhapsodic reminiscences of Leona Queyrouze Barel—*The Idyl: My Personal Reminiscences of Lafcadio Hearn* (Tokyo: Hokuseido Press, 1933)—and the essential memoirs by Setsuko Koizumi—*Reminiscences of Lafcadio Hearn* (Boston and New York: Houghton Mifflin Co., 1918)—and Kazuo Koizumi—*Father and I: Memories of Lafcadio Hearn* (Boston and New York: Houghton Mifflin Co., 1935). Invaluable collections of Hearn's newspaper articles, sketches, and feuilletons have been edited independently by Albert Mordell, Charles Woodward Hutson, and William S. Johnson, and important anthologies of Hearn's writings have been assembled by Henry Goodman, Kenneth Rexroth, and Francis King. The author has even been the subject of a series of racy, and now found to be forged, letters by a "Countess Annetta Halliday Antonia of Detroit, Michigan," who claimed to have met Hearn when she was a young girl spending time, for no discernible reason, in Cincinnati and New Orleans, and whom Lafcadio supposedly referred to as his "Pagan" prior to her marriage to an Italian, Count Alessandro Giuseppe

Valerio-Antonia: *Letters to a Pagan* (Detroit: R. B. Powers, 1933). Kazuo Koizumi
was so taken with these letters that he translated them into Japanese. The pagan
"Countess," however, was shown to be nonexistent, the "Count" suppositious,
and the letters irrefutably a forgery by Albert Mordell in " 'Letters to a Pagan'
Not by Hearn," first published in *Today's Japan* 5 (1) (1955–60, 5th Anniversary
Edition): 89–98.

Throughout my book, I have, whenever possible, consulted both primary and
secondary sources. I have reprinted Hearn's articles, sketches, and tales from
the first editions of his books and respected the writer's idiosyncratic use of
punctuation and much of his idiosyncratic spelling.

Until about the 1930s, the word "Negro" with a small "n" was in general use.
I have taken the liberty, retroactively, of capitalizing this noun in Lafcadio's
writings. In transliterating Japanese into English, Lafcadio Hearn followed the
nineteenth-century Hepburn system. I have followed Hearn's example.

Elizabeth Bisland's *Life and Letters of Lafcadio Hearn* and *The Japanese Letters
of Lafcadio Hearn*—edited by her and published in one volume by Houghton
Mifflin in 1910—were eventually slightly expanded and divided into shorter
volumes, and came to make up the concluding *four* volumes of the sixteen-
volume *Writings of Lafcadio Hearn,* published by Houghton Mifflin in 1922. Because the pagination of *Life and Letters* and *Japanese Letters* therefore differs
markedly from that of Volumes 13–16 of the *Writings*—the first quarter of *Japanese Letters* (which makes up Volume 16 of the *Writings*) has been included at
the end of Volume 15, for example, I have, throughout the Source Notes, simply
supplied the reader with the dates given by Hearn for each of the letters quoted
from in my text, thereby facilitating reference to the individual letters in *any* of
the above editions.

Finally, in my informal listing and discussion of primary and secondary
sources, I have used the following abbreviations:

ABBREVIATIONS

(Complete bibliographical information about those works written by Lafcadio
Hearn and referred to in the following Abbreviations and Source Notes can
be found in the Chronological Bibliography.)

A.F.	Alethea (Mattie) Foley
B.H.C.	Basil Hall Chamberlain
C	*Chita: A Memory of Last Island*
C.Com	Cincinnati *Commercial*
C.En	Cincinnati *Enquirer*
E.B.	Elizabeth Bisland
E.H.	Ellwood Hendrick
E&R	*Exotics and Retrospectives*

F&I	Kazuo Koizumi, *Father and I: Memories of Lafcadio Hearn* (Boston and New York: Houghton Mifflin Co., 1935)
G	*Glimpses of Unfamiliar Japan*
GB-F	Gleanings in Buddha-Fields
G.M.G.	George M. Gould
H.E.K.	Henry E. Krehbiel
H.W.	Henry Watkin
I	Leona Queyrouze Barel, *The Idyl: My Personal Reminiscences of Lafcadio Hearn* (Tokyo: Hokuseido Press, 1933)
JL	*The Japanese Letters of Lafcadio Hearn*
K	*Kotto*
K:H&E	*Kokoro: Hints and Echoes of Japanese Inner Life*
K.K.	Kazuo Koizumi
L.H.	Lafcadio Hearn
LH	Elizabeth Stevenson, *Lafcadio Hearn*
LHAD	Edward Tinker, *Lafcadio Hearn's American Days*
LH:CL	Nina H. Kennard, *Lafcadio Hearn: Containing Some Letters from Lafcadio Hearn to His Half-Sister, Mrs. Atkinson*
LL	Elizabeth Bisland, *The Life and Letters of Lafcadio Hearn*
LR	*Letters from the Raven: Being the Correspondence of Lafcadio Hearn with Henry Watkin*
"NDL"	"Newly Discovered Letters from Lafcadio Hearn to Dr. Rudolph Matas," ed. Ichiro Nishizaki
N.O.*It*	New Orleans *Item*
N.O.*T-D*	New Orleans *Times-Democrat*
OE	*Out of the East*
RLH	Setsuko Koizumi, *Reminiscences of Lafcadio Hearn* (Boston and New York: Houghton Mifflin Co., 1918)
R.M.	Rudolph Matas
S	*Shadowings*
S.K.	Setsu Koizumi
TY	*Two Years in the French West Indies*
Y	*Youma: The Story of a West-Indian Slave*
YH	O. W. Frost, *Young Hearn*

INTRODUCTION

Charles Dater Weldon (1844–1935) was an illustrator and watercolorist who studied in Cleveland, New York, London, and Paris. An associate of the National Academy of Design and the American Watercolor Society, he was on the staff of Harper and Brothers when he met and traveled to Vancouver and Yokohama with L.H., with whom he eventually quarreled about the amount of money each should receive for their collaboration on articles for *Harper's Weekly*.

The lines of Charles Baudelaire's poetry are quoted in Marguerite Yourcenar's *With Open Eyes*, translated by Arthur Goldhammer (Boston: Beacon Press, 1984), p. 257.

The remarks by Kenneth Rexroth (1905–1982) concerning L.H. as a prose stylist and as a still-relevant informant about contemporary Japanese life are taken from his introduction to *The Buddhist Writings of Lafcadio Hearn* (Santa Barbara: Ross-Erikson, Inc., 1977), pp. xi–xii.

Stefan Zweig's glowing comments about L. H. were in response to the publication of *Das Japanbuch,* a collection of Hearn's writings translated by Berta Franzos (Frankfurt-am-Main: Rutten and Loening, 1911). The earlier appearance of a German edition of *Kokoro* (1905) contained a Foreword by Hugo von Hofmannsthal, in which he talks of Lafcadio's "rare love: . . . the love that partakes of the inner life of the beloved country."

L.H.'s hope for "a United Orient" to counter "our cruel Western Civilization" was expressed in a December 1895 letter to E.H. (*LL,* II).

The assertions about the "flexibility" of contemporary Japan are taken from an interview with the social critic Shuichi Kato that appeared in *New Perspectives Quarterly* 6 (3) (Fall 1988), pp. 52–54.

Yone Noguchi's and Professor Inazo Nitobe's opinions about L. H. are quoted in *Selected Writings of Lafcadio Hearn,* edited by Henry Goodman, p. 17, and in Edward Thomas's *Lafcadio Hearn* (Boston: Houghton Mifflin Co., 1912), pp. 90–91. Albert Mordell's remark about Hearn and Japan is made on the last page of his introduction to *Occidental Gleanings,* p. lxxvi.

Marguerite Yourcenar's definition of "a wanderer" is stated in *With Open Eyes,* p. 257.

The poet Charles Olson proposed his idea about Ulysses and his journey as an archetype of the Western experience in his study of Melville, *Call Me Ishmael* (San Francisco: City Lights Books, 1947), pp. 113–19.

Constantine P. Cavafy—the pen name of C. P. Kavafis (1863–1933)—lived most of his life in Alexandria, where he was born.

PROLOGUE: THE DREAM OF A SUMMER DAY

Lafcadio Hearn's account of his trip to Nagasaki in the summer of 1893, his "escape" to a traditional Japanese inn (the House of Urashima), and his journey from there to his home in Kumamoto are recounted in a letter written to Basil Hall Chamberlain on July 22, 1893 (*JL*), as well as in Hearn's reverie "The Dream of a Summer Day" (*OE*). In this reverie also appears the writer's retelling of the story of Urashima, the boy who goes to live in the Dragon Palace under the sea. This tale was not only Lafcadio's favorite Japanese story, it is even today "Japan's favorite story," according to Hayao Kawai, a Jungian analyst and professor at Kyoto University. Dr. Kawai's book *The Japanese Psyche: Major Motifs in the Fairy Tales of Japan* (Dallas: Spring Publications, Inc., 1988) contains a lengthy discussion of the Urashima tale, which the author connects to the Jungian archetype of the *puer aeternus* (Divine or Eternal Child). In the light of Hearn's comments about and meditations on youth and old age in "The Dream of a Summer Day," Dr. Kawai's remarks seem especially illuminating: "Often an eternal youth spends his time in the unconscious world, and therefore you might say he does not age. . . . That the membrane between inner and outer

. . . is paper-thin—like a *fusuma* (sliding room-divider) or *shoji* (a paper door-window)—reflects the nature of the Japanese ego. Established by successfully 'killing the mother,' the Western ego clearly distinguishes between conscious and unconscious and between I and thou—grasping things objectively. In comparison, Japanese consciousness tries to grasp the whole as an undifferentiated state by always making borders vague" (pp. 102–104).

PART ONE

CHAPTER 1: BLUE GHOST

My remarks about the ancient Greek gods, Apollo and Aphrodite in particular, are drawn primarily from my readings of Hesiod's *The Homeric Hymns;* Walter F. Otto's *The Homeric Gods,* trans. Moses Hadas (New York: Pantheon Books, 1954); and Walter Burkert's *Greek Religion,* trans. John Raffan (Cambridge, Mass.: Harvard University Press, 1985).

In his *Heroides,* Ovid drew on the Leucadian legend of Sappho's suicide leap. With a kind of sentimental cruelty, Ovid portrays the Greek poetess as a small, dark woman "of a certain age," creatively exhausted and obsessed by her unrequited love for the young ferryman, Phaon, who has recently deserted her for several younger Sicilian girls. Her desire burning like a "field afire," Sappho seeks out Apollo's temple on the high cliff of Leucadia; pledges her lyre to the god; looks down from the precipice, declaring, "Venus, born from the sea, offers the sea for a lover"; then throws herself, *deshabillé,* from the edge and floats lightly to her death on Cupid's wings.

Lafcadio Hearn's distinctive punctuation (specifically, his use of dashes followed by commas or semicolons) is often "corrected" and standardized by many of his biographers and editors. The original publications of the important letters Lafcadio wrote from New York City in 1890 to his rediscovered brother James D. Hearn—then living in Ohio—suffer from this kind of editing, as well as from misdating: "Lafcadio Hearn's Brother," ed. Henry T. Kneeland, *Atlantic Monthly* 131 (1) (January 1923): 20–27; "Letters of Lafcadio Hearn to His Brother," ed. E. C. Beck, *The English Journal* 20 (1931): 287–92. The excerpts I have used from these letters are based on the original copies in the Houghton Library, Harvard University.

James Hearn had written to Lafcadio after seeing a photo of him in a Cleveland newspaper. Deeply suspicious of this overture, Lafcadio replied to the "supposed" brother, addressing him as "Dear Sir," and demanded answers to questions like: "What is your full name? . . . What was your mother's name prior to her marriage? . . . Of what place was she a native? . . . Where is she?" James wrote back, confessing he could answer only one or two of Lafcadio's queries, but finally convinced Lafcadio of their common lineage. (Especially convincing was James's possession of a portrait photograph of Charles Hearn.) One should remember that Lafcadio had seen his brother only once when James was seven years old. In 1871 he, like his older brother, had emigrated to America—first to Chicago, and then to Ohio, where he and his family rented a small

farm. (He later moved to St. Louis, Michigan.) As in the story of the feuding
Biblical brothers Jacob and Esau, Lafcadio was devoted to the memory of his
mother, James to his father. After Lafcadio's death, James Hearn wrote their half-
sister Minnie Atkinson: "He may have been a genius in his line, but genius is
akin to madness, and I do really think that dark, passionate Greek mother's
blood had a taint in it. For me, instead of nobler aspirations and thoughts, it
begat extremes of hate and love—a shrinking and sensitive morbid nature.
Whatever of the man I have in me comes from our common father. . . . If we
had the good old Celtic and Saxon blood in us, it would have been better for
those dependent on us" (quoted in *LH:CL,* p. 101).

For the dates and details of the stories of the courtship of Rosa Cassimati and
Charles Hearn, of Lafcadio's birth, and of his childhood idyll on Leucadia with
his mother, I have depended mainly on *YH.*

Lafcadio's wish "to melt utterly away forever" into "that infinite Blue Ghost"
appears in his novel *Chita* and is expressed in slightly different fashion in
several letters to his New Orleans friends Dr. Rudolph Matas and Page Baker
(see Part Two, Chapter 7) and to Henry Watkin (Part Four, Chapter 2).

The concluding words to this chapter (about "a magical time") are those of
the previously quoted "The Dream of a Summer Day" (*OE*).

CHAPTER 2: PARADISE LOST

This chapter—like the following one—draws mainly on *YH, LL, LH,* and *LH:CL.*
Lafcadio confessed having slapped his mother's face when he was a child to
his half-sister Minnie Atkinson (in a letter reprinted in *LH:CL,* pp. 13–14).

The second of three girls born in India to Charles and Alicia Goslin Hearn,
Mrs. Minnie Atkinson was the only one of the three who ever received replies
from her half-brother to the letters each of the sisters had sent to Japan in the
early 1890s. Lafcadio's correspondence with Minnie Atkinson—occasionally cen-
sored by both the recipient and the biographer Nina Kennard—appeared in
LH:CL, as do the list of derivations of the name *Hearn* (p. 15).

Lafcadio's recounting of his first (and last) encounter with his younger brother
appears in one of the 1890 letters to James Hearn (see Notes for the preceding
chapter). His description of his fear of ghosts is from taken both a letter dated
December 1893 to B.H.C. (*JL*) and from "The Child's Room," one of several
autobiographical sketches Lafcadio wrote in 1902, two years before his death
(*LL,* I, p. 16). (Please note that Lafcadio Hearn's letters are occasionally dated
only with the year—though usually with at least the month and the year, and,
later in his life, with the month, the day, and the year. The Source Notes supply
whatever dating information Lafcadio himself provided.)

CHAPTER 3: RENAISSANCE

Lafcadio's account of his discovery of the book containing drawings of the
ancient Greek gods, goddesses, fauns, satyrs, etc., is excerpted from his autobiographical sketch "Idolatry," which first appeared in *LL,* I, pp. 24–25. His

account of his childhood summers in Wales appeared in his letter of August 21, 1894, to B.H.C. (*JL*).

CHAPTER 4: SHADES OF THE PRISON-HOUSE

Lafcadio expressed his opinion of Catholic education in a letter (August 30, 1893) to B.H.C. (*JL*). The comments about the Institution Ecclésiastique by Guy de Maupassant occur in the short story "Une Surprise," first published in the French journal *Gil Blas* (May 15, 1883). Lafcadio's admission of his provocative confession to the college priest appears in an undated letter to George M. Gould, who published it in his book *Concerning Lafcadio Hearn* (Philadelphia: George W. Jacobs and Co., 1908). Lafcadio's pantheistic reverie appears in his essay "Of Moon-Desire" (*E&R*). The reminiscences of Achilles Daunt about his school chum "Paddy Hearn" were published in *LH:CL* (pp. 63–65). Lafcadio's own reminiscences of schoolmate Daunt are preserved in a January 1895 letter to E.H. (*LL*, I). His remark about his fascination with "the Odd, the Queer, the Strange . . ." appears in a letter of June 29, 1884, to W. D. O'Connor (*LL*, I). His nightmarish descriptions of life in London's East End are found in a letter to Minnie Atkinson (*LH:CL*) and in paraphrased remarks of Achilles Daunt (quoted in *LL*, I, p. 37).

The lines by Algernon Charles Swinburne ("Thou hast conquered, O pale Galilean . . .") are from that writer's 1866 poem "Hymn to Proserpine."

CHAPTER 5: IN THE LAND OF OPPORTUNITY

Readers of Toni Morrison's novel *Beloved* may recall that the ex-slave heroine of the book, Sethe, lives with the remnants (and revenants) of her family in a ghost-haunted, gray-and-white house that existed on the semirural outskirts of Cincinnati during the 1870s—the same period in which Lafcadio Hearn resided in that city. His own description of the hayloft where he found shelter from the streets is in one of his autobiographical sketches entitled "Stars," first published in *LL*, I, pp. 33–34. His reminiscences of Henry Watkin were remarks made in an August 21, 1894, letter to B.H.C. (*JL*). His early notes to H. W. appear in *LR* (pp. 29–32). And his remark about "Everybody who does me a wrong . . ." is quoted in *LH:CL* (p. 68), and is later repeated and expanded upon in a September 1895 letter to B.H.C. (*JL*).

CHAPTER 6: A SENSATIONAL REPORTER

John A. Cockerill's recollections of his first meeting with Lafcadio appear in Cockerill's essay-review "Lafcadio Hearn: The Author of *Kokoro*," *Current Literature* XIX (6) (June 1896). A reconstruction of all of the articles Hearn wrote about the Tanyard Murder can be found in Jon Christopher Hughes's *The Tanyard Murder: On the Case with Lafcadio Hearn*.

Lafcadio was a staff writer for both the Cincinnati *Enquirer* and the Cincinnati *Commercial*. For the former, Hearn contributed "Feminine Curiosity—A Female Blackguard's Lecture to Prurient Sisters" (January 22, 1874), "Among the Spirits" (January 25, 1874), and "Skulls and Skeletons" (August 30, 1874). For the latter paper, Lafcadio wrote "Haceldama" (September 5, 1875), "Balm of Gilead" (October 3, 1875), "Notes on the Utilization of Human Remains" (November 7, 1875), "The Demi-Monde of the Antique World" (November 28, 1875), and "Gibbeted" (August 26, 1876).

For its exhaustive and informative account of the history of the sensationalist nineteenth-century American penny press, I consulted David S. Reynolds's *Beneath the American Renaissance* (New York: Alfred A. Knopf, 1988).

CHAPTER 7: BLACK AND WHITE

Much of my discussion on antimiscegenation laws in the United States is based on J. A. Rogers's *Sex and Race* (St. Petersburg, Florida: Helga M. Rogers, 1942), volume 2.

Lafcadio's portrait/description of Mattie Foley (and her uncanny "ghost-seeing") appeared with the title "Some Strange Experience" in *C.Com* (September 26, 1875), though Mattie is not identified by name, nor is her relationship to the writer spelled out.

In 1906, having heard that Lafcadio had left a "vast fortune" upon his death, Mattie, then fifty years old and still living in Cincinnati, instituted a suit, claiming that she was Hearn's widow—since she had never obtained a divorce—and requesting a share of the writer's literary estate. The New York *Sun* picked up the story and published a lengthy, sensationalistic, mean-spirited editorial—possibly written by one of Lafcadio's disgruntled ex-friends—that began:

> It will surprise no one who knew Lafcadio Hearn at all well to hear that a Negro woman in Cincinnati now claims recognition as his widow and seeks to obtain, as such, a share of the American royalties on his remarkable literary work. Hearn spent several years in the Ohio city, and it is sufficiently notorious that in his purely private and domestic relations he consorted with colored people only. . . .
>
> Hearn [lived] in the downtown river front quarter of New Orleans with Negroes—not the ordinary "corn-field" type, but the Congo priestesses and prophetesses; as a matter of fact with no less a personage than Marie [Laveau], the "Voudoo Queen." . . . From the West Indies Hearn went to Japan, where he formed some sort of domestic relation with a native; and he died there in 1904. . . .
>
> His appearance was forbidding, if not actually repulsive. Only about five feet tall, with one eye totally blind and the other so disabled that he had to hold papers within an inch in order to decipher them; always ill-dressed, unkempt, slovenly; with the face of a weasel and the manners of an oaf; he was nevertheless one of the most brilliant and picturesque writers of his day, a profound, versatile and poetic thinker, one of the greatest masters of occult languages and literature the Christian world [!] has ever known.
>
> That Hearn lived with the Cincinnati Negress in an intimate domestic relation is easily imaginable. That he actually went through the form of a legal marriage his acquaintances will believe with difficulty. If throughout his career in the United States he ever paid tribute to any convention whatever, the men who came nearest to knowing him have never heard of it.

It should be mentioned that the New Orleans *Times-Democrat* and the New

York *Tribune* both took the *Sun* editorial to task for its misstatements and disparaging remarks. Lafcadio did, for instance, "go through the form of a marriage" with Mattie Foley; but according to Ohio law at that time, the marriage was illegal. Mattie, moreover, had later married a man named John Kleintank. The Ohio court therefore threw out Mattie's lawsuit. A detailed report on this entire episode can be found in Oscar Lewis's *Hearn and His Biographers: The Record of a Literary Controversy* (San Francisco: The Westgate Press, 1930).

For the *C.Com*, Lafcadio wrote "Steeple Climbers" (May 26, 1876) and "Frost Fancies" (December 10, 1876). Of the twelve articles in which he examined the life of the inhabitants of Bucktown and the Levee, the *C.Com* published "Pariah People/Outcast Life by Night in the East End/The Underground Dens of Bucktown and the People Who Live in Them" (August 22, 1875) and "Levee Life/ Haunts and Pastimes of the Roustabouts/Their Original Songs and Peculiar Dances" (March 17, 1876). All twelve of Hearn's sketches of and articles about Cincinnati's post–Civil War black ghetto life have been collected in *Children of the Levee*, ed. O. W. Frost.

CHAPTER 8: SWALLOW FLYING SOUTH

Lafcadio's translations of Théophile Gautier's stories were eventually published under the title *One of Cleopatra's Nights and Other Fantastic Romances* (1882).

L. H.'s first series of letters to H. W. were written from Memphis, Tennessee, in October and November 1877 (*LR*), pp. 36–39, and reveal his depressed state of mind as he waited for the steamer to New Orleans.

L. H. later described his experience with the drunken man and the kitten to his son Kazuo (*F&I*, p. 11), and to Ellwood Hendrick, *Percolator Papers* (New York: Harper and Brothers, 1919), pp. 190–91.

Lafcadio's description of his boat trip down the Mississippi, which he wrote in New Orleans on November 14, 1877, appeared in the *C.Com* with the title "Memphis to New Orleans" (November 23, 1877).

PART TWO

CHAPTER 1: THE BRIDE STRIPPED BARE

Lafcadio's first impressions of New Orleans were expressed in his fourteen "letters" to the *C.Com*, which were published between 1877 and 1878, and signed under the name Ozias Midwinter. Lafcadio chose this *nom de plume* as a private joke after reading Wilkie Collins's *Armadale* (1866). In this novel, the author describes the character of Ozias—an illegitimate son—as a dark, foreign-looking young man with "preternaturally large and wild" eyes, who runs away from a school where he has been tormented by both students and teachers to live with a gypsy thief. Ozias subsists on menial jobs, and at the age of twenty— friendless, parentless—he confronts his sense of frustration and self-failure. (It is not difficult to see how Lafcadio might have identified with such a character.)

From the "Ozias Midwinter" letters, I have, in Chapter 1, quoted from the letters of November 26, 1877; December 10, 1877; December 22, 1877; and January 7, 1878 (all from the *C.Com*).

My discussion of Lafcadio's notions of the connections between beauty and decay/sadness/death draws on Hearn's occasional essays on and translations of Gautier and Baudelaire; the sentiments he expresses about the intermingling of love and death in his *Fantastics* sketches; and Mario Praz's classic study *The Romantic Agony*, trans. Angus Davidson (Oxford, England: Oxford University Press, 1933).

CHAPTER 2: STARTING OVER

This chapter—like the following ones in Part 2—are indebted for much of their information to *LH* and particularly to *LHAD*.

Lafcadio's discouraging remarks to H.W. about New Orleans appear in *LR*, pp. 44–45 and pp. 54–55. Hearn's lengthy letter to H.W. concerning the former's approaching twenty-eighth birthday—a letter that might have been by Ozias Midwinter himself!—can be found in *LR*, pp. 47–52.

The line of poetry by Friedrich Hölderlin (1770–1843)—"Danger itself fosters the rescuing power" *("Wo aber Gefahr ist, wächst/Das Rettende auch")*—is taken from the poem "Patmos" (1802). Lafcadio's comment about man getting "right down in the dirt" appears in *LR*, p. 54. Colonel John Fairfax's first impression of Hearn is quoted in John S. Kendall's "Lafcadio Hearn in New Orleans, I, On the *Item.*" *Double Dealer* III (17) (May 1922): 238.

Lafcadio describes his "new journalistic life" in an 1878 letter to H.E.K. in *LL*,I. His sketch, "The City of Dreams," appeared in the N.O.*It* (March 9, 1879).

Hearn's controversial praise of Buddhism (in particular, the "higher Buddhism" in contrast to "esoteric" or "neo-"Buddhism, which he thought was corrupted with spiritualistic "humbug" and superstitious beliefs) appeared in a number of editorials both in the N.O.*It* and the N.O.*T-D*. He wrote even more enthusiastically about the subject ("What are the heavens of all Christian fancies, after all, but Nirvana? . . . ") in an 1883 letter to W. D. O'Connor (*LL*, I).

Hearn's "distrusting" attitude toward his friends is described by Julia Wetherall (Mrs. Marion Baker) in *LHAD*, p. 362. His complaint about his ocular troubles was communicated to H.W. in *LR*, p. 70. The book review/editorial "Artistic Value of Myopia" was first published in the N.O.*T-D* (February 7, 1887). His translation of passages from Pierre Loti's *Le Mariage de Loti* appeared in the N.O.*T-D* (October 17, 1880).

CHAPTER 3: CREOLE DAYS

At the beginning of his fifth year in New Orleans, Lafcadio wrote of his mood and state of mind to H.W. in *LR*, p. 77. He described his Spanish lessons with his eccentric Mexican Spanish-language tutor in an 1879 letter to H.E.K. (*LL*,I), and suggested his ideas concerning the opportunity to study and his approach to reading in an 1883 letter to a progressive Boston minister, the Reverend Wayland D. Ball (*LL*,I).

Lafcadio's two-part article "The Creole Patois" was published in *Harper's Weekly* (January 10 and 17, 1885). The Creole street-cries appeared in the N.O.*It* (August 25, 1880). The Creole patois ditties were included in one of Hearn's "Ozias Midwinter" letters in the *C.Com* (February 18, 1878). Lafcadio's collection of Creole proverbs in six Creole dialects were turned into his book *"Gombo Zhèbes"* (1885). And his impressionistic description of traditional French Creole life, "A Creole Courtyard," appeared in the N.O.*It* (November 11, 1879).

CHAPTER 4: VOODOO NIGHTS

Lafcadio's obituary/essay on Jean Montanet, "The Last of the Voudoos," appeared in *Harper's Weekly* (November 7, 1885).

My discussion of the life of Marie Laveau and of voodoo culture in nineteenth-century New Orleans is based primarily on Robert Tallant's *Voodoo in New Orleans* (London: Collier-Macmillan, 1962); *Historical Sketch Book and Guide to New Orleans* (see Chronological Bibliography); Albert J. Raboteau's *Slave Religion* (New York: Oxford University Press, 1978); Zora Neale Hurston's *Mules and Men*, first published 1935 (Bloomington and London: Indiana University Press, 1978)—especially valuable for Hurston's description of her own voodoo initiation ceremony led by a supposed descendant of Marie Laveau; Robert Farris Thompson's *Flash of the Spirit* (New York: Random House, 1983); "Hear that Long Snake Moan," in Michael Ventura's *Shadow Dancing* (Los Angeles: Jeremy P. Tarcher, 1985); Francine Prose's novel *Marie Laveau* (New York: Berkley Publishing Corporation, 1977), which deals with the rivalry between Marie and Jean Montanet; and *LHAD*.

Lafcadio's essay "New Orleans Superstitions," based, in part on his conversations with Marie Leveau and with her daughter Marie, was published in *Harper's Weekly* (December 25, 1886).

CHAPTER 5: SOME FRIENDS ALONG THE WAY

Lafcadio's characterization of himself as a "demophobe" appears in an 1887 letter to H.E.K. (*LL*,I), and his admission of his "susceptibilities, weaknesses, sensitivenesses" was given in an 1888 letter to Dr. George Gould (*LL*,I). Hearn's encounter with the six-year-old boy who called him Dick Dead Eye is reported in *LHAD*, p. 91. Lafcadio's obscene characterization of his onetime friend and "very noble and lovable" boss, Page Baker, as a toilet bowl can be found in an April 30, 1888, letter to Dr. Rudolph Matas in "NDL."

Elizabeth Bisland first read Lafcadio's *Fantastics* sketch "A Dead Love" in the N.O.*It* (October 21, 1880). His ambivalent remarks about his first impressions of "Miss Bessie Bisland" appear in *LHAD*, p. 175. His later, more adoring comments concerning her are quoted in *LH:CL*, p. 152, and in letters he wrote to her from Japan (see Part 4, Chapter 8). For her part, Elizabeth Bisland's long, perceptive description of Hearn during his New Orleans days appears in *LL*,I, pp. 72–74.

George Washington Cable's story "Jean-ah Poquelin," Lafcadio's introduction to this writer's work, can be found in Cable's first collection of stories, *Old*

Creole Days (1879). After Cable's 1884 national reading tour with Mark Twain, Lafcadio developed a sibling-type rivalry with Cable, which is evident in an 1885 letter to H.E.K. (*LL*,I). Cable's unhappiness over the demise of French Creole culture and society is made clear in his remarks quoted in Louis D. Rubin, Jr.'s *George W. Cable: The Life and Times of a Southern Heretic* (New York: Pegasus, 1969).

The legendary life of Père Adrien Emmanuel Rouquette is recounted in almost all histories of the state of Louisiana. Lafcadio's glowing review of Rouquette's *La Nouvelle Atala* (1879) appears in the N.O.*It* (February 25, 1879) under the heading "A Louisana Idyl." Hearn was supposed to have objected strongly to the priest's polemical, racist pamphlet attacking G. W. Cable's novel *The Grandissimes*. (The anonymous pamphlet was entitled *Critical Dialogue Between Aboo and Caboo on a New Book; or, A Grandissime Ascension,* and was cited by Joel Chandler Harris in the Atlanta *Constitution* of February 20, 1881, as an example of the South's fear and denial of inescapable truths.

A detailed account of William D. O'Connor's marital problems and the temporary breakup of his friendship with Walt Whitman can be found in Justin Kaplan's *Walt Whitman: A Life* (New York: Simon and Schuster, 1980). The selections from the letters written by Lafcadio to O'Connor date from 1883–87, and appear in *LL*,I.

Dr. Rudolph Matas's comments about his first encounters with Lafcadio are quoted in the introduction to *Fantastics and Other Fancies,* pp. 16–19, edited by Charles Woodward Hutson. Hearn's Arabic-type flourishes and phrases in his early notes to R.M. appear in "NDL," p. 86. Lafcadio's article on Creole medicine and folk remedies, "The Creole Doctor," drew on information he obtained from R.M., his wife, as well as one or two of Hearn's black Creole landladies; it was published in the New York *Tribune* (January 3, 1886).

Lafcadio's statements regarding the "several little cities" contained within New Orleans appeared in the N.O.*It* (March 23, 1879). His deprecation of the "parlour" ("That Parlour!") was also written for the *Item* (September 28, 1881). Hearn conveyed his ecstatic opinion of Herbert Spencer's philosophy in an April 1886 letter to O'Connor (*LL*,I), as well as in talks with Leona Queyrouze, who recalled them in *I*. Lafcadio's "memory of long ago" is quoted in *LH:CL*, pp. 163–64.

For the story of Lafcadio's nocturnal excursions with Mrs. Margaret Courtney's nephew Denny Corcoran, I am indebted to *LHAD*—even today the only book that has explored the "other" side of Hearn's life in New Orleans. The tale Lafcadio recounts to twelve-year-old Ella Courtney is quoted in *LHAD*, pp. 198–99. Lafcadio's "News of Ants" appeared in the N.O.*T-D* (August 27, 1882). His notions concerning the relationship between sexuality and history are expressed in a letter of November 1882 to Rev. Wayland D. Ball (*LL*,I), and his theories about the differences between French and American literature in his editorial "The Sexual Idea in French Literature," published in the N.O.*It* (June 17, 1881). An overwrought passage like "Acres upon acres of silvered corpses . . ." appears in the story "Torn Letters" that was published in the N.O.*T-D* (September 14, 1884). The embarrassed confession of Don Lafcadio is quoted in *LHAD*, p. 215.

CHAPTER 6: IN THE SHADOW OF THE ETHIOPIAN

Lafcadio's confidences to H.W. are found in *LR*, pp. 58–59. His joyous March 1884 letter to O'Connor appears in *LL*,I. The famous (or infamous) letter to H.E.K.—dated "New Orleans, 1880" (*LL*,I)—contains the sentence "I eat and drink and sleep with members of the races you detest like the son of Odin that you are." Of German descent, Henry E. Krehbiel (1854–1923) was the music editor for the Cincinnati *Gazette* (1874–1880) and the New York *Tribune* (1880–1923), where he championed the then mostly unpopular music of Brahms and Wagner; wrote books on Wagnerian drama and Afro-American folk songs; and edited, rewrote, and translated Thayer's three-volume biography of Beethoven.

H.E.K.'s story of Lafcadio and Jere Cochran in a Cincinnati bordello is quoted in Oscar Lewis's *Hearn and His Biographers*, p. 74. Julia Wetherall's assertion about Lafcadio's "strongly sensual nature" is published in *LHAD*, p. 362. Albert Mordell's contention that an inordinately busy schedule made it impossible for L.H. to engage in "dissipation" and associate with "low company" appears in his introduction to *Occidental Gleanings*, p. xxxix. E. L. Tinker's attribution of Lafcadio's ebulliency at New Orleans's quadroon balls to his "Defective Personality" appears in *LHAD*, p. 95. (For background on the history of the quadroon balls I drew on *The Federal Writers' Project Guide to 1930s New Orleans*, first edition 1938 (New York: Pantheon Books, 1983); *Historical Sketch Book and Guide to New Orleans*; J. A. Rogers' *Sex and Race*, volume 2; and *LHAD*.

Nina Kennard explains L.H.'s "abnormal . . . fancy" for black women by reference to his "barbaric ancestry" (*LH:CL*, p. 103). Elizabeth Stevenson sees its cause in Lafcadio's inferiority complex and fear of women who were his intellectual equals (*LH*, p. 25). For a discussion of the Cohn/Deutsch biography of Rudolph Matas with its vitriolic attitudes toward Hearn, see the essay "Lafcadio Hearn and Dr. Rudolph Matas" in Albert Mordell's *Discoveries: Essays on Lafcadio Hearn* (Tokyo: Orient/West Incorporated Publishers, 1964), as well as Mordell's "The 'Lady's' Unrequited Love for Hearn" in this same collection of essays, a thorough investigation of the forty-one-year-old Mrs. Ellen Freeman's obsession for the then twenty-six-year-old Cincinnati journalist. (See also a selection of L.H.'s letters to Mrs. Freeman in the last section of *LR*.) Lafcadio's complaints about "the churches, the societies," etc. that made it impossible for him to enter "a woman's society" are communicated in a letter to H.W. in *LR*, p. 81.

The statement by the English writer E. S. Abdy on "the bugbear of amalgamation" is quoted in Rogers, *Sex and Race*, volume 2, p. 191; so, too, is the quote by Fanny Kemble, p. 184. Lafcadio's editorial/essay, "Fair Women and Dark Women," appeared in the N.O.*It* (August 25, 1878). His radical opinions on the superior beauty of black skin in comparison with white skin were expressed in a letter of March 6, 1894, to B.H.C. in *JL*, pp. 270–72.

Although rumors of Lafcadio's supposed liaison with Marie Laveau (then in her late eighties!) or her daughter are utterly unfounded, there is evidence that Lafcadio did become infatuated with at least one voodoo enchantress during his early years in New Orleans. Caught in what he knew was a dangerous entanglement, he wrote to a friend: "I became passionately in love before I knew it;

and then!—It required all the reason and all the strength I could summon to save myself; but it took me months to do it—she came to me in dreams and made me feel her shadowy caresses. Don't think I am exaggerating. You have no idea of the strange fascination possessed by some of these *serpent women*" (*LHAD*, p. 96).

CHAPTER 7: THE MAN WHO LOVED ISLANDS

Lafcadio expressed his longings for nature in *LR*, p. 79. His report on the settlement of Tagalog fishermen, "Saint Malo," was published in *Harper's Weekly* (March 3, 1883). His journey into the Teche country resulted in the travel article "The Garden of Paradise," which appeared in the N.O.*T-D* (March 27, 1883). Lafcadio's joyful remarks after arriving on Grand Isle were communicated in letters to Rudolph Matas ("NDL," p. 87) and to Mrs. Courtney (*LHAD*, p. 222). His October 1884 note to H.E.K. (*LL*,I) tells of his sudden romantic attachment for the young Basque girl Marie; and the lines from Tennyson he quotes ("I will take some savage woman . . .") are from the poem *Locksley Hall* (1842). Hearn's letter of regret to Page Baker on having to leave Grand Isle is quoted by E.B. in *LL*,I, pp. 87–88. Lafcadio informs R.M. of his impatient wait for "the poet's pentecost" ("NDL," p. 87). Its arrival inspired the writing of the novel *Chita: A Memory of Lost Island* (1889), a long passage of which (from Part III, Chapter 2) is presented here.

CHAPTER 8: RESTLESS FAREWELL

Lafcadio's early sense of weariness with New Orleans was expressed in an 1880 letter to H.E.K. (*LL*,I). His notion concerning the pleasantness of the *"first relations with people"* was suggested in an 1887 letter to George M. Gould (*LL*,I). Hearn talks of his "spirit of restlessness" in an 1880 letter to H.E.K. (*LL*,I). Mexico and El Dorado, he tells H.W., are two of the places he is dreaming of visiting (*LR*, pp. 67, 75). Lafcadio states his desire to be "a literary Columbus" in an 1883 letter to H.E.K. (*LL*,I).

In Herman Melville's *Israel Potter,* the character of Paul Jones is the author's "fascinating but terrible symbol for the American character" (F. O. Matthiessen). Lafcadio wrote to H.W. about "little phantoms of men," and compared newspapermen with "[a] grain[s] of mustard seed" (in *LR*, pp. 82, 46). He complained to O'Connor in an August 1883 letter of the emasculating effect of journalism on one's writing style (*LL*,I), and he commented to H.E.K. in an 1882 letter about the treadmill effect of daily trade (*LL*,I). In the same letter to H.E.K., Lafcadio presented the "bohemian ideal of the holy fire of art" as an alternative to the mundaneness of the journalistic grind.

Lafcadio's encounter and relationship with Leona Queyrouze is described and detailed in Queyrouze's memoir (*I*).

"This quaint and ruinous city . . . this land of perfume and dreams": such was Lafcadio's characterization of New Orleans in a letter he wrote to H.E.K. in 1879 (*LL*,I).

PART THREE

CHAPTER 1: PARADISE REGAINED

Lafcadio's letter from New York City to H.W. appears in *LR*, pp. 84–86. Walt Whitman's words about "Manahatta"—his autochthonous name for Manhattan—are quoted in Justin Kaplan's *Walt Whitman: A Life*, p. 107. Hearn's observations about the fly aboard the S. S. *Barracouta* were noted in his article "A Midsummer Trip to the Tropics," which appeared later in *TY*. His first delirious impressions of St. Pierre, Martinique, were conveyed in a letter to R.M. ("NDL," pp. 91–92).

Back in Metuchen, New Jersey, L.H. wrote his vitriolic letter about Page Baker (see Source Note to Part Two, Chapter 5), and informed H.W. of his plans to return to the West Indies (*LR*, pp. 89–90). After returning to St. Pierre, he described the port town to R.M. in "NDL," pp. 92–94, and wrote of his vision of the inhabitants of St. Pierre, as if they were ancient Pompeiians reborn on this paradisaical isle, in his essay *"Les Porteuses"* (in *TY*.) Hearn mentioned his need to observe and write at his own pace in a letter (dated "Winter, 1887") to Henry Alden (in *New Hearn Letters from the French West Indies*, p. 63). L.H. discussed the "racial complexity and diversity" of the people of Martinique in his article/essays "A Study of Half-Breed Races in the West Indies" (published in the June 1890 issue of *Cosmopolitan*) and "West Indian Society of Many Colorings" (in the July 1890 issue of *Cosmopolitan*).

Lafcadio's essays *"Les Porteuses"* and *"La Grande Anse"* were collected in *TY*.

L.H. admits in a July 17, 1888, letter to Alden that he lacked the true fiction writer's gift (*New Hearn Letters*, p. 78). His equivocal remarks concerning his domestic arrangements in St. Pierre were coyly shared with R.M. in "NDL," p. 114. His portrait of his mistress Cyrillia (*"Ma Bonne"*) appears in *TY*.

L.H.'s contradictory attitudes toward the tropics are revealed in a series of letters: To E.B. (January 1889) he expressed his aversion to the cold ("all kinds of cold!!!!"); to R.M. he complained about being enervated by the tropical heat ("NDL," p. 107); to the ophthalmologist George M. Gould (October 1888) he railed at the "deformities" of "civilization's" manners and behavior and referred (June 1888) to the "aggressive characteristics" in the "nervous centers of the world's activity" (Gould and Bisland letters in *LL,*1). Ultimately, Lafcadio expresses to R.M. his regret on leaving Martinique ("NDL," pp. 107, 117).

The passage quoted here from Hearn's novel *Youma* (1890) is taken from pp. 130–31 of *Y*'s first edition.

CHAPTER 2: NERVOUS CENTERS

Lafcadio's May 1889 note to Joseph Tunison appears in *LL,*1. G.M.G.'s diagnosis of Hearn's right eye is quoted in Chapter VI ("Lafcadio Hearn") of his *Biographic Clinics* IV (Philadelphia: 1906). Here he propounds his theory that "intellect is largely, almost entirely, the product of vision," which predates by about a hundred years that of the British ophthalmologist Patrick Trevor-Roper. In the latter's book, *World Through Blunted Sight* (London and New York: The

Penguin Press, 1988), Trevor-Roper contends that defective vision (myopia, cataracts, etc.) deeply affected the work of Keats, Turner, and Monet; and he suggests that myopia, in particular, motivated artists like Tennyson, Joyce, Schubert, and Cézanne to lead lives of introspection and relative isolation. (Lafcadio's own essay of 1887, "Artistic Value of Myopia"—see Part 2, Chapter 2—had pointed to the positive aspects of nearsightedness for writers and painters.) In the chapter "Getting a Soul" from Gould's *Concerning Lafcadio Hearn* (Philadelphia: George W. Jacobs and Co., 1908), pp. 307–308, the ophthalmologist's puritanical theories about beauty and desire are discussed. L.H.'s own reflections about the process of "sensual perceptions" becoming refined and evolving into "moral ones" appeared in an 1888 letter that he himself wrote to Gould (*LL*,1). Hearn's expressions of contrition and self-criticism were sent from Philadelphia to Henry Alden on July 3, 1889 (quoted in *LHAD*, p. 310), as well as in a letter to Gould (quoted in *LH*, p. 180). G.M.G.'s self-congratulatory comments about Lafcadio's story "Karma" appear in *Concerning Lafcadio Hearn*, p. 18. L.H. finally accused Gould of stealing his ideas, and then wrote a sarcastic note of apology—requested by George Gould—to Mrs. Gould. (Both letters are dated November 1889 and exist on microfilm in the Edmund C. Stedman Collection, Rare Book and Manuscript Library, Columbia University.)

Lafcadio had earlier described the Navarro Apartments in a letter to R.M. ("NDL," p. 90). Ellwood Hendrick commented on what the out-of-place L.H. was wearing at Alice Wellington Rollins's dinner party, and on what he and Hearn talked about that evening after the party, in "Lafcadio Hearn," *The Nation* 116 (April 11, 1923): 432. The story of E.H. and L.H. at Jay Gould's New York mansion is recounted in *LHAD*, pp. 321–22. Lafcadio's remark about E.B. being like "a silkmoth" was imparted to R.M. ("NDL," p. 90), and his statement about her being like "a witch" and "hasheesh" was made to George Gould at the end of 1889, in a letter now on microfilm in the Stedman Collection, Columbia University.

L.H.'s declaration to H.W. about wanting to visit Japan appears in *LR*, p. 69. His account of the Japanese ink-brush paintings that he admired at the New Orleans Exposition was published in *Harper's Weekly* (January 31, 1885). Hearn wrote to Gould in 1889 about Lowell's *The Soul of the Far East* (*LL*,1).

Walt Whitman's lines ("Inquiring, tireless . . .") come from the 1860 version of *Leaves of Grass*.

L.H.'s proposal to Harper and Brothers for a book about Japan is quoted in *LHAD*, pp. 328–29.

Whenever Elizabeth Bisland reprints one of Lafcadio's letters to her in *LL*, she makes it a point always to omit her name, so that the identifying heading to each of these letters mysteriously reads: "To—." L.H.'s note to her, when she had already left for a trip around the world, is dated November 1889 (*LL*,1). The letter Hearn wrote to her just hours before he left for Japan is dated March 7–8, 1890 (*LL*,1).

PART FOUR

CHAPTER 1: IN FAIRYLAND

The quote from Gaston Bachelard comes from his book *The Poetics of Reverie*, trans. Daniel Russell (Boston: Beacon Press, 1971), p. 124.

Basil Hall Chamberlain's advice to L.H. is contained in the first sentence of Lafcadio's essay "My First Day in the Orient," whose text is reprinted from *G*, the first book that Hearn wrote in Japan.

CHAPTER 2: IN THE PROVINCE OF THE GODS

In this chapter, as in the other chapters of Part 4, I have drawn much information from Elizabeth Stevenson's well-researched *LH*.

Lafcadio expressed his joy at being in "the land of dreams" to both H.W. (*LR*, p. 94) and E.B. in a letter dated 1890 (*LL*,II).

The translations of verse by Sappho and Lady Murasaki Shikibu, both by Kenneth Rexroth, were published in *Poems from the Greek Anthology* (Ann Arbor: The University of Michigan Press, 1962), p. 100, and in *One Hundred Poems from the Japanese* (New York: New Directions, 1955), p. 56. The quote by Guy Davenport is taken from his introduction to *Archilochus Sappho Alkman*, p. 1. L.H.'s remark about escaping "out of Western civilization into Japanese life" is contained in a letter of May 22, 1891, and his recollection of weeks spent in Carey's hotel appears in a letter of May 16, 1894—both to B.H.C. (*JL*). His profane 1890 letter cutting his ties with both Harper and Brothers and Henry Alden is in the Harper Collection of the Pierpont Morgan Library. L.H.'s remarks to his first student in Japan, Edward B. Clarke, were recalled in the latter's book *Stray Leaves: Essays and Sketches* (Tokyo: Kenkyusha Company, 1936).

Hearn expressed his desire to simplify and pare down his prose style in a series of letters (January 1893; February 6, 1893; February 18, 1894) to B.H.C. (*JL*). The literary advice of Matsuo Bashō (1644–1694) is quoted in Nobuyuki Yuasa's introduction to his translation of Issa's *The Year of My Life* (Berkeley and Los Angeles: University of California Press, 1960), pp. 16–18. Lafcadio's questioning whether it is in fact an "inestimable privilege" to be "reborn [as] a human being" is raised in his essay "Gaki," published in *K*.

Theodore Roosevelt's declaration is taken from the first volume of his six-volume work *The Winning of the West* (New York: The Literature Publishing Company, 1905), pp. 1–4; and Albert Beveridge's from Claude G. Bowers, *Beveridge and the Progressive Era* (New York: Literary Guild, 1932), p. 69. L.H.'s opinion of missionaries is stated here in a letter dated May 1899 (*LL*,II) to Mrs. Ernest Fenollosa, the wife of a famous American art critic, collector of Oriental art, and poet, with whom L.H. broke off ties (see Part 4, Chapter 7). Robert Louis Stevenson's quite similar opinions about missionaries appeared in his posthumously published *In the South Seas* (London: Chatto and Windus, 1900).

L.H. wrote to B.H.C. about the beauty of Shintō ideas concerning ancestor worship (April 1891—*LL*,II); about his having submitted to "the flesh-pots of Egypt" (*i.e.*, Western food) (June 1981—*JL*); and about the "interminable small etiquette" of Japanese life (September 4, 1891—*JL*).

Hearn formulated Pierre Loti's approach to descriptive writing in the former's essay "The Most Original of Modern Novelists: Pierre Loti," first published in the N.O.T-D on December 7, 1884.

"The Chief City of the Province of the Gods" appeared in OE.

CHAPTER 3: A WEDDING IN MATSUE

Lafcadio aired his complaint about the early and bitter Matsue winter to B.H.C. in a letter of January 1891 (JL). The notion that "cold quickens egotism" is to be found in L.H.'s essay "Dust" in GB-F.

The passages quoted here from Loti's Madame Chrysanthème (1888) are in the English translation of Laura Ensor (Paris: Edouard Guillaume et Cie., 1889), pp. 121–22, 323. L.H.'s unusually dismissive remarks about Loti were written in a February 18, 1893, letter to B.H.C. (JL).

In New Orleans, L.H. had told Julia Wetherall of the unimportance he placed on "intellectual companionship" in the matter of choosing a wife (LHAD, p. 341). In this regard, Dr. Anthony Storr, in his book Solitude: A Return to the Self (New York: The Free Press, 1988), pointedly states: "Some bereaved or very isolated children abandon any hope of making lasting intimate attachments, and only risk embarking upon relationships which are not so close. . . . Creative artists are quite likely to choose relationships which will further their work, rather than relationships which are intrinsically rewarding, and their spouses may well find that marital relations take second place" (pp. 106–107). Lafcadio's preference for a "sweet Japanese girl" over the "diamond-hard" American woman is stated in a July 1891 letter to B.H.C. (LL,II), and his suggestion that marriage resolves the problem of the eternal longing for the Eternal Feminine is stated in a November 1892 letter to E.H. (LL,II). L.H.'s comments on geishas were made in a June 1892 letter to Page Baker (LL,II). Hearn's response to the novel by William Mallock sent to him by Ellwood Hendrick and his statement about the influence on him of "the magnetism of another faith" both appear in an April 1892 letter to E.H. (LL,II).

Lafcadio's essay "In Yokohama" is taken from his book OE.

Setsu Koizumi gives her early impressions of Lafcadio in RLH, pp. 11, 42–43.

The passage quoted here from "In a Japanese Garden" is the last section of Hearn's autobiographical essay published in G.

CHAPTER 4: LITTLE SPRING, EIGHT CLOUDS

The section quoted here from "The Dream of a Summer Day" appears in OE.

Lafcadio announced the news of the birth of his son Kazuo to E.H. in a letter dated November 1893 (LL,II), and informed Page Baker (with whom he had reconciled)—in a letter of April 1895 that "the whole universe changes" when one "has a child and loves it" (LL,II).

"I wish I could fly out of Meiji forever . . ." L.H. exclaimed to Sentarō Nishida, the dean of the Middle School in Matsue and his first Japanese friend, in a letter of November 1893 (LL,II).

The passage from "The Stone Buddha" quoted here is from OE.

Hearn wrote to B.H.C. of his satisfaction with his new glass *shoji* on February 18, 1893 (*JL*). "Bits of Life and Death," sections of which are printed here, was published in *OE*.

L.H. stated his liability to his new family—the "nine lives depending on my work"—in a January 1892 letter to E.H. (*LL*,II). His detailed account of a "typical day" of the Koizumi clan was given, in confidence, in an October 11, 1893, letter to B.H.C. (*JL*).

Hearn wrote about the "aggressive selfishness" concomitant with the Occidental notions of "personality and individuality" in April 1891 (*JL*). Contemporary discussions of this theme can be found in the work of such authors as David Riesman and C. Wright Mills, Paul Goodman and Philip Slater—the last of whom, in his book *Earthwalk* (New York: Anchor Press/Doubleday, 1974), suggests what L.H. had intuited almost a hundred years previously: that the cult of individualism inevitably led to a society "founded on unstable, fragmentary, transient, competitive, and unco-ordinated relationships" (pp. 55–56, 82–100). See also the recent *Habits of the Heart: Individualism and Commitment in American Life*, by Robert N. Bellah *et al.* (Berkeley and Los Angeles: University of California Press, 1986).

Hearn's "A Conservative" was published in *K:H&E*.

L.H. reports on the patriotic attitude of his students to B.H.C. in a May 1896 letter (*LL*,II). Lafcadio's response to Chamberlain's questioning *him* about the vehemence of his pro-Japanese sentiments is made in a letter of October 31, 1893 (*JL*); and his explanation, in a June 24, 1894, letter, to his half-sister, Minnie Atkinson, of the reasons for Japan's increasing military strength and its growing anti-Western feelings is quoted in *LH:CL*, p. 259. Hearn's comments about Japan, Russia, China, and Scandinavia appear in "A Letter from Japan" (dated August 1, 1904), posthumously published in Lafcadio's *The Romance of the Milky Way*.

S.K.'s responding to her husband's proud assertion that he had "nothing Western about him" by pointing to his nose is in *RLH*, p. 55.

CHAPTER 5: THE PATH

Just before leaving Kumamoto for Kobe at the end of 1894, L.H. sent an aged H.W. and his daughter, Effie, a letter (*LR*, pp. 96–101). Lafcadio's editorials from this period are collected in *Editorials from the "Kobe Chronicle"* (1913). He had earlier revealed to B.H.C. in a number of letters—including June 1891; August 1891; December 21, 1892; February 6, 1893 (in both *LL*,II and *JL*)—that his inspiration was waning, that he was "fizzed out." He even, for a moment, felt homesick for the West (see letter of July 15, 1894—*JL*). L.H. described to Chamberlain his recipe for "forcing" work (in a letter of January 23, 1893—*JL*), a method he had once, to E.H., compared to that of the industrious ants (in a letter dated 1892—and *JL*); to the latter he wrote a letter in January 1895 remarking that he could finally say that he had gained "a little in the path" (*LL*,II). Lafcadio told W. B. Mason of his longing for the "primitive west coast" where the ancient gods were still alive (August 1892—*JL*) and had asked B.H.C., in a letter dated February 16, 1894 (*JL*), "What is there, finally, to love in Japan except what is passing away?"

L.H. recounted his second visit to the little temple in Yokohama in his essay "In Yokohama" (*OE*).

CHAPTER 6: TOKYO STORY

Lafcadio stated his opinion of Tokyo ("the most horrible place in Japan") in two letters to E.H. dated January 1895 (*LL*,II); and he commented to Sentarō Nishida in January 1895 (*LL*,II) that his wife thought of Tokyo the way "a French lady thinks of Paris." Setsu recalls the Buddhist temple that L.H. loved to visit behind their first Tokyo home in *RLH*, pp. 27–28. L.H. talked of consoling himself by "plunging into the study of Buddhism" in an August 6, 1892, letter to W. B. Mason (*J L*). Some of his theoretical essays about Buddhism—"By Force of Karma" and "The Idea of Pre-existence," for example—were published in *K:H&E*. "Otokichi's Daruma," reprinted with Lafcadio's drawings, is taken from Hearn's *A Japanese Miscellany*.

L.H. expressed his anxiety about his oldest son, K.K., to E.B. in a letter of January 1900 (*LL*,II), and also to Sentarō Nishida in a letter of August 1894 (*LL*,II); and he informed E.H., in September 1895, that Kazuo claimed to have been a doctor "in his former birth" (*LL*,II).

K.K.'s remembrances of his father's teaching methods are elaborated in Chapter 4 of *F&I*, pp. 127–67. The selections reprinted here from the ten-year-old Kazuo's *Copybook* have been chosen from Chapter 4 of K.K.'s *Re-Echo*, edited by Nancy Jane Fellers (Caldwell, Idaho: The Caxton Printers, Ltd., 1957), pp. 125–30).

The opinions concerning L.H.'s teaching abilities of his students and colleagues at the Imperial University of Tokyo are quoted in *LH*, p. 288. Hearn's own opinions about various English poets and novelists are drawn from the three-volume *Complete Lectures*, edited by Ryuji Tanabe *et al.* (1932–34). The lecture by Professor Hearn reprinted here, "The Value of the Supernatural in Fiction," is taken from the version appearing in the second of the two-volume *Interpretations of Literature*, edited by John Erskine, pp. 90–103.

Setsu recollects telling ghost stories to L.H. at night in *RLH*, pp. 36–40. Lafcadio's "The Story of Mimi-Nashi-Hōïchi" was first published in *Kwaidan*, as was his tale "Ohidori." To B.H.C. he expressed his profound admiration for the fairy tales of Hans Christian Andersen (in a letter dated 1895—*LL*,II).

L.H.'s wistful conversation with his wife about the *uguisu* in the garden of their second Tokyo home is recounted in *RLH*, p. 32. The "changings" brought about by the New Japan were "ugly and sad," Lafcadio stated to E.H. in a letter dated 1902 (*LL*,II); and he complained, in September 1899, to Mitchell McDonald about his friend's overindulgent hospitality (*LL*,II). L.H.'s essay "Insect-Musicians" appeared in *E&R*, his first book for his new publisher, Little, Brown and Company. Having argued with and left Houghton Mifflin in 1897, Lafcadio wrote a letter dated November 1898 (*LL*,II) to McDonald: "*Temporarily, I am thus independent.*"

CHAPTER 7: "ALMOST" JAPANESE

Hearn's Whitmanesque-sounding "The largest thought accepts all . . ." is from a letter, written about 1894, to E.H., which is now in the possession of the Hearn Collection, New York Public Library. The explanations of the symbolism of the white heron/black crow come, in part, from J. C. Cooper's *An Illustrated Encyclopaedia of Traditional Symbols* (London: Thames and Hudson, 1978). Hearn's notion of the human being as a ghost is put forth in the last sentence of his essay "Nirvana," published in *GB-F*. And in a letter dated July 30, 1892 (JL), Lafcadio referred to W. B. Mason as an amiable ghost.

Several commentators on L.H.'s life have pointed to his dismissive letter of December 1898 to Ernest Fenollosa in order to support their claim that Hearn's lifelong paranoia (and social boorishness) increased markedly during his last years in Japan. In this particular rejecting but polite letter to Fenollosa, Lafcadio makes no secret of his urgent need for time alone in order to write. (Without announcing it, he was also aware of his deteriorating health.) As a further counterweight to his critics' argument, moreover, one might cite the following observation made by the Tibetan Buddhist teacher Chögyam Trungpa in his lecture "Working with Negativity" that appears in *The Myth of Freedom* (Boston and London: Shambhala, 1976), p. 77: "It is said in the tantric tradition that, if you do not destroy when necessary, you are breaking the vow of compassion which actually commits you to destroying frivolousness. Therefore, keeping to the path does not necessarily mean only trying to be good and not offending anyone. . . . That does not work, that is not the point. If anyone gets abruptly in our path, we just push them out because their intrusion was frivolous."

CHAPTER 8: RESTLESS GHOST

"Revery"—Hearn's meditation on mother-love and physical dissolution—and "Kusa-Hibari"—his tribute to his tiny musical grass-lark (cricket)—are both reprinted from *K*.

Lafcadio's last days are described by his wife in *RLH*, pp. 73–83, and by K.K. in *F&I*, pp. 204–208. Setsu draws up a list of what had been her husband's favorite and least favorite things in this world (in *RLH*, pp. 84–85). Kazuo reports on the aftermath of his father's cremation in *F&I*, p. 126. L.H.'s discussion of the *kaimyō*, the Buddhist names given to the spirits of the dead, can be found in sections 4 and 5 of his essay "The Literature of the Dead" in *E&R*.

"Of what concern, then, the next disintegration?" L.H. asks in his essay "Dust," from *GB-F*.

The Writings of Lafcadio Hearn: A Chronological Bibliography

Lafcadio Hearn did not have an easy time with his magazine editors and book publishers, nor they with him. His general complaint was that they dealt with articles and books "precisely as they might deal in pork or hay." His particular—and certainly a reasonable—objection was that he was not, as a rule, allowed to go over his galleys. "I feel that I cannot any longer endure the pain of seeing myself in print as somebody else," he complained in an 1888 letter to Henry Alden, the editor of *Harper's Magazine*. "The whole 'style' of the composing room,—the changes,—the changes by omission and punctuation and re-paragraphing and condensation,—destitute me of all personality to an extent that discourages me utterly. No kindness and no money can help me to bear the torture of it. . . ." This was the main issue over which Lafcadio broke his connection with *Harper's Magazine* and Harper and Brothers when he moved to Japan. But even there, when his new publisher, Houghton Mifflin Co., *did* send him book galleys, Lafcadio spoke of "the *feeling* their correspondence gives me of tricky business or of personal ill-feeling."

The letters Lafcadio composed to his publishers are among the most vitriolic and scurrilous he ever wrote ("Oh!" he once declared, "—how I want to sound my barbaric yawp!"), and his friends often tried to dissuade him from sending a particularly pointed and intemperate note to one or another of his editors. Lafcadio's wife, Setsu, learned to hide those letters written during her husband's most ferocious and yawpish moods in a drawer, then show them to him a week later—at which time Lafcadio always thanked her for her clearheadedness and farsightedness.

In his lifetime, Lafcadio Hearn witnessed the publication of twenty of his books, but he was hardly his own best literary agent. He paid a New York publisher $150 to bring out his first work, a translation of Théophile Gautier's *One of Cleopatra's Nights and Other Fantastic Romances* (1882). Until he went to Japan, he was never given an advance or paid expenses for his nonjournalistic writing. And it was only with his two novels, *Chita* and *Youma*, and with *Two Years in the French West Indies*, that he began to receive minimal royalties. ("Would I were living in the days of the Caliphs!" he declared to his friend Ellwood Hendrick, "—sure to receive a purse of 1000 pieces of gold, and two beautiful singing-girls every time I wrote anything good. I might be bowstrung, but then—what a time I should have before it!")

Since his death, close to a hundred volumes of Lafcadio's own work, as well as his translations from the French, have been published in English, mostly in collections and anthologies (with sometimes overlapping material) of his newspaper articles, sketches, and editorials. His lectures on literature and culture, gleaned from the notes of his Japanese students, and his innumerable (and memorable) letters to colleagues, friends, and foes, have also been issued.

Except for the twelve major books he wrote in Japan—and several excellent anthologies (*Writings from Japan*, edited by Francis King; *Selected Writings*, edited by Henry Goodman; *The Buddhist Writings of Lafcadio Hearn*, edited by Kenneth Rexroth)—most of Hearn's pre-1890s work has been difficult to obtain, at least since the 1930s. In the past ten years or so, however, reprint houses have begun publishing—mostly in limited, facsimile editions—a number of the volumes listed below, along with many previously out-of-print biographies of Hearn, attesting to the beginnings of a resurgence of interest in this author.

One of Cleopatra's Nights and Other Fantastic Romances, by Théophile Gautier, trans. Lafcadio Hearn. New York: R. Worthington, 1882.

Stray Leaves from Strange Literature. Boston: J. R. Osgood and Co., 1884.

La Cuisine Créole: A Collection of Culinary Recipes. New York: Will H. Coleman, n.d. [1885].

"Gombo Zhèbes": A Little Dictionary of Creole Proverbs, Selected from Six Creole Dialects. New York: W. H. Coleman, 1885.

Historical Sketch Book and Guide to New Orleans, edited by several New Orleans journalists, including L. H. New York: Will H. Coleman, 1885.

Some Chinese Ghosts. Boston: Roberts Brothers, 1887.

Chita: A Memory of Lost Island. New York: Harper and Brothers, 1889.

The Crime of Sylvestre Bonnard, by Anatole France, trans. Lafcadio Hearn. New York: Harper and Brothers, 1890.

Two Years in the French West Indies. New York: Harper and Brothers, 1890.

Youma: The Story of a West-Indian Slave. New York: Harper and Brothers, 1890.

Glimpses of Unfamiliar Japan, 2 volumes. Boston: Houghton Mifflin Co., 1894.

Out of the East: Reveries and Studies in New Japan. Boston: Houghton Mifflin Co., 1895.

Kokoro: Hints and Echoes of Japanese Inner Life. Boston: Houghton Mifflin Co., 1896.

Gleanings in Buddha-Fields: Studies of Hand and Soul in the Far East. Boston: Houghton Mifflin Co., 1897.

Exotics and Retrospectives. Boston: Little, Brown and Co., 1898.

Japanese Fairy Tales, printed in color by hand from Japanese woodblocks, 5 volumes. Tokyo: Hasegawa, 1898–1922.

In Ghostly Japan. Boston: Little, Brown and Co., 1899.

Shadowings. Boston: Little, Brown and Co., 1900.

A Japanese Miscellany. Boston: Little, Brown and Co., 1901.

Kotto: Being Japanese Curios, with Sundry Cobwebs. New York: The Macmillan Co., 1902.

Kwaidan: Stories and Studies of Strange Things. Boston: Houghton Mifflin Co., 1904.

Japan: An Attempt at Interpretation. New York: The Macmillan Co., 1904.

The Romance of the Milky Way, and Other Studies and Stories. Boston: Houghton Mifflin Co., 1905.

"Letters of a Poet to a Musician: Letters from Hearn to H. E. Krehbiel." *Critic* 48–49 (April 1906): 309–18.

The Life and Letters of Lafcadio Hearn, 2 volumes, by Elizabeth Bisland. Boston: Houghton Mifflin Co., 1906.

Letters from the Raven: Being the Correspondence of Lafcadio Hearn with Henry Watkin, ed. Milton Bronner. New York: Brentano's, 1907.

The Japanese Letters of Lafcadio Hearn, ed. Elizabeth Bisland. Boston: Houghton Mifflin Co., 1910.

The Temptation of St. Anthony, by Gustave Flaubert, trans. Lafcadio Hearn. New York and Seattle: Alice Harriman Co., 1910.

Leaves from the Diary of an Impressionist, ed. Ferris Greenslet. Boston: Houghton Mifflin Co., 1911.

Editorials from the "Kobe Chronicle," Japanese Editorial Writings. New York: Privately printed, 1911.

Fantastics and Other Fancies, ed. Charles Woodward Hutson. Boston: Houghton Mifflin Co., 1914.

Japanese Lyrics. Boston: Houghton Mifflin Co., 1915.

Life and Literature, ed. John Erskine. New York: Dodd, Mead and Co., Inc., 1917.

Karma. New York: Boni and Liveright, 1918.

Hearn Memorial Translations (in Japanese), 9 volumes. Tokyo: Hokuseido Press, 1920–23.

"Some Martinique Letters of Lafcadio Hearn." *Harper's Magazine* 142 (March 1921).

Books and Habits, From the Lectures of Lafcadio Hearn. New York: Dodd, Mead and Co., Inc., 1921.

The Writings of Lafcadio Hearn, 16 volumes. Boston: Houghton Mifflin Co., 1922.

An American Miscellany, Articles and Stories Now First Collected, 2 volumes, ed. Albert Mordell. New York: Dodd, Mead and Co., Inc. 1924.

Creole Sketches, ed. Charles Woodward Hutson. Boston: Houghton Mifflin Co., 1924.

Saint Anthony, and Other Stories, by Guy de Maupassant, trans. Lafcadio Hearn, ed. Albert Mordell. New York: Albert and Charles Boni, 1924.

Occidental Gleanings: Sketches and Essays Now First Collected, 2 volumes, ed. Albert Mordell. New York: Dodd, Mead and Co., Inc., 1925.

Some New Letters and Writings of Lafcadio Hearn, ed. Sanki Ichikawa. Tokyo: Kenkyusha, Ltd., 1925.

Complete Lectures on Art, Literature, and Philosophy, eds. R. Tanabe and others. Tokyo: Hokuseido Press, 1925–34.

Editorials: New Orleans Journalistic Writings, ed. Charles Woodward Hutson. Boston: Houghton Mifflin Co., 1926.

Interpretations of Literature, 2 volumes, ed. John Erskine. New York: Dodd, Mead and Co., Inc., 1926.

"Insects and Greek Poetry." New York: W. E. Ridge, 1926.

Talks to Writers, ed. John Erskine. New York: Dodd, Mead and Co., Inc., 1927.

Adventures of Walter Schnaffs, by Guy de Maupassant, trans. Lafcadio Hearn, ed. Albert Mordell. Tokyo: Hokuseido Press, 1931.

"Letters of Lafcadio Hearn to His Brother," ed. E. C. Beck. *English Journal* XX (1931): 287–92; and *American Literature* IV (1932): 167–73.

Stories from Pierre Loti, trans. Lafcadio Hearn, ed. Albert Mordell. Tokyo: Hokuseido Press, 1933.

Stories from Emile Zola, trans. Lafcadio Hearn, ed. Albert Mordell. Tokyo: Hokuseido Press, 1935.

Sketches and Tales from the French, trans. Lafcadio Hearn, ed. Albert Mordell. Tokyo: Hokuseido Press, 1935.

Unfamiliar Lafcadio Hearn, ed. Kenneth Porter Kirkwood. Tokyo: Hokuseido Press, 1936.

Barbarous Barbers and Other Stories, ed. Ichiro Nishizaki. Tokyo: Hokuseido Press, 1939.

Buying Christmas Toys, and Other Essays, ed. Ichiro Nishizaki. Tokyo: Hokuseido Press, 1939.

Literary Essays, ed. Ichiro Nishizaki. Tokyo: Hokuseido Press, 1939.

The New Radiance and Other Scientific Sketches, ed. Ichiro Nishizaki. Tokyo: Hokuseido Press, 1939.

Oriental Articles, ed. Ichiro Nishizaki. Tokyo: Hokuseido Press, 1939.

Selected Writings of Lafcadio Hearn, ed. Henry Goodman. New York: The Citadel Press, 1949.

Selected Writings of Lafcadio Hearn, edited by the Hearn Centennial Committee, Tokyo, published for the English Literary Society of Japan by Kenkyusha, Ltd., 1953.

"Newly Discovered Letters from Lafcadio Hearn to Dr. Rudolph Matas," ed. Ichiro Nishizaki, Ochanomizu University, Tokyo. *Studies in Arts and Cultures* 8 (March 1956): 85–118.

Children of the Levee, ed. O. W. Frost. Lexington, Kentucky: University of Kentucky Press, 1957.

New Hearn Letters from the French West Indies, by Ichiro Nishizaki. Reprinted from Ochanomizu University, Tokyo, *Studies in Arts and Cultures* 12 (June 1959): 59–110.

Lafcadio Hearn: From Hoki to Oko—The Development from His Notes to the Final Version—Appendix: The Contents of Hearn's Notes, by Hisashi Kajitani. Reprinted from the Collection of Essays in Commemoration of the Tenth Anniversary [1959] of Shimane University (Human Science), February 1960.

"Two Unpublished Hearn Letters," ed. O. W. Frost. *Today's Japan* 5 (1) (1955-60: Fifth Anniversary issue): 43–48.

Memoranda for the Lectures at Tokyo Imperial University. New York: AMS Press, 1975.

The Buddhist Writings of Lafcadio Hearn, ed. Kenneth Rexroth. Santa Barbara: Ross-Erikson, Inc., 1977.

Lafcadio Hearn: Selected Writings 1872–1877, ed. William S. Johnson. Indianapolis: Woodruff Publications, 1979.

The Tanyard Murder: On the Case with Lafcadio Hearn, Jon Christopher Hughes. Washington, D.C.: University Press of America, 1982.

Writings from Japan, ed. Francis King. New York: Penguin Books, 1984.

The Great Interpreter: An Anthology of Lafcadio Hearn, eds. Louis Allen and Jean Wilson. Ashford, Kent: Norbury Publications, Ltd., 1988.

A NOTE ABOUT THE AUTHOR

Jonathan Cott is the author of ten previous books, among them
Pipers at the Gates of Dawn: The Wisdom of Children's Litera-
ture, Conversations with Glenn Gould, The Search for Omm
Sety, *and two collections of conversations*—Forever Young *and*
Visions and Voices. *He is a contributing editor of* Rolling Stone
magazine and Parabola: The Magazine of Myth and Tradition.
He lives in New York City.

A NOTE ON THE TYPE

The text of this book was set in Berkeley Oldstyle, a typeface
designed by Tony Stan based on a face originally developed by
Frederick Goudy in 1938 for the University of California Press
at Berkeley.
Composed by Creative Graphics, Inc., Allentown, Pennsylvania
Printed and bound by R. R. Donnelley & Sons,
Harrisonburg, Virginia
Designed by Iris Weinstein